W9-AQX-853

Adverbs, Vowels,
and Other Objects
of Wonder

WITHDRAWN

James D. McCawley

# Adverbs, Vowels, and Other Objects of Wonder

The University of Chicago Press
Chicago and London

RITTER LIBRARY
BALDWIN - WALLACE COLLEGE

JAMES D. MCCAWLEY is professor of linguistics
at the University of Chicago. He is the author
of *The Phonological Component of a Grammar
of Japanese* and *Grammar and Meaning* and is
the editor of *Notes from the Linguistic
Underground.*

The University of Chicago Press, Chicago 60637
The University of Chicago Press, Ltd., London

© 1979 by The University of Chicago
All rights reserved. Published 1979
Printed in the United States of America
83 82 81 80 79   5 4 3 2 1

*Library of Congress Cataloging in Publication Data*
McCawley, James D.
    Adverbs, vowels, and other objects of wonder.
    Bibliography: p.
    Includes index.
    1. Linguistics—Collected works. I. Title.
P27.M245            410            78-11608
ISBN 0-226-55615-8

# Contents

v

# Preface

This collection of papers written between 1965 and 1977 is broader in its range of topics than was my earlier collection, *Grammar and Meaning*, which was confined to papers on syntax and semantics. In view of the fact that the latter volume contains nearly everything that I had written on those topics up to 1971, the papers on syntax and semantics in the volume are generally more recent than the phonology papers; indeed, of the papers collected here, those written before 1972 all deal with phonology, either exclusively or in relation to questions of the history or the theoretical foundations of linguistics. The papers are grouped into four sections of roughly equal length: phonology, syntax and semantics, the lexicon, and foundations of linguistics; the papers in each section are arranged in the order in which they were written, which often does not agree with the order of their publication. One major systematic omission from this volume is my critical studies of the approach to syntax and semantics found in recent works by Chomsky, such as my 103-page review of (and commentary on) Chomsky's *Studies on Semantics in Generative Grammar* (McCawley 1975*b*) and my remarks on Jackendoff's treatment of anaphora and reference (McCawley 1976*c*); the principal reasons for this omission are that the most important item in this area is so long as to leave little room for the inclusion of other papers and that I am considering collecting the papers in this area in a separate volume.

As in *Grammar and Meaning*, I have added to the various papers annotations in which I make retractions, point out additional facts that I had failed to take into account in the original paper, or comment on subsequent research on the problems dealt with. The annotations are bracketed to distinguish them from the notes of the original papers. Otherwise I have confined the editing of the papers to stylistic improvements, the replacement of occasional ill-chosen examples by other examples that make the same point better, deletion of passages that duplicate material found elsewhere in this volume, some minor changes in terminology and notation to achieve consistency with other papers in the volume, and the replacement of the original bibliographic citations by references to a master bibliography that appears at the end of the volume.[1]

The point of view that I take in the papers on syntax and semantics and on the lexicon is essentially the same as that which I took in most of the papers in *Grammar and Meaning:* I reject the distinction between 'transformation' and 'semantic interpretation rule' and the notion of the 'grammaticality' of a sentence considered apart from its meaning, use, and context and take the grammarian's business to be the formulation of rules that specify what devices the language allows for the expression of the various possible meanings, subject to whatever contextual constraints (linguistic or extralinguistic) may be imposed on the use of those devices. However, whereas a large proportion of *Grammar and Meaning* consisted of arguments for that approach, here I do not present arguments for it (except in "On Identifying the Remains of Deceased Clauses" and to a much lesser extent in "On Interpreting the Theme of This Conference") but merely assume it. I do not mean to suggest by this that I am so arrogant as to regard all the controversies over claims that I and other 'generative semanticists' have made about the unity of syntax and semantics as having been settled in our favor. Rather, I simply think that for further discussion of those questions to be productive, the disputants need a much broader and deeper understanding of the relevant factual areas than any of them (myself included) had around 1970. Indeed, a large proportion of my energies since the early 1970s has been devoted to exploratory work on the lexicon and in logic, with a view toward replacing the sweeping and often rash generalizations in my earlier work about the relationship of grammar to logical structure and the lexicon by more detailed proposals whose backing was less anecdotal. This work has resulted neither in major recantations nor in a satisfactory statement of how logic, syntax, and lexical semantics fit together. The principal respect in which my thinking on this question has changed during the 1970s is something that unfortunately is largely ignored in this book: except in a passage in "Lexicographic Notes on English Quantifiers" and in a couple of annotations, I have not dealt here with Grice's notion of 'conversational implicature', which I have come to realize has profound implications for the development of both lexical semantics and a linguistically appropriate notion of logical structure. Specifically, Grice has shown that many things that sentences convey are not parts of the meaning of the sentence but rather result from the interaction of the meaning and form of the sentence with principles of cooperation. For example, *Either Springfield or Peoria is the capital of Illinois* conveys that the speaker does not know whether it is

Springfield or Peoria that is the capital; but that is only because if he did know, he would be going out of his way to be uninformative by saying *either Springfield or Peoria* instead of the shorter and more informative *Springfield*. Grice's approach allows one to account for a broad range of details of what various lexical items convey and restrictions on their use, without incorporating those details into the dictionary entries of the various lexical items or into the semantic structures of sentences in which those lexical items are used; see Heringer 1976 and McCawley 1978*a, b* for a number of analyses in which restrictions on the use of various lexical items are explained away as consequences of principles of cooperation, and in particular, for a demonstration that a semantically complex lexical item may have exactly the same meaning as a syntactically complex 'paraphrase' (in the sense of making the same contribution to semantic structure) and yet not convey the same thing, by virtue of Grice's 'maxim of manner', which requires that one be no more verbose than is appropriate and which can be exploited to make the more verbose of two equivalent expressions convey something other than what the less verbose one does.

If there is a single theme that unites the essays contained in this book, it is that there is more diversity in language and in ways of looking at language than linguists have generally recognized. In saying that linguists have underestimated the diversity of language, I do not mean to advocate the position that "languages could differ from one another without limit and in unpredictable ways" (Joos 1958:96). Quite the contrary: I think that it is only by doing serious work on language universals that one can identify the differences among languages rather than merely seeing amorphous diversity everywhere. A linguist who holds that languages can differ unpredictably and without limit is at a great disadvantage with regard to determining *what* the differences among languages are: he cannot view linguistic phenomena close up because he has no reason for choosing linguistic phenomena that are worth the time and expense of close-up viewing. (By the same token, someone who regards most human activities as sinful is poorly equipped to recognize real evil when he sees it.) The linguist armed with a knowledge of language universals, by contrast, is able to identify analogues to phenomena in other languages that are known to be sites of interlinguistic variation and to investigate those phenomena in great depth. Such in-depth investigation frequently turns up additional interlinguistic differences (e.g., additional factors that can but need not affect whether a constituent can be relativized) that would have gone unnoticed if linguists had not had reason to examine certain very specific classes of facts in great detail.

The failure of linguists to recognize the diversity of ways of looking at language is quite comparable to the popularity of simplistic schemes of classifying political views, such as the popular belief in a dimension of 'left' versus 'right', with political views supposedly differing mainly in the value on that scale that one takes as an ideal, or the even more popular superstition that one can classify minds in terms of scores on IQ tests. In both politics and linguistics there are a huge number of independent or only loosely dependent issues and a broad range of combinations of positions on those issues are attested. Those holding common combinations of positions are not more consistent than those holding uncommon ones, only more docile. It is of course inevitable that certain combinations of positions will be common and others uncommon in a scientific community: the traditions of the community are passed on in the form of a body of respected and successful problem solutions (what Kuhn [1970] calls 'exemplars'), with 'normal science' consisting in finding new instances of, analogues to, and combinations of the 'exemplars', and scientific education transmitting to the students all components of the exemplars (deadwood as well as the central ideas), along with the implicit judgment that the problems that the exemplars solve are the most important problems. But it is worth the linguist's while to recognize that the ideas commonly held in the scientific community to which he belongs are often independent of one another and that it is absurd to lump into a group of 'enemies' (you might call them 'structuralists' or the like) persons who have in common only that they disagree with some of your favorite ideas, or to lump into a group of 'precursors' (you might call them 'rationalist grammarians' or the like) earlier scholars who have in common only that they said things suggesting agreement with some ideas that you cherish. Recognizing the independence of different ideas is important not merely in order to achieve a just appreciation of other scholars but also as an aid to making sense of current controversies. I note in this connection that there are a number of cases in which authors have argued for some complex set of ideas (say, an 'interpretive theory of anaphora') by offering arguments for a particular idea of that set (say, the idea that pronouns can't all be derived from copies of their antecedents) but interpreting those arguments as providing support for the whole package (in this case, as if they supported the claim that syntactic rules are not sensitive to coreference); see McCawley 1975b: 259–60 for criticism of this precise illegitimate argument for a 'package' of ideas. I am pleased to have this book open with one article demonstrating that Edward Sapir was further removed from generative phonology than generative phonologists have often maintained and another article showing that William Dwight Whitney was less of a structuralist and more of a generative phonologist than is often thought the case, though it pains me to state these points in those terms: I object to taking stereotypes of 'generative phonology' and 'structuralism' as the standards in terms of which past scholars' approaches to language are evaluated.

Many persons have helped me to put the essays collected here into their present form; they are too numerous to list, even if my memory were up to the task of enumerating them all, but I hereby thank the great number of linguists who have given me the benefit of their comments at conferences, in classes, at guest lectures, and in informal bull sessions, in places as diverse as Turku, Finland, Melbourne, Australia, and Seoul, Korea. I wish especially to thank my students and colleagues at the University of Chicago for their longstanding and exemplary service as sounding boards, especially to the many students before whom I presented fetal forms of most of the papers that are collected here (and of many other papers that I have aborted): what confidence I have in the papers published here stems in large part from my realization that papers that have survived presentation before such exacting audiences can't be completely bungled.

# I  Phonology

# I    Sapir's Phonologic Representation

The name of Edward Sapir has been invoked many times recently as a precursor of modern generative phonology. For a typical example, note Chomsky (1964:87), where after introducing the term 'systematic phonemic' to denote the representation which forms the input to the phonological component of a transformational grammar, Chomsky states "The level of systematic phonemics is, essentially, the 'phonological orthography' of Sapir" (p. 87). In this paper I will examine the question of the extent to which a segment in one of Sapir's phonologic representations can be identified with a segment in the dictionary representation of a morpheme in a transformational grammar.

I first note one obvious respect in which Sapir's representations agree with those of generative phonology, namely that both are 'mentalistic', in the sense of being advanced as hypotheses as to the speaker's tacit knowledge of his language. In both cases, only two segmental representations are considered of significance: an 'underlying' or 'phonologic' representation which represents the speaker's 'mental image' of the various morphemes, and a phonetic representation which corresponds to the actual articulations made by the vocal organs in producing utterances. No systematic significance is attached to any 'intermediate' representation[1] such as a phonemic representation in the sense of, for example, Bloch and Trager 1942, although in both Sapir and transformational grammar, 'underlying' phonological representations are converted into phonetic representations through several intermediate stages, since some 'rules' apply to the output of other 'rules'. That the representations which Sapir called 'phonemic' or 'phonologic' were not 'phonemic' as the term is used in the 'Neo-Bloomfieldian' tradition of Bloch and Trager is apparent from a perusal of

Reprinted by permission from *International Journal of American Linguistics* 33 (1967): 106–11.

almost any of Sapir's grammars; to cite an example, in his Takelma grammar, Sapir (1922) gives four forms of the verb *to shoot* which he observes are all pronounced [sãk'] but have different phonologic representations.

While Sapir's phonologic representations were not bound by such constraints as the biuniqueness, linearity,[2] and invariance which characterize the phonemic representations of neo-Bloomfieldian linguists, Sapir nonetheless subjected his phonologic representations to certain other constraints which have the effect of making the set of possible analyses for Sapir radically different from the set of possible analyses in generative phonology. The most important of these constraints comes to light if one considers the diagrams which Sapir often used in his discussions of phonological systems. These diagrams are tables of the phonetic segments which occur in a language, with parentheses around certain of those segments.

| p | | t | k |
|---|---|---|---|
| p′ | | t′ | k′ |
| (b) | | (d) | (g) |
| f | θ | s | x |
| (v) | (ð) | (z) | (γ) |

(From Sapir 1925:38.)

Sapir calls the unparenthesized symbols 'organic' segments and uses them in his phonologic representations; the parenthesized segments are called 'inorganic' and treated as variants of the 'organic' segments. Thus, Sapir has two inventories of segments, the full phonetic inventory and the 'organic' or 'phonologic' inventory, the latter inventory being a subset of the former. Sapir (1921) makes this fairly explicit: "Back of the purely objective system of sounds that is peculiar to a language and which can be arrived at only by a painstaking phonetic analysis, there is a *more restricted* "*inner*" or "*ideal*" system which, while perhaps equally unconscious to the naive speaker, can far more readily be brought to his consciousness as a finished pattern, a psychological mechanism" (p. 55; emphasis added). It should be noted that the constraint that the phonologic inventory be a subset of the phonetic inventory, a constraint which Sapir adhered to virtually without exception, would exclude a large subclass of the possible analyses of generative phonology, namely those analyses in which some underlying contrast is always neutralized phonetically. For example, Yokuts (Kuroda 1967) has only three different long vowels phonetically: [ō, ā, ē]; however, it is necessary to regard phonetic [ō] in Yokuts as representing two different underlying vowels, /ō/ and /ū/, because of the fact that for the purposes of Yokuts vowel harmony, certain occurrences of [ō] function as high vowels but other occurrences function as low vowels.

|  | passive<br>aorist | dubitative | underlying<br>form of stem |
|---|---|---|---|
| *care for* | gopit | gopol | gop |
| *swear* | muṭhun | muṭal | muṭ |
| *take in* | gōbit | gōbol | gōb |
| *steal* | ʔōṭʔut | ʔōṭʔal | ʔūṭʔ |

Vowel becomes rounded after rounded vowel of same height.

The constraint under which Sapir operated would exclude the analysis just suggested for Yokuts, which would involve setting up an underlying /ū/ in a language in which no phonetic [ū] occurs.

The only possible exception which I have been able to find to my assertion that Sapir's phonologic segment inventory is always a subset of his phonetic inventory is one extremely late work, the dictionary and grammatical sketch appended to *Nootka Texts*, done in collaboration with Morris Swadesh and published in 1939, the year of Sapir's death. Sapir and Swadesh's dictionary representations of Nootka morphemes contain several symbols which do not correspond to segment types which occur phonetically in the language, for example, their symbol for a [p] which alternates with an [m] and their symbols for vowels of 'variable length', which are long except when they occur in a word where they are preceded by two or more syllables, in which case they are short. However, since these symbols serve solely to abbreviate lists of allomorphs and are not interpretable as phonetic symbols in any language, let alone in Nootka, it is not clear that Sapir would have called these dictionary representations 'phonologic'.

My conjecture that Sapir would not have applied the word 'phonologic' to such representations relates to another aspect of my assertion that Sapir's phonologic segment inventory is a subset of his phonetic segment inventory. That assertion is to be interpreted in the really literal sense that not merely does he allow no underlying contrasts which are never realized as such, but also every phonologic segment type is identified with a phonetic segment type. The concept of 'archisegment', that is, a segment which is unspecified for some feature or features of articulation, was totally foreign to Sapir. Thus, for example, in describing a language such as Haida, where obstruents are predictably voiced in intervocalic position and predictably voiceless elsewhere, Sapir treats all obstruents as being phonologically voiceless and regards the voiced obstruents as arising through a 'euphonic law' which changes voiceless articulation into voiced in intervocalic position. It should be noted that in this respect Sapir's position is diametrically opposed to that of Bloomfield's *Language* (1933):[3] Bloomfield's 'phonemes' are 'archisegments' unspecified for predictable features such as the voicing of the above example. Thus, Sapir's phonologic representations are converted into phonetic representations by changing articulations into different articulations, whereas Bloomfield's phonemic representations, with one exception which I will note, are converted into phonetic representations by the filling in of unspecified articulations. The one class of exceptions to this assertion about Bloomfield is noteworthy, namely that in cases such as vowel reduction, where a phonological rule creates a new segment type in which two or more different underlying segment types are neutralized, Bloomfield will write the underlying segment symbol in his 'phonemic' transcriptions; he thus allows the Russian phonemic symbols /a, o/[4] and the English phonemic symbols /i, e, etc./ all to be pronounced [ə] when unstressed, as in his transcriptions /'gorot/, /goro'da/, /'biznes/, /'sekretejrij/.[5] However, Bloomfield does this only in cases where the neutralization creates a new segment type; in cases such as the devoicing of final obstruents in German and Russian, where the neutralization converts one already existing segment type into another, he allows, for example, only /bunt/ as the phonemic transcription of the words for *association* and *colorful*, rather than allowing 'phonemic' transcriptions /bund/ and /bunt/ respectively. I conjecture on the basis of these observations that if Bloomfield had been presented with a dialect which was exactly like standard German except that it had two stop series, voiced unaspirated and voiceless aspirated, which were neutralized in final position into a third phonetic type, voiceless unaspirated, Bloomfield would have allowed the distinct 'phonemic' transcriptions /bund/ and /bunt$^h$/ for the two homophonous words [bunt]. In cases such as the reduced vowel, Bloomfield inconsistently replaced his conception of a phoneme as an archisegment by a conception reminiscent of Sapir's charts with parentheses, which attempts to identify phonetic types as variants of other phonetic types.

In connection with the point that Sapir's phonologic segments are 'fully specified' for all articulatory features, it is worth noting the following passage: "In watching my Nootka interpreter write his language, I often had the curious feeling that he was transcribing an *ideal flow of phonetic elements* which he heard, inadequately from a purely objective standpoint, as the intention of the actual rumble of speech" (1921:56; emphasis added). Note also another passage where Sapir comes close to the notion 'archisegment' but then, through a terminological equivocation, replaces it by his conception of 'fully specified' 'organic' segments and variants of those segments: "the *t* of *time* is indeed noticeably different from that of *sting*, but the difference, to the consciousness of an English-speaking person, is quite irrelevant. It has no 'value'. If we compare the *t*-sounds of Haida, the Indian language spoken in the Queen Charlotte Islands, we find that precisely the same difference of articulation has a real value. In a word such as *sting* 'two', the *t* is pronounced precisely as in English, but in *st'a* 'from', the *t* is clearly 'aspirated', like that of *time*. In other words, an objective difference that is irrelevant in English is of functional value in Haida. . . . The objective comparison of sounds in two or more languages is, then, of no psychological or historical significance unless those sounds are first 'weighted', unless their phonetic 'values' are determined" (pp. 54–55). Sapir starts off by talking about the 'value' of the difference between two sounds, but then lapses into talking about the 'values' of the sounds themselves.

In one respect, Sapir's conception of segments in phonologic representations as 'fully specified' is reminiscent of such papers as Jakobson 1949, where Jakobson gives segment inventories with feature specifications in terms of pluses and blanks but no minuses.[6] Jakobson held at that time that a blank for a feature specification was equivalent to a minus and that the optimum representation was that which minimized the number of pluses in the segment inventory. But to treat blanks as equivalent to minuses implies that leaving out a plus in the representation of a segment is equivalent to representing it by the opposite value, yielding not an archisegment but a fully specified less highly marked segment, for example, representing a voiced segment as voiceless; rules converting these representations into phonetic representation would have the effect of converting articulations into different articulations, exactly as in Sapir.

I turn next to a point which was described well by Harris (1951*b*) in his review of Sapir's *Selected Writings*. Harris describes a hypothetical language in which there are no vowel sequences phonetically and a glottal stop intervenes whenever a morpheme which otherwise ends in a vowel precedes a morpheme which otherwise begins with a vowel. Harris states, "Sapir would say that no two vowels could come together (within a morpheme) and that when a particular morpheme conjunction would have the effect of bringing two vowels together a glottal stop comes in as a protective mechanism to keep them apart." When I first read this passage, I was amazed by Harris's total neglect of another possible analysis, namely that in which *all* intervocalic glottal stops, the morpheme-internal ones as well as those at morpheme boundary, are inserted by a rule. However, on reflection I am inclined to say that in neglecting that solution Harris was doing as Sapir would have done and that the solution which Harris ascribes to Sapir, namely treating only intermorphemic glottal stops as inserted by a rule, would indeed have been Sapir's solution. Two characteristics of Sapir's work play a role here: first, that any characteristic common to all the alternants of a morpheme will appear in Sapir's phonologic representation of it, so that if a morpheme always possesses a medial glottal stop, Sapir will write that segment in his phonologic representations even if there is a phonological rule of the language which would insert it anyway, and secondly, that Sapir would conversely treat one single phenomenon as two if its effects were manifested both in the alternations of some morphemes and in the constant shapes of others. A good example of this last point is that in the Southern Paiute grammar, Sapir (1930)[7] divides stem morphemes into three types: spirantizing, nasalizing, and geminating, which he indicates by so-called process markers $^s$, $^n$, and $^g$. However, the 'spirantizing' process marker is totally unnecessary, since spirantization is what happens to all intervocalic stops in Paiute: the 'spirantizing morphemes' are simply morphemes which end in a vowel, and when an affix beginning with a stop and a vowel gets added, the stop becomes spirantized by exactly the same phenomenon which spirantizes morpheme-internal intervocalic stops.[8]

A final respect in which Sapir's phonological analyses differ from those of modern generative phonology relates to the representation of segments by features or, alternatively, to the assembling of segment types into classes. This topic is perhaps the only one where Sapir, whose writings are usually models of clarity, is guilty of unusual vagueness, inconsistency, and ex post facto rationalization. One of the reasons why Sapir encounters difficulty in this area is his rejection of any universal phonetic theory. This rejection stems from a total failure on his part to conceive of the possibility of basing a universal phonetic theory on relative rather than absolute features; indeed, he used the terms 'universal' and 'absolute' as if they were interchangeable (e.g., 1925:36). In place of the universal phonetics which he rejects, Sapir (1925:42) says that classes are to be set up on the basis of distribution (e.g., the English segments which can occur after initial [s] would form a class) or of role in phonological alternations (e.g., English [f, θ, s] form a class since they but not other segments alternate with voiced counterparts) or of phonetic parallelism (e.g., Sapir cites the fact that English [p, t, k] have voiced counterparts as reason for their belonging together as a class). However, there are many ways in which this characterization of phonological class is unsatisfactory. First of all, the latter two criteria for class membership seem either to rely on the universal phonetics which Sapir rejects or to involve circularity: how can one refer to the voiced counterpart of something if classes such as 'voiced stop' are what he is trying to define? Secondly, there is no evidence that Sapir ever went systematically through a language and set up classes on the basis of these criteria; it is hard to imagine how they could be used to justify, for example, the class of voiceless spirants [f, θ, s, š] in English. Third, and most importantly, Sapir's notion of class is such as to imply that class relationships between segments will remain the same through a 'derivation' (if I may use such a word here). This fact is the basis of the failure of Sapir's (1925) attempt to explain historical 'drift' by suggesting that historical drift tends to be in terms of the segment classes set up by criteria such as those listed above. Recall the discussion of English and Spanish [s], [θ], and [ð] in "Sound Patterns." Sapir notes that [s] and [θ] often merge in Spanish dialects but not in English and that [θ] and [ð] often merge in English but not in Spanish and states, "We do not in English feel that θ is to be found in the neighborhood, as it were, of *s*, but that it is very close to ð. In Spanish, θ is not far from *s* but not at all close to ð." Sapir cites no distributional or other facts to explain these feelings, but there is one fairly obvious fact that he might have cited to explain a difference between the role of [θ] in Spanish and English, namely that Spanish [θ] but not English [θ] alternates with velars, for example, [diɣo]/[deθir]. Thus, as far as this alternation is concerned, [θ] goes in a class with the velars. However, the fact that it counts as a velar at one point in the grammar doesn't prevent it from counting as a dental at another point in the grammar, since, contrary to Sapir's claim about [θ] and [ð], [θ] does indeed get voiced to [ð] when it is in the environment for the voicing assimilation rule, as, for example, in [huðgar]. In generative phonological terms, what is going on here is simply that [θ]'s are underlying velars which a rule of the phonology turns into dentals in a certain environment; from that point on in the grammar they are dentals and not velars and are so treated by all subsequent phonological rules. Cases such as this are extremely common; for example, Finnish [v] functions as a semivowel in the 'earlier' phonological rules but as an obstruent in the 'later' phonological rules; with Finnish [h], the situation is reversed. Sapir's notion of 'class of segments' prevents him from making such distinctions and forces him, as it were, to describe a three-dimensional object in terms appropriate to a two-dimensional projection of it.[9]

I close with the observation that Sapir's own work may thus be confirmation of the Sapir-Whorf hypothesis, in that one who speaks in terms of unit 'sounds' rather than in terms of complexes of features can hardly fail to be led by this manner of speaking to introduce a notion of 'class of sounds' which does not allow a segment to change its class membership during the course of a derivation. The history of linguistics might have been vastly different if Sapir had learned to interpret the names p, t, k, and so on syntactically as common nouns (thus represented semantically as conjunctions of properties) rather than as proper nouns (represented semantically as individuals).

# 2 The Phonological Theory behind Whitney's *Sanskrit Grammar*

William Dwight Whitney's *Sanskrit Grammar* was written long before linguists realized that grammars were really the subject matter of linguistics; indeed, Bloomfield (1926) may have been the first linguist to realize that one of the linguist's basic tasks is to characterize in general terms the nature of the different kinds of representation involved in linguistic description and of the systems of rules which relate the different representations (morphemic, phonemic, etc.) of an utterance.[1] As may be expected, neither the *Grammar* itself not Whitney's various works on general linguistics (1867, 1875) contain any explicit discussion of the considerations involved in Whitney's selection of the 'base forms' by which he cites morphemes or of the relationship between the 'rules' of the grammar and the representations of utterances. It is my purpose in this paper to determine on the basis of the *Sanskrit Grammar* Whitney's answers to these questions which he never explicitly treated.

Before taking up those questions, however, it will be necessary for me to justify my implicit assertion that Whitney intended his *Sanskrit Grammar* as a grammar in the sense of twentieth-century linguistics, that is, as a synchronic rather than a historical description of the language: a specification of what is possible in a given variety of a language (or possibly in several varieties of the language, as is the case in the *Sanskrit Grammar*) and an explanation of those facts by the postulation of mechanisms which are operative within that variety of the language rather than merely by the the chronicling of the historical events which brought about those facts. Whitney makes admirably clear that his grammar is a synchronic rather than a diachronic study by numerous passages in which he contrasts his

Reprinted by permission from *Languages and Areas: Studies Presented to George V. Bobrinskoy* (Chicago: Division of the Humanities, University of Chicago, 1967), pp. 77–85. Copyright 1967 by Division of Humanities, The University of Chicago.

description with a historical description. For example, in § 155, Whitney states, "In a few roots, when a final sonant aspirate [/$g^h$, $d^h$, $b^h$/;[2] also /h/, as representing an original /$g^h$/] thus loses its aspiration, the initial sonant consonant /g, d, or b/ *becomes aspirate*" (emphasis added). Thus Whitney sets up a synchronic rule making initial stops aspirated even though (as is clear from the following sentence) he was aware that the segments in question were historically aspirates which had lost their aspiration: "That is to say, the original aspirate of such roots is restored, when its presence does not interfere with the euphonic law, of comparatively recent origin, which (in Sanskrit as in Greek) forbids a root to both begin and end with an aspirate." Likewise, Whitney mentions the historical fact that Sanskrit palatals derive historically from velars but accounts for the velar/palatal alternation, which arose historically through the change of velars into palatals before front vowels, not by giving a rule converting velars into palatals but instead by giving a rule (actually, several rules) which convert palatals into velars; note his remark (§ 43): "In some situations, the original guttural shows itself—or, as it appears from the point of view of Sanskrit, the palatal reverts to its original guttural." Similarly, Whitney observes that the alveo-palatal spirant /ś/ derives historically from a /k/, thus bringing about a /k/-/ś/ alternation, but describes the alternation in his grammar as a change of underlying /ś/ to /k/ and not vice versa; note his statement (§ 218b): "a /ś/ remains unchanged before /p/ in the compound viśpáti." Historically, the /ś/ is certainly not "unchanged" : it was originally /k/ and then became /ś/; however, "from the point of view of Sanskrit" it is "unchanged" in that it is not subject to the change of /ś/ to /k/ which is one of the synchronic rules of Sanskrit (at least, as formulated by Whitney; my citation of various "rules of Sanskrit" should not be interpreted as implying that I believe that the rules in question would be part of a "descriptively adequate" (Chomsky 1964:63) grammar of Sanskrit: Whitney's grammar leaves room for improvement, although that fact is of no concern to me here, since my subject matter is Whitney's theoretical position rather than the Sanskrit language). The many examples such as these in the *Sanskrit Grammar* make it clear that for Whitney a grammar of a language is a purely synchronic description and that whatever mentions he makes of the history of the language are intended as asides rather than as part of the grammar proper.

I turn now to the question of the types of representation which Whitney uses in the *Sanskrit Grammar*. There are many places in the *Grammar* where Whitney gives two representations side by side, for example (§ 127):

rājendra (rāja-indra)
hitopadeśaḥ (hita-upadeśaḥ)

The left-hand representation is essentially a phonetic transcription: in chapter 2, Whitney describes the articulations which he believed corresponded to the different alphabetic symbols which he used, and his extensive discussion of the "true"pronunciation of certain alphabetic symbols whose phonetic value is not universally agreed upon (e.g., in §§ 37c and 70a) makes it especially clear that each symbol in this representation was to correspond to a definite articulation. It is not a phonemic transcription, since, for example, voiced /h/ and voiceless /ḥ/ are written differently even though in complementary distribution.

The representation inside parentheses in the above examples is an underlying representation, involving a decomposition of the form into immediate constituents and a representation of each of those constituents as a sequence of segments which are converted by "phonological rules" into the representation on the left. There is considerable variation, however, in how far under Whitney's underlying representations lie. Some of the underlying representations are "base forms" of individual morphemes; other underlying representations involve composite items (such as upadeśaḥ in the above example) which have already been subjected to various phonological rules. Since the composite items can themselves be decomposed into immediate constituents and these constituents given a segmental underlying representation, presumably for Whitney each utterance would eventually derive from a "tree" indicating the immediate constituency relationships between the parts of the utterance, where each "terminal node" in the tree is a morpheme represented as a sequence of "underlying" segments (which may be altered, elided, or subjected to additions in the course of the application of the phonological rules). Whitney, of course, never exhibits such a "tree"; however, a "tree" such as I have just described would be the logical consequence of his universal practice of representing the various words and phrases with which he deals in terms of their immediate constituents.

Whitney's use of segments in the underlying representation of morphemes (and larger constituents) is subject to several constraints, of which the following are the principal ones:

1. The inventory of segments involved in underlying representations is contained within the inventory of segments involved in phonetic representations. In other words, only those alphabetic symbols which appear in the phonetic representation of the language are admitted in underlying representations. There are several occasions on which Whitney treats situations which lend themselves to a treatment involving an underlying contrast which is neutralized in the phonetic output; in each case Whitney avoids such a solution and treats the alternation by giving long (possibly open-ended) lists of morphemes. Note, for example, § 219: "final /j/ is in one

set of words treated like /c/ and in another set like /ś/ . . . To the former or yuj-class belong . . . about twenty roots and radical stems [Whitney lists them]; also, stems formed with the suffixes /aj/ and /ij/ . . . ; and ṛtvij. . . . To the latter or mṛj-class belong only about one-third as many [Whitney lists them]." Rather than setting up underlying forms which distinguish two different /j/'s, one the voiced counterpart of /c/ and the other the voiced counterpart of /ś/, and considering the difference in the behavior of the morphemes yuj/yukti and mṛj/marṣṭi to correspond to an underlying difference between the final segments, Whitney makes that difference a feature of the entire morpheme. In a rather intriguing passage on the next page of the *Grammar*, Whitney refers to the possibility of having a segment type which never occurs on the phonetic level; after discussing the different behavior of two classes of morphemes ending in /h/, one in which the /h/ behaves like the voiced aspirate counterpart of /c/ and the other in which it behaves like the voiced aspirate counterpart of /ś/, Whitney states, "This is as if we have to assume as a transition sound a sonant aspirate lingual /ẓʰ/, with the euphonic effects of a lingual and of a sonant aspirate, itself disappearing under the law of the existing language which admits no sonant sibilant." The especially interesting point in this quotation is Whitney's description of the /ẓʰ/ as a *transition sound*: presumably, something which may serve as an intermediate stage between the underlying form and the phonetic form, but is not admissible into the basic form of a morpheme. Whitney gives no evidence that he even considered the possibility of representing morphemes by basic forms involving segments such as /ẓʰ/, which would participate in an underlying contrast with other segments but coalesce with other segments in the phonetic output.

2. Indeed, Whitney generally appears to operate under the much stronger constraint that the base form of a morpheme must be identical with one of the phonetic forms which it actually manifests. For example, in the passage from § 155 quoted above, Whitney fails to consider the possibility of distinguishing those roots whose initial consonant is aspirated when the final becomes deaspirated (the initial being otherwise unaspirated *bodʰate/bʰotsyati*) from those in which the initial voiced stop is always unaspirated (*dabʰus/dipsati*)[2] by assigning the one class underlying forms beginning with an aspirate (e.g., *bʰudʰ*, a combination of segments which would otherwise never occur in the language) and the other class underlying forms with an unaspirated initial (*dabʰ*). He instead assigns to both types of morphemes underlying forms having a voiced unaspirate for the initial and gives the rule of § 155 which aspirates the initial segment of the morphemes of a certain list whenever the final consonant of that morpheme becomes unaspirated. Note that Whitney fails to consider the nonoccurring /bʰudʰ/ as the underlying form despite his knowledge that /bʰudʰ/ was

indeed the form from which the morpheme historically derives (§ 155a). In this connection, note also Whitney's remark (§ 240b) "didéva, . . . , etc. from √dīv; tiṣṭʰeva from √ṣṭʰīv; srevāyāmi, srévuka, from √srīv . . . on account of which it is, doubtless, that these roots are written with /iv/ (div, etc.) by the Hindu grammarians, although they nowhere show a short /i/, in either verb-forms or derivatives." This passage is quoted from a section dealing with the insertion of /a/ ("guna"); insertion of /a/ in /div/ would yield underlying /daiv/ = phonetic /dev/ in forms such as /didéva/; however, Whitney excludes the possibility of an underlying form /div/ because of the fact that short /i/ is never (phonetically) manifested anywhere in the paradigm.

As indicated above, Whitney's phonological rules do not convert underlying representations directly into phonetic form but rather involve the passage through several intermediate stages. References to intermediate stages of derivations are numerous. To cite a number of them: "A guna-vowel differs from the corresponding simple vowel by a prefixed /a/-element, which is combined with the other according to the usual rules" (§ 235a); thus, for example, underlying /i/ becomes /ai/ by the gunation rule, which in turn yields /e/ by the "usual rules" for vowel combination. "Final /ś/ reverts to its original /k/, in internal combination, only before the /s/ of a verbal stem or ending (whence by 180 /kṣ/); before /t/ and /tʰ/ it everywhere becomes /ṣ/ (whence by 197, /ṣṭ/ and /ṣṭʰ/". (§ 218); thus, /śs/ is converted into /kṣ/ through an intermediate state of /ks/, /śt/ is converted into /ṣṭ/ through an intermediate stage of /ṣt/, and /śtʰ/ is converted into /ṣṭʰ/ through an intermediate stage of /ṣtʰ/. "In general, only one consonant, of whatever kind, is allowed to stand at the end of a word; if two or more would etymologically occur there, the last is dropped, and again the last, and so on, till only one remains. Thus /tudants/ becomes /tudant/, and this /tudan/; /udañc-s/ becomes /udañk/, and this /udañ/; and /acʰāntst/ . . . is in like manner reduced to /acʰān/" (§ 150). "When successive words like /indra ā ihi/ are to be combined, the first combination, to /indrā/ is made first, and the result is /indre hi/ (not /indrāi hi/, from /indra e hi/)" (§ 127b). "For all the processes of external combination—that is to say, in composition and sentence-collocation—a stem-final or word-final is in general to be regarded as having, not its etymological form, but that given it by the rules as to permitted finals. From this, however, are to be excepted the /s/ and /r/: the various transformations of these sounds have nothing to do with the visarga to which as finals before a pause they have—doubtless at a comparatively recent period of phonetic history—come to be reduced" (§ 152). The last quotation refers to two intermediate stages between the basic representation and the phonetic representation of an utterance: the "rules as to permitted finals" (exclusive of the rules converting /s, r/ before pause into /ḥ/, the "visarga" of the above passage) apply, yielding an intermediate stage which serves as input to the "processes of external combination," which yield another intermediate stage which serves as the input to the rule converting /s, r/ before pause into /ḥ/.

While Whitney thus makes it abundantly clear that his rules are to apply sequentially, that is, that rules generally operate not on the basic forms of morphemes but on the results obtained by applying other rules, he leaves very unclear the question of how the rules are organized. The order of presentation of the rules bears no relation to the order in which they apply; for example, while the quotation from § 235a cited above makes it clear that the gunation rule applies before the rules simplifying vowel sequences, the latter are discussed (§§ 125–31) long before the former. Furthermore, as was pointed out by Morris Halle (1962), appropriate ordering of the rules which Whitney cites makes certain rules completely superfluous. Halle treats the following rules from Whitney:

(1) Two similar simple vowels, short or long, coalesce and form the corresponding long vowel . . . [§ 126].

(2) An *a*-vowel combines with a following *i*-vowel to *e*; with a *u*-vowel, to *o* . . . [§ 127].

(3) The *i*-vowels, the *u*-vowels, and the *ṛ* before a dissimilar vowel or diphthong are each converted into its corresponding semi-vowel, *y*, or *v*, or *r* . . . [§ 129].

(4) Of a diphthong, the final *i*- or *u*- element is changed into its corresponding semi-vowel, *y* or *v*, before any vowel or diphthong: thus *e* really *ai* . . .) becomes *ay*, and *o* (that is *au* . . .) becomes *av* . . . [§ 131].

Halle observes that

If the first three rules are applied in the order (1), (3), (2), two important economies can be effected. First, in rule (3), the qualification 'before a dissimilar vowel or diphthong' can be simplified to 'before a vowel,' for at the point where rule (3) applies, only sequences of dissimilar vowels remain, since rule (1) replaces all sequences of identical vowels by single long vowels. Moreover, rule (4) can be dispensed with altogether. Since rule (3) converts /i/ and /u/ in position before a vowel into /y/ and /v/, respectively, no sequences of /ai/ and /au/ in position before a vowel will ever be turned into /e/ or /o/, respectively, by the subsequent application of rule (2). Inasmuch as rule (2) is the only source of /e/ and /o/ in the language, there is now no need for rule (4), whose sole function is to convert /e/ and /o/ into /ay and /av/ in those cases where by the proposed ordering of the rules, /e/ and /o/ could not have arisen. [1962:58]

While it will indeed turn out that Whitney's grammar is in some cases ambiguous, to the extent that, for the rules to yield the derivations cited by Whitney, an ordering would have to be imposed on the rules, which Whitney does not specify, nonetheless much of the sequence of rule application is independent of any imposition of ordering on the rules and indeed follows from a mechanism implicit in Whitney's presentation. Specifically, Whitney's citation of "underlying forms" which are intermediate stages corresponding to the immediate constituents of the forms under discussion suggests a cyclic mode of application, wherein the rules apply first to the "innermost" constituents, then to the next larger constituents, and so on.[3] The mode of rule application on each constituent seems to be that any rule which will adjust an "inadmissible sequence"(e.g., a /ś/ & /s/ sequence at the junction of two constituents) in the constituent is applied; then if any other "inadmissible sequence" remains or has just been created by the rule just applied (e.g., the /ks/ which has resulted from /śs/), the rule adjusting it is applied; and so on, until no more "inadmissible sequences" remain in the constituent; then the derivation passes on to the next larger constituent. It should be noted that if the system of rules applies cyclically and consists precisely of rules for adjusting "inadmissible sequences" (understood as the sequences which are excluded in the phonetic representations), then at each stage of the derivation there will be little choice as to which rule may apply, even if the rules are taken to be unordered. The need to choose between rules arises only when a constituent contains two or more "inadmissible sequences." Whitney's rules appear to be such that if a constituent contains two nonoverlapping inadmissible sequences, the same result will arise no matter which one is adjusted first. Thus, given cyclic application, the only place where the unorderedness of Whitney's rules causes an indeterminacy as to the total effect of the rules is in the case of a constituent containing two overlapping inadmissible sequences (and, in particular, a single sequence which is inadmissible for two separate reasons). One place where this arises is in /#udañc#/, where both /ñc#/[4] and /c#/ are inadmissible, the one because there are no final consonant clusters and the other because there are no final palatals. To get the sequence of steps cited by Whitney in § 150 (udanc-s → udañk → udañ), it will be necessary for the stage /#udañc#/ (which arises from the adjustment of inadmissible /cs#/ by the deletion of the /s/) first to be subjected to the adjustment of inadmissible /c#/ to /k#/ rather than by the adjustment of the equally inadmissible sequence /ñc#/ by deletion of the /c/; in the resulting sequence /#udañk#/, both /ñk/ and /ñk#/ are inadmissible, the one by virtue of the nasal not being homorganic with the following stop and the other by virtue of the consonant cluster being final; the adjustment of the former inadmissibility (yielding /ñk#/) will have to precede the adjustment of the latter inadmissibility (yielding finally /ñ#/); any sequence of rule applications other than the above ([1] final palatal → velar, [2] nasal assimilates, [3] final clusters simplify) would yield the incorrect result *udañ*. However, examples such as these are sufficiently hard to find that Whitney may well be excused for having failed to realize that ordering of rules is necessary even under cyclic application.

The cyclic mode of application which I am ascribing to Whitney will insure that the "rules as to permitted finals" will have applied before the "rules of external combination" (cf. the quote from § 152); given a constituent of the form # A # B #, the application of the rules to the constituents A and B will have included the application of the "rules as to permitted finals," since each of those constituents is indeed bounded by word boundaries, so that when the rules are applied to the constituent AB the rules as to permitted finals will have already applied to A and B. Similarly, the "rules as to permitted finals" will have already applied before the rule converting /s, r/ before pause into /ḥ/ can apply, since the latter applies only to a constituent bounded by "phrase boundary" (or pause); the immediate constituents of such a constituent will be bounded by word boundary rather than by phrase boundary and thus when the phonological rules apply to them, the "rules as to permitted finals" will be applicable but the rule converting /s, r/ into /ḥ/ will not.

Note further that under the mode of rule application and notion of rule which I ascribe to Whitney, the rule (4) which Halle eliminates indeed cannot be eliminated from the grammar: the /au/ of an underlying form /bʰau/ would be an "inadmissible sequence" and would be converted into /o/ even if it were contained in a larger constituent in which it was followed by a vowel (e.g., bʰau & a = bʰava); when the cycle applied to that larger constituent, there would no longer be any sequence /au/, and a rule such as 4 would be needed to restore it. In order to make the rules operate in such a way that rule 4 would still be unnecessary, it would be necessary to modify the mode of rule application in some way so as to postpone the application of rule 2 until after the other rules affecting vowel sequences have applied, which could be done by modifying rule 2 so as to make it apply only when "phrase boundary" is present. However, such a modification runs completely counter to Whitney's actual practice: his rules require the presence of a boundary element only when that boundary element plays a role in determining the admissibility or inadmissibility of a sequence of segments; since /ai/ and /au/ are inadmissible regardless of whether they are adjacent to phrase boundary, Whitney would be forced to say as much, thus making rule 4 necessary.

It should be noted, finally, that this notion of rule and mode of rule application provides a motivation for (and indeed entails) the otherwise quite arbitrary constraints noted above which Whitney operates under. If each constituent is to be subjected to the same system of rules for adjusting inadmissible sequences of segments, then no advantage is gained by having a base form containing a phonetically nonoccurring segment, since if it did contain such a segment, the rules of the language would convert it to something else before they applied to any larger constituent containing that morpheme. Similarly, if an underlying form /b$^h$ud$^h$/ were set up, the "euphonic law" which eliminates inadmissible C$^h$VC$^h$ sequences by deaspirating the first consonant would have already applied before the larger constituent (e.g., b$^h$otsyati) which contained the environment for the deaspiration of the second segment would be reached, so that no advantage would be gained by setting up underlying /b$^h$ud$^h$/, and a rule would be necessary to aspirate the initial stops of forms such as /b$^h$otsyati/. Moreover, this interpretation makes it clear why the "transition sound" /ẓ$^h$/ which Whitney suggests in § 219 would have to be precisely that: a segment created by the phonological rules rather than one present from the beginning. If the /ẓ$^h$/ were present at the beginning, it would be converted into /h/ when the rules are applied to the morpheme itself, so that it would have to be reintroduced by a phonological rule in those combinations which behave "as if" there were "a sonant lingual aspirate" before the junction between the constituents.

I thus sum up my interpretation of Whitney's position as follows: the phonological rules of a language are rules which replace "inadmissible" segments and segment sequences by other segments or sequences, where the same items are taken to be inadmissible regardless of how "deep" or "shallow" they appear in the "derivation" (keeping in mind, however, that boundaries are involved in the admissibility of segments and sequences: /nt/ is admissible but /nt#/ is not; /s#/ is admissible but /s%/ is not); the rules operate in cyclic fashion, first the innermost constituents being adjusted to admissibility, then the constituents of which these are immediate constituents, then the constituents of which those are immediate constituents, and so on. In applying the rules to any particular constituent, the mode of application is "random sequential":[5] any rule applicable to the constituent is applied, then any rule applicable to the result thus obtained, then any rule which is then applicable, until no more rules are applicable.

Two consequences of the position which I ascribe to Whitney should be pointed out. First, the entities involved in Whitney's transcriptions (as in those of many later linguists such as Boas and Sapir) are not "archisegments" such as Bloomfield's and Bloch's phoneme and Trubetzkoy's archiphoneme (entities characterized only by those features of pronunciation which are "distinctive") but are rather "fully specified" segments corresponding to particular articulations. Thus a rule of phonology for

Whitney, Boas, or Sapir is not something which fills in a predictable and hitherto unspecified feature of articulation but rather something which replaces one articulation by a different articulation. Second, the grammar is "monolevel" [6] in that the various representations of an utterance involve units chosen from a single inventory rather than two or more separate inventories such as are found in the works of the recent structuralists, who insist on a sharp distinction between phonetic units, phonemic units, and morphophonemic units, and consistently criticize any "mixing of levels." Thus, Whitney is being perfectly consistent in referring to underlying segments as "sounds." Whitney's position in this respect is very similar to that of generative phonologists, for whom all phonological representations, be they input, output, or intermediate, are of the same formal nature, namely matrices of feature specifications involving exactly the same set of features. The principal differences between Whitney and the generative phonologists are thus (1) his use of unanalyzed segments rather than features as the fundamental units of phonology, (2) his requirements that all stages of the derivation of an utterance be made to conform to the same restrictions on permitted segments and sequences which are met by phonetic representations (generative phonology, by contrast, allows such restrictions to be postponed until after the operation of the phonological cycle, so that a large part of the phonology may operate in terms of segments and combinations of segments which never occur phonetically in the language), and (3) the explicit ordering of the rules of phonology by generative phonologists, as against Whitney's failure to indicate any ordering even in the cases where it is important, although (as was shown above) the first two points make ordering of rules less crucial to Whitney than it is in generative phonology. [7]

# 3 The Role of a Phonological Feature System in a Theory of Language

The system of phonological features used in Halle's *The Sound Pattern of Russian* is essentially the same as that presented in Jakobson, Fant, and Halle's *Preliminaries to Speech Analysis* eight years earlier. However, the system of features played a very different role in the theoretical frameworks of these two works. In *Preliminaries*, as in Jakobson's other phonological writings, the features are intended as *distinctive* features: they are intended as a universal system of "phonemic" representation, that is, a system for representing contrasts between the utterances of any language. Jakobson sought a feature system which was not only universal but also minimal; he thus presents many cross-linguistic complementary distribution arguments for uniting various different oppositions into a single feature, for example, uniting the oppositions rounded/unrounded and pharyngealized/non-pharyngealized into the single feature flat/plain.

If a phonemic representation as envisioned by Jakobson were incorporated into a full grammar of a language, that is, a device which specifies how semantic representation is paired with phonetic representation in that language, that grammar would have to contain both a *phonological component*, which would assign a phonemic representation to the "surface syntactic" representation of each utterance, and a *feature interpretation component*, which would specify the relationship between phonemic representation and phonetic representation in that language. The feature interpretation component would presumably have to involve (*a*) rules predicting "nondistinctive" values of the universal features (e.g., rules which specify the nondistinctive voicelessness of final obstruents in Russian and the nondistinctive voicedness of obstruents which are followed by a voiced obstruent), (*b*) rules stating which of the possible realizations of

Reprinted by permission from *Phonological Theory*, ed. V. Makkai (New York: Holt, Rinehart and Winston, 1972), pp 522–28. Copyright © 1972 by Holt, Rinehart and Winston, Inc.

each of the universal features is utilized in a given language (e.g., a rule of English that the feature of flatness is realized as lip-rounding rather than as pharyngealization), and (c) rules specifying "ideal values" for physical parameters involved in the realization of those features (e.g., a rule in Serbo-Croatian that a long vowel is about $1\frac{1}{2}$ times as long as a short vowel, as opposed to Czech, in which a long vowel is about $2\frac{1}{2}$ times as long as a short vowel).

*The Sound Pattern of Russian*, while utilizing almost the same feature system which Jakobson had set up for universal representation of phonemic oppositions, rejected the notion of phonemic representation. In that work Halle describes the phonological component of a grammar as consisting of an ordered system of rules for the conversion of "surface syntactic" representation into "systematic phonetic" representation. Here the "surface syntactic" representation of an utterance indicates what morphemes are involved in the utterance, what sequence they come in, how they are grouped together, and what syntactic category the various groups belong to, and each morpheme is represented as a sequence of segments, each segment being a set of "underlying" specifications for phonological features. The "systematic phonetic" representation of an utterance is a representation in which each segment is assigned a value of + or − for each of the universal features, regardless of whether that value is "distinctive." The full grammar of a language would thus involve both a phonological component (which Halle describes in great detail) and a feature interpretation component (which he largely ignores), although the feature interpretation component would now only perform the second and third of the three functions listed above and would have for its input the "systematic phonetic" representation rather than a "phonemic" representation. The phonological rules operate in terms of the same system of features on which both the underlying representation of morphemes and the "systematic phonetic" representation of utterances are based. Each rule specifies the class of segments affected in terms of a formula involving those features and specifies its effect as certain changes in the feature composition of the affected segment, as in the Korean rule

$$\begin{bmatrix} +\text{obstruent} \\ +\text{closure} \\ -\text{tense} \end{bmatrix} \rightarrow [+\text{voiced}] \text{ in env. } [+\text{voiced}] \text{——} [+\text{voiced}]$$

which changes to + the voicing specification of a nontense stop or affricate which is preceded by a voiced segment and followed by a voiced segment, as in [pat] + [etta] → [padetta] 'received'.[1]

Since Halle's purposes in *Sound Pattern* and subsequent works are so different from those of Jakobson in *Preliminaries*, the question obviously arises of whether Jakobson's features are adequate for Halle's purpose. It should first be noted that there are a couple of respects in which the feature system of *Preliminaries* is inadequate even for Jakobson's purposes, in that there are languages possessing contrasts which cannot be represented in that feature system. For example, the feature system of *Preliminaries* contains a feature of *stridency*, which is supposed to represent both the difference between affricates and ordinary stops and the difference between the "noisy" spirants [f, s, š, x] and the "less" noisy spirants [ɸ, θ, ś, ç]; however, the existence of languages such as Chipewyan, which has a three-way contrast between [t, tθ, tˢ], shows that the difference between stops and affricates and the difference between "noisier" and "less noisy" places of articulation are two independent dimensions on which sounds may differ and thus may not be subsumed under a single feature, as in *Preliminaries*. Using the terms "delayed release" and "proximal"[2] to denote these two oppositions, the segments in question may be represented as

|                 | θ | s | t (dental) | t (alveolar) | tθ | tˢ |
|-----------------|---|---|---|---|----|----|
| closure         | − | − | + | + | + | + |
| delayed release | − | − | − | − | + | + |
| proximal        | − | + | − | + | − | + |

The above is an example of a case in which distinct articulatory oppositions which Jakobson subsumed under one feature may in fact not be so subsumed within an adequate universal theory of phonology. It is interesting to note that such may be the case even when the two articulatory oppositions never function as independent dimensions of contrast. Consider the feature of "flatness," under which Jakobson subsumes the articulatory oppositions of lip-rounding and pharyngealization. Arabic has an opposition between plain and pharyngealized consonants and has a three-vowel system [i, a, u], of which [u] is rounded; vowels are pharyngealized when adjacent to a pharyngealized consonant. Consider what phonological rules and "feature interpretation rules" would be needed to represent these facts within a theory in which the phonological component of the grammar operates in terms of the flat/nonflat opposition and "rounded" and "pharyngealized" figure only in the feature interpretation component. The phonological component would have to contain the rule

$$[+\text{syllabic}] \rightarrow [+\text{flat}] \text{ in env.} \left\{ \begin{array}{l} \underline{\quad} \begin{bmatrix} +\text{flat} \\ -\text{syllabic} \end{bmatrix} \\ \begin{bmatrix} +\text{flat} \\ -\text{syllabic} \end{bmatrix} \underline{\quad} \end{array} \right\}$$

and the feature interpretation component would have to specify that "flat" is interpreted as "pharyngealized" when attached to a consonant or to a front or low vowel, as "rounded" when attached to a high back vowel, and as "rounded plus pharyngealized" when attached to a high back vowel which is adjacent to a [+flat] consonant. But note that this means that the generalization "vowel is pharyngealized when adjacent to pharyngealized consonant" must in effect be stated twice, once in the phonological component and once in the feature interpretation component. Thus, a theory of phonology in which pharyngealization and rounding are treated as the same feature throughout the phonological component suffers from exactly the same defect which Halle (1959: 22–23) pointed out in theories which require underlying forms to be converted into phonetic representation through an intermediate stage of "taxonomic phonemic" representation: in each case the theory may force one to treat a single phonological process as if it were rather two unrelated processes in two separate components of the grammar. I accordingly conclude that even if there are no languages in which rounding and pharyngealization function as independent oppositions, a theory which treats them as separate must still be held superior to a theory which subsumes them under a single feature.

The above examples have related to the superiority of one feature system over another on the basis of the representations which it gives as output of the phonological component, in the one case because of the inability of one of the systems to distinguish things which contrast at that level, in the other case because the mode of representation forces the feature interpretation component to duplicate rules which are already part of the phonological component. However, a system of features may be superior to another on grounds relating exclusively to the phonological component, namely relating to the role which the features play in specifying the classes of segments to which the various rules apply and the effects which these segments are subjected to. An instructive example in this connection is the comparison of the features "compact" and "diffuse" with alternative features which could be employed to represent the same contrasts. The feature of "diffuseness" has been used to oppose high vowels and alveolar, dental, and labial consonants (which are all designated as [+diffuse]) to low and mid vowels and palatal and velar consonants (which are all [−diffuse]). The feature of compactness has been used to separate the low vowels ([+compact]) from the mid and high vowels ([−compact]); there has been no uniformity on the assignment of values for compactness to consonants, which in some works (Halle 1964b) are taken as unspecified for compactness, whereas in others (Halle 1959) the [+diffuse] consonants are said to be [−compact] and the [−diffuse] consonants [+compact]. Suppose that a theory of language involving the feature of diffuseness is compared with an otherwise identical theory in which diffuseness is replaced by a feature in which consonants are matched with vowels in precisely the opposition fashion, that it, a theory which differs from the former by having instead of diffuseness a feature called "high" which opposes high vowels and velar and palatal consonants ([+high]) to mid and low vowels and alveolar, dental, and labial consonants ([−high]). Crucial for choosing between these two theories is a consideration of phonological rules in which either a class containing both consonants and vowels is involved in the rule or a vowel or consonant has an unambiguously "assimilative" effect on a consonant or vowel, respectively: in the former case if the one feature system allows the class to be specified with a single feature value (say, [+high]), then the other will require a disjunction involving another feature also (say, "diffuse consonantal or nondiffuse nonconsonantal"), thus providing evidence that it is the features of the former system that are functional in the rule; in the latter case the effect of the rule will in the one system be to make the two segments agree in the value of the feature in question, in the other system to disagree, thus giving evidence that the former system more correctly characterizes the notion "assimilation."

In every case which I have been able to find which is of relevance to the choice between these two theories, evidence is provided for the superiority of "high" over "diffuse." (1) In Sanskrit [s] becomes retroflexed after [i, u, r, k]. Since Sanskrit [r] has palatal place of articulation and since palatal and velar consonants other than [k, r] become something else before [s] (i.e., all consonants become voiceless and unaspirated before [s] and palatal obstruents become velars), the rule can be expressed as

$$\begin{bmatrix} +\text{obstruent} \\ -\text{grave} \\ -\text{closure} \end{bmatrix} \rightarrow [+\text{high}] \text{ in env. } [+\text{high}] \text{ ——}$$

that is, it is simply an assimilation of the feature of highness. If this rule were expressed in terms of diffuseness rather than highness, it would appear to do two quite distinct things: to assimilate diffuseness after a nondiffuse consonant and to dissimilate diffuseness after a diffuse vowel.[3] (2) In Maxakalí, a language spoken in Brazil, there are phonological processes by which a vowel is added after a word-final stop and the stop is either weakened or deleted entirely (Gudschinsky, Popovich, and Popovich 1970). The vowels added are as follows: after [p], add [ē]; after [t], add [a]; after [č], add [i]; after [k], add [ɨ]. Note that the vowel added has the same "highness," that is, the opposite diffuseness to the consonant to which it is added. Moreover, the choice of vowel is determined by an "assimilation": less movement is required on the organs of speech in passing from [p] to [ē], and so on, than would be required in passing to vowels of the opposite highness (i.e., the same diffuseness) as the consonant: [pɨ], [ti], [ča], [kė]. Thus the theory with highness instead of diffuseness correctly represents the assimilatory nature of this vowel insertion rule. (3) The extremely common phonological rule by which [ty] becomes [č] is universally classed as an assimilation and, in terms of the theory with highness, consists of the stop taking on the [+high] specification of the glide; however, in terms of the theory with diffuseness this change looks like a dissimilation: [t] and [y] are [+diffuse] but [č] is [−diffuse]. (4) In the Ripuarian dialect group of German, which includes the dialect of Köln, dentals have become velars after high vowels, as in [huŋk] 'dog', [kiŋk] 'child', [lük] 'people', [tˢik] 'time', corresponding to standard German *Hund, Kind, Leute, Zeit* (Schirmunski 1962:121).This change is also an assimilation of highness.

Not only are there cases such as the above which argue for classing high vowels together with velar and palatal rather than dental and labial consonants and to my knowledge no cases which argue for the opposite classification, but it it quite easy to give a uniform articulatory characterization of the [+high] segments: they are the segments whose primary constriction or closure is above a line drawn from the rear of the alveolar ridge to the uvula,[4] whereas a uniform articulatory characterization of the "diffuse" segments may well be impossible; the articulatory definitions which have been proposed for it either do not define the class of segments enumerated above[5] or do not provide a criterion which applies uniformly to consonants and vowels.[6]

In this connection, it is worth bringing up the other feature in *Preliminaries* whose articulatory definition has never been satisfactory, namely "vocalic." The definitions in Halle (1964*b*) ("vocalic sounds are pronounced with a periodic excitation and with an open oral cavity, i.e., one in which the most extreme degree of narrowness is a constriction"; "consonantal sounds are pronounced with occlusion or contact in the central path through the oral cavity") appear to preclude a segment from being both [+vocalic] and [+consonantal]; nevertheless, these two features are supposed to "produce a quadripartite division of the sounds of speech into (1) vowels, which are vocalic and nonconsonantal; (2) liquids . . . , which are vocalic and consonantal; (3) consonants, which are nonvocalic and consonantal; and (4) glides . . . , which are nonvocalic and nonconsonantal" (Halle 1964*b*:327).

One clear defect of the feature system of *Preliminaries* is that it provides no way of representing the difference between syllabic and nonsyllabic liquids and nasals. Since there are languages in which utterances may differ solely by virtue of the syllabicity or nonsyllabicity of a liquid or nasal (e.g., in many dialects of English the verbal noun *gambling* has a nonsyllabic [l] but the present participle *gambling* has a syllabic [l]), an adequate phonological theory must provide some feature to distinguish between these segments. Leaving aside the difficult question of giving an articulatory characterization of syllabicity, I note that it is the only systematic distinction between vowels and glides and moreover that there are many cases in which an alternation between vowel and glide is governed by exactly the same rule which governs an alternation between syllabic liquid or nasal and nonsyllabic liquid or nasal; for example, Sanskrit has a rule by which high vowels become glides and syllabic liquids become nonsyllabic when a vowel follows. I accordingly propose to scrap the feature of "vocalic" and assert that the features "consonantal," "syllabic," and "obstruent" more adequately distinguish between the principal classes of segments:

|              | vowels | glides | syllabic nasals, liquids | non-syllabic nasals, liquids | stops, spirants, affricates |
|--------------|--------|--------|--------------------------|------------------------------|-----------------------------|
| syllabic     | +      | −      | +                        | −                            | −                           |
| consonantal  | −      | −      | +                        | +                            | +                           |
| obstruent    | −      | −      | −                        | −                            | +                           |

This system of representation has several advantages over that in terms of "vocalic," among them (*a*) the fact that it makes nonsyllabic liquids closer in feature composition to glides than to vowels (rather than vice versa, as in the system with "vocalic"), which fits well the fact that alternations between nonsyllabic liquid and glide are extremely common but alternations between nonsyllabic liquid and vowel are quite rare; and (*b*) in the extremely common case in which the underlying forms of the morphemes of a language are all of the form "CVCV . . . ," the system with "syllabic" allows that generalization to be reflected in a redundancy rule which specifies every odd-numbered segment as [−syllabic] and every even-numbered segment as [+syllabic], whereas in the system with "vocalic," all that could be predicted about vocalicness is that even-numbered segments are [+vocalic] and odd-numbered [−consonantal] segments are [−vocalic], that is, the generalization about morpheme shape would make the vocalicness specification of glides redundant but would not make redundant any feature specification in a liquid, nasal, or obstruent.

It should be clear from the preceding portions of this paper that the optimum feature system for a theory of language such as that of *The Sound Pattern of Russian* and subsequent works will involve a considerably greater number of features than appear in *Preliminaries* and *Sound Pattern of Russian*. Indeed, on the basis of arguments such as those which I have presented above, Chomsky and Halle conclude in *Sound Pattern of English* that a system containing over twice as many features as that of *Prelimi-*

*naries* is needed to provide for adequate phonological description. Since the values of $n$ binary features may be combined in $2^n$ different ways, the question immediately arises of whether there are as many segment types as can in principle be represented by a system of features such as that of *Sound Pattern of English*, that is $2^{25} = 33,554,432$. Clearly there are not: there are very sharp constraints on the way that feature specifications may combine, and the number of combinations which will appear in the "systematic phonetic representations" of natural languages is probably no more than a couple of thousand. The fact that the feature systems (even that of *Preliminaries*) of generative phonological works allow in principle a class of feature combinations which is astronomically larger than the class which will appear in phonetic representations has been taken by some (e.g., Householder 1965) as a defect of generative phonology. However, this fact merely shows that the goals of the phonologist and the electrical engineer cannot be met within the same representation: a representation in terms of the categories which play a role in phonology will not be an "optimal coding"; of course, there is no reason to expect it to be.

In actual fact, the restrictions on feature combinations which I mentioned above play an important role in the functioning of the phonological component of a language. Briefly, the universal constraints on feature combinations provide a mechanism whereby a phonological rule may have effects other than those mentioned in the rule: when a rule introduces a feature specification into a segment, the segment is adjusted so as to acquire all other feature specifications which are implied by that feature specification and the universal constraints. For example, there is a universal constraint excluding the combination of features $\begin{bmatrix} -\text{released} \\ +\text{aspirated} \end{bmatrix}$. When a rule makes a segment [−released], that segment is automatically also made [−aspirated]; likewise, a rule which makes a segment [+aspirated] would also make it [+released]. An excellent example of the important role which this principle may play in phonology is given by the following facts from Korean.

In syllable-final position in Korean the only segments which occur phonetically are [l], nasals, and unreleased stops. Corresponding to this fact, many underlying contrasts are neutralized when a consonant comes to be in syllable-final position; for example, underlying /nač/ 'day', /nač$^h$/ 'face', and /nas/ 'sickle', which are distinct in the locative ([naǰe], [nač$^h$e], [nase]), become homophonous in isolation: [nat⁻] (where ⁻ means "unreleased"). In this alternation, underlying obstruents become unaspirated and lax, and in addition, underlying /s, č, h/ all become [t⁻]. There are universal constraints excluding the feature combinations

$\begin{bmatrix} -\text{released} \\ +\text{aspirated} \end{bmatrix}$ and $\begin{bmatrix} -\text{released} \\ -\text{closure} \end{bmatrix}$. Consequently, a rule which made consonants in syllable-final position [−released] would automatically make them also [−aspirated] and [+closure]. Thus the effect of the rule

$$[-\text{syllabic}] \rightarrow [-\text{released}] \text{ in env. } \underline{\qquad} \left\{ \begin{matrix} [-\text{syllabic}] \\ \# \end{matrix} \right\}$$

(# means word boundary) would be to turn [s, č, h] into [t⁻, ť⁻, ʔ] respectively, where [ť⁻] denotes an unreleased apico-palatal stop. The eventual effect is obtained as the result of subsequent rules which turn a glottal stop into an apical stop and which make unreleased apical stops dental:

$$\begin{bmatrix} -\text{consonantal} \\ +\text{closure} \end{bmatrix} \rightarrow [-\text{grave}]$$

$$\begin{bmatrix} -\text{grave} \\ -\text{released} \end{bmatrix} \rightarrow [-\text{high}]$$

Korean is traditionally regarded as having a single underlying liquid, which is pronounced as flapped [r] intervocally and as [l] in syllable-final position or in a geminate; an underlying liquid at the beginning of a word is either deleted or turned into [n], depending on whether or not it is palatalized. Examples: [kʰal] 'knife', [kʰare] 'knife (loc.)'; [täro] 'highway', [nobyen] 'roadside'; [isu] 'mileage', [oryi] 'five miles'. There are not only verbs in which morpheme-final [r] alternates with [l]: [algo] 'know and', [aretta] 'knew', but also a large class of verbs in which morpheme-final [r] alternates with [t⁻]: [mut⁻ko] 'inquire and', [muretta] 'inquired'. The latter verbs are traditionally regarded as irregular; however, the rules given already plus the universal constraints make it possible to assign to these verbs an underlying representation such that these alternations automatically arise. Specifically, note that [t⁻] is what would arise by the universal constraints from an underlying flapped [r] which was made unreleased. Thus, if Korean is analyzed as having two distinct underlying liquids, /l/ and /r/, and the two verbs are represented as underlying /al/ and /mur/, the rules given already would yield all the desired forms. Note further that because of the rules alluded to whereby an intervocalic liquid becomes [r] and a word-initial liquid either is deleted or turns into [n], morpheme-final is the one underlying position in which an underlying distinction between /l/ and /r/ could ever have any phonological effect. Since an underlying feature specification for laterality,[7] which distinguishes /l/ from /r/, plays no role in the phonological rules of Korean unless it is in morpheme-final position, all occurrences of liquids in other positions may be left unspecified for laterality in their underlying forms, and the value realized phonetically would be inserted by one of the rules just mentioned. Consider now the fact that not only are there verbs which display the normal alternation between syllable-final [p⁻] and intervocalic [b]: [čep⁻] 'to fold', [čebe] 'to fold and', but there are also verbs which display an alternation between [p⁻] and [w]: [kip⁻] 'to mend', [kiwe] 'to mend and'. Here again underlying forms can be set up which will automatically yield the correct results thanks to the universal constraints: /čep/, /kiw/. When it is made unreleased, underlying /w/ becomes a stop as a result of the universal constraints.

An interesting point to note concerning the above discussion is that the treatment of Korean which I propose requires that "released" play a role within the phonological component. This fact is noteworthy since no cases have been reported of a language in which the difference between released and unreleased stops is distinctive. I point this out in order to emphasize that the system of features which play a role within the phonological component is anything but the extremely limited class of largely "distinctive" features which it until recently was generally assumed to be, and that the phonological component, rather than affecting the "more distinctive" features in the "earlier" rules and the "less distinctive" features in the "later" rules, as is sometimes supposed, must operate in terms of highly "nondistinctive" features even in early rules of the grammar, such as the rule making syllable-final consonants unreleased.

In conclusion, it would be worthwhile to reconsider for a moment the role which the "feature interpretation component" plays in a grammar. Of the three functions which it would play in a grammar containing a "taxonomic phonemic" level of representation, one becomes unnecessary if that level is rejected. Of the two remaining functions, the domain of one, namely that of choosing between alternative modes in which a feature may be realized, has been reduced considerably in the process of the above arguments. Indeed, there remain no clear cases in which anything is gained by considering two distinct articulatory features to be identified with the same feature of universal phonology. Accordingly, then, the task of the feature interpretation component of a grammar can probably be restricted to that of supplying ideal values to the physical parameters in which the features which function in the phonological component manifest themselves.

# 4    Length and Voicing in Tübatulabal

This paper is largely an exercise in lily-gilding. It will be a restatement and revision of an analysis for which I have always felt nothing but awe, namely, the masterful and elegant analysis of the really bewildering facts of vowel length in Tübatulabal (a Uto-Aztecan language of California) which Morris Swadesh and C. F. Voegelin proposed in their 1939 paper "A problem in phonological alternation."[1]

I will begin by giving as close an approximation of the rules stated in and implied by Swadesh and Voegelin's paper as is possible within the framework of ordered rules applying to segments that are represented as sets of feature specifications, pointing out the few places where differences between Swadesh and Voegelin's theoretical framework and mine will force the restatement to be something other than a purely mechanical process of translation. I will then propose some small but, I think, interesting revisions in their analysis.

I will go through the rules of the restatement of Swadesh and Voegelin in the order in which they would have to apply, to the extent that I have managed to establish that.[2] The ordering relations that I have established are indicated by arcs joining rule numbers:

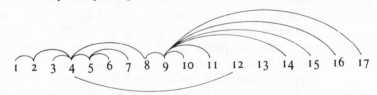

Rule 1:

$$\text{`R' [ \quad ]. 1} \rightarrow 0$$

'R' is lost if followed by any segment. This rule has to do with the symbol

Reprinted by permission from *Chicago Linguistic Society* 5 (1969): 407–15. Copyright © 1969 by Department of Linguistics, University of Chicago.

'R', which Swadesh and Voegelin write at the end of certain morphemes so as to protect a vowel at the end of the morpheme from undergoing the rule that deletes final vowels (my rule 5). Of the underlying segments that Swadesh and Voegelin set up, R is the only one whose full feature composition is not implicit in their analysis, although they note at the end of their paper that it could be identified with the glottal stop. Since R is never pronounced, their analysis implies a rule deleting all R's (or, taking up their suggestion, all morpheme-final glottal stops). However, a consideration of rule ordering shows that it is impossible for all the R's to be deleted by the same rule. The deletion of nonfinal R's must precede rule 2, the rule which simplifies vowel sequences:

> (underlying) bələ:laR + ina 'arrive' + causative
> (by rule 1)   bələ:la + ina
> (by rule 2)   bələ:l + ina
> ( > pələ:lin by later rules)

But rule 2 must precede rule 4, which lengthens alternate short vowels, rule 4 must precede rule 5, which deletes final vowels, and rule 5 must precede the deletion of final R since the very reason why R was set up was to protect the final vowel of the morphemes in question from being deleted by rule 5. Thus final R's would have to be deleted by a much later rule than the rule which deletes word-medial R's. This is my principal reason for feeling that Swadesh and Voegelin's use of R yields no great advantage over just treating the morphemes in question as ending in a vowel but being exceptions to rule 5. It is worth noting that setting up final R violates the otherwise valid generalization that the underlying forms of Tübatulabal verb stems always end in vowels.[3]

Rule 2:

$$\begin{bmatrix} + \text{ syllabic} \\ \langle + \text{ long} \rangle \end{bmatrix} [+ \text{ syllabic}]. \quad \begin{array}{c} \langle 2 \rightarrow [+ \text{ long}] \rangle \\ 1 \rightarrow 0 \end{array}$$

A vowel sequence formed at morpheme boundary becomes a single vowel which has the quality of the second vowel and which is long if the first vowel is long. One respect in which this rule acts different from Swadesh and Voegelin's is that Swadesh and Voegelin treat the vowel of the affix as replacing the final vowel of the preceding morpheme and accordingly write the morpheme boundary in a different place: pələ:li + n, as opposed to my pələ:l + in. I know of no rule of Tübatulabal which crucially depends on the place of morpheme boundary in such words and which could thus give evidence as to which of the two alternatives is correct.

Rule 3:

$$\begin{bmatrix} + \text{ syllabic} \\ - \text{ long} \end{bmatrix} \begin{bmatrix} - \text{ syllabic} \\ - \text{ consonantal} \\ + \text{ closure} \\ + \text{ voice} \end{bmatrix} \begin{bmatrix} + \text{ syllabic} \\ - \text{ long} \end{bmatrix}. \quad 2 \rightarrow 0$$

Rule 3 does not correspond directly to any of Swadesh and Voegelin's rules. An interesting difference between their theoretical framework and mine makes it necessary for me to divide up between two rules what a single rule of theirs accomplished. Their rule of contraction converts a VʔV sequence into a single vowel under certain circumstances. Specifically, they state that contraction 'takes place between light vowels separated only by a ʔ. . . . The quality of the contract vowel is that of the second of the two component vowels, as is seen in u:ša:n ( < *u:šuʔa:na), and the quantity is long if one of the components is long, short if both are short'. By 'light', Swadesh and Voegelin mean underlying short; their reference to 'short' has to do with vowel length after the application of rule 4, since the clause 'if one of the components is long' could only refer to length introduced by rule 4. Thus their statement of the conditions under which contraction takes place is in terms of the situation before rule 4 applies, and their statement of its effect is in terms of the situation after rule 4 applies. Since a single rule in the variety of generative phonology that I assume here cannot refer to earlier or later stages of a derivation, the closest to a restatement of Swadesh and Voegelin's rule that can be made in this framework will be to replace it by two rules, one which applies before rule 4, deleting the glottal stop and thus insuring that contraction will take place, and one which applies after rule 4, simplifying vowel sequences (which will have all resulted from rule 3) and assigning length to the resulting vowel on the basis of the lengths that have resulted from rule 4. The derivation of u:ša:n is then as follows:

    u + šuʔa + ana perfective + 'dry$_{tr}$' + benefactive
(2) u + šuʔ + ana
(3) u + šu + ana
(4) u: + šu + a:na
(5) u: + šu + a:n
(12) u: + š + a:n

Rule 4, which I formulate below, attempts to restate the central idea of Swadesh and Voegelin's ingenious account of vowel length in Tübatulabal. Swadesh and Voegelin set up both underlying short and underlying long vowels (which they call 'light' and 'heavy', respectively) and both underlying voiced and underlying voiceless consonants (which they call 'neutral' and 'shortening', respectively). Many of the underlying voiced/voiceless distinctions are neutralized in the phonemic representations which their rules generate; the assignment of these consonants to an underlying voiced or voiceless series is on the basis of their interaction with a rule (my 9) which shortens vowels before voiceless consonants. Vowel length is governed by a rule which lengthens alternate short vowels except when next to a long vowel; vowels which are followed by an underlying voiceless consonant and which are thus always pronounced short are assigned to the underlying short or long series depending on whether they inhibit the lengthening of adjacent vowels. I will give rule 4 in two forms, one involving only the notational devices of what may be called 'orthodox' generative phonology

$$\left.\begin{bmatrix}+\text{syll}\\+\text{long}\end{bmatrix}\begin{bmatrix}-\text{syll}\end{bmatrix}_0\overset{\#}{\begin{bmatrix}+\text{syll}\\-\text{long}\end{bmatrix}}\right\}\left(\begin{bmatrix}-\text{syll}\end{bmatrix}_0\begin{bmatrix}+\text{syll}\\-\text{long}\end{bmatrix}\begin{bmatrix}-\text{syll}\end{bmatrix}_0\begin{bmatrix}+\text{syll}\\-\text{long}\end{bmatrix}\right)_0$$

$$\begin{bmatrix}-\text{syll}\end{bmatrix}_0\begin{bmatrix}+\text{syll}\end{bmatrix}\begin{bmatrix}-\text{syll}\end{bmatrix}_0\begin{Bmatrix}\#\\\begin{bmatrix}+\text{syll}\\-\text{long}\end{bmatrix}\end{Bmatrix}$$

$$\downarrow$$

$$[+\text{long}]$$

and a second (which it should be clear that I prefer), which makes use of three controversial devices: negative environments, 'mirror-image' environments (which I indicate by@, i.e.,@before the structural description of a rule indicates that only adjacency and not left-to-right order is significant; several examples of 'mirror-image' environment are given in Bach 1968 and Harms 1968), and left-to-right iterative application of a rule, that is, application of a rule first to the leftmost segments, then those next to the right, and so on, as opposed to the 'orthodox' position that all applications of a single rule are 'simultaneous'.[4] These devices allow the rule to take the form 'lengthen vowel except when next to long vowel':

LR iterative. $[+\text{syll}] \rightarrow [+\text{long}]$ except in env.@___$[-\text{syll}]_0\begin{bmatrix}+\text{syll}\\+\text{long}\end{bmatrix}$

For example, in a six-syllable word with only underlying short vowels such as ta:wəgi:nana:la 'to go along causing him to see' (< dawəga + ina + ana + laR), rule 4 would lengthen the first vowel, since it is not next to a long vowel, but would not affect the second vowel since its application to the first vowel has left the second vowel next to a long vowel; it would then lengthen the third vowel, which is not adjacent to a long vowel, but would not affect the fourth vowel, which its application to the third vowel has left next to a long vowel; similarly, the fifth but not the sixth vowel is lengthened.

Rule 5:

$$[+ \text{syll}] \#. \quad 1 \rightarrow 0$$

Example: dawəga 'see'
(4) da:wəga:
(5) da:wəg
(> ta:wək; cf. ta:wəgat 'sees')

A final vowel is deleted. Verb stems normally do not exhibit a final vowel when used without an affix as infinitives, or when followed by vowel-initial affixes such as the causative, benefactive, and passive. However, a verb stem exhibits a final vowel if followed by a consonant-initial affix such as the imperfective or the imperative. This vowel must be treated as part of the stem and is deleted when either final or followed by a vowel; rules 5 and 2 delete it in these two cases.

Rule 6:

$$\begin{bmatrix} - \text{syll} \\ - \text{cons} \\ - \text{clos} \\ + \text{obstr} \end{bmatrix} \begin{bmatrix} - \text{syll} \\ - \text{obstr} \end{bmatrix} \#. \quad 12 \rightarrow 21$$

Example: muhyu 'celebrate'
(4) mu:hyu
(5) mu:hy
(6) mu:yh

A final cluster of h plus liquid, nasal, or semivowel metathesizes.

Rule 7:

$$\begin{bmatrix} - \text{syll} \\ + \text{cons} \\ - \text{obst} \end{bmatrix} \begin{bmatrix} - \text{syll} \\ - \text{cons} \\ + \text{clos} \end{bmatrix} [ \quad ]. \quad 2 \rightarrow 0$$

Example: halʔə: + t 'sit' + imperfective
(7) halə: + t
(9) halə + t (cf. halʔ)

Glottal stop is lost if nonfinal and preceded by liquid or nasal.

Rule 8:

$$[- \text{cons}] \begin{bmatrix} - \text{syll} \\ - \text{cons} \\ + \text{clos} \\ - \text{voice} \end{bmatrix} \phi \, [- \text{syll}]. \quad 3 \rightarrow \begin{bmatrix} 1 \\ + \text{syll} \\ - \text{long} \end{bmatrix}$$

Example: lo:ʒgi:n 'take off strip of bark'[5]
  (8) lo:ʒogi:n
  (> loʔogi:n)

An epenthetic vowel is inserted into certain clusters of ʔ plus consonant. The segment preceding the glottal stop may be either a vowel or a semi-vowel, and the epenthetic vowel is homorganic with it. Rule 8 follows rule 5, since the lengthening of alternate short vowels takes place as if the epenthetic vowel were absent.

Rule 9:

$$[+ \text{syll}] \begin{bmatrix} - \text{syll} \\ - \text{voice} \end{bmatrix}. \quad \text{1} \rightarrow [- \text{long}]$$

Example: dəWəLə + ana 'fix' + benefactive
  (2) dəWəL + ana
  (4) də:WəL + a:na
  (5) də:WəL + a:n
  (9) dəWəL + a:n
  (> təwəla:n; cf. ə:dəwəlan 'fixed for him')

This is the rule alluded to above which shortens vowels before voiceless consonants.

Rule 10:

$$R \#. \quad \text{1} \rightarrow \text{o}$$

This is the rule alluded to above which deletes 'R' in word-final position. It follows rule 9, since Swadesh and Voegelin treat R as a voiceless consonant and make it responsible for the fact that word-final vowels are short.

Rule 11:

$$\alpha \# \begin{bmatrix} + \text{obs} \\ + \text{clos} \end{bmatrix}. \quad \text{2} \rightarrow [- \text{voice}]$$

A stop or affricate at the beginning or end of a word is devoiced.

Rule 12:

$$\begin{bmatrix} + \text{syll} \\ \langle + \text{long} \rangle \end{bmatrix} [+ \text{syll}]. \quad \begin{matrix} < \text{2} \rightarrow [+ \text{long}] > \\ \text{1} \rightarrow \text{o} \end{matrix}$$

If two vowels occur in a row, the first is lost; if the first is long, the second becomes long. This rule was discussed above in connection with contraction. It should be noted that it is identical with rule 2, which is especially striking since they both have a somewhat peculiar effect. However, it is easy to demonstrate that rule 2 must precede rule 4 and rule 12 must follow it, so that there is no way of combining rules 2 and 12 into a single rule. Moreover, a rule such as 2/12 cannot be an 'anywhere rule' (a rule which can apply at any point in a derivation where its structural description is met), since it would yield incorrect forms if allowed to apply between rules 3 and 4.

Rule 13:

$$\# \begin{bmatrix} - \text{ syll} \\ - \text{ cons} \\ + \text{ clos} \end{bmatrix}. \quad 2 \to 0$$

An initial glottal stop is deleted.

Rule 14:

$$\begin{bmatrix} + \text{ clos} \\ + \text{ obst} \\ + \text{ cons} \end{bmatrix} \begin{bmatrix} - \text{ syll} \\ - \text{ cons} \\ - \text{ obst} \end{bmatrix}. \quad 1 \to [- \text{ voice}]$$

Example: ta:dwaR + l 'man'
  (2) ta:dwa + l
  (14) ta:twa + l

This rule, which devoices a stop or affricate before w (or y? I have no examples), is neither formulated nor mentioned by Swadesh or Voegelin but is necessitated by their giving underlying forms ta:dwaR and či:ǯ wana:bə:R which contain voiced sources for voiceless stops and affricates; their analysis necessitates such underlying forms because the voiceless stop or affricate pronounced in these forms is preceded by a long vowel.

Rule 15:

$$\begin{bmatrix} - \text{ syll} \\ - \text{ obstr} \end{bmatrix} \to [+ \text{ voice}]$$

Rule 16:

$$\begin{bmatrix} - \text{ syll} \\ - \text{ cons} \\ + \text{ obstr} \end{bmatrix} \to [- \text{ voice}]$$

Rule 17:

$$\begin{bmatrix} + \text{ obstr} \\ - \text{ clos} \end{bmatrix} \to [- \text{ voice}]$$

Rules 15–17 are not stated by Swadesh and Voegelin but are implied by their treatment, since their underlying voicing distinction must be wiped out in those segments which do not exhibit a surface voicing distinction. Rule 15 makes liquids, nasals, y's and w's voiced, rule 16 makes h's and ʔ's voiceless, and rule 17 makes š voiceless.

The faults that can be found with Swadesh and Voegelin's analysis are remarkably few. I will proceed now to find them.

Rule 13 is superfluous and is indeed merely an artifact of Swadesh and Voegelin's rules, which are supposed to generate phonemic and not phonetic representations. Swadesh and Voegelin's system of phonemic representation writes initial vowels where glottal stop plus vowel is actually pronounced. Since the glottal stops that the morphophonemic rule 13 deletes would have to be put back in again by an allophonic rule, both rules can be dispensed with. I will thus henceforth write initial glottal stops in accordance with what I gather is the pronunciation.[6]

Among the segments which Swadesh and Voegelin must set up both voiced and voiceless sources for, because of differences in the application of the rule that shortens vowels before underlying voiced consonants, is the glottal stop. They set up a voiceless glottal stop in ?a:ga 'open the mouth' because of the short vowel in the reduplicative prefix: (?a:gina:n ?a?a:gina:n) but a voiced glottal stop in ?u:da 'united' because the vowel of the reduplicative prefix remains long: (?u:dina:n ?u:?u:dina:n). A voiced glottal stop, however, is an anatomical impossibility: the vocal cords cannot be both pressed shut and vibrating at the same time. Does the fact that this analysis leads one to set up voiced glottal stops mean that proposed constraints whereby all stages in a derivation must be 'pronounceable'[7] are misguided and must be rejected? Or is there an alternative analysis which keeps the advantages of the Swadesh-Voegelin analysis but does without voiced glottal stops?

I will argue for the latter position by showing that facts about the phonetics of Tübatulabal which Voegelin described in his 1935 grammar but he and Swadesh did not take into account in their 1939 paper support an alternative analysis in which something other than voice is the underlying distinction betwen the two series of consonants which they set up. Voegelin (1935:61) states, "Voiceless plosives (except ?) and affricates, nasal consonants, and *l* are always geminated after vowels having the value of one mora. Fricatives and semivowels are likewise geminated, but this is a theoretical ideal. In actual practice, fricatives and semivowels are most consistently geminated after vowels which are stressed." All of the consonants that Swadesh and Voegelin set up as underlying voiceless are preceded in surface phonetics by short vowels, as a result of rule 9, and thus are pronounced geminate, except that ? is always pronounced short, and fricatives (including h) and semivowels are optionally pronounced short. Thus the consonants which Swadesh and Voegelin set up as underlying voiceless are usually pronounced geminate, and the consonants which Swadesh and Voegelin set up as underlying voiced are usually pronounced short (although they too are geminate if the preceding vowel is short, except that voiced stops and affricates are never long). Since the surface phonetic distinction between long and short consonants to a large degree matches Swadesh and Voegelin's underlying voiced/voiceless distinction, the possibility suggests itself of taking consonant length rather than voicing as the underlying distinction and predicting the voicing of stops and affricates on the basis of their length rather than vice versa. I thus propose an analysis which has long p and short p where Swadesh and Voegelin have p and b, long ʔ and short ʔ where Swadesh and Voegelin have voiceless ʔ and voiced ʔ, and so on.

If length rather than voicing is taken as the underlying distinction between the two series of consonants, the following revisions of the above rules will be necessary. Rules 3 and 8 will have to refer to short and long rather than voiced and voiceless glottal stop. Rule 9, instead of shortening vowels before voiceless consonants, will shorten vowels before long consonants. Rule 11 will have to be replaced by something which neutralizes the length of initial and final consonants. According to Voegelin, initial and final consonants are short, except that final stops and affricates are long. The grammar thus requires a rule which shortens initial and final consonants and a rule lengthening final stops and affricates:

Rule 18:

$$@[ \qquad ] \#. \quad 1 \rightarrow [- \text{ long}]$$

Rule 19:

$$\begin{bmatrix} + \text{ obst} \\ + \text{ clos} \end{bmatrix} \#. \quad 1 \rightarrow [+ \text{ long}]$$

Rule 18 has been formulated so as to apply to all segments, not just consonants; it thus insures that all final vowels are short (cf. the discussion of 'R' above). Rules 15–17 are then unnecessary. However, a rule will have to be added to the grammar that voices those stops and affricates that are pronounced voiced:

Rule 20:

$$[+ \text{ voice}] \begin{bmatrix} + \text{ obst} \\ + \text{ clos} \\ - \text{ long} \end{bmatrix} [+ \text{ syll}]. \quad 2 \rightarrow [+ \text{ voice}]$$

By formulating rule 20 so as to be applicable to nasal-stop-vowel sequences but not to vowel-stop-semivowel sequences, I have made rule 14 unnecessary. The following rules relating to consonant length are also needed:

Rule 21:

$$\begin{bmatrix} + \text{ syll} \\ - \text{ long} \end{bmatrix} [- \text{ syll}] [+ \text{ syll}]. \quad 2 \rightarrow [+ \text{ long}] \text{ except } \begin{bmatrix} + \text{ obst} \\ + \text{ clos} \end{bmatrix}$$

(An intervocalic consonant other than a stop or affricate becomes long if preceded by a short vowel.)

Rule 22:

$$\begin{bmatrix} -\ \text{syll} \\ -\ \text{clos} \end{bmatrix} \text{optionally} \rightarrow [-\text{long}]$$

(Spirants and semivowels are optionally shortened.)

Rule 23:

$$\begin{bmatrix} -\text{syll} \\ -\ \text{cons} \\ +\ \text{clos} \end{bmatrix} \rightarrow [-\ \text{long}]$$

(ʔ becomes short.) The order relations established among the rules of the revised analysis are:

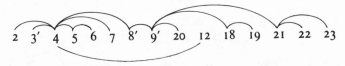

$$2 \quad 3' \quad 4 \quad 5 \quad 6 \quad 7 \quad 8' \quad 9' \quad 20 \quad 12 \quad 18 \quad 19 \quad 21 \quad 22 \quad 23$$

It should also be noted that many conceivable combinations of segments in Swadesh and Voegelin's inventory of underlying segments do not appear to be possible in underlying forms of Tübatulabal morphemes. For example, there are morphemes which cause Swadesh and Voegelin to set up underlying *Mš* but none which would require underlying *mš*, which is to say that all surface occurrences of [mš] are preceded by short vowels. In fact, most consonant clusters in Tübatulabal can only be preceded by short vowels, that is, most consonant clusters act in the same way that long consonants do. A particularly striking case of this generalization is given by the reduplicative prefix when it is applied to something that begins $C_{\text{short}}VN$. In this case the reduplicative prefix has a nasal after its vowel, as in *kin-/ʔiŋgin* 'bring, brought'. When the reduplicative prefix contains a nasal, its vowel is always short, which is to say that the combination of prefix nasal and root consonant acts like a long consonant in shortening the preceding vowel. However, I have not yet found a way of distinguishing all the consonant clusters that shorten the preceding vowel from all those that do not; I thus have not attempted the reformulation of rule 9 that I suspect to be necessary.[8]

I conclude that my proposed revision retains all the advantages of Swadesh and Vogelin's analysis and adds a couple of extra ones, namely, avoidance of unpronounceable underlying segments, a slight simplification of the rules, and a system of representation that at least offers some hope of identifying the shortening of the vowel in a ʔVN prefix with the more general shortening discovered by Swadesh and Voegelin. I would like to close by mentioning one noteworthy aspect of my proposed revision in Swadesh and Voegelin's analysis, namely, the change in the underlying segment inventory. Until I hit on the idea of taking length rather than voicing as the feature distinguishing the two underlying series of consonants, I had always cited Tübatulabal in my phonology courses as an example of a language whose underlying segment inventory is wildly different from its surface segment inventory. However, under the revised analysis, the underlying segment inventory turns out to be virtually identical to the surface phonetic inventory, at least as far as the consonants are concerned.

# 5   Some Tonal Systems That Come Close to Being Pitch-Accent Systems But Don't Quite Make It

In an earlier paper (McCawley 1964a), I proposed two criteria for distinguishing between pitch as it is involved in a true 'tone language' and pitch as it is involved in a 'pitch-accent' system.[1] The first criterion had to do with the lexical information relating to-pitch: if the underlying form of each morpheme requires at most the specification of the location of some pitch phenomenon (e.g., the location of a high pitch or of a drop in pitch), the language has a pitch-accent system and is not a tone language; if a morpheme generally requires an underlying form in which each syllable must be specified for an underlying tone (so that the number of potential underlying tonal contrasts increases geometrically with the number of syllables, as compared with the pitch-accent case, where it only increases arithmetically with the number of syllables), the language is a tone language. The second criterion had to do with the rules that affect pitch. In a language with a pitch-accent system, the rules affecting pitch are accent reduction rules, that is, rules that make one element of a phrase or word predominate by eliminating or 'weakening' the accentual phenomena elsewhere. For example, in standard Japanese, which has a pitch-accent system and requires underlying forms that specify the place (if any) where the morpheme in question can contribute a fall in pitch, the first fall in pitch in each phrase predominates:

> hana' & ma'de → hana' made   'up to the flower'
> hana & ma'de → hana ma'de   'up to the nose'

Accent reduction involves action at a distance: in principle, an accent reduction can remove or reduce accents arbitrarily many syllables away from the accent that is made to predominate. By contrast, rules affecting

Reprinted by permission from *Chicago Linguistic Society* 6 (1970): 526–32. Copyright © 1970 by Chicago Linguistic Society.

pitch in a tone language are the same kinds of assimilations and dissimilations that affect ordinary segmental features such as vowel height, continuance, and voicing. For example, there is the well-known Mandarin Chinese rule whereby a low tone becomes a rising tone before another low tone (dissimilation) and another Mandarin rule that optionally turns a rising tone into a high tone when it is preceded by a tone that ends high (i.e., a high or a rising tone) and followed by a stressed syllable (assimilation).

This paper will be devoted to exploring the inadequacies and incoherencies in the above typology. One inadequacy that I had already noted in McCawley 1964*a* is that there are languages that require underlying forms in which the amount of underlying tonal information required in a dictionary entry is independent of the length of the morpheme (e.g., in the Japanese dialects of western Kyushu, the only tonal distinction that need be marked in the dictionary entry of a morpheme is whether it imposes a 'falling' or a 'level' melody on the entire phrase it begins) and languages in which the underlying form of a morpheme must contain some tonal information in addition to the location of an accentual phenomenon, though not specifications of the tones of all the syllables (e.g., in the Japanese dialect of Kyoto, the underlying form of a noun must indicate not only where, if anywhere, it contributes a drop in pitch, but also whether the noun starts on a high or on a low pitch).

There is some reason to treat an initial low pitch in Kyoto Japanese as corresponding to an underlying fall in pitch at the beginning of the item in question. First, low-beginning words are preceded by a drop in pitch if something high-pitched precedes them, for example, ùsàgí 'rabbit', ánó ùsàgí 'that rabbit'. Second, if initial low pitch is interpreted as a preposed drop in pitch, a single rule suffices to insert the (predictable) accent of adjectives, even though monosyllabic adjectives start low and longer adjectives start high, for example,

'yo-i   L-H      'good' (-*i* = present tense)
a'ka-i   HL-L    'red'
yawara'ka-i   HHHL-L   'soft'

Thus, Kyoto nouns can be treated as having up to two underlying accents: an accent before the word or not, and an accent on one of the syllables of the word or not:[2]

'usagi LLH 'rabbit'      kata'na HHL 'sword'
katati HHH 'form'        'tuba'sa LHL 'wings'

However, the drop in pitch corresponding to initial low pitch is not affected by the accent reduction rules that apply in Kyoto, for example, the rule that puts accent on the second element of a noun compound with a 'long' second member:

'tanu'ki 'badger' + o'yazi 'old man' → 'tanuki-o'yazi 'cunning old man'

Another language which, like Kyoto Japanese, has 'accent reduction' rules but whose morphemes' tonal behavior requires more than just the location of an accentual phenomenon to appear in their dictionary entries is Ịjọ, a language of Nigeria (Williamson 1965, 1968). In Ịjọ, subject to a couple of qualifications, the first word of a phrase determines the tonal pattern that appears on the phrase. As in Kyoto Japanese, there is a distinctive difference between words that begin on a high pitch and those that begin on a low pitch. There is the extra wrinkle that a morpheme can contribute a fall in pitch that occurs not on the morpheme itself but one syllable after it, for example,

|       |            |            |                |
|-------|------------|------------|----------------|
| dírí  | 'medicine' | dírí gúọ́  | 'make medicine' |
| bùrú  | 'yam'      | bùrù gbòró | 'plant yams'   |
| wárị  | 'house'    | wárị kọ́rị | 'build houses' |
| kèní  | 'one'      | kènì sárì  | 'once'         |

If one felt impelled to set up underlying forms for these items as if they were words of Kyoto Japanese, the underlying forms would be /diri, 'buru, warị', 'keni'/, where ' again means drop in pitch. This proposal requires that the grammar contain an accent shift rule: warị' + kọrị → warị kọ'rị. Besides the above types of nouns, there are also nouns that impose a low tone on everything after them, for example, ògórì 'bushcow', ògórì bà-mì 'killed a bushcow'. The data at my disposal are not sufficient to allow me to decide whether these nouns can also be fit into the mold of Kyoto, that is, underlying forms with at most two 'accents', one before the item and one on one of its syllables (e.g., /'o'gori/, assuming the accent shift rule to be applicable here too); the data given in Williamson 1965 suggest that there is a greater profusion of tonal shapes than is consistent with this proposal. In any event, Ịjọ does not clearly fit the criteria that I gave in my earlier paper for either 'tone language' or 'pitch-accent language'. It clearly requires underlying forms in which more has to be specified than the location of an accentual phenomenon, but it still has a rule of accent reduction and a rule of accent shift such as are found with stress or with pitch accent.[3]

Another language whose tonal system does not fit neatly into the typology of McCawley 1964a is Ganda, a Bantu language spoken in Uganda. In Ganda, the underlying forms required by morphemes are a textbook case of what I said about 'pitch-accent languages'. Indeed, pretty much the same statements can be made about pitch information in the underlying forms of Ganda as in the case of standard Japanese: in both languages, verbs divide into two tonal classes regardless of length (Japanese accented and unaccented verbs, Ganda high-tone and low-tone verbs); in both languages, the underlying form of a noun must specify where (if anywhere) a high pitch is followed by a low pitch, and that information is sufficient to predict its tonal behavior.[4] However, whereas in Japanese the surface pitch shape can likewise be specified simply by saying where (if anywhere) pitch drops, in Ganda there is a tremendous profusion of surface tonal forms: in surface phonology, the pitch of polymorphemic Ganda words can differ not only as regards where there is a drop in pitch but also as regards whether the word starts on a high tone or on a low tone, how many initial low-pitched syllables there are before the pitch becomes high, and how many low-pitched syllables there are after a drop in pitch before the pitch rises. The profusion of surface tonal possibilities in Ganda arises as a result of the tonal rules of the language, which, aside from one early accent reduction rule, are all of the types that are characteristic of tone languages; for example, there is a rule whereby a sequence of high tones after a high tone becomes low, a rule whereby a sequence of low tones between two high tones becomes high, and a rule whereby all but the first of a sequence of low tones, except for low tones derived from highs by the dissimilation rule, become high.[5]

Thus, the available facts contradict a putative language universal that I assumed in setting up the second criterion for what a tone language is, namely, the assumption that rules that assimilate and dissimilate pitches do not occur in the same grammars as do accent reduction rules. Although these two types of rules can in fact occur in the same grammar, I know of no facts that would contradict a weaker universal principle about their cooccurrence, namely, the hypothesis that if the tonal phenomena in a language are governed by both kinds of rules, the accent reduction rules occur earlier in the grammar than the assimilations and dissimilations of pitch. If this conjecture is correct, then it will not be possible to classify languages into 'tone languages' and 'pitch-accent languages' in a non-arbitrary way, but it will be possible to speak of a language as having a pitch-accent system up to some point in the ordering of its rules and having a tonal system from that point on. Languages could then be classified according to how early in their grammars they become tone languages. For example, Mandarin Chinese is a tone language throughout the entire grammar, Ganda is a tone language starting from a very early point in the ordering of its rules (as far as I know, the rule that deaccents a noun before a possessive is the only accent reduction rule in Ganda; see Cole 1967:71), and, as I am about to argue, standard Japanese is a tone language starting from a very late point in its derivations. In fact, not all rules affecting Japanese accent are of the accent reduction type. Consider, for example,

the appearance of accent in contracted forms of unaccented verb plus
unaccented auxiliary verb:

$$\text{itte iru} \rightarrow \text{itte\'ru} \quad \text{'is going'}$$

I maintain that this occurrence of accent arises in the same way that a
number of cases of downstep in African languages arise. Downstep in
African languages generally (perhaps always)[6] arises through assimilations
or deletions that apply after rules assigning pitch levels to high and low
tones. A high tone after a low is assigned a pitch level below that of a high
before the low, and downstep arises if the low of a HLH sequence is either
deleted or assimilated up to the level of one of the highs:

Tonga  bà-lí-bà-láng-ìdè
  → $\text{ba}^2\text{li}^5\text{ba}^1\text{la}^4\text{ngi}^0\text{de}^0$    (the numbers here indicate pitch levels)
  → $\text{ba}^2\text{li}^5\text{ba}^4\text{la}^4\text{ngi}^0\text{de}^0$    (by assimilation)
  = bàlí'bálángìdè    (' here indicates downstep)

I propose that in Japanese, consecutive high pitches become successively
lower in pitch (even if no low intervenes between the highs) and that the
rule assigning successively lower pitches to highs precedes the rule that
deletes the initial vowel of *iru*. Since the amount by which pitch drops in
Japanese is quite small, a major or minor second, it is of the same magni-
tude as the difference in pitch between the first and third of three consecutive high pitches, and if the pitch assignment rule to which I have been
referring precedes the contraction rule, the drop in pitch between the *te* of
*itte* and the *ru* is indistinguishable from the drop in pitch that manifests
accent.[7] In addition, Japanese has a phenomenon whereby accents are
eliminated not through an accent reduction rule but through pitch assignment rules, namely, the loss of accent noted by Kawakami (1965) in words
with a final accented long vowel on which interrogative intonation is
imposed, for example *iku desyo'o* 'will probably go' but [ìkú désyóő] 'Do
you think (he) will go?' (″ denotes extra-high pitch). The raised pitch
imposed on the final mora of *desyo'o* cancels out any phonetic manifestation of its underlying accent.

One sort of tonal system that does not fit into this revised typology is
that of the Japanese dialects of southern and western Kyushu, where each
morpheme imposes one of two melodies on any phrase which it begins, as
in the following data from the dialect of Kagoshima:[8]

hî, hí gà 'day'    kùrúmà, kùrùmá gà 'vehicle' (falling melody)
hí, hì gá 'fire'   àbùrá, àbùrà gá   'oil'     (level melody)

Although I have described pitch assignment in Kagoshima (McCawley
1968*a*) in terms of rules such as 1, which put high pitch directly on specific

syllables, I now think that it must rather be described in terms of rules such as 2, which impose an entire melody as a unit on the phrase:[9]

1. Syllable → [+ high] / % [+ Falling] X ⎯⎯ Syllable %
2. % [+ Falling] X % → $L_0$ H L
   % [− Falling] X % → $L_0$ H

My reason for preferring 2 is that the HL sequence created by a falling morpheme appears even when the phrase contains fewer than the two syllables that 1 calls for; in that case the single syllable bears a high-low falling pitch, as in the isolation form of 'day' cited above. The interpretation of pitch assignment rules such as 2 is that each pitch is to be assigned to whatever the pitch-bearing unit is (in Kagoshima it is the syllable, but in the nearby and almost identical dialect of Koshikijima it is the mora), except where dearth of such units forces the obligatory pitches to be combined on a single unit. This kind of pitch assignment rule appears to be necessary to describe verb conjugation in Bantu languages such as Tiv (McCawley 1970a), where each tense will correspond to a formula such as $\widehat{LB}$ H $H_0$ (B = 'Basic' and the ligature indicates that the two tones are combined on a single syllable), which imposes a sequence of low tone and the basic high or low tone on the first syllable, followed by an obligatory high tone (which goes on the second syllable if there is one and becomes the third of a sequence of three tones on a single syllable in the case of a monosyllabic verb), with any subsequent syllables getting a high pitch. These formulas, in conjunction with the rules that adjust pitch sequences, explain why in some tenses the tonal distinction between high-toned and low-toned verbs is neutralized in monosyllabic verbs but not in disyllabic or trisyllabic verbs. The $\widehat{LHH}$ and $\widehat{LLH}$ sequences which the above formula would yield when applied to a monosyllabic high- or low-toned verb, respectively, both are realized phonetically as downstep plus high, in accordance with general rules of the assignment of pitch level and assimilation of rising pitches up to the level of the end of the syllable.

Since at no stage of derivations in Kagoshima Japanese will there be any representation involving accented syllables—before the pitch assignment rules apply, tonal information will appear in the form of morpheme features, and afterwards every syllable is supplied with a pitch—Kagoshima Japanese can be described as being a tone language from a certain point in the derivation on, and neither a tone language nor a pitch-accent language prior to that. While standard Japanese verbs and adjectives, like Kagoshima morphemes in general, require lexical entries in which tonal information is in the form of a single binary morpheme feature ('accented' verbs vs. 'unaccented'), the rule which converts this information into features of segments or of syllables does not (as in Kagoshima) assign pitch levels but rather specifies a certain syllable as accented. From that point on in the derivations, standard Japanese verbs have the same kind of tonal representation as do nouns, namely, with a syllable being specified as the accented one, and behave exactly the same way with respect to accent reduction rules as do nouns; in Kagoshima, a representation specifying one syllable as the accented one is never called for at any stage of the derivation.

It is well established that many cases of downstep must be derived synchronically from an underlying high-low-high sequence as follows:

   a. Specific tone levels are assigned to high and low tones by means of rules whereby consecutive highs are on the same pitch, consecutive lows are on the same pitch, and the interval down from a high to a following low exceeds the interval up from a low to a following high (i.e., highs are 'lowered' after a low),

   b. Certain low tones are then either removed or assimilated to the level of a following high or (less commonly) a preceding high, for example,[1]

Twi:       mé ɔ̀bó → me$^5$ ɔ$^2$bo$^4$ → me$^5$ bo$^4$ = mé 'bó 'my stone'
             [Schachter and Fromkin 1968:110]

Tonga:    bàlíbàlángìdè → be$^2$li$^5$ba$^1$la$^4$ngi$^0$de$^0$ → ba$^2$li$^5$ba$^4$la$^4$ngi$^0$de$^0$
             = bàlí'bálángìdè 'they look at them' [Meeussen 1963:73]

Shambala: mìví mìhyá → mi$^2$vi$^5$ mi$^1$hya$^4$ → mi$^2$vi$^5$ mi$^5$hya$^4$ = mìví mí'hyá 'new arrows' (Spaandonck 1967:47]

The example of deletion in Twi involved deletion of the syllable that bore the low tone responsible for the lowering of the subsequent highs. A hypothetical example where a tone rather than its bearer was deleted would be bâmá → ba$^{5-2}$ma$^4$ → ba$^5$ma$^4$, in which one of a sequence of tones on the same syllable is lost but the syllable otherwise remains unchanged. In this note I will explore the consequences of analyzing downstep in Tiv as arising from deleted low tones which in underlying structure are parts of tone sequences on single syllables.[2] My source of data and of many features of the analysis will be Arnott's important paper of 1964.

Reprinted by permission from *Studies in African Linguistics* 1 (1970): 123–30. Copyright 1970 by the Regents of the University of California.

Arnott presents examples both of (1) downstep contributed by the item following the downstep and of (2) downstep contributed by the item preceding the downstep:

> (1) í    lú    kwá              gá      'It was not a ring of huts'
>      it   was   ring of huts    not
>      í    lú    'kwá gá                 'It was not a leaf'
>      it   was   leaf  not
> (2) í    lú    tóhó gá                  'It was not grass'
>      it   was   grass not
>      ká    'tóhó gá                     'It is not grass'
>      it is  grass not

To derive these forms, Arnott set up underlying forms with preposed and postposed downsteps, which I propose to reinterpret as follows:

> Arnott   reinterpretation
> kwá      kwá               'ring of huts'
> 'kwá     kwă               'leaf'
> lú       lú                recent past copula
> ká'      kâ                'it is'

The reinterpretation makes it necessary to have rules which eliminate the low part of a rising or falling tone sequence on a single syllable. Since the only rising tones in Tiv are on syllables ending in a sonorant or a voiced spirant (e.g., bĕr 'pond' [Abraham 1940:3]) and since the formulation of tonal rules for conjugation will provide reason for treating such final sonorants and voiced spirants as if they were separate syllables with their own tone (e.g. bĕr = bèř), Tiv must be analyzed as having no surface rising-toned syllables. Thus, a rule which deleted the low part of underlying rising-toned syllables such as I propose for /kwă/ 'leaf' would not affect anything other than what I want it to affect. There do exist true falling-toned syllables in Tiv, so that there can not simply be a rule which deletes the low part of every high-low sequence on a single syllable. However, Arnott points out that precisely the words which contribute a following downstep when followed by a high pitch are pronounced with a final falling pitch when at the end of a phrase:[3]

> mbá 'kásév    'there are women'
> kásév mbâ     'there are women'

Thus, the rule deleting the low part of a high-low sequence on a single syllable is only applicable non-finally, and my underlying form for items contributing a following downstep is identical with their phrase-final alternant.

The proposal to use combinations of high and low to represent down-step allows appreciable simplification in the rules which assign tone to the various forms of the verb. I have reproduced below, with slight differences in notation and layout, the tabulation of tones given by Arnott for high-toned and low-toned verbs of one, two, and three syllables. I have ignored the distinction between the large H's and L's which Arnott used to represent the tones on full syllables and the small H's and L's which he used to represent tones on the tone-bearing final voiced consonants which occur in four of the tenses, for example, yévéséǹ 'used to run away'. I have also treated the geminate vowels of the Habitual 3, Habitual 4, and Past Habitual of monosyllabic verbs as units. Thus, I treat vááǹ 'comes (Habitual 3)' as exemplifying the formula HH rather than Arnott's HHн.

Consider first the General Past. The downstep plus high of the first syllable of high-toned verbs will be represented as a low-high sequence on that syllable. Since the low tone on the first syllable of low-toned verbs can equally well be represented as a sequence of two low tones on that syllable, the following generalization can be made about General Pasts: the first

|  | 1-syllable | | 2-syllable | | 3-syllable | |
|---|---|---|---|---|---|---|
|  | High | Low | High | Low | High | Low |
| General Past | 'H | L | 'H L | L L | 'H L L | L L L |
| Recent Past A | 'H | 'H | 'H H | L H | 'H H L | L H L |
| Recent Past B | H | H | H H | H 'H | H H L | H H L |
| Subjunctive | | | same as Recent Past B | | | |
| Habitual 1 | 'H | 'H | 'H H | L H | H H L | L H L |
| Habitual 2 | 'H' | 'H' | 'H H' | L H' | 'H H H | nonexistent |
| Habitual 3 | 'H H | 'H H | 'H H H | L H H | 'H H H (H) | L H H (H) |
| Habitual 4 | H L | H L | H H L | H H L | H H H L | H H H L |
| Past Habitual | 'H L | 'H L | 'H H L | L H L | 'H H H L | L H H L |
| Continuous | H L | H L | H L L | H L L | H L L | H L L |
| Imperative | H | H | H L | L H | H H L | L H L |
| Future | 'H | L | H L | L L | H L L | L L L |

syllable has a low tone plus the basic tone of the verb (i.e., high in the case of a high-toned verb and low in the case of a low-toned verb), and any subsequent syllables are on a low tone. I summarize this generalization with the formula $\widehat{LB}\, L_0$. In this formula, the tie indicates being in the same syllable, and the subscript 0, to be read 'zero or more', means that if there are any subsequent syllables, lows are to be put on all of them.

Consider now the Recent Past A. Disyllabic verbs obviously fit the formula $\widehat{LB}\, H$ and trisyllabic verbs the formula $\widehat{LB}\, H\, L$. A single formula which covers both of these cases and also the monosyllabic case can be set up by regarding the $\widehat{LB}$ and H of the last two formulas as obligatorily present in the Recent Past A but the L of the trisyllabic case as merely filling up leftover syllables. If L͡B and H were combined on a single syllable, 'H would result regardless of whether B were H or L: both L͡HH and L͡LH would bring about lowering of the H('s), and the rule about deleting the low part of a rising tonal sequence would leave the equivalent results 'H͡H and 'H. Thus, the following formula covers all Recent Past A's, regardless of number of syllables: L͡B H $L_0$. The proper interpretation of these formulas requires the convention that when a formula containing two syllables' worth of obligatory tonal material is applied to a monosyllabic form, these tones are stuck together on that single syllable (note that tones with the subscript o are not involved in this convention: they are only assigned to whatever syllables are left over after the obligatory material has been assigned).

A single formula is also possible for the Habitual 3. Since the first syllable of disyllabic and trisyllabic verbs can be interpreted as L͡B and the subsequent syllables are all high, the formula L͡B $H_0$ suggests itself. That formula will not do for the monosyllabic case, since it would incorrectly predict *L H for a monosyllabic low-toned verb. To get a formula that covers this case too, it is necessary to regard two H's as obligatorily present in this tense and only the final H of trisyllabic verbs as 'filler' material. The formula is thus L͡B H H $H_0$. The convention about combining tones on a single syllable if there are not enough separate syllables to accommodate them will have to be refined slightly in order to insure correct application of this formula to monosyllabic verbs (note that a monosyllabic verb has a disyllabic Habitual 3): when three syllables' worth of obligatory material is distributed over two syllables, it is necessary to combine the tone in the middle with the preceding tone rather than the following tone, since otherwise *L H would result as the Habitual 3 of a monosyllabic low-toned verb.

In six of the twelve tenses, a single formula covers all cases, and in three of the remaining tenses a formula covering two of the three verb lengths is possible. As in the formulas given by Arnott (1964:49) it is nowhere necessary to give separate formulas for high-toned and low-toned verbs, and in only one instance (the Imperative of disyllabic verbs) is it necessary to resort to an at all ad hoc notational device to avoid treating high-toned and low-toned verbs by different formulas. The formulas are:

| | |
|---|---|
| General Past | L͡B $L_0$ |
| Recent Past A | L͡B H $L_0$ |
| Recent Past B | H (1-syll), H B͡H (2-syll), H H L (3-syll) |
| Subjunctive | (same as Recent Past B) |

Habitual 1       $\widehat{LB}$ H, except B H L (3-syll)
Habitual 2       $\widehat{LB}$ $\widehat{HL}$, except $\widehat{LB}$ H H (3-syll)
Habitual 3       $\widehat{LB}$ H H $H_0$
Habitual 4       $H_0$ L
Past Habitual    $\widehat{LB}$ H $H_0$ L
Continuous       H $L_0$
Imperative       H(1-syll), B $\check{B}$ (2-syll; $\check{B}$ = opposite of basic tone),
                 B H L (3-syll)
Future           B $L_0$, except $\widehat{LB}$ (1-syll).

The treatment of downstep in Tiv as arising from the lowering effect of underlying low tones that are eventually deleted partially explains one striking feature of the Tiv verb paradigms, namely that there are several tenses in which the contrast between high-toned and low-toned verbs is neutralized only in monosyllabic verbs, but there are no tenses in which it is neutralized only in disyllabic verbs or only in trisyllabic verbs. The above discussion shows that in a tense which is covered by a single formula, tonal contrasts which are manifested in verbs of two or more syllables are neutralized in monosyllabic verbs if the combining of two syllables' worth of tones on a single syllable sandwiches the basic tone between a low and a high.

# Some Tonga Tone Rules

Many Bantu languages have a surface contrast between high and low tones which exactly matches an underlying high/low tone contrast, but there are others in which the relationship between surface and underlying tones is far from obvious. In Tonga, Bangubangu, and Sukuma, for example, underlying tone contrasts are manifested not on the syllable that bears them but elsewhere in the phrase: for example, in Bangubangu an underlying high tone is generally manifested as a high tone on the following syllable (Meeussen 1954, McCawley 1973*b*), and in Sukuma an underlying high tone is manifested as a high tone one, two, or three syllables later (Richardson 1959). In these languages it is often far from obvious which member of an underlying tone contrast should be designated "underlying high" and "underlying low." Thus, many scholars (Meeussen 1954, 1963; Stevick 1969) have avoided such terms, preferring "determinant" and "neutral", where determinant is that underlying tone which (under at least some conditions) causes deviations from the "least marked" tonal contour (which generally is level low pitch).

The Tonga paradigm that follows, representing the present tense affirmative, shows that in at least some forms the interchange of *tu-* 'we' and *ba-* 'they', or of *-mu-* 'him' and *-ba-* 'them', or of *-lang-* 'look at' and *-bon-* 'see' may result in a difference in tone on an adjacent syllable, even though none of these morphemes has a constant tonal effect throughout the whole paradigm:

1. 'we/they V'   'we/they V him'   'we/they V them'
   tu-la-lang-a   tu-la-mu-lang-a   tu-la-ba-lang-a
   ba-la-lang-a   ba-la-mu-lang-a   ba-lá-ba-lang-a
   tu-la-bon-a    tu-la-mu-bon-a    tu-la-ba-bon-a
   ba-lá-bon-a    ba-lá-mú-bon-a    ba-lá-ba-bon-a

Reprinted by permission from *A Festschrift for Morris Halle*, ed. Stephen R. Anderson and Paul Kiparsky (New York: Holt, Rinehart and Winston, 1973), pp. 140–52. Copyright © 1973 by Holt, Rinehart and Winston, inc.

Meeussen noted that these morphemes can be assigned to two groups, "determinant" and "neutral", in such a way that the high tones which appear in the paradigm are on those neutral syllables which are between determinants. In the examples given, determinants appear in boldface type:

2. tu-la-lang-a    tu-la-mu-lang-a    tu-la-**ba**-lang-a
   **ba**-la-lang-a    **ba**-la-mu-lang-a    **ba**-lá-**ba**-lang-a
   tu-la-bon-a    tu-la-mu-bon-a    tu-la-**ba**-bon-a
   **ba**-lá-bon-a    **ba**-lá-mú-bon-a    **ba**-lá-**ba**-bon-a

Under the assumption that all "neutrals" correspond to one underlying tone and all "determinants" to another and that the underlying tones in an underlying two-tone system must be "high" and "low," the question arises whether "determinant" is underlying high or underlying low. If it is underlying low, then rather than a rule being necessary to do something to neutrals that are between determinants (they will simply retain their underlying high tone), a rule will be needed to lower neutrals that are not between determinants. We can formulate this rule, which I call "terminal lowering" (where $\|$ denotes phrase boundary), as:[1]

3. Terminal Lowering    $H^n \rightarrow L^n \; / \; \left\{ \begin{matrix} \|\text{---} \\ \text{---}\| \end{matrix} \right\}$

On the other hand, if "determinant" is underlying high, it will be necessary to change the tone not only on neutrals that are between determinants but also on the determinants that they are between. This would all have to be done by a single rule such as:[2]

4. $H(L^n H) \rightarrow L(H^n L)$

Otherwise, global rules will be necessary: if the lows between the highs are made high before the highs are made low, the rule that makes the highs (determinants) low will have to distinguish underlying highs from derived highs, that is, it will have to make reference to a stage of the derivation earlier than its input.

Though the choice between "determinant" = "high" and "determinant" = "low" is far from clear, I will adopt the alternative that lets one do without global rules, that is, I will take the position that determinants are underlying lows.[3]

There are a number of phonological rules which will have to be discussed before taking up the more complicated tonal phenomena to be treated here. The negative form *tabalángi* 'they do not look at' provides reason for taking the suffix -*i* to be a determinant. Thus, we can now assign tone correctly to all but one of the negative forms:

5. 'they do not V'      'they do not V him'      'they do not V them'
   ta-ba-láng-i      ta-ba-mú-láng-i      ta-ba-bá-láng-i
   ta-ba-bon-i      ta-ba-mú-bon-i      ta-ba-ba-bon-i

The one form whose tone is not accounted for is *tababálángi* 'they do not look at them', where the incorporated object *-ba-* is pronounced high even though it is known to be determinant. Such forms as this led Meeussen to posit a dissimilation rule which makes a determinant neutral after another determinant. In the framework adopted here, this rule would appear as:

6. Dissimilation      $L \rightarrow H / L$ ____

As formulated, this rule would be applicable not only to *tababálángi* but also to *tabababoni* (which ends with four consecutive determinants) and *tulababona* 'we see them' (in which the third and fourth syllables are determinant). However, if "dissimilation" is ordered before terminal lowering (3), the correct forms will result, as shown:[4]

7. tá-bà-bà-láng-ì   tá-bà-bàbòn-ì   tú-lá-bà-bòn-á
         bá                  bá-bón-í              bón      Dissimilation
   tà                  tà      bà-bòn-ì tù-là      bòn-à   Terminal Lowering
   tà-bà-bá-láng-ì   tà-bà-bà-bòn-ì   tù-là-bà-bòn-à

A second phenomenon illustrated by present negative forms is that in many tenses[5] the underlying tone contrast on the agreement marker is neutralized. With the agreement marker *tu-* 'we' the tones in the negative present tense are exactly the same as with *ba-* 'they': *tatubálángi* 'we do not look at'. There is thus some rule which, prior to dissimilation, imposes a tone (in this case a low tone) on the agreement marker in various tenses. Details of this rule will be given later.

A further phenomenon which appears in various forms is "downstep," as in the present perfect affirmative form *balí'bálángide* 'they have looked at them'. Downstep (indicated by ') consists of a lowering of the pitch of subsequent highs relative to the pitch of preceding highs: *-balang-* in the last example is on a slightly lower pitch than *-li-*; by contrast, in *balímúlángide* 'they have looked at him', *-li-*, *-mu-*, and *-lang-* are all on the same pitch. Tonga seems amenable to the analysis originally proposed by Stewart (1964, cited in Schachter and Fromkin 1968: 110) for downstep in Twi. According to this, downstep arises from HLH sequences via (*a*) pitch assignment rules which make H after L lower in pitch than H before L (that is, the drop in pitch from H to a following L exceeds the rise in pitch from L to a following H) followed by (*b*) rules which either eliminate L between H's or assimilate L between H's to the pitch of one of the surrounding H's. The form in question appears to be a case of assimilation,

and, indeed, all forms in which the tone rules given so far would yield . . .
HLH . . . in fact exhibit . . . H'HH . . . . Thus *balí'bálángide* appears
to demand the deviation in 8, where the interval between *li*⁵ and *ba*⁴
constitutes downstep (with lower numbers standing for lower pitch):

8. bà-lí-bà-láng-ìdé

| | |
|---|---|
| – | Dissimilation |
| è | Terminal Lowering |
| ba³li⁵ba²la⁴ngi¹de¹ | Pitch Assignment |
| ba⁴ | Assimilation |
| ba³li⁵ba⁴la⁴ngi¹de¹ | |

The major portion of this paper will be devoted to the topic of initial and
final high pitches, which according to the rules given so far ought not to be
possible. In the course of discussing this question, it will be necessary to
take up in detail the relationship of "preinitial" morphemes (morphemes
which precede the agreement marker) to the neutralization of tonal
contrasts in agreement markers.

I am aware of four classes of circumstances in which an initial syllable
in Tonga is on a high pitch. The first of these apparently corresponds to a
minor restriction on Terminal Lowering. Consider the full paradigm for
the present perfect affirmative (where -*siy*- is 'leave behind'):

9. 'we/they have V-ed'   'we/they have V-ed him'   'we/they have V-ed
                                                      them'

| | | |
|---|---|---|
| túlí-láng-ide | tú-lí-mú-láng-ide | tu-li-ba-láng-ide |
| ba-lí-láng-ide | ba-lí-mú-láng-ide | ba-lí-'bá-láng-ide |
| tu-li-siy-ide | tu-li-mu-siy-ide | tu-li-ba-siy-ide |
| ba-lí-siy-ide | ba-lí-mú-siy-ide | ba-lí-ba-siy-ide |

The first two forms of the first line have an initial sequence of high syllables,
rather than being entirely low pitched as the rules given so far would
predict them to be. This phenomenon occurs only when a neutral verb root
is preceded by only neutral elements. Some further examples are:

10. ndí-lí-mú-tóbel-ide     'I have followed him'
    ndí-lí-mú-yándaul-ide   'I have looked for him'

Since the perfect morpheme *ide* has the property of making determinant
the "extension," that is, the part of the verb stem after its first syllable, the
class of forms under discussion here can be characterized as those in which
a sequence of underlying high pitches terminates in a high-pitched verb-
root syllable followed by a low tone. The clause of Meeussen's pitch
assignment rules which covers this case is equivalent to the restriction on
terminal lowering that is built into the revised statement of the rule:

11. Terminal Lowering$_2$    $H^n \rightarrow L^n \,/ \left\{ \begin{array}{l} \| \underline{\hspace{1em}} \text{ except } / \underline{\hspace{1em}} \text{ root } L \\ \underline{\hspace{1em}} \| \end{array} \right\}$

The second case of initial high pitches is the imperative. An imperative consists of a bare verb stem followed by the suffix -a, the former pronounced on a high pitch and the latter on a low pitch:

12. láng-a  'look at!'     tóbél-a  'follow!'     yándáúl-a  'look for!'
    bón-a   'see!'        sílík-a  'treat!      swíílíl-a  'listen to!'
                                   (medically)'

The verbs in the first line are neutral, those in the second line determinant. Meeussen analyzed imperatives as having an initial segmentless determinant. This would neutralize tonal contrasts in the verb since dissimilation would make the first syllable of a determinant verb neutral. To get this proposal to work, Meeussen had to treat the suffix not as a single vowel but as an underlying geminate, the first element of which is neutral and the second determinant: a determinant is needed so that neutral -lang-, for example, can be between two determinants and thus pronounced high, but that determinant cannot immediately follow the verb stem since Dissimilation would then apply to the suffix of determinant -bon-a, for example, and the whole word would end up on a low tone. Meeussen's proposal thus corresponds to the derivations in:

13. φ-bòn-áà  φ-láng-áà
    bón       –           Dissimilation
    –         –           Terminal Lowering
         à        à       Contraction
    bón-à     láng-à

The correct formulation of the contraction rule(s) is a major problem which will come up again later in this paper.

Since the hortative (which may be used as an imperative and which is indeed the only way of expressing an imperative when there is an incorporated object) causes the agreement marker to be made determinant, the proposal of an initial segmentless determinant is fairly plausible: it posits the tone which would be there if an agreement marker were overtly present.

A third case of initial high pitches involves preinitial morphemes. All preinitials have fixed tone. Meeussen (1963) calls high-pitched preinitials determinant and low-pitched preinitials neutral on the grounds that "a low preinitial never [is] followed by a high . . . ; a high preinitial should be viewed as a determinant . . . since the following syllables are high before a primary[6] determinant" (p. 75). This is illustrated by the data in 14, in which = marks the boundary between preinitial and agreement marker and boldface type indicates what Meeussen takes to be determinant (in both tenses neutral tone is imposed on the agreement marker):

14. í = bá-bon-ide 'they who have seen'
ni = nd-a-mú-bon-a (< ni = ndi-a- . . . ) 'if I had seen him (today)'

If í = were neutral, the result should be *ibabonide; if ni = were determinant, the result should be *nindámúbona or *nindá'múbona, depending on certain details in the contraction rule. Attempting to recast this proposal of Meeussen's in terms of "high" and "low" rather than "determinant" and "neutral" puts one in something of a quandary. On the one hand, we can propose that determinant preinitials have the same underlying tone as other determinants, namely, low, in which case a rule will be needed to reverse the pitch of preinitials. On the other hand, we can say that the dissimilation rule, assuming that it operates in the examples in 15 in the way that Meeussen indicates, has to turn a low into high after a low nonpreinitial or a high preinitial but not after a low preinitial, so that tu-, -a-, and -bon- or -silik- all become high pitched:

15. ni = tu-a-bon-aa (/ní = tù-à-bòn-áà/) → nítwábóna 'when we saw (today)'
tiyi = tu-a-silik-aa (/tìyí = tù-à-sìlík-áà/) → tiyítwásílíka 'we did not treat (today)'

Either way, Terminal Lowering would have to be inhibited from making a preinitial low.

One is hoisted firmly onto one horn of this dilemma by a consideration of the one morpheme in Tonga which is a preinitial in some tenses but not in others, namely, the negative marker ta. Ta is preinitial except in the following tenses, where it follows the agreement marker: tenses that have another preinitial, subjunctive tenses, and past participles. Preinitials always impose a tone on the agreement marker (which immediately follows the preinitial). The subjunctive tenses and the past participles are the only tenses in which there is no preinitial but a tone is imposed on the agreement marker anyway. Thus, there is reason to posit a segmentally zero preinitial in the subjunctive and the past participles. Then a tone is imposed on the agreement marker if and only if there is a preinitial (and the preinitial determines which tone is imposed on the agreement marker), and, furthermore, ta- will appear after the agreement marker if and only if there is some preinitial other than ta- present.

Meeussen attributes three different tonal behaviors to ta in various tenses: he treats it as neutral when preinitial and as determinant when it follows the agreement marker, except in the present subjunctive, where he says that it is given the opposite underlying tone from the root (that is, it is determinant with a neutral root and vice versa). However, an alternative analysis is available which eliminates this third case. The forms in the present subjunctive are:

16. 'that we not V'      'that we not V him'      'that we not V them'
    tu-tá-tóbel-i        tu-tá-mú-tóbel-i         tu-tá-bá-tóbel-i
    tu-tá-silik-i        tu-tá-mú-silik-i         tu-tá-ba-silik-i

If present subjunctive negatives are derived from underlying forms in which *ta* is determinant (as it normally is when it follows the agreement marker), the agreement marker is determinant (as in other subjunctive tenses), and the suffix *-i* is determinant (as in other negative present tenses), then the resulting output would differ from the forms in 16 only to the extent that *tutásiliki* and *tutábasiliki* would all be low, rather than having *ta* high. *Ta* in fact has surface high pitch not only in all present subjunctive negative forms but in all subjunctive negative forms. Thus the correct pitches result if *ta* is taken to be a determinant and there is a rule ordered after Terminal Lowering which makes *ta* high pitched in the subjunctive. Under this proposal *ta* is neutral if preinitial and determinant otherwise. Under the assumption that *ta* has the same underlying tone regardless of where it occurs and that the earlier decision to treat nonpreinitial determinants as underlying lows is correct, we arrive at the conclusion that the underlying tones of preinitials are identical to their surface tones. That is, [í = ], which Meeussen called "determinant," is an underlying high tone, and [tà = ] and the conditional [nì = ], which Meeussen called "neutral," are underlying low tones.

The most reasonable approach to getting off the horn of the dilemma is to see if an alternative analysis is possible in which the dissimilation rule does not apply to examples such as those of 15. To investigate this possibility, I will have to examine the various preinitials and the tones which they impose on the agreement marker. In 17 the preinitials have been arranged in three groups according to the tonal sequence across the = boundary in Meeussen's analysis:

17a. D = N   i 'direct relative'       í = bá-láng-a 'they who looked at'
             ni 'potential'            ní = nd-a-lang-a 'I would have
                                       looked at'
  b. N = D   ka 'hortative'            ka = mu-láng-a 'let him look at'
             aa 'hortative'            á = 'tú-láng-e 'let him look at'
             φ 'subjunctive'           tu-láng-e 'that we look at'
             ta 'negative'             ta = tu-láng-i 'we do not look at'
             kaa 'present participle'  ká = 'tú-láng-a 'we looking at'
             φ 'past participle'       tw-á-láng-a 'we having looked at'
             ni 'conditional'[7]       ni = nd-a-lang-a 'if I had looked at'

   c. D = D   tiyi 'negative'              tiyí = tw-á-sílík-a 'we did not
                                           treat'
         ni 'temporal'                     ní = tw-á-láng-a 'when we looked
                                           at'
         n . . . 'indirect relative' [8]   n-cí = tw-á-láng-a 'which we
                                           looked at'

It is only with the three morphemes of group c that Meeussen has
occasion to treat the preinitial as conditioning Dissimilation. Note that
more is involved than just the surface tone of the agreement marker. In
*tiyí = twásílíka*, *-a-* must be determinant if dissimilation is to make *-sil-* of
*-silik-* high, and *-tu-* (which is neutral in tenses without a preinitial) must
be determinant if *-a-*, which has just been shown to be determinant, is to be
pronounced on a high pitch; and if something such as Dissimilation does
not apply to make *-tu-* high, the result will involve downstep: *\*tiyí =
'twásílíka*. The only alternative that I can see to the peculiar formulation
of Dissimilation which this would require is to say that an extra rule is
involved in the cases where Meeussen has a preinitial conditioning Dissimilation, for example, a rule ordered after Dissimilation (and before Terminal
Lowering) which would make the agreement marker high after the morphemes of group c. One peculiarity here is that the extra rule would cause
the three morphemes to impose on the agreement marker the opposite of
the tone that they had imposed on it by an earlier rule. For a slightly
improved approach, suppose for the moment that groups a and b are all
the preinitials that there are. Then the rule by which preinitials impose a
tone on the agreement marker can be taken to be a simple assimilation rule:

18. preinitial assimilation       syllable → $\alpha$H/$\alpha$H = ____

This rule would not suffice to handle group c: the obvious proposal of
treating the morphemes of group c as having an extra tone which is
assimilated onto the agreement marker (*tìyî =*, *nî =*) will not work, since
precisely that kind of underlying form is needed for the tonal behavior of
[á = ] and [ká = ] of group b, which are followed by downstep, whereas the
items of group c are not.

Rather than treating the preinitials of group c as exceptional to two
different rules that impose a tone on the following syllable (one rule
coming before dissimilation and one after it), it is possible to incorporate
all of the irregularity into a single rule by saying that these preinitials in
fact make the agreement marker "neutral" (that is, behave like group a
with respect to assimilation) but are subject to a later rule (ordered after
dissimilation) which makes the morpheme after the agreement marker
(always the infix *-a-* in the cases in question) high pitched. We would then
have the derivations:

19. í=bà-láng-áà    kà=mú-láng-áà    ní=tú-à-bòn-áà
      bá                    mù                    (tú)               Preinitial
      –                      –                       bón               Dissimilation
                                                     á                 Minor Raising
              à                       à                         à       Contraction
    í=bálángà      kà=mùlángà      ní=twábónà

The fourth case in which an initial syllable in Tonga may be high pitched involves noun prefixes. There are no underlying tone contrasts in noun prefixes, the tone on the prefix being determined by the noun to which it is attached. Consider the forms:

20. i-ma-tongo   'ruins'
    í-má-kani    'news'
    í-mú-súne    'ox'

These examples consist of i-, which begins the so-called "double prefix," followed by the prefix proper, followed by the noun. Since infinitives in Bantu languages are morphologically nouns, they provide material that is essential for making the analysis of nouns consistent with that of verbs. The prefix of an infinitive is low before a neutral verb and high before a determinant verb:

21. i-ku-lang-a   'to look at'
    í-kú-bon-a    'to see'

Of the devices that have been used to derive word-initial tones in previous examples, the only one which would work here is that of positing a segmentless low tone at the beginning of the word: since the prefix is not high before all verbs, it cannot be exempted from Terminal Lowering in the way that preinitials are, and since the prefix is high before determinant and not neutral verbs, the initial high cannot be ascribed to the restriction which exempts from the first clause of Terminal Lowering sequences of neutrals terminating in a neutral verb root followed by a determinant. I thus tentatively assign to the nouns in 20 the underlying forms and derivations in:[9]

22. ɸ-í-má-tóngó   ɸ-í-má-kàní   ɸ-í-mú-súnè
      ì-mà-tòngò         ì              –              terminal lowering
      ì-mà-tòngò     í-má-kànì     í-mú-súnè

Such underlying forms yield correct result for the genitive construction, which is made up of the head noun followed by a word that consists of an agreement marker of the class of the head noun, a linking element -a-, and the dependent noun with its own single prefix. In the examples in 23, each of the two nouns is given in its isolation form, and then a genitive construction is given with the first noun as head:

23.  í-kú-boko                              'arm'
     í-mú-kaintu                            'woman'
     í-kú-'bókó kw-á-'mú-kaintu             'woman's arm'
     < ɸ-í-kú-bòkó kú-à-mú-kàíntú
     í-bú-lwazi                             'disease'
     í-n-kuku                               'fowl'
     í-bú-'lwázi bw-á-n-kuku                'disease of fowl'
     < ɸ-í-bú-lwàzí bú-à-ń-kùkú[10]
     í-kú-boko                              'arm'
     i-mu-sankwa                            'boy'
     í-kú-'bókó kw-á-mu-sankwa              'boy's arm'
     < ɸ-í-kú-bòkó kú-à-mú-sánkwá
     í-mú-súne                              'ox'
     í-mú-nene                              'old man'
     í-mú-sú'né w-á-'mú-nene                'old man's ox'
     < ɸ-í-mú-súnè ú-à-mú-nèné
     í-cí-sálu                              'hide'
     í-mú-súne                              'ox'
     í-cí-sá'lú c-á'mú-súne                 'hide of ox'
     < ɸ-í-cí-sálù cí-à-mú-súnè
     i-mu-limo                              'work'
     í-mú-límó 'w-á-mú-kaintu               'woman's work'
     < ɸ-í-mú-límó ú-à-mú-kàíntú
     í-mú-límó w-a-mu-sankwa                'boy's work'
     < ɸ-í-mú-límó ú-à-mú-sánkwá

Note that Terminal Lowering does not apply to *i-mu-limo* when a genitive follows, which shows that phrase boundary rather than word boundary is indeed the environment for this rule.

I turn now to cases where a phrase-final high pitch occurs in Tonga. Aside from two enclitics (Carter 1962; 15) about which I have nothing to say, I know of three classes of cases where this occurs, all of which involve relatively short nouns and verbs. In a large number of tenses, forms occur in which a monosyllabic determinant verb stem is preceded by downstep and followed by a high-pitched suffix, as in *tiyí = bá-ká-'bón-á* 'they did not see (yesterday)'. Before pitch assignment, these forms of course have the verb stem low and the suffix high. In all of the tenses in question, Meeussen's analysis involves an underlying geminate suffix whose first component is neutral and whose second is determinant. Forms with a determinant incorporated object show it to be necessary to treat the suffix as -*áà* in the tense just cited, the hesternal negative:

24. tiyí=bá-ká-'bá-láng-a < tìyí=bà-ká-bà-láng-áà
    tiyí=bá-ká-'bá-bón-a < tìyí=bà-ká-bà-bòn-áà

There must be a determinant after -*lang*- for it to end up on a high pitch. However, the determinant cannot come directly after the verb stem since it would then be subject to Dissimilation in the forms with -*bon*-, and the resulting -HH sequence would become -LL by Terminal Lowering, yielding \**tiyí=bá-ká-ba-bon-a*. The final high pitch on *tiyí=bá-ká-'bón-á* (and the other forms alluded to) can thus be accounted for by appropriate formulation of the contraction rules: rather than a V́V̀ suffix always yielding a low output (as it has in all the examples up to now), it yields a low output after a high pitch and a high output after a low pitch:[11]

25.  tìyí=bà-ká-bòn-áà   tìyí=bà-ká-bà-bòn-áà
       bá                    bá              Preinitial Assimilation
       –                     bón             Dissimilation
            á                    à           Contraction
     tìyí=bá-ká-bòn-á     tìyí=bá-ká-bà-bòn-à

Contraction, or at least the case of it which applies to V́V̀ after V̀, must then apply later than Terminal Lowering so that the high pitch which it leaves will not yet be final when Terminal Lowering applies.

The second case where a final high pitch occurs involves what I will refer to as "nonsyllabic verbs," that is, verbs whose stem has the surface form of a single consonant, as in:

26. tu-la-ty-a  'we pour'
    tu-la-p-a   'we give'

The fragmentary data that I have seen on the perfect tenses of these verbs (Carter 1962: 51–52) suggests that, just as in Ganda (Tucker 1967: *xxiv*), the verbs have underlying CV forms whose vowel is lost everywhere except in the perfect tenses. One reason for wanting to set up underlying forms with vowels is that these verbs bear underlying tonal contrasts and thus would otherwise conflict with the apparently valid claim that tones in underlying forms can be borne only by syllables or moras. The tonal contrast between -*ty*- and -*p*- is illustrated by the forms in 27, in which the tonal behavior of the present tense marker -*la*- is exactly the same as with neutral and determinant verbs that have a CVC shape:

27. ba-la-ty-a  'they pour'  (cf. ba-la-lang-a  'they look at')
    ba-lá-p-a   'they give'  (cf. ba-lá-bon-a   'they see')

There are a rather large number of forms in which nonsyllabic verbs may end on a high pitch, for example:

28. ty-á  'pour!'    ka-mu-ty-á  'let him pour'
    p-á   'give!'    ka-mu-p-á   'let him give'

As shown in the derivations in 29, such forms require extra clauses of the contraction rule(s) to cover three-tone sequences but otherwise cause no problems:

29. ɸ-tí-áà   ɸ-pè-áà   kà=mú-tí-áà   ká=mú-pè-áà
                 mù               mù          Preinitial Assimila-
                                                  tion
                                          pé      Dissimilation
    tyá      pá        tyá           pá          Contraction
    ty-á     p-á       kà-mù-ty-á    kà-mù-p-á

Evidently, V́V́V̀ yields V́ and, as the contrasting examples in 30 indicate, V̀V́V̀ (the left-hand form) yields V̀:

30. 'let him give me'    'let him give them'
    kà=mú-ndí-pá-áà   kà=mú-bà-pè-áà   Preinitial Assimilation
         mù                 mù
                         bá-pé          Dissimilation
         pà                 pá          Contraction
    kà-mù-ndí-p-à     kà-mù-bá-p-á

I wish I could report here that these proposals correctly predict all final high tones after nonsyllabic verb stems. However, there remain a large number of forms which I am unable to account for without, for example, taking certain suffixes to have a different form after a nonsyllabic stem. The subjunctive form *tu-tá-bá-p-i* 'that we not give them', for instance, remains a mystery: the expected underlying form ɸ=*tú-tà-bà-pè-ì* should yield \**tu-tá-ba-p-i* (by, among other rules, the one that makes *ta* high in subjunctives).

The last case of final high pitch which I know of involves monosyllabic nouns. Just like two-syllable nouns, one-syllable nouns exhibit a three-way tonal contrast:

31. i-bu-su  'flour'
    í-bú-si  'smoke'
    í-má-lí  'money'

The first and second of these examples can obviously be derived from ɸ-*i-bú-sú* and ɸ-*i-bú-sì*, respectively. However, there is no obvious underlying form for 'money' which would make it tonally distinct from 'flour'. One possibility is to treat the final vowel as a geminate, *-líì*; but this would force a revision of the contraction rules since in their present formulation they would make *-líì* low-pitched after the high-pitched *-má-*. Moreover, such a proposal would involve setting up a combination of segments which otherwise does not occur in nouns and indeed is required only in verb suffixes and preinitials.[12]

While both one- and two-syllable nouns fall into three tonal types, the number of tonal distinctions for nouns in general increases with the number of syllables. For example, there are five possibilities for three-syllable nouns:[13]

32.                          PRESUMED
     PRONUNCIATION          UNDERLYING FORM
     í-mú-cáyíli   'driver'   cáyílì
     í-n-'káláya   'rust'     kàláya
     í-n-gówani    'hat'      gówàni
     i-m-bilila    'incense'  bílílá
     í-cí-jatizyo  'handle'   jàtizyo

Since the rules of Tonga are such that the eight logical possibilities for tones on three syllables can yield only five surface distinctions (LHH, LLH, and LLL would all yield the pitch of *ící-jatizyo*, and HLH and HLL would both yield the pitch of *í-n-gówani*),[14] it would appear as if pitches were freely combinable in underlying forms of nouns. However, if the possible tonal underlying forms for nouns were simply the different assignments of H or L to each syllable, there would be only two tonal possibilities for monosyllabic nouns rather than the three that actually occur. The only alternative that I can think of which might avoid this problem involves a rather drastic change in the underlying forms for Tonga, namely, representing the tonal behavior of morphemes not in terms of high and low pitches on the various syllables but in terms of places where pitch falls, as in my treatment of Japanese (McCawley 1968*a*), especially the dialects of the Kansai area (Kyōto, Kōchi, Hyōgo, etc.). In these dialects, nouns differ as to whether they begin on a high or a low pitch and as to where, if anywhere, there is a fall in pitch. Using ' to represent fall in pitch and also using a preposed ' to represent initial low pitch (which is reasonable in that there is in fact a fall in pitch at the boundary between a high pitched item, a demonstrative, for example, and a following initial low pitch), the accentual possibilities for three-syllable nouns in Hyōgo Japanese are:[15]

33. PRONUNCIATION[16]                           UNDERLYING FORM

| | | |
|---|---|---|
| kúrúmá; kúrúmá gá | 'vehicle' | kuruma |
| ùsàgí; ùsàgì gá | 'rabbit' | 'usagi |
| ábùrà; ábùrà gà | 'oil' | a'bura |
| ázúkì; ázúkì gà | 'red bean' | azu'ki |
| ùsírò; ùsírò gà | 'rear' | 'usi'ro |

Any Hyōgo noun contains at most two "accents," one before it and one within it. There are no three-syllable or longer nouns in Hyōgo Japanese which have a final accent. However, this possibility does occur in one- and two-syllable nouns, as shown:

34. PRONUNCIATION                           UNDERLYING FORM

| | | |
|---|---|---|
| é; é gá | 'picture' | e |
| hî; hí gà | 'day' | hi' |
| hǐ; hì gá | 'fire' | 'hi |
| úsí; úsí gá | 'cow' | usi |
| ìtó; ìtò gá | 'thread' | 'ito |
| ótò; ótò gà | 'sound' | o'to |
| àmê; àmé gà | 'rain' | 'ame' |

If Tonga nouns are represented using ' to indicate fall in pitch, the possibilities for one- and three-syllable nouns exactly match those for Hyōgo Japanese, and the possibilities for two-syllable nouns differ only to the extent of there being no Tonga counterpart to words such as *ámê* which are both preaccented and final-accented:

35. 
| | |
|---|---|
| su | 'flour' |
| 'si | 'smoke' |
| li' | 'money' |
| tongo | 'ruins' |
| 'kani | 'news' |
| su'ne | 'ox' |
| bilila | 'incense' |
| 'jatizyo | 'handle' |
| go'wani | 'hat' |
| cayi'li | 'driver' |
| 'kala'ya | 'rust' |

I will not redo all the rules in accordance with this proposal since my principal reason for suggesting it relates to the underlying representations of nouns, and the information which I have about nouns in Tonga, particularly nouns of more than three syllables, is too fragmentary to serve as a basis for anything. There seem to be no major problems in recasting the rules presented earlier in terms of "accents"; for example, Dissimilation would delete an accent that is one syllable after an accent. One attractive feature of this proposal is that, since it allows the possibility of a three-way contrast in suffixes containing a single vowel (-a, -'a, -a'), it appears to make unnecessary the underlying geminates which Meeussen set up for suffixes such as that of the imperative (which can be represented as -*a'* rather than -*áà*) and for certain preinitials. The low tone on these morphemes could be attributed to a rule which retracts final accent by one syllable except when either (*a*) the retraction would cause there to be accents on two consecutive syllables[17] or (*b*) the retraction would move the accent off a monosyllabic noun (or verb?). There would thus be derivations such as:

36. 'see!'        'they did not see'     'they did not see them'
    '⌀-'bon-a'   'tiyi='ba-ka-bon-a'   'tiyi='ba-ka-'ba-'bon-a'
    '⌀-bon-a'    –                      bon-a'  Dissimila-
                                                tion
    '⌀-bo'n-a    –                      bo'n-a   Retraction
    bónà         tìyí=báká'bóná         tìyí=báká'bábónà

Morphemes other than nouns, suffixes, and preinitials would come in only two underlying tonal types, namely, preaccented and unaccented.[18]

# II    Syntax and Semantics

# 8 Two Notes on Comparatives

*1. Before and 'Semicomparatives'*

Geis (1970) has argued that *before*-clauses have an underlying structure in which *earlier than* occurs (and similarly, *after*-clauses have an underlying structure containing *later than*). For Geis, the following two examples have the same underlying structure:

1a. Bill went home before Frank did.
 b. Bill went home at a time which was earlier than the time at which Frank went home.

There are, however, other sentences in which *before* does not correspond to *earlier than*:

2. I'll go hungry before I'll accept a farthing from you.

If one says 2, he is not asserting that the time at which he will go hungry is earlier than the time at which he will accept a farthing from you, but that he would rather go hungry than accept a farthing from you.

The 'semicomparatives' *would rather* and *prefer* have a much narrower range of possibilities for reduction of the *than*-clause than do comparatives proper:[1]

3a. I enjoy eating popadums more than (I enjoy) smoking pot.
 b. I prefer eating popadums to smoking pot.
 c. I prefer to eat popadums than to smoke pot.
 d. I would rather each popadums than smoke pot.
 e. I enjoy playing cards more than Sam (does).
 f. *I prefer playing cards than Sam (does).
 g. *I prefer to play cards than Sam (does).
 h. *I would rather play cards than Sam (would).

Published by permission; to appear in *Linguistic and Literary Studies in Honor of Archibald A. Hill*, vol. 2, ed. E Polome et al. (Lisse: Peter de Ridder).

This difference is paralleled in the two kinds of *before*-clauses: example 4 is ambiguous between a comparative sense (which asserts that my resignation will precede my wife's and presupposes that both of us will resign) and a semicomparative sense (which asserts that I would rather resign than let my wife resign and does not presuppose that either of us will resign), while 5 can have only the comparative sense.[2]

4. I'll resign before my wife does.

5. I'll resign before my wife.

This fact strongly supports Geis's analysis of sentences like 1a as comparatives: the comparative reduction rule cannot be formulated as simply applying to comparatives and to *before*- and *after*-clauses, since it applies only to those *before*-clauses that are comparatives. An adequate formulation of comparative reduction requires an underlying structure in which the *before*-clauses of 1a and the like are represented as comparatives and those of 2 are not.

## 2. Comparatives and Predicate NP's

In Chomsky 1965:180–81, there is some inconclusive discussion of pairs of sentences like 6 and 7, which Chomsky notes are not synonymous in that, for example, 6b presupposes that Mary is a man (the * here marks conflict between that presupposition and the rest of the sentence, given normal use of the proper names), but 6a does not.

6a. John is a man who is taller than Mary.
   b. *John is a taller man than Mary.

7a. This is an inkwell which is older than the Parthenon.
   b. *This is an older inkwell than the Parthenon.

There is in fact much more of a difference between such pairs of sentences than Chomsky pointed out. Sentences 8a and b differ not only as regards whether there is a presupposition that Frank is a midget but also as regards how tall Tom is asserted to be.

8a. Tom is a midget who is shorter than Frank.
   b. Tom is a shorter midget than Frank.

There is nothing in 8a to preclude Tom's being a tall midget (e.g., about 4'5" tall), but in 8b, Tom is asserted to be a short midget, as is, in addition, Frank. Sentences 9a and b differ as regards what mental characteristic is being ascribed to the two persons.

9a. Lionel is a lawyer who is smarter than Albert.
   b. Lionel is a smarter lawyer than Albert.

In 9a, nothing is said about Lionel's abilities as a lawyer (nor about those of Albert, who need not even be a lawyer), and Lionel is being compared with Albert in intelligence as a whole, not in the specific kinds of intelligence that are involved in excellence as a lawyer, whereas in 9b, it is only the latter kind(s) of intelligence that is/are at issue. Indeed, 10 is not contradictory:

10. Albert is smarter than Lionel, but Lionel is a smarter lawyer than Albert.

Finally, for certain choices of the noun, the sentence of the b-pattern may be extremely odd even though there is nothing wrong with the corresponding sentence of the a-pattern:

11a. Lionel is a lawyer who is taller than Albert.
  b. ?Lionel is a taller lawyer than Albert.

12a. Genevieve is an oboe teacher who is sexier than Harriet.
  b. ?Genevieve is a sexier oboe teacher than Harriet.

13a. Max is a chicken plucker who is more honest than Dick.
  b. ?Max is a more honest chicken plucker than Dick.

What makes 11b, 12b, and 13b odd is that they falsely suggest that lawyers are taller than ordinary people, that oboe teachers are sexier, and that chicken pluckers are more honest, or that there is a special kind of tallness for lawyers or the like.

These facts all point to the incorrectness of an assumption that is at the bottom of Chomsky's perplexity at the nonsynonymy of 6a and 6b, namely, his assumption that the comparative in 6b is the comparative of an adjective. I propose that all the b-sentences involve the comparative of a predicate NP rather than of an adjective, which is to say that 6a and b are appropriately paraphrased respectively by 14a and b.[3]

14a. John is a man such that the extent to which he is tall exceeds the extent to which Mary is tall.
  b. The extent to which John is a tall man exceeds the extent to which Mary is a tall man.

The observations made about 8b and 9b are immediate consequences of the hypothesis that 8b compares the extent to which Tom is a short midget with the extent to which Frank is and 9b compares the extent to which Lionel is a smart lawyer with the extent to which Albert is.

I would indeed claim, following Ross 1967, that the underlying structure of comparatives is along the lines of 14b: *exceed* combined with two NP's of the form the *extent to which S*. Since there is nothing anomalous about the S of *the extent to which S* having a predicate NP rather than a predicate adjective, Ross's proposal would allow for the derivation of comparatives from structures containing *the extent to which John is a smart lawyer* or *the extent to which John is a lawyer*, provided that it is supplemented by rules to put the comparative morpheme in the right place in the various cases:

15a.  John is TALLER than Bill.
   b.  John is MORE of A LAWYER than Bill.
   c.  John is *a* SMARTER *lawyer* than Bill.

The reason for the oddity of 11b–13b is that it makes no sense to speak of *the extent to which Lionel is a tall lawyer* unless there is a different standard of tallness than for ordinary people or there is a special kind of tallness for lawyers.

What I have said implies that the Adjective-preposing rule proposed in Smith 1961 and assumed in Chomsky 1965 (according to which, e.g., *a tall man* is derived form *\*a man tall*, the latter in turn derived by relative clause reduction from *a man who is tall*) should not be applicable to comparatives at all: if it were, 8b would be ambiguous between the sense discussed above and the sense of 8a. The conclusion that adjective-preposing is not applicable to comparatives is confirmed by the fact that 16a and b have only the sense in which the *big* of *big beer drinker* is adverbial ('Belgians drink beer more than Frenchmen do') and not that in which *big* is interpreted as a reduced relative clause ('Belgians are beer drinkers who are larger than Frenchmen'), whereas 17a and b are ambiguous between those two senses:

16a.  Belgians are bigger beer drinkers than Frenchmen are.
   b.  Europeans are heavier smokers than Americans are.

17a.  Belgians are big beer drinkers.
   b.  Europeans are heavy smokers.

There is in fact an independent reason for believing that comparatives do not have the constituent structure which is necessary for Adjective preposing to be applicable. Normally, an adjective allows adjective preposing only if it is at the end of its 'VP' (Lakoff 1970:122–23), and material that is within the VP does not undergo the rule that moves adverbial elements to the beginning of the clause.[4]

18a.  John is prudent in financial matters.
   b.  John is proud of his achievements.

19a.  John is a prudent man in financial matters.
   b.  *John is a proud man of his achievements.

20a. In financial matters, John is prudent.

  b. *Of his achievements, John is proud.

Note that *taller than Frank* behaves like *proud of his achievements*, not like *prudent in financial matters*:

21 *Than Frank, Bill is taller.,

which means that *than Frank* is in the VP and thus that *taller* in *taller than Frank* should not undergo Adjective proposing. I reject as fallacious my earlier argument (McCawley 1964*b*) that because of the difference in grammaticality between 22a and b, the derived constituent structures of 22c and d must differ in the same way as do those of 18a and b:

22a. John is a more intelligent man than Bill.

  b. *John is a more sick man than depraved.

  c. John is more intelligent than Bill.

  d. John is more sick than depraved.

In 22a, adjective preposing has applied to *intelligent* and not to *more intelligent*, and thus the grammaticality of 22a implies nothing about the constituent structure of 22c. The ungrammaticality of 22b results from the fact that it can arise neither from reduction of a relative clause containing a 'qualitative comparison', since *more sick than depraved* does not have the appropriate constituent structure, nor from 'qualitative comparison' of a structure containing *intelligent man*, since in a qualitative comparison based on a predicate NP, *more* precedes the article:

23. John is more a sick man than $\begin{cases} \text{depraved.} \\ \text{a depraved man.} \end{cases}$

# 9     Fodor on Where the Action Is

This paper is concerned with Jerry A. Fodor's critique (Fodor 1972) of the logical structures proposed in Donald Davidson's "The Logical Form of Action Sentences" (Davidson 1967a). I will have nothing to say below about the parts of Fodor's paper that deal with the proposals of Davidson's "Truth and Meaning" (Davidson 1967b). I am inclined to agree with Fodor's conclusion that (contra Davidson) a truth definition for a natural language need not reveal the logical structure of the sentences of the language, though my reasons are quite different from those which Fodor gives. Fodor mentions only the fact that trivial truth definitions are possible; however, even disregarding trivial definitions, I would maintain that a wide range of putative 'logical forms' can be consistent with the same assignment of truth values and that the choice among alternative systems of 'logical form' must be made on the basis of whether they allow rules of inference and rules of grammar to be stated in full generality.[1]

Davidson proposed that the logical structure of every action clause involves reference to an action, for example, that the logical structure of 1 is along the lines of 2:

1. Amundsen flew to the North Pole in 1926.

2. $(\exists x)$ [Fly(Amundsen, the North Pole, x) & In(x, 1926)].

'Fly' is conceived of as a three-place predicate, with the third place being the action. In this and several other examples, Davidson treated an adverb as conjoined with what it 'modifies' (with a quantifier around the whole lot) and claimed to have thereby solved Kenny's (1963) problem of 'variable polyadicity': he does not have to treat *fly* as having a different number of arguments in 1 than in

3. Amundsen flew to the North Pole.

Reprinted by permission from *Monist* 57 (1973): 396–407. © 1973 by The Open Court Publishing Co.

In addition he is able to show that 3 follows from 1 on the basis of standard rules of inference. Davidson, unfortunately, did not make clear whether he wanted to treat *all* adverbs as being conjuncts in logical structure. He could easily be suspected of holding that view, since he proposes a conjunctive treatment for one kind of adverb that seems an unlikely candidate for such a treatment; specifically, he analyzes 4a as 4b:[2]

4a. I flew my spaceship to the moon.
 b. $(\exists\ x)$ [Fly(I, my spaceship, x) & To(x, the moon)].

Fodor takes Davidson as holding that 'Adverbs in action sentences report properties of events, and the logical form of an action sentence containing adverbial modifiers is a conjunction' (Fodor 1972:51). He refers to the formula $(\exists\ x)$ [V ($p_1, p_2, \ldots, p_n, x$) & Dx] as 'Davidson's canonical form for a simple action sentence containing an adverbial modifier'. I maintain that the position which Fodor attributes to Davidson is absurd and moreover is inconsistent with Davidson's view of actions.

Fodor states that Davidson would have to analyze one or other of 5a–b as 5c:

5a. Clearly, John spoke.
 b. John spoke clearly.
 c. $(\exists\ x)$ [Speak(John, x) & Clear(x)].

He then objects against Davidson that whichever is analyzed as 5c, Davidson will have no analysis available for the other. I will consider first the proposal that 5a has the logical structure 5c, which Fodor finds a plausible analysis. If that proposal is accepted, then sentential adverbs such as *clearly* will play a different role in the logical structure of action sentences such as 5a than they do in other sentences such as

6a. Clearly, John is incompetent.
 b. Obviously, all of the conspirators have fled.
 c. Probably, no one is more stupid than Max.

To put it slightly differently, the possibility of combining these adverbs with a sentence has nothing to do with whether the sentence is an 'action sentence'; however, the analysis of 5a as 5c would mean that in action sentences such adverbs are combined in logical structure with something (the action) to which they are irrelevant and which is not even present in the logical structure of other sentences in which such adverbs occur. Second, the analysis of 5a as 5c is inconsistent with a rather basic claim that Davidson has made about actions: that John's pulling the trigger, his firing the gun, his shooting his mother-in-law, his killing his mother-in-law, and his murdering his mother-in-law are not five different actions but a single action described five different ways. If combined with the analysis of 5a as 5c, Davidson's claims about actions would yield the absurd result that the following argument is valid:

John's pulling the trigger is the same action as his murdering his mother-in-law.
Clearly, John pulled the trigger.
Therefore, clearly, John murdered his mother-in-law.

To uphold Davidson's view of actions without committing oneself to the validity of this argument, it is necessary to interpret sentential adverbs such as *clearly* as being predicated not of an action but of something else, and the most obvious proposal is that *clearly* (or, better, *clear*) is predicated of a proposition.[3]

The analysis of 5b as 5c encounters the kinds of problems treated by Parsons (1972), who draws on unpublished work of John Wallace. Just as *The doctor administered the medicine through a tube* does not entail *The doctor cured the patient through a tube*, under the assumption that the doctor's administering the medicine is the same action as his curing the patient, so *John spoke clearly* does not entail *\*John convinced me clearly* under the assumption that John's speaking and his convincing me are the same action.

Fodor claims that examples 5a–b show that the role of adverbs in logical structure cannot be reduced to a combination of quantification and conjunction. It should be evident from my last two paragraphs that I agreed with him about that much. However, that is where my agreement with him ends. Fodor's description of the difference between the modifiers of 5a and 5b is as follows: 'The adverbial phrase may modify the *entire* sentence, or it may modify (just) the verb phrase of the sentence. [5a] would seem to be a case of the first kind of relation and [5b] to be a case of the second' (1972:56). As a description of the surface structure of the sentences, this is fine; however, Fodor makes clear that he means that as a description of the deep syntactic structure as well.[4] Fodor's conception of deep structure is thus something not far removed from surface structure and a long way removed from logical form. I would expect someone who held such a view of deep structure also to hold that the relation between deep structure and logical form is rather complex. Curiously, Fodor seems to assume throughout that the relationship must be rather simple: that modifiers in deep structure must correspond either to conjoined sentences (if they modify a sentence) or to members of some homogeneous class of hitherto unidentified logical elements (if they modify anything other than a sentence). Such an assumption is embodied in the following passage: 'The other way of putting the point is that there are a number of important differences between the syntax of natural languages and the syntax of the standard logical formalisms. Among these is the fact that natural languages acknowledge modifiers both on sentences and on constituents, whereas the standard formalisms acknowledge only the former' (1972:61).[5] Fodor proceeds to give up all hope of an analysis of 'constituent modifiers' in terms of conjoining *and embedding* of sentences, without even mentioning the literature discussed by Davidson in "Logical Form," for example, von Wright's (1963) analysis of *I went from San Francisco to Pittsburgh* as 'I caused [(I be in San Francisco) to become (I be in Pittsburgh)]'. While the specific proposals of G. H. von Wright, Anthony Kenny, Roderick Chisholm and others that Davidson took up are all highly programmatic and solid arguments against them can be constructed, Fodor is hardly in a position to reject approaches of that type as categorically unworthy of consideration, the attitude which his silence suggests he takes. Fodor also appears to believe that a modifier in a deep structure must correspond to a 'modifier' (which for him appears to include 'predicate') in logical structure. He thus fails to consider analyses (like that of von Wright cited above) in which a surface modifier (e.g., *from San Francisco*) corresponds to (part of) an *embedded clause*.

Von Wright's proposal was an attempt at analyzing the logical structure of a complex clause in terms of just predicates and indices, where predicates are allowed to take propositions as arguments. I maintain that all of Fodor's putative examples of 'constituent modification' are amenable to such an analysis, provided that the logic is enriched so as to admit presuppositions and descriptions of sets, which presumably any serious proposal for the logical form of sentences of natural languages would have to admit. Consider first Fodor's putative example of 'constituent negation':

7a. It was not John who left his house.
 b. It was not his house that John left.

The 'problems for the standard formalisms' which Fodor sees in 7 have nothing to do with negation but are inherent in the sentences of which 7a–b are obviously the negations:

8a. It was John who left his house.
 b. It was his house that John left.

What Fodor says about 7 is equally applicable to 8: 'It is arguable that [they] are logically equivalent, but it is pretty clear that the differ in their presuppositions' (1972:62). Any analysis which distinguishes 8a from 8b on the basis of their differences in presuppositions can immediately be converted into an equally good analysis of 7a and 7b, with the negation in 7a–b being ordinary sentence negation.[6]

Fodor's remaining examples of 'constituent modification' are the following:

9a. John spoke clearly.
 b. John will do the job in a minute. (the sense in which 'a minute' is the duration of the job)
 c. John cooked the meal slowly. (the sense in which 'slowly' gives the rate at which the meal cooks, not the rate at which John does the cooking)
 d. John aimed his gun at the target. (the sense which implies that if John fires the gun and all goes well, the bullet will hit the target)
 e. John made the model by hand.
 f. John owns a typical Georgian house.
 g. John bakes well.
 h. John left the umbrella at the station.

In 9a, what is being said to be clear is the speech that John produced; compare the nominalized version *John's speech was clear*. *Speak* allows a surface direct object only to a limited extent (e.g., *John spoke those words calmly*), but it is fairly clear that *John's speech* is logically an object-nominalization of *speak*; I accordingly propose that the logical structure of 9a is:[7]

10. $(\exists x)$ $(\iota y\colon \text{Speak}(\text{John}, y, x))\text{Clear}(y)$.

A serious proposal for the logical structure of 9b will have to amount to a proposal for the logical structure of 'accomplishment' expressions, in the sense of Vendler 1957. An 'accomplishment' is a combination of an 'activity' and an 'achievement' (again, in Vendler's sense):

11a. Bill combed his hair for two minutes. (activity)
  b. Mike combed his hair in two minutes. (accomplishment)

For example, the difference between 11a and 11b is that in 11b the combing terminates with the event (= 'achievement') of its becoming the case that his hair is in place, whereas 11a makes no reference to any culmination of the activity; when two minutes had passed, Bill's combing stopped and Mike's combing finished. *In two minutes* conveys the information that the interval from the beginning of the activity to its culmination is equal to (or less than) two minutes.[8] I conjecture that the logical form of *John ran a mile in five minutes* is something like

12. $(\exists x)$ (John do x & x consist of running & x end with (John has gone a mile in x) & x last five minutes).

In that case, the logical form of 9b would be (leaving out anything corresponding to *will*):

13. (∃ x) (John do x & x end with (the job is done) & x last a minute).

There is no analogue to the second conjunct of 12, since *do the job* leaves the nature of the activity unspecified.

Example 9c is a case of the phenomenon (discussed at some length in McCawley 1971a, 1973) of an adverb modifying not the clause in which it appears but a clause which is embedded in the logical structure of that clause. If *John cooked the meal* is assigned a logical structure 'John did something which caused the meal to cook', the logical structure of 9c would differ only by the addition of *slowly* as a modifier of the clause 'the meal cooks.' Example 9d allows a similar analysis except that there the adverb is not really a modifier of the embedded clause: the logical structure would be 'John did something which caused the gun to be aimed at the target'. *Aimed* is here an adjective, not a participle. Note that a gun can be aimed at the target without anyone having aimed it at the target, just as a sign can be nailed to a door without anyone having nailed it there (it is nailed to the door if there are nails extending through it and into the door, holding it in place, regardless of how the nails got there, whether by a person hammering them in with a solid object or pushing them in with his bare hands or by a miracle in which God made nails appear out of nowhere; one can say that a person nailed something to the door only if he hammered the nails in; see McCawley 1971a.[9]

Example 9e is open to the kind of analysis proposed in Lakoff 1968, according to which instrument expressions reflect a logical structure involving the three-place predicate *use* (as in *He used a knife in peeling the potatoes*). The logical structure of 9e would also have to involve *only*: 9e says not only that John used his hands but that he used no other source of power; and the variable bound by *only* would have to range over 'sources of power': 9e implies that John didn't use a lathe, but it does not imply that he didn't use a knife. In this case, a 'Davidsonian' analysis is quite plausible: 'use' can perfectly well be taken to be a relation between an agent, an instrument, and an action, though it of course could not be taken to be a one-place predicate of an action such as figures in the 'canonical form' which Fodor attributes to Davidson.[10]

In 9f, *typical* refers not to a property of the house but to a relationship between the house and the class of thing that it is said to typify. Thus, the logical structure of 9f will have to involve reference to that class, for example,[11]

14. (∃ x) (Own(John,x) & Typical(x, {y: y is a Georgian house})).

Example 9g is a generic sentence, and I am no more prepared to propose a logical structure for it than for any other generic sentence.[12] It is a generic counterpart to such nongeneric sentences as

15. John baked that pie well.

Or more idiomatically,

16. John did a good job of baking that pie.,

Both can be paraphrased as 'Whenever John bakes, he typically/usually does it well'. This paraphrase refers to an act type ('baking') and involves a variable ranging over acts of that type and suggests that *good* (or *well*) in 9h and 15–16 is a two-place predicate that is predicated of a person and an action. In combination with Davidson's conception of actions, this analysis yields absurd results. For example, it implies that (in the case discussed in connection with 7) if John pulled the trigger well he fired the gun well.[13] I am not sure which should be held to be the culprit: the proposed analysis of *good* or Davidson's conception of actions. This is the first example I have examined which has given me serious doubts that it is correct to identify John's pulling the trigger with his firing the gun: it brings out that there is more to firing the gun well than pulling the trigger; for example, aiming the gun; one can be an expert at pulling triggers but still be incompetent at aiming guns and thus be competent at *discharging* guns and still be imcompetent at *hitting targets*. Thus pulling the trigger well, that is, with a steady squeeze and without jerking, is a necessary but not sufficient condition of being a good marksman.

I suspect that it is in fact necessary to distinguish between the action of pulling the trigger and the action of firing the gun but am more confident that the action of firing the gun is the same as the action of shooting his mother-in-law. Being in no position to resolve this question, I will leave it up in the air, expressing the hope that those who are interested in the analysis of actions will have something to say soon about *John fired the gun well*, and the like.

Example 9h is similar to 9c and 9d, though it is less obvious what its logical structure is. Example 9h refers to John's doing something which causes the umbrella to remain at the station and implies that until John performed that action the umbrella was with him. The following thus seems a reasonable guess as to the logical structure of 9h:

17. ($\exists$ x) [Do(John, x) & Cause(x, (Become(Not(With(the umbrella, John))))) & (for some interval after x, At(the umbrella, the station))].

I must emphasize that in proposing the above formulas as candidates for the logical structure of 9a–h, I have done little more than make conjectures. Any proposed logical structure requires justification on the basis of its interaction with logic (i.e., does it, plus otherwise valid rules of inference, suffice to yield all and only the inferences which it is appropriate to draw from the sentence whose content it is supposed to represent?) and linguistics (i.e., can rules for the relationship between logical form and surface structure be formulated which take in the sentences in question as special cases and are consistent with previously established rules and with otherwise valid generalizations about grammatical rules and their organization?).[14] It would not surprise me at all if all of the above formulas turned out to be deficient in many details or if some of them turned out to be incorrigibly wrong; I have not done sufficient work on most of the problems involved in 9a–h to be in a position to make proposals that I would take really seriously. My chief reason for presenting them is to show that plausible proposals which analyze away all of Fodor's putative cases of 'constituent modification' are not hard to come by and that Fodor was thus overly hasty in rejecting the kind of analysis presented by Davidson. Fodor's examples show something which hardly anyone would contest: that classical first-order predicate calculus is insufficient to represent the content of all the sentences of a natural language. However, they do not raise any obvious problems for predicate calculus with presuppositions, sets, and propositional arguments. Fodor has not demonstrated that the notion 'constituent modification' is relevant to anything other than surface structure and relatively superficial stages of syntactic derivations.

I note finally that in the course of this paper I have proposed three different analyses for three things that are traditionally called 'manner adverbs' (*John spoke* CLEARLY; *John cooked the meal* SLOWLY; *John bakes* WELL); I would propose a fourth analysis for *John spoke* CALMLY, in which calmness is predicated not of John's action nor of John's speech but of John. I do not consider my failure to provide a uniform analysis of manner adverbs to be a defect of my proposals; rather I regard 'manner adverb' as a pseudocategory which has been accepted only because the analysis and classification of adverbs so far has been done so superficially, both by linguists and by logicians.

# 10    On Identifying the Remains
of Deceased Clauses

The verb *want* occurs followed by a variety of material:

1a. Max wants Shirley to kiss him.
 b. Max wants to eat a banana.
 c. Max wants a lollipop.

Numerous transformational grammarians have argued that sentences of the forms 1a and 1b involve the same kind of underlying structure, namely one in which *want* has a sentence object, and differ only as regards whether the subject of the embedded sentence is deleted. Specifically, a rule of Equi-NP-deletion is posited, which deletes the subject of the complement of *want* if it is identical to the subject of *want*:

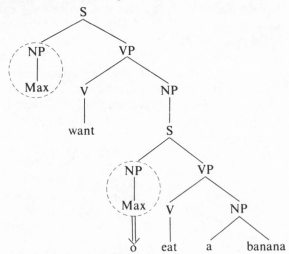

I will argue below that sentences of the form 1c also have an underlying structure in which *want* has a sentential object and that the surface object

Reprinted by permission from *Language Research* 9 (1974): 73–85.

of *want* in 1c is in fact the residue of an embedded clause.[1] I will be concerned first with demonstrating that there *is* an underlying embedded clause in sentences like 1c, and then with determining exactly what that clause is. There is in fact a fairly obvious analysis of 1c in which *want* has a sentential object, namely that in which it has the same underlying structure as *Max wants to have a lollipop* and undergoes not only Equi-NP-deletion but also deletion of the verb of the embedded clause, and it is in fact that analysis (or at least, something very close to it) which I will be presenting justification for.

The first argument that the surface object in sentences like 1c is the residue of an embedded clause has to do with time adverbs, such as those in

2. Bill wants your apartment $\begin{cases} \text{until June.} \\ \text{for 6 months.} \\ \text{while you're in Botswana.} \end{cases}$

The time adverbs in 2 do not give the time when the wanting takes place, as is especially clear when one considers sentences such as

3. Right now Bill wants your apartment until June, but tomorrow he'll probably want it until October.

In 3 there is another time adverb which explicity indicates another time as the time when the wanting takes place. If an embedded clause such as *Bill have your apartment* is posited, that clause can serve as the scope of the time adverb (i.e., in 2, *until June* is not the time when Bill's wanting takes place but the time when Bill is to have your apartment if his wish is to be satisfied). Without such an embedded clause, there is nothing that the time adverbs can plausibly be taken as modifying.

Two other arguments are closely related to this one. First, positing an underlying sentence object with *want* allows a ready explanation of why clauses with *want* can have two time adverbs, as contrasted with verbs such as *paint*, for which such an analysis would be senseless and which allow only one time adverb:

4a. A week ago Bill wanted your car yesterday.
 b. *A week ago Bill painted your car yesterday.

Secondly, the hypothesis allows one to explain which of the two time adverbs controls the tense of *want*. In simple sentences, *yesterday* allows past tense but not future tense, and *tomorrow* allows future tense but not past tense:

5a. Yesterday I played 10 Scarlatti sonatas.
 a′. *Yesterday I'll play 10 Scarlatti sonatas.
 b. Tomorrow I'll play 10 Scarlatti sonatas.
 b′. *Tomorrow I played 10 Scarlatti sonatas.

In the following sentence,[2] the tense is determined by *yesterday*, not by *tomorrow*:

6a. Yesterday Bill wanted your bicycle tomorrow.
  b. *Yesterday Bill will want your bicycle tomorrow.

If *want* in fact has a sentence object, the only coherent interpretation of the adverbs in 6a is that in which *yesterday* modifies the main clause and *tomorrow* the embedded clause. Each time adverb controls the tense of the clause that it modifies, and thus *yesterday* rather than *tomorrow* controls the tense of *want* in 6a. The hypothesis that 1c arises through deletion from a structure with a sentence thus gives one a way of predicting when *tomorrow* can co-occur with a past tense verb.

The next argument is based on facts that are more within the domain of logic than of what is usually regarded as grammar. The sentence *Max wanted a lollipop* is ambiguous between a 'referential' sense which implies that there is a lollipop such that Max wanted it, and a 'nonreferential' sense which does not imply that. The referential sense has to do with a desire to have a specific lollipop: having that specific lollipop will satisfy Max's desire and having any other lollipop will not suffice to satisfy it. The nonreferential sense has to do with a desire that will be satisfied when Max has a lollipop, regardless of the identity of the lollipop. Quine (1960: 154–56), discussing examples such as *Ernest is looking for a lion*, observed that that apparently simple sentence displays the same ambiguity as does the complex sentence *Ernest is trying to find a lion* and that the logical properties of the former can be accounted for in a natural way if one analyzes it as having the same logical structure as the latter. Specifically, let us assume that logicians are correct in representing the content of a simple sentence such as *Sam kicked a dog* by factoring out a quantifier and an associated noun:

7. (Some $x$ : $x$ is a dog) (Sam kicked $x$)

which may be recast in tree form as

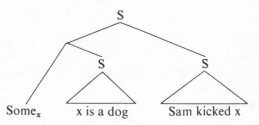

When applied to a complex sentence such as *Ernest tried to find a lion*, this factorization could take place on either the main or the subordinate clause, yielding the structures 8a and 8b. Structure 8a is a natural way to represent the referential interpretation and the nonreferential interpretation, since in each case the complement of *try* correctly matches the conditions for success of the attempt, and only 8a implies the existence of a lion that figures in Ernest's attempt; Quine thus proposes these structures as representing the logical structure of the two senses of *Ernest is trying to find a lion* (and also of the two senses of *Ernest is looking for a lion*).

8a.

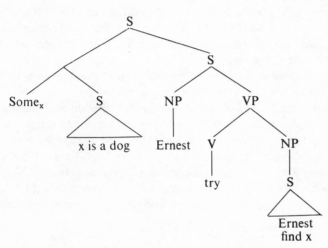

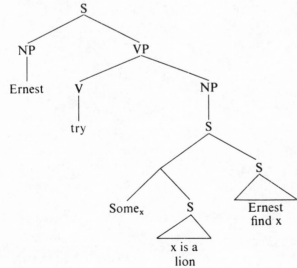

Note, however, that Quine's mode of representing the content of the non-referential interpretation is possible only if there is an embedded clause to serve as the scope of the quantifier. Thus, positing an underlying sentential object in 1c allows one in a natural way to represent its nonreferential interpretation and correctly predicts that *Max wanted a lollipop* allows a nonreferential interpretation but *Max ate a lollipop*, in which it would be absured to posit a sentential object, does not.[3]

The last argument had to do with whether a quantifier applied to the main clause or the hypothesized subordinate clause, and the first group of arguments had to do with whether an adverb applies to the main clause or the hypothesized subordinate clause. A similar argument can be made having to do with conjoining. If *want* in fact has a sentential object in 1c, then there is nothing in principle to prevent both of the structures 9a and 9b from being realized as *Max wants a cup and a saucer*.

In 9a, both $S_1$ and $S_2$ would undergo Equi-NP-deletion and deletion of *have* and then $S_0$ would undergo conjunction reduction; in 9b, $S_1$ would undergo conjunction reduction, yielding *Max have a cup and a saucer*, and then $S_0$ would be of the appropriate form to undergo Equi-NP-deletion and deletion of *have*. *Max wants a cup and a saucer* is in fact ambiguous between a sense that fits 9a and one that fits 9b: in the one case it refers to two independent desires, one for a cup and one for a saucer, and in the

9a.

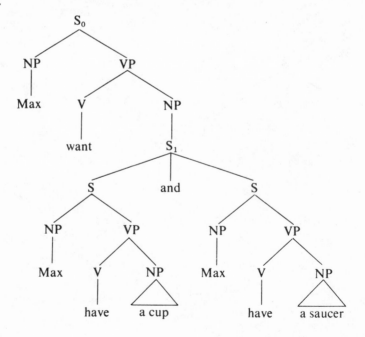

b.

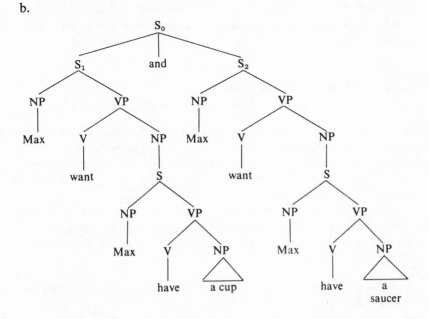

other case it refers to a single desire which is satisfied by Max's having both a cup and a saucer.[4] The same is true of conjunction with *or*: *Max wants a Cadillac or a Volkswagen* is ambiguous between a sense that implies that either he wants a Cadillac or he wants a Volkswagen (parallel to 9a) and a sense that refers to a single desire which will be satisfied when he has either a Cadillac or a Volkswagen (parallel to 9b). Not only does the hypothetical subordinate clause provide a natural way of distinguishing between these two interpretations, but it also allows one to maintain the otherwise valid generalization that constituents conjoined with *or* always arise through conjunction reduction from conjoined sentences.[5] Unless *want* has an underlying sentence object, there is no way in which *a Cadillac or a Volkswagen* could be derived by conjunction reduction in the sense which refers to a single desire, since that sense does not mean the same as *Max wants a Cadillac or he wants a Volkswagen*.

The next argument has to do with the pronoun-antecedent relation. At first glance, the antecedent of *it* in 10a appears to be a *horse*; however, if the antecedent were *a horse*, then replacement of *a horse* by something of a different gender or number ought to give rise to a different pronoun, though in fact it does not:

10a. Joe wants a horse, but his mother won't allow it.
  b. Joe wants some horses, but his mother won't allow it/*them.
  c. Joe wants a wife, but his mother won't allow it/*her/*one.

In addition, if the antecedent of *it* were *a horse*, then it ought to be possible to use *allow* with an object that refers to a horse; however, *allow* requires a sentential object:

11. Joe's mother won't allow $\begin{cases} \text{*Dobbin.} \\ \text{*that horse.} \\ \text{Joe to have a horse.} \end{cases}$

All of these facts are explained if *want* is taken as having an underlying sentence object: the antecedent of *it* in 10 can then be taken to be the sentence *Joe have a horse*, the pronoun will be *it*, since sentences count as neuter singular, and *allow* will not require anything other than the kind of object that it usually takes.

A further fact about pronominalization also supports the analysis with a sentential object, namely, that the following sentence is interpreted as having a referential object if the pronoun is *them* and a nonreferential object if the pronoun is *that*:[6]

12. Bill wants a Cadillac and a Volkswagen, and his girl friend wants them/ that too.

*That* can serve as the pronominal form of a sentence, but *them* cannot. *Them* would have to refer to the Cadillac and the Volkswagen, which it could do only if the quantifier(s) binding *Cadillac* and *Volkswagen* has/have the whole sentence as scope, in which case *a Cadillac* and *a Volkswagen* have a referential interpretation.

I will henceforth take it as established that *want* has a sentential object in sentences like *Max wants a lollipop* and turn to the question of exactly what the deleted verb is. The question divides into a number of subsidiary questions: (*a*) Is there one specific verb that has been deleted, or can any of several verbs be deleted, that is, can sentences with *want* be ambiguous as to what verb has been deleted? (*b*) Is a word of English deleted, or is some semantic material deleted? This latter question has to be asked if one accepts the framework that I currently do, in which a grammar is a single system of rules that relate semantic structures to surface structures via intermediate stages. The grammar includes not only deletion rules, movement rules, and copying rules, but also rules that combine semantic units into complex units, and lexical insertion rules, which associate morphemes of the specific language to complexes of semantic material. Since there is no reason to expect that the lexical insertion rules will apply before all deletion rules (nor that they will apply after all deletion rules), it cannot be assumed from the outset either that a word of English is deleted or that semantic material is deleted.

The following sentences appear to be ambiguous as to what has been deleted:

13a. I want more money than Sam has.
   b. Bill wants six children.
   c. Sam wants a million dollars.

These sentences allow semantically distinct paraphrases involving *have* and *get*. This is perhaps clearest in the case of 13c. Assume that Sam currently has $900,000. The sense paraphraseable as *Sam wants to have a million dollars* implies that Sam's desire will be satisfied if he increases his present wealth by $100,000; the sense paraphraseable as *Sam wants to get a million dollars* implies that Sam's desire will not be satisfied unless he gets a million dollars over and above the $900,000 that he already has. This is a real ambiguity, since the distinction between the two senses is respected by rules of grammar; for example,

14. Sam wants a million dollars, and so does Bert.

This sentence is appropriate in the case where each of them wants to have a million dollars or in the case where each of them wants to get a million dollars over and above what he presently has, but not in the case where one of them wants to have a million dollars and the other wants to get a million dollars.

The second question raises a more general question: how could you tell whether lexical material or semantic material has been deleted? I have been able to think of only one way of determining which kind of material is deleted: to look at cases where words and meanings do not match neatly (e.g., idiomatic uses of a word, or cases where a word that normally may express the meaning in question is not allowed) and see whether it is the word or the meaning that determines whether deletion may take place. For example, one could argue that the word *have* is deleted by showing that for every sentence of the form *Max wants to have X*, no matter how idiomatic the combination *have X* is, there is a sentence *Max wants X* which expresses the same meaning. Or one could argue that semantic material meaning 'possess' is deleted by showing that a sentence *Max wants to VX* has an equivalent *Max wants X* if and only if 'V' expresses the notion 'possess' but that no one verb with that meaning was appropriate in all examples. On the basis of a not very thorough tabulation of sentence with *want*, I have concluded that in one class of sentences the English verb *have* is deleted and in another class semantic material meaning 'obtain' is deleted. The following sentences illustrate idiomatic uses of *have* from which *have* has been deleted.

15. I don't want a heart attack.
    I just want a good time.
    I want a word with you.
    I want sweetbreads for dinner tonight.

*Have* in *have a heart attack, have a good time, have a word with X*, and *have X for dinner* does not express the notion of possession but rather a variety of meanings that do not appear to be subsumable under one semantic generalization. Not quite all sentences of the form *Max wants to have X* allow deletion of *have*; for example, corresponding to the idioms *have a ball* and *have it out with*, there are no such sentences as

16. *I want a ball.
    *I want it out with Fred.

However, such cases appear to be rare enough that one can maintain that, subject to a few exceptions, all sentences of the form *X wants to have Y* allow deletion of the word *have*, not of some corresponding semantic material.

The following sentences indicate that it is not always *have* that is deleted:

17. I want $10 from you by Friday.
    Fabian wanted advice from me.
    The boss wanted some originality from his employees.
    I want $50,000 a year.

To many speakers, all of these sentences sound somewhat awkward if *have* is supplied, though there is no awkwardness with *get* or such synonyms of it as *receive* or *obtain*:

18. I want to get/?have $10 from you by Friday.
    Fabian wanted to get/?have advice from me.
    The boss wanted to get/?have some originality from his employees.
    I want to get/?have $50,000 a year.

While each of the *have* sentences is felt to be perfectly acceptable by quite a lot of speakers, the existence of significant numbers of speakers who find them distinctly odd is enough to show that the acceptability of sentences with *have* does not fully parallel the acceptability of sentences with a deleted verb. Moreover, what is deleted in sentences like 17 can only be characterized semantically, not lexically, since idiomatic and 'nonbasic' senses of *get* and *receive* cannot be deleted:

19. I want to get up at 10:00.
    I want to get elected treasurer.
    I want to receive Warsaw on my radio.

20. *I want up at 10:00.
    *I want elected treasurer.
    *I want Warsaw on my radio.

It is hardly a pleasing result that in one class of cases a word is deleted and in others semantic material is deleted; however, no other result seems to fit the facts.[7]

So far I have talked only about the verb *want*. There are many other verbs which sometimes take an infinite object and sometimes a 'simple' object, and it is generally possible to give the same kinds of arguments as in the case of *want* that the 'simple' object results from deleting material from an underlying sentential object. Such verbs include *promise, offer, ask for*, and *hope for*. For example, *Fred asked Sam for a cigar or a cigarette* has the same ambiguity as does *Max wants a Cadillac or a Volkswagen*, and an embedded clause is necessary to represent the sense which implies that Fred asked that Sam either give him a cigar or give him a cigarette. However, the details of the deletion vary from verb to verb. With *promise*, Equi-NP-deletion is contingent on identity with the subject, that is, *Max promised Shirley to wash the dishes* refers to Max's washing the dishes, not to Shirley's washing them.

21. Max promised Shirley a Cadillac.

However, if 21 involved Equi-NP-deletion plus deletion of *have*, it ought to mean that Max promised Shirley that he would have a Cadillac, whereas it actually means that he promised her that she would have one. Thus, either 21 involves Equi-NP-deletion that is controlled by a NP other than that which normally controls it, or it involves deletion not of *have*, but of, say, *give* plus its indirect object (i.e., it would be derived from *Max promised Shirley to give her a Cadillac*).

I will conclude this paper by pointing out that the kinds of arguments that I gave above for the existence of an underlying subordinate clause are applicable not only to the relatively innocuous cases where a subordinate clause loses its identity through an optional deletion of its verb, but also to cases that must be analyzed not in terms of deletion but in terms of the incorporation of material into the meaning of a semantically complex verb. Consider, for example, the following example, from Masaru Kajita:

22. Yesterday Bill lent me his bicycle until tomorrow.

The same kinds of arguments as before show that *until tomorrow* modifies a subordinate clause. However, 22 cannot arise through deletion of a verb since *lend* does not allow a sentential complement:

23. *Yesterday Bill lent me to have his bicycle until tomorrow.

The only plausible way to set up a subordinate clause for *until tomorrow* to modify is to decompose *lend* into 'allow to have' (plus additional material indicating, e.g., that the transfer of possession is temporary) and to take *until tomorrow* as modifying the clause 'I have Bill's bicycle', which would be a constituent of the semantic structure of *Bill lent me his bicycle*. A further example of an adverb which modifies a semantic constituent of a word is found in *Max closed the door temporarily*: *temporarily* gives not the time that Max's action of closing the door took place but the time that the door was to remain closed. Only if *Max closed the door* is analyzed along the lines of *Max caused (the door be closed)*[8] is there a constituent that *temporarily* can plausibly be taken as modifying. This involves taking the adjective *closed* as semantically and syntactically more basic than the transitive verb *close*. While that may be disquieting in view of the fact that *closed* obviously divides morphologically into the verb *close* and an ending, it is a fact of life that morphological complexity does not always match syntactic and semantic complexity. Jespersen, for example, has observed that *true* is to *truth* as *beautiful* is to *beauty*, that is, if *truth* is not only morphologically but also syntactically a derivative of *true*, then *beauty* is syntactically a derivative of *beautiful*, even though morphologically it is a constituent of *beautiful*. One final example of an adverb modifying part of the meaning of a word comes from Robert Binnick 1968:

24. The sheriff of Nottingham jailed Robin Hood for four years.

This example is ambiguous as to what *for four years* modifies. In the less likely interpretation, *for four years* modifies the main clause *The Sheriff of Nottingham jailed Robin Hood*, and that clause must be given an iterative interpretation: that for four years the sheriff kept repeatedly jailing Robin Hood, only to have him break out of jail. In the more likely interpretation, *for four years* gives the time that Robin Hood is to be in jail, and the verb *jail* must be decomposed into something like *cause to be in jail*, so as to provide a clause for the adverb to modify (namely *Robin Hood be in jail*).[9] Exactly the same is true if the verb *jail* is replaced by *incarcerate*: *The sheriff of Nottingham incarcerated Robin Hood for four years* has the same set of interpretations as does 24 and thus requires an underlying structure containing a clause that means 'Robin Hood is in jail'. The fact that the verb *jail* has a corresponding noun *jail* but the verb *incarcerate* has no corresponding noun *carcer* thus has no bearing on how these sentences are to be analyzed.

I will conclude by making explicit the message of this commercial: the same kinds of considerations which support the innocuous and relatively uncontroversial deletion of *have* in *Max wants a lollipop*, an analysis which is perfectly consistent with the theory of Chomsky 1965, in which syntax and semantics are strictly segregated, also supports analyses like those of *lend* and *incarcerate*, in which the semantic constituents of words play a significant role in syntax. It thus appears that unless one is to restrict the domain of syntax so that it does not include such things as modification relations, which have traditionally been taken without questions as within the domain of syntax, one must give up any boundary between syntax and semantics.

# The Category Status
## of English Modals

Jackendoff (1972:100) states that modals and 'true verbs' in English display 'totally different syntactic behavior'. I will argue here that none of the five differences that he cites provide much support for his policy of assigning modals to a separate syntactic category and that the analysis which he adopts does not have some virtues that he ascribes to it.[1]

"Modals do not undergo number agreement, though all verbs do" (1). This is not quite true, as witness the combinations *thou canst, thou may'st.* English modals (like those of Old English and modern German) have the morphological irregularity of having a zero ending in the third person singular. They give the illusion of not undergoing person and number agreement only because the one subject with which they exhibit a non-zero agreement marker is archaic. While few children these days grow up hearing *thou canst,* and the like, once people are exposed to *thou* and its agreement marker they appear to have no hesitation in putting it on a modal (and, by the same token, no tendency to put it on *not* or on adjectives). If the occurrence of non-zero agreement markers is a criterion for verbhood, then learning to say *thou canst* should involve changing the category of *can* in one's internalized grammar from 'Modal' to 'Verb'. I question, however, that anything more is involved than learning that *thou* takes *-st* as its agreement marker.

"Modals do not occur together, and they do not appear in gerunds and infinitives" (2, 3). The second of these facts provides the explanation of the first: the verb following a modal is in the infinite form and, since modals do not have an infinitive form, cannot itself be a modal. More generally, English modals have highly defective paradigms, exhibiting at most present and past forms.[2] Even those (such as Jackendoff) who hesitate to call the verb after a modal an infinitive could hardly call it a present or past tense

Reprinted by permission from *Foundations of Language* 12 (1975): 597–601.

form. Thus in any event facts 2 and 3 are special cases of a generalization which is a matter of morphology rather than syntax. Given a universal output constraint against surface structures that contain nonexistent forms, there is no need to accommodate the defectiveness of the paradigms of modals by any special treatment in the base rules.

"Modals also differ from all main verbs but *be* and some uses of *have* in that they undergo subject-aux inversion, precede *not* and block *do*-support" (4). Though this is a difference between modals and most 'true verbs', Jackendoff's remark indicates that two 'true verbs' behave in the way that modals do. Moreover, there is dialect variation as regards which uses of *have* behave in which way. There is thus at least some irregularity involved, and the facts are amenable to a description in terms of a minor rule which sets up a structural difference that conditions the way in which Subject-aux inversion, Negative placement, and *Do*-support apply in the two types of cases. The obvious minor rule to propose is one which adjoins *be*, a modal, or certain uses of *have* to an immediately preceding tense, and the appropriate formulations of Subject-aux inversion and Negative-placement call respectively for moving a V over an immediately preceding NP (as in the figure below)[3] and for right-adjoining a *not* to an immediately following V. Setting up a category distinction between modal and verb contributes nothing to the analysis of these phenomena.

"If the surface main clause in sentences with modals is to be a deep structure complement clause, modals must govern a rule deleting the complementizer, since none shows up at the surface" (5). Jackendoff himself observes that there are 'true verbs' exhibiting precisely this characteristic:

> Harry made John wash the dishes every night.
> Betty heard Sue walk into the bathroom.

However, he points out that these verbs allow prepositional phrases in place of the complement, whereas modals do not:

> Harry made John into a nervous wreck.
> Betty heard Sue in the bathroom.
> *John may into a nervous wreck.

And he notes that those 'true verbs' which do not allow a prepositional phrase or noun phrase in place of the complement do not allow deletion of the complementizer:

> Fred seems to/*ϕ enjoy swimming.

But this means that whether the absence of complementizers after modals is a difference between them and 'true verbs' depend on whether the absence of nonmodal verbs which require a surface complement and allow deletion of the complementizer is not just an accident, comparable to the fact that all Japanese verb roots ending in /t/ (all eight of them) are

Raising

Auxiliary Adjunction

Inversion

Affix-hopping

Derivation of *Is Bill sleeping?*

accented. Would the adition to the language of verbs of that type imply any change in English grammar? I rather doubt it: however, Jackendoff's argument seems to imply that the introduction into English of a verb used as follows would be reason to reanalyze *can*, and the like, as 'V' rather than 'Modal':

> Denny glorched Luke (*to) go upstairs.
> *Denny glorched Luke into the living room.

This completes the list of things that Jackendoff offers as arguments against analyzing modals as verbs.[4] He then proceeds to adopt a variant of the *Syntactic structures* analysis, observing that it "captures the syntactic disparity quite accurately, with no use of the notion 'exception' at all. The only cost of this analysis is the addition of the node Modal in the base rules."

While Jackendoff's analysis 'captures' the syntactic disparities that he has mentioned, it fails to capture many other similar disparities, for example, that between *can* and *must* (*can* has a past tense, *must* does not) or that between *make* and *cause* (*make* is subject to complementizer deletion, *cause* is not). Jackendoff has provided no criterion for determining which captive facts fit into which cellblocks of a grammatical prison. Is there any reason why the disparities between *can* and *must* should not be captured in terms of base rules that assign them to different categories? It is not at all clear that Jackendoff's largely unstated policy on identity of category would yield just the two categories 'V' and 'Modal' rather than a large number of quite small categories.

Notwithstanding Jackendoff's disdain for the notion of 'exception', both the *Syntactic structures* analysis and Jackendoff's variant of it actually make crucial use of that notion. In the former the rules of Subject-aux inversion, and the like, involve the list {Modal, *be, have*}[5] and in the latter the rule adjoining *be* and certain uses of *have* to a preceding tense simply lists the items that are to be moved. The fact that there is no use of 'exception features' such as [+subject-aux inversion] is of no particular significance, since these lists accomplish exactly the same thing that such a feature would: they indicate an 'arbitrary bifurcation' between those items which undergo the rule and those which do not.

Jackendoff's reference to 'cost' is misleading, since it assumes a notion of 'cost' in which certain linguistically significant pieces of information are assigned no cost. Specifically, no 'cost' is assigned to the information as to *where* the modal is among the constituents of the S, and thus a phrase structure rule putting modals at the end of the S would cost no more than one putting them after the subject. The analysis of modals as verbs entails that modals will occur in a position where verbs can occur (thus, in English, after the subject and before any objects), whereas the *Syntactic structures* analysis puts modals in their position only by fiat. The defective morphology of modals provides the explanation of why they not only occur in a position where verbs can occur but are restricted to being the *first* verb of a tensed clause.[6]

Remarks on What Can Cause What

This is an informal, incomplete, and inconclusive exploration of the notions of causation that are involved in the meanings of English sentences, with some attention to the question of what kinds of things the various notions of causation are relations between.

I will begin by pointing out that the notion "causative verb" covers an area that is not obviously homogeneous. For example, different causative verbs differ with regard to aspect:

1a. *John shot Mary at 2:37* P.M. ("achievement," in the classificatory scheme of Vendler, 1957)
   b. *John boiled the eggs for 5 minutes.* ("activity")
   c. *John dressed the child in 5 minutes.* ("accomplishment")

These aspectual differences presumably are predictable from the semantic structures of these sentences and, indeed, from the verbs' contribution to the semantic structure. Let us see how this works. Sentence 1b is in some sense a causative of *The eggs are boiling* and 1c a causative of *The child is dressed*. I say *The eggs are boiling* rather than *The eggs are boiled*, since 1b is noncommittal as to whether the activity ends with the eggs in a cooked state. I say *The child is dressed* rather than *The child dresses*, since in 1c it is only John who serves as agent; 1c is exactly parallel to *Susie dressed her doll in five minutes*, in which there is no chance of the direct object's serving as an agent. Both 1b and 1c refer to a 5-minute stretch, but the relationship of the "caused" proposition to that 5-minute stretch is different in the two cases: 1b says that at every instant of the 5-minute stretch the eggs are boiling, whereas 1c says that the child is dressed when the 5-minute stretch ends but implies that he is not (fully) dressed before the 5-minute stretch

Reprinted by permission from *The Grammar of Causative Constructions*, Syntax and Semantics 6 (New York: Academic Press, 1976) pp. 117–29. Copyright © 1976 by Academic Press, Inc.

ends. Thus, in 1c the "caused" proposition is a condition with which the activity culminates, whereas in 1b the "caused" proposition is a condition that the activity maintains at each instant. In 1a, there is not an activity but simply an action. The discharging of a bullet that pierces Mary's body is an event, not a proposition, and 1a refers to John's performing an action that leads directly (i.e., without intervening actions) to the event of the gun's discharging. There are, of course, two propositions involved in the description of that event, namely, that the gun discharged a bullet and that the bullet pierced Mary's body. However, the relationship of shooting Mary to the event(s) of the gun's discharging a bullet and the bullet's piercing Mary's body is different from the relationship of putting clothes on the child to its culmination in the child's being fully dressed. While an adverb like *in 5 minutes* is appropriate in the case of *dress*, it is not appropriate in the case of *shoot* unless the adverb is taken to give the time that elapsed before John performed the action rather than the time that elapsed in his performing it:

2. *?John shot Mary in half a second.*

In addition to an activity sense, *boil* also allows an accomplishment sense, as in:

3. *John boiled the eggs in 3 minutes.*

Here, the implied culmination is *The eggs are cooked*. However, it is a culmination tacked onto the same activity that *boil* describes in 1b: At each instant of the 3-minute stretch the eggs are boiling, and at the end they are cooked. Many verbs have paired activity/accomplishment uses, for example:

4a. *Harold combed his hair for 5 minutes.* (activity)
 b. *Harold combed his hair in 5 minutes.* (accomplishment)

In such cases, the implied culmination is the normal goal associated with the activity, for example, the person's hair's being presentable, in the case of 4b. Whether such a use is possible may vary with the object NP, since that NP may have a bearing on whether there is a normal goal for the activity:

5a. *??Oscar squeezed the tennis ball in 20 seconds.*
 b. *Oscar squeezed the orange in 20 seconds.* (implies: extracted all the juice in 20 seconds)

Sentence 3 appears to involve both the causal relation involved in 1b and that involved in 1c. The activity (which, of course, need not be much of an activity—it can consist in just standing by the stove and watching that the gas does not go out and that the water does not boil away) is at each point causing the eggs to be boiling, and the total activity causes the eggs to be cooked. Simply to give these notions names, I will call them "continuous causation" and "culmination," respectively. Other examples involving continuous causation are:

6a. *Bert drove the car for two hours.*
  b. *I was only able to support Paul's weight for a few seconds.*

Each of these sentences refers to an activity that at each instant is causing a certain condition to be the case (it is actually more natural to say "to remain the case"): in 6a that the car is "locomoting," in 6b that Paul does not fall.

The kind of causation involved in 1a appears to coincide with what Shibatani (1973) has referred to as "ballistic causation," and I will retain his term unless he objects. These three kinds of causation combine with the following kinds of things:

7. Ballistic causation:    action/event        event
   Continuous causation:  each instant of a process  state
   Culmination:        an entire process     state

I say that in culmination the process causes a state rather than an event, since there need not be an event describable as the child's becoming dressed.

Ballistic causation can often be expressed using the verb *make*:

8. *The blow that Mary received made her lose consciousness.*
  *The explosion made the building shake.*

Note that, in these examples, what appears as the subject of *make* is a description of an event and is related only indirectly to a sentence. This is in line with my claim that the "subject" of ballistic causation is an action or event rather than a state. Shibatani lists a number of other kinds of causatives in which more than one agent is involved and classifies them using intersecting features:

9a. Directive coercive: *John made Mary kiss him.*
  b. Directive noncoercive: *John had Mary wash his socks.*
  c. Nondirective manipulative: *John chased Mary into the garden.*[1]

These examples all involve reference to an action or an activity on John's part. Sentence 9b is actually noncommital as to whether coercion was involved.[2] Besides the dimensions of coercion, 9b differs from 9a aspectually —9b refers to the result of John's action rather than to the action itself:

10a. *When I entered the room, John was making/?\*having Mary kiss him.*
  b. *It took John 5 minutes to make/?\*have Mary kiss him.*
  c. *John made Mary kiss him by threatening her with a knife.*
  c'. *\*John had Mary wash his socks by telling her that he needed clean socks.*

Sentence 9c involves both continuous causation and culmination: it means that John, by running toward Mary, caused her to run away from him, until she was in the garden. It is like *John boiled the eggs in 3 minutes*, except that the continuously caused "state" is the state of an activity going on, that is, that Mary is running away from John. Note that while progressives are formed from activities, they themselves are states. Since I have little beyond isolated observations about these kinds of causative, I will drop them at this point and turn to other types of causative sentences that have not figured in recent linguistic controversies, and ask what can be said about them.

To begin with, let us consider a use of the word *cause* that can be found on any page of a daily newspaper, for example:

11. *Smoking causes cancer.*

This sentence evidently involves a lot of ellipsis, and an analysis of it will have to begin with undoing the ellipsis. First of all, cancer does not exist all by itself but only as suffered by an organism, which suggests that the meaning of 11 is the same as that of *Smoking causes people to develop cancer*. In this case, the understood subject of *smoking* is evidently the same as that of *develop*, though that sort of identity will not prevail in all cases; for example, *Pollution causes cancer* does not imply that polluters are more susceptible to cancer than others. Sentence 11 is a generic sentence, and I do not propose in this paper to unravel the well-known mysteries of generic sentences (see Lawler, 1972, 1973*a*, *b*). As a makeshift, let me simply paraphrase the generic with *There frequently are cases in which . . .*, thus yielding a paraphrase:

12. *There frequently are cases in which a person's smoking causes him to develop cancer.*

The notion of causation found here, I maintain, is quite different from those discussed earlier. It cannot be ballistic causation, since it makes little sense to speak of an event of a person's developing cancer and still less sense to speak of an event in which smoking causes him to develop cancer. You do not take your 8397th drag and have a tumor suddenly appear. It is not continuous causation either (since cancers presumably do not start developing the moment one starts smoking, nor stop developing the moment one stops smoking), and it is not "culmination" (since the development of a cancer does not terminate the smoking).

Discussions of causation by philosophers often involve attempts to analyze it in terms of counterfactuals; for example, a highly sophisticated proposal of this type is given by Lewis (1973*b*). Such an analysis seems quite reasonable in this case:

13. *There frequently are cases in which a person develops cancer and if he hadn't smoked, he wouldn't have developed cancer.*

This kind of paraphrase is often rejected because of difficulties that it encounters with what might be called "causal overkill." Strictly speaking, *If Schwartz hadn't smoked, he wouldn't have developed cancer* implies not merely that if he had not smoked, he would not have developed the lung cancer that he did develop; it also implies that he would not have developed brain cancer or laryngeal cancer or prostate cancer. But that is not part of the meaning of 11: Someone who says that smoking causes cancer does not necessarily hold that those people whose cancers are due to smoking would have been immune to all forms of cancer if they had not smoked. In this case, there is a simple solution to the problem: Instead of analyzing 11 as *There frequently are cases in which . . .* , analyze it as *There frequently occur cancers such that if the patient had not smoked, he would not have developed that particular cancer.* This involves ontological permissiveness, which Quine, for example, would never tolerate: quantifying over cancers (cancer tokens, this is, not cancer types). It also leads to a peculiar but perhaps correct notion of identity. Suppose that there is a drug, call it glorpaline, that is known to prolong for about a week the lives of patients in the terminal stages of brain cancer. Suppose that a doctor treating such a patient decides not to give him glorpaline. The patient dies, but if he had been given glorpaline, he presumably would not have died until about a week later. What is the cause of death? Is it brain cancer or is it lack of glorpaline? It will not do just to say "Brain cancer, because if he hadn't had brain cancer, he wouldn't have died, but even if he had been given glorpaline, he would have died anyway." That will not work, since all men are mortal, and even those who never have brain cancer will die sooner or later. Saying that the cause of death is brain cancer amounts to identifying the patient's real death with some hypothetical deaths but not with others: If he were given glorpaline, he would die the same death, though a week later; but if he had not developed brain cancer, he would die a different death. A similar solution is possible for the familiar puzzle (Hospers 1967:307) of the man who is pushed off the top of the Empire State Building and, as he falls, is shot through the heart by a person on the 89th floor and dies of the wound before he hits the ground. While one cannot say that Flanagan would not have died if Schultz had not shot him (since Flanagan would have died anyways as soon as he hit the pavement), one can still say that Flanagan would not have died that particular death if Schultz had not shot him. For the moment, I am content to say that the counterfactual paraphrase can be reconciled with "causal overkill" by appropriate choice of the entities involved, and ontological scruples be damned.[3]

Lewis (1973a) has proposed an ingenious analysis of counterfactuals in terms of possible worlds. Lewis argues that many important logical properties of counterfactuals, for example, their failure to obey laws of contraposition or of transitivity, are accounted for if a notion of "closeness between" possible worlds is set up and "if $p$ were the case, then $q$ would be the case" is taken to mean that in the words in which $p$ is the case that are closest to the real world, $q$ is also the case; that is, there is a world $w$ such that $p$ is true in $w$, and $q$ is true in all worlds at least as close to the real world as $w$ in which $p$ is true. This analysis captures neatly the notion of "other things being equal," which is an essential part of counterfactuals: When you say that you would have enjoyed yourself more if Shirley had come to the party, you are only referring to worlds that differ from the real world by as little as is necessary to accommodate the counterfactual proposition that Shirley came to the party—you are not saying anything about remote worlds in which, for example, Shirley comes to the party but you are being held captive on Baffin Island and forced to watch reruns of Pepsodent commercials all your waking hours.

Lewis uses $p \;\Box\!\!\rightarrow q$ to symbolize the relationship that in the closest worlds in which $p$ is true, $q$ is also true. I propose giving this relationship the name "local entailment."

When applied to the analysis of 11, Lewis's proposal yields *There frequently occur cancers such that in the closest worlds in which the patient did not smoke, he did not develop that cancer*. This seems reasonable at first glance. However, in recent unpublished work, Dowty has proposed an alternative that, though it may seem far less reasonable at first glance, turns out to be far more reasonable at second or third glance.[4] Specifically, he has proposed analyzing $S_1$ *caused* $S_2$ not as 14a but as 14b:

14a. $S_2$ *and* $(\sim S_1 \;\Box\!\!\rightarrow\; \sim S_2)$
   b. $S_2$ *and* $(\sim S_2 \;\Box\!\!\rightarrow\; \sim S_1)$

In view of the supposed paraphrase relation between counterfactual conditionals and local entailment, 14b at first sounds ludicrous: Dowty seems to be saying that 11 means not that if certain cancer patients had not smoked, they would not have developed cancer but, rather, that if they had not developed cancer, they would not have smoked, which suggests the wrong time sequence between the smoking and the cancer. However, this absurdity is only apparent, since local entailment is in fact of broader applicability than is the counterfactual conditional, and it is only the counterfactual analog of 14b, not 14b itself, that is absurd. Example 14a says that in the closest worlds in which the patient did not smoke he did not develop cancer; 14b says that in the closest worlds in which he did not develop cancer, he did not smoke. Dowty maintains that the latter fits the meaning of *cause* better than does the former: When you speak of someone's smoking causing him to develop cancer, you are contrasting the real world not with its closest counterparts in which that person does not smoke but with its closest counterparts in which he does not develop cancer. What is relevant is not how easily he could have given up smoking but how easily he could have avoided cancer.

The discussion of 15 in Hart and Honoré 1959[5] shows that 14b is also better than 14a as an analysis of *because*:

15. *The roses died because the gardener didn't water them.*

If *because* is to be identified with some sense of *cause*, $S_1$ *caused* $S_2$ will have to correspond to $S_2$ *because* $S_1$. Thus, the analog of 14a for 15 is *The roses died, and if the gardener had watered them, they wouldn't have died.* This would, of course, be true in the circumstances in which one would say 15. However, the following would also be true: *If Yogi Berra had watered the roses, they wouldn't have died; if Chou-En-Lai had watered the roses, they wouldn't have died; if Linda Lovelace had watered the roses they wouldn't have died.* Nonetheless, if the gardener was entrusted with the care of the roses, it would be correct to say that they died because the gardener did not water them but not to say that they died because Yogi Berra or Chou En-Lai or Linda Lovelace did not water them. Hart and Honoré say that this is because the gardener's not watering the roses is a deviation from normalcy, whereas Yogi Berra's not watering your roses is not a deviation from normalcy. This observation fits perfectly with 14b. If Hart and Honoré's notion of deviation from normalcy is identified with Lewis's notion of distance from the real world, 14b becomes *In the most normal worlds in which the roses did not die, the gardener watered them.* A world in which your gardener waters your roses is very normal, that is very close to the real world, whereas a world in which Linda Lovelace waters them is quite remote from the real world.[6]

One qualification will have to be added. Consider the following sentence:

16. *It isn't the nicotine that causes cancer—it's the tars.*

By Dowty's proposal, the second part of 16 should assert that in the closest worlds in which someone did not develop cancer he did not consume tars, and the first part should deny that in the closest worlds in which he did not develop cancer he did not consume nicotine. But this would appear to conflict with the proposition that the closest worlds in which he does not develop cancer are those in which he does not smoke and, thus, consumes neither nicotine nor tars. Is there an easier way to avoid consumption of

tars then just to stop smoking? Dowty's analysis for 16 makes sense only
relative to a restricted class of possible worlds: those in which the person
smokes and, thus, the question of nicotine versus tars arises.

The class of worlds that one can consider relevant for making a causal
claim can in fact vary wildly from one occasion to another, and accordingly,
one can perfectly well assign several distinct causes to something without
contradicting himself. This point was made with particular clarity by
Collingwood (1938):

> A car skids while cornering at a certain point, turns turtle, and bursts
> into flame. From the car-driver's point of view, the cause of the accident
> was cornering too fast, and the lesson is that one must drive more care-
> fully. From the county surveyor's point of view, the cause was a defective
> road surface, and the lesson is that one must make skid-proof roads. From
> the motor-manufacturer's point of view, the cause was defective design,
> and the lesson is that one must place the center of gravity lower. [Pp.
> 92–93]

The different propositions $S_1$ *causes* $S_2$ that are involved in this passage do
not reflect different judgments as to the facts of the accident, nor different
beliefs with regard to how cars, drivers, and roads function. Rather, they
differ only with regard to the differences that one is for the moment
admitting between the real world and possible alternatives to it. It is
immaterial that three different persons are referred to in this passage. The
driver, without in any way contradicting himself, could assert on one
occasion that the crash occurred because he was driving too fast, on
another occasion that it occurred because the road was poorly designed,
and on a third occasion that it occurred because the car had too high a
center of gravity.

My reason for belaboring this point is that this kind of relativity to point
of view or to rhetorical context is not a characteristic of the notions of
causation discussed earlier in this chapter. Irrespective of what alternatives
to the real world one considers relevant or irrelevant to the discussion at
hand, in describing a situation in which a gun has gone off, one contradicts
himself if he says on one occasion that John fired the gun, on another
occasion that Mary fired the gun, and on another occasion that Yogi Berra
fired the gun. If John performed the act of squeezing the trigger with
sufficient force so that the gun went off, he fired the gun, regardless of
whether Mary had told him to squeeze the trigger or whether he was
distressed over Yogi Berra's choice of pinch hitters. If John merely let his
finger rest around the trigger and Mary pushed his finger against the trigger,
it is Mary rather than John who fires the gun. The notion of causation
involved in an analysis of *fire* into *do something that causes* (*a firearm*) *to*

*discharge* has to do with an act, and in deciding on the truth of the sentence *John fired the gun* the only matters relevant are those of what acts John performed and the relationsip of those acts to the event of the gun's going off.

Having come to the conclusion that several distinct notions of causation can play a role in the meanings of sentences, I should raise the question of whether it is merely accidental that the word *cause* is used with reference to all of them. I will conclude this study by proposing that these different senses of *cause* share an important characteristic that may provide the basis of the existence of a single word to cover all of them. Each proposition A *cause* B, whatever the sense of *cause* and whatever the nature of the A and B, can be associated in a natural way with a proposition $S_1$ *cause* $S_2$, which it implies and which involves the sense of *cause* that is analyzable in terms of local entailment. For example, suppose that *John killed Bill* is analyzed as *John did something which caused it to become the case that Bill is not alive*. The causal proposition involved in the analysis, *x caused* (*Become* (*Not* (*Alive* (*Bill*)))), where *x* denotes John's action, implies *Because John did x, Bill ceased to be alive*, which is, in turn, analyzable as *Bill died, and in the closest worlds in which Bill did not die, John did not do x*. Causal propositions are not all of the same type, but there is a single type of causal proposition that is implied by all other types.

## Appendix

If A causes both B and C, with B preceding C, will the "epiphenomenon" B spuriously count as a cause of C according to Dowty's proposal? In the closest worlds in which C does not occur, A does not occur, so presumably B also would not occur (a world in which some alternative cause brought B about would generally be further from the real world than the closest worlds in which C does not occur), so does not *B causes C* spuriously come out true?

There are two separate questions to be asked here: Does *B causes C* come out true, and if it does, is that a defect of the analysis? To arrive at tentative answers to these questions, I will take up two situations that illustrate different roles that epiphenomena may play.

*Scenario 1*: John and Mary are standing on opposite side of a glass door. Mary picks up a gun, points it at John, and fires (A). The bullet goes through the glass (B) and then through John's heart, whereupon he dies instantly (C).

*Scenario 2*: Cpl. Nguyen fires an antiaircraft cannon (A). The sound wakes up Pvt. Lien, who had been sleeping nearby (B). The missile discharged by the cannon strikes Lt. Saunders' plane (C).

In scenario 1, evidently $\sim$C $\square\!\!\rightarrow$ $\sim$B is true: By assumption, in the closest worlds in which John did not die the particular death in question, Mary did not fire the gun, and in those worlds the bullet did not go through the glass, since it would take a greater departure from reality for the bullet to go through the glass without Mary's firing the gun. However, in this case it is not particularly counterintuitive to say that John's dea h occurred because the glass broke (or, rather, because that particular vent of the glass breaking took place). As in Collingwood's case of the a to accident, one has the freedom to treat different factors as constants and assign different causes accordingly; from the point of view of a manufacturer of bulletproof glass, it would, indeed, be quite natural to say that John died because the glass broke.

In scenario 2, no point of view, not even that of a manufacturer of sleeping pills, could make plausible the statement that Lt. Saunders' plane was hit because Pvt. Lien woke up. The closest worlds in which Lt. Saunders' plane is not hit by the missile are presumably those in which Cpl. Nguyen's aim is a little off but in which the sound of the cannon going off is still enough to wake up Pvt. Lien. But suppose that we exercise our right to hold certain factors constant and consider only worlds in which the excellence of Cpl. Nguyen's aim is the same as in the real world. Can we then assert that $\sim$C $\square\!\!\rightarrow$ $\sim$B, that is, that (according to Dowty's proposal) Pvt. Lien's waking up caused Lt. Saunders' plane to be hit? To say that, one would have to say that in the closest of the remaining worlds in which Lt. Saunders' plane is not hit, Pvt. Lien does not wake up, that is, that there is a world $w$ in which Lt. Saunders' plane is not hit and Pvt. Lien does not wake up that is closer to the real world than all worlds in which Lt. Saunders' plane is not hit and Pvt. Lien does wake up. Given the way that the world works (e.g., loud noises wake people up), the only likely candidate for such a world is one in which the cannon does not go off when Cpl. Nguyen does whatever one does in firing an antiaircraft cannon. Is that world closer to the real world than all worlds in which the plane is not hit and Pvt. Lien does wake up? Presumably it would be if the cannon's failing to go off is more likely than any other factor that could prevent the plane from being hit (e.g., a bird flying into the path of the missile or Lt. Saunders doing an unexpected dive).

This looks like bad news for Dowty's proposal: Given reasonable assumptions about closeness between worlds plus the option of holding certain characteristics constant, which was needed anyway to get Dowty's proposal to accord with ordinary usage of *cause*, we ought to be able to say *Pvt. Lien's waking up caused Lt. Saunders' plane to be hit*; but that remains absurd even in the context of the given assumptions. What then? Should the original analysis of *Because p, q* as $\sim$p $\square\!\!\rightarrow$ $\sim$q be resurrected?

Or should the two proposals be combined (as in Abbott, 1974) in an analysis of *Because p, q* as $(\sim p \;\square\!\!\rightarrow\; \sim q) \wedge (\sim q \;\square\!\!\rightarrow\; \sim p)$? Sadly, these proposals appear to be no help in this case, since $\sim B \;\square\!\!\rightarrow\; \sim C$ would still be true, at least on the extra assumption that the cannon going off is the thing most likely to cause Pvt. Lien to wake up: In the closest worlds in which Pvt. Lien does not wake up, the cannon has not gone off and Lt. Saunders' plane has not been hit.

Alternatively, one could try retaining Dowty's analysis but reinterpreting the notion of "closeness" between possible worlds. I have made frequent references to probability and have spoken of a world $w'$ being further than a world $w$ from the real world because the "defining property" of $w'$ is less probable than the defining property of $w$[7] (e.g., $w'$ is a world just like the real world except that a bird flies into the path of the missile and the missile does not hit the plane; $w$ is a world just like the real world except that the cannon does not go off, the missile does not even leave the cannon, much less hit the plane, and Pvt. Lien does not wake up). This choice of language suggests that closeness between worlds is given in terms of a numerical measure of distance that is intimately related to probability; that, in turn, suggests that all distances are "commensurable": Given two worlds $w_1$ and $w_2$, both distinct from the real world, either $w_1$ will be further from the real world than is $w_2$ or it will be closer to the real world than is $w_2$ or it will be the same distance from the real world as is $w_2$. Suppose, however, that the notion of "closeness" is explicated in terms of graph theory rather than of metric geometry. Suppose that if one world differs from another just by an atomic "deviation" (plus the minimum additional differences necessary to ensure consistency), an "arc" connecting the two worlds is set up. A "path" from one world to another is a sequence of arcs that take one step by step from the one world to the other. Define $w_1$ *dominates* $w_2$ to mean *There is a minimal path from $w_1$ to the real world that passes through $w_2$.*[8] Finally, suppose that $p \;\square\!\!\rightarrow\; q$ is now taken to mean *For every world w such that p is true in w but not in any world dominated by w, q is true in w.* In that case, $\sim C \;\square\!\!\rightarrow\; \sim B$ is false: Let $w$ be a world differing from the real world only in that a bird had flown into the path of the missile, deflecting it so that it missed the plane. Then $\sim C$ is true in $w$, $w$ does not dominate any world in which $\sim C$ is true, but $\sim B$ is still false, which means that $\sim C \;\square\!\!\rightarrow\; \sim B$ is false.

This revision appears to make epiphenomena causes only when they ought to be; that is, in cases like scenario 1 the epiphenomenon is a cause, but in those like scenario 2 it is not. But does it accomplish this at the expense of losing the distinction between *The roses died because the gardener didn't water them* and *The roses died because Yogi Berra didn't water them*? While you would have to make quite a few changes in the real world to get to a world in which Yogi Berra waters your roses (e.g., he would have to learn the location of your roses) but very few to get to a world in which your gardener waters your roses, those two worlds are evidently still incommensurable, and so both causal propositions evidently would come out true. I have fairly strong visceral feelings that the revised notion of closeness can be further revised so as to avoid this disconcerting consequence, but I will postpone undertaking further revisions until I have done sufficient additional meditation.

# 13 Morphological Indeterminacy in Underlying Syntactic Structure

The existing transformational literature does not accord morphology anywhere near the status that many other linguistic theories give to it. Indeed, it is not much of an exaggeration to say that transformational studies make morphology a part of syntax when that is feasible and ignore it when it is not.[1] In particular, the choice among different personal pronouns has been reduced to the same mechanisms that choose among different nouns or different verbs: pronouns have been treated as either present as such in base structures, in which case they for all practical purposes are treated as nouns, or as derived from copies of their antecedents, in which case the choice of the particular pronoun has been taken to reflect features of the NP from which it is derived.

This policy is at the bottom of a type of argument that has appeared frequently in the recent literature, illustrated by one of Chomsky's arguments (1971:211) that coreference is determined late in derivations rather than being specified throughout derivations. Following Dougherty (1970a), Chomsky takes *each other* as arising through the steps indicated informally in:

1. Each of those students hates the others.
   → Those students each hate the others.
   → Those students hate each other.

However, when the first of these steps is applied in a case like 2a, a structure having different coreference possibilities results:

2a. Each of those men loves his brothers.
  b. Those men each love his brothers.

Reprinted by permission from *1975 Mid-America Linguistics Conference*, ed. Frances Ingeman (Lawrence: Linguistics Department, University of Kansas, 1976), pp. 317–26. Copyright © 1976 by the Linguistics Department, University of Kansas.

In 2a, *his* can refer back to the subject, but in 2b it can only refer to something in the previous discourse. Thus, Chomsky concludes, *each*-movement changes the possibilities for coreference and coreference must be predicted by an interpretive rule sentitive to a stage of derivations after that at which *each*-movement applies.

A question that naturally arises here is why Chomsky wishes to relate 2a to 2b and not to 3:

3. Those men each hate their brothers.

(See Partee 1971, where precisely that question is raised). Note, however, that the latter possibility is not at all easy to accommodate in Chomsky's framework. Either the form of the pronoun must be changed subsequent to *each*-movement (4a) or *each*-movement must apply to structures containing a nonpronominal NP that is subsequently pronominalized (4b):

4a. Each of the men loves his brothers.
    →      The men each love his brothers.
    →                 their
  b. Each of the men loves that man's brothers.
    →    *The men each love that man's brothers.
    →             *those men's
    →             their

(The *'s in 4b relate to an interpretation in which *that man* or *those men* refers back to the subject.) Either you would have to change a singular pronoun into a plural (but under what conditions?) or you would have to change a singular anaphoric NP into the corresponding plural (but under what conditions, and how could you insure that it will then obligatorily be pronominalized, whereas pronominalization was optional if you didn't do *each*-movement?). Moreover, 3 does not mean exactly the same as 2a, since 2a implies that the men have more than one brother each, whereas 3 is noncommittal as to how many brothers each man has. Thus, it is not clear that there is a viable alternative to having *each*-movement relate 2a to 2b rather than to 3.

Note, however, an important unstated premise of Chomsky's argument and the above addenda to it: the assumption that at every stage of the derivation all nouns and pronouns are determinate as to number, that is, either are explicitly singular or are explicitly plural, with no NP's unspecified as to number. The bulk of this paper will be concerned with alternatives which allow one to reject that premise and to relate 2a to 3 in terms of derivations having NP's that are unspecified for number (and for that matter, for person, gender, and definiteness) until fairly late in the derivation.

It should be remarked at the outset, though, that the standard transformational policy on pronoun choice is a direct consequence of the
standard conception of a transformational derivation, in which a transformation can be sensitive only to information present in its input structure
(not, e.g., to more remote syntactic structures, or to semantic structure, or
to factors outside of the derivation altogether). In English, the distinctions
among nominative, accusative, and genitive case in pronouns are in fact
predictable from information present in some stage of derivations (cf.
Klima 1964), namely, whether a NP is 'in subject position' and whether
it is 'in determiner position', and there has accordingly been no hesitation
among transformational grammarians to take NP's in deep structure as
unspecified for case and to take case specifications as inserted in the course
of the derivation. However, the number of a noun or pronoun and the
person and gender of a pronoun are not predictable from structural
configurations at some stage of derivations: what number a NP has
depends on whether it purports to refer to one or more than one individual
(subject to the qualification that some nouns are idiosyncratically plural
regardless of their purported reference), what person a pronoun is depends
on whether its purported reference includes the speaker and on whether it
includes the addressee, and what gender a pronoun has depends on whether
it purports to refer to a male person, a female person, or something else
(again with qualifications about nouns that have idiosyncratic gender).
Thus, for person and number to be 'predictable', NP's would have to
carry a specification of purported reference throughout the derivation, and
the specifications of reference would have to be rich enough to indicate not
only referential identity and nonidentity but also referential inclusion, to
distinguish the speaker and the addressee from each other and from other
purported referents (i.e., in effect, the performative analysis would have to
be adopted); for gender of pronouns to be predictable, whatever underlies
any third person singular pronoun would have to include information as
to the sex of the purported referent.

Adherents of 'standard transformational grammar' have generally
rejected all but the most rudimentary indications of reference within
syntactic structure and have accordingly taken all NP's as specified for
person and number in deep structure, and in Chomsky 1965 the base
component is taken as providing a gender specification for every noun in
deep structure. Thus, 'standard transformational grammar' yields two
possibilities for the derivation of pronouns: any personal pronoun either
is derived from a repetition of its antecedent (in which case its person,[2]
number, and gender are features of the item that underlies it, and it is
derived by a transformation that wipes out all of a NP except for those
features, under a condition of identity with another NP) or it is not derived

from a repetition of its antecedent, in which case it is an underlying complex of person, number, and gender features, which is to say that it is a pronoun from the outset of the derivation.

The way in which standard transformational grammar allows pronouns to be derived from copies of their antecedents has a serious flaw, however, namely that it requires the positing of spurious ambiguities. For example (as I pointed out in McCawley 1968*b*), some occurrences of *neighbor* would have to be specified as 'male' and others as 'female' if the grammar is to derive the sentences

5a. My neighbor hurt himself.
 b. My neighbor hurt herself.

However, available tests for ambiguity indicate that *neighbor* is unspecified with regard to sex, rather than ambiguous, even in examples like 5. Note that 6a is possible regardless of the sex of the two neighbors, and for many speakers 6b is acceptable regardless of the sex of the neighbor:[3]

6a. Lee is my neighbor, and so is Robin.
 b. My cousin hurt himself, and so did my neighbor.

In addition, conjunction reduction on the structure underlying 7a is applicable despite the difference in sex:

7a. My cousin hurt himself, and my neighbor hurt herself, too.
 b. My cousin and my neighbor hurt themselves.

Similar examples can be constructed showing that if all NP's are determinate as to number in deep structure, than spurious ambiguities must be posited. For example, 8a is unspecified rather than ambiguous with regard to whether each composer wrote more than one quartet, but if the conjunction reduction giving rise to 8a were not carried out, the resulting sentence would have to specify whether one or more than one quartet was involved in each case:

8a. The quartets of Eierkopf and Misthaufen are beautiful.
 b. The quartet(s) of Eierkopf is/are beautiful, and the quartet(s) of Misthaufen is/are beautiful.

My claim that 8a is derived by an application of conjunction reduction which ignores the difference between singular *quartet* and plural *quartets* is derived by conjunction reduction, since there is no other way that the passivization and *tough*-movement that they exhibit could take place, are also noncommittal as to whether either composer wrote more than one quartet:

9a. The quartets of Eierkopf and Misthaufen are in public domain and
have been copyrighted by Misthaufen's widow, respectively.
  b. The quartets of Eierkopf and Misthaufen are respectively exquisitely
beautiful and unbearably difficult to listen to.

Note also 10, in which VP-deletion has applied despite the fact that the
deleted VP, which would have surfaced as *love their wives*, involves
different number in both the determiner and the noun than in the corresponding words of the antecedent *loves his wife*:

10a. John loves his wife, and my two brothers love their wives too.
  b. John loves his wife, and my two brothers do too.[4]

The most commonly adopted way out of these difficulties has been
simply to deny that any anaphoric devices are derived by transformations
from copies of their antecedents; this is the approach adopted most
explicitly by Jakendoff (1972), and by Chomsky, Dougherty, and other
adherents of the 'extended standard theory'. For this to provide a real way
out, it would be necessary for one also to reject the transformation of
conjunction reduction since some of the spurious ambiguities that arise
when all NP's are determinate as to person, number, and gender in deep
structure result through the application of conjunction reduction. While an
analysis allegedly doing without conjunction reduction has been advanced
by Dougherty (1970a:856–66), that analysis really just recasts conjunction
reduction in a different form, rather than eliminating it; in particular,
Dougherty's analysis provides no way to derive 9b other than from a deep
structure in which there are a sentence referring to the quartet(s) of
Eierkopf and a sentence referring to the quartet(s) of Misthaufen, with a
separate underlying occurrence of *quartet* for each composer.[5]

I wish to propose here an alternative way out, one which may be
necessary even from the point of view of the 'extended standard theory',
namely, that the features relevant to choice among pronouns have nothing
to do with deep structure, that is, that nouns are unspecified with regard to
number, and pronouns with regard to person, number, and gender, until
a fairly late stage of derivations, and that only for the nouns and pronouns
which are present at that and later stages do the person, number, and
gender features play any role in the interpretation of the sentence or the
conditions for its appropriate use.[6]

Under this proposal, the following sentences would all have derivations
involving conjunction reduction:

11a. John and I love *our* mothers.
  b. You and John love *your* mothers.
  c. Bill and John love *their* mothers.

The choice of the pronoun would be based on its purported referent: if it includes the speaker, it is first person, if it includes the addressee but not the speaker, it is second person, and otherwise it is third person. With regard to this point, it is immaterial whether the pronoun is derived from a full NP; if it is, the pronominalization transformation would eliminate that NP except for its referential index, and the pronoun would be chosen on the basis of referential inclusion relations. In the case of pronouns with an antecedent, the pronoun is chosen to agree with the antecedent. Any grammatical idiosyncracies of the antecedent (such as grammatical gender, or the idiosyncratic plural of *shears* and *overalls*) are reflected in the choice of the pronoun. The different pronoun choice between 2a and 3 reflects a difference in antecedent: in 2a, the antecedent of the pronoun is *each of those men*, which is grammatically singular; *each*-movement destroys that NP, leaving only *those men* as a possible antecedent, and thus requiring the third person plural pronoun *their*.

An extension of this proposal provides a way of countering an objection that could be raised to the derivation 1.[7] If all nouns have a specific number in deep structure, then *other* would have to be singular in the deep structures of some instances of *each other* and plural in other instances:

12a. Each of the two boys helped the other/*others.
 b. Each of the three boys helped the others/*other.

Thus, *each other* in 13 would be ambiguous as to whether it had a singular source or a plural source (corresponding to whether *the boys* are two or more than two):

13. The boys helped each other.

However, this is a spurious ambiguity, since *each other* with a singular source and *each other* with a plural source count as identical:

14. Mary and Susan helped each other, and so did Tom, Dick, and Harry.

The proposal of morphologically indeterminate underlying structures allows all occurrences of *each other* to be derived from a source that is unspecified as to number and thus allows the two occurrences of *each other* in 14 to be derived from sources that differ only in referential indices. However, if the steps forming *each other* are not carried out, a number must be assigned to *other* on the basis of the size of the set that it refers to, which means that a singular is required in 12a but a plural in 12b (since for any member of a two-element set there is only one other member, whereas for any member of a three-element set there are two other members).

A further morphological indeterminacy suggest itself when one observes that 13 is noncommittal as to whether each boy helped all of the other boys; 13 in fact is appropriate even when each boy helped only one other boy. I propose that the structure underlying *each other* is indeterminate not only with respect to plurality but with respect to definiteness as well, that is, that the structure underlying 13 is not 'Each of the boys helped the others' or '. . . helped the other' or '. . . helped others' or '. . . helped another', but rather '. . . helped other', where *other* is unspecified both with regard to number and with regard to definiteness. More specifically, underlying 13 there would be a structure containing an existential quantifier in the pristine form in which it occurs in formal logic: 'there is a y $\neq$ x such that x helped y', totally noncommittal as to whether there is more than one such y, or as to whether there is anyone whom x did not help. The definite article is forced on the speaker in 12a, since with regard to either member of a two-element set, one 'other' is all the others that there are; there need not be anything in the structure underlying 12a that corresponds to the article.

Let me finally turn to two problems that to my knowledge have not been discussed in the literature, which an analysis in terms of morphologically indeterminate underlying structure may cast some light on. Observe first that 15 is appropriate even in the case where Harry has only one wife:

15. Ahmed loves his wives, and so does Harry.

The repeated structure involves a universal quantifier ('for all x such that x is wife of Ahmed, Ahmed loves x, and for all y such that y is wife of Harry, Harry loves y') Since *wife* appears overtly in the first clause, it must be supplied with a grammatical number, thus forcing the speaker to commit himself as to Ahmed's having more than one wife; however, the underlying occurrence of *wife* in the second conjunct does not surface and can thus remain indeterminate as to number, that is, it does not commit the speaker as to how many wives Harry has. Suppose, however, that the order of the conjuncts in 15 were reversed:

16. Harry loves his wife, and so does Ahmed.

Here it is not possible to interpret the second conjunct as meaning that Ahmed loves his wives—it can only be 'Ahmed loves his wife'. I am not at all clear why this should be the case. Perhaps for some reason *Harry loves his wife* cannot be interpreted as containing a universal quantifier and thus that *Ahmed loves his wives* cannot be (sloppily) identical to it; and perhaps here I have further evidence for my conjecture (McCawley 1968c) that it is plural and not singular that is the unmarked number.

The second and final problem relates to 'reduced passives'.[8] The most popular account of a reduced passive such as 17a derives it from a structure with *someone* or *something* as subject (thus, the same structure would underlie 17a as 17b) by passivization plus deletion of an indefinite *by*-phrase:

17a. Fred was attacked.
  b. Someone attacked Fred.

However, indefinite pronouns are not indefinite enough. For example, it has often been observed that reduced passives are possible even when the verb demands a 'semantically plural' subject and thus does not admit *someone*:

18a. The fort was being surrounded.
  b. *Someone was surrounding the fort.

There is a further respect in which indefinite pronouns are not indefinite enough, which is illustrated in the ludicrousness of relating 19a to 19b:

19a. Chomsky's *Syntactic Structures* was written in 1955.
  b. Someone wrote Chomsky's *Syntactic Structures* in 1955.

The *someone* of 19b must be interpreted as noncoreferential with *Chomsky*; it implies that someone other than Chomsky wrote *Syntactic Structures*. However, 19a is completely noncommittal as to the authorship of *Syntactic Structures*: it could be used equally appropriately by someone who believes the real author to be Chomsky as by someone who thinks it was written by Bernard Bloch (but who nonetheless persists in calling it 'Chomsky's *Syntactic Structures*', much in the way that people persist in speaking of 'Purcell's trumpet voluntary' even though they know that it is really by Jeremiah Clarke).

There is an important difference between 19a and 19b which I suspect is responsible for their different implications as to who wrote *Syntactic Structures*, namely, that the *someone* of 19b can serve as the antecedent of a pronoun (you could follow it with *But nobody has figured out who he was*), whereas the underlying subject of 19a cannot serve as the antecedent of a pronoun. The *someone* of 19b serves two functions: it both expresses an existential quantifier (i.e., asserts the existence of a person such that person wrote Chomsky's *Syntactic Structures* in 1955) and provides a constant that can be referred back to in subsequent discourse.[9] As a result of the principles of sportsmanly behavior in language use that are associated with Grice's name, distinct NP's are taken as noncoreferential unless the speaker indicates somehow that they are to be taken as coreferential. The following approach to the difference between 19a and 19b is thus open to us: we can take 19a and 19b as both corresponding to an underlying structure with an existentially quantified NP; in 19b, the means chosen of expressing that existential quantifier will be misleading unless one holds that the author of *Syntactic Structures* is not (or may not be) Chomsky; however, in 19a, there is nothing about the sentence to lead the hearer into believing that the author is not Chomsky. I have concluded with this example, since it illustrates that indeterminacy covers a broader range of matters than just the choice among alternatives of a paradigm, as well as illustrating the interplay between conversational implicature and the presence or absence in surface structure of some crucial word or morpheme. I suspect that there are more such interactions, but at the moment I am just starting to look for them.

# 14 Evolutionary Parallels between Montague Grammar and Transformational Grammar

In reading various works by Richard Montague and by Montague grammarians, I have frequently had a feeling of déjà vu: that I was watching a recapitulation of developments that had taken place in transformational grammar ten to fifteen years earlier. This paper will be devoted to exploring a number of respects in which Montague grammar has encountered problems, both pseudo and real, that arose in the early development of transformational grammar, and in which quite parallel considerations have been invoked or could be invoked by both transformational grammarians and Montague grammarians in choosing horns on quite parallel dilemmas.

I will begin by sketching Montague grammar in a way that will set the stage for what follows. In 'classical' Montague grammar, a description of a language consists of four parts. First, there is a lexicon, which consists of a list of the 'lexical items' of the language (or at least, those lexical items that are not in effect always 'transformationally introduced'), each provided with a syntactic category and a translation into intensional logic, for example,[1]

1. *walk*: t/T (essentially, 'intransitive verb')
   $(\lambda x)$walk' $(x)$

Second, there is a set of syntactic rules, specifying what the 'derived' members of each syntactic category are (the lexicon specifies what the 'basic' members, if any, are). Syntactic rules have the following general form, where $P_A$ stands for the set of strings that are of category A:[2]

2. If $\alpha \in P_A$ and $\beta \in P_B$, than $f(\alpha,\beta) \in P_C$.

Reprinted by permission from *Northeastern Linguistic Society* 7 (1977): 219–32.

Montague imposed no restriction on what the $f$ of such a rule could be. In many cases, the $f$ was simply concatenation, as in a rule that might be expressed (using linguistically familiar names for categories rather than Montague-style category names) as:

3. If $\alpha \in P_{Prep}$ and $\beta \in P_{NP}$, than $\alpha\beta \in P_{PP}$.

When the $f$ is concatenation, the syntactic rule amounts to a phrase structure rule, as in 3, which has the content of the phrase structure rule PP $\rightarrow$ Prep NP. However, the $f$ need not be mere concatenation, and Montague gave several rules that combine the content of a phrase structure rule with the content of one or more transformations. For example, his rule for combining a NP with a VP to yield a sentence (1974:251) was a combination of the phrase structure rule S $\rightarrow$ NP VP and an agreement rule that makes the verb form conform to the choice of the NP:[3]

4. S4. If $\alpha \in P_{t/IV}$ and $\delta \in P_{IV}$, then $\alpha\delta' \in P_t$, where $\delta'$ is the result of replacing the first verb (i.e., member of $B_{IV}$, $B_{TV}$, $B_{IV/t}$, or $B_{IV//IV}$) in $\delta$ by its third person singular form.

Similarly, his rule S14 combined a phrase structure rule S $\rightarrow$ NP S with a transformation of 'quantifier lowering',[4] plus pronominalization of those occurrences of the bound variable other than that for which the NP is substituted:

5. S14. If $\alpha \in P_T$ and $\phi \in P_t$, then $F_{10,n}(\alpha,\phi) \in P_t$, where
(i) if $\alpha$ does not have the form $he_k$, then $F_{10,n}(\alpha,\phi)$ comes from $\phi$ by replacing the first occurrence of $he_n$ or $him_n$ by $\alpha$ and all other occurrences of $he_n/him_n$ by $he/she/it$ or $him/her/it$, respectively, according as the gender of the first $B_{CN}$ or $B_T$ in $\alpha$ is masc/fem/neuter:
(ii) if $\alpha = he_k$, then $F_{10,n}(\alpha,\phi)$ comes from $\phi$ by replacing all occurrences of $he_n/him_n$ by $he_k/him_k$, respectively.

'Classical' Montague grammar does not allow one to separate the agreement rule involved in 4 from the phrase structure rule, since there is no provision for such a thing as an obligatory rule. Each of the syntactic rules tells how you can construct *surface* members of the given category, and if you have a rule saying you can form a S by combining a NP with a VP, without any agreement, that rule says that *That dog bark* is a S, regardless of whether you also have a rule saying you can form a S from a S by making its verb agree with its subject, as in 6a. The only way you could in effect make a rule obligatory would be by proliferating categories, that is, by saying that a S that had not undergone agreement belonged to a different category (call it, say, t'), in which case you could have rules according to which *That dog bark* was not a well-formed S, though it was a well-formed representative of another category, as in 6b. It is to Montague's credit that he avoided 'solutions' of that type: rather than allowing an arbitrary alphabet of categories, he restricted his categories to those expressible in terms of his two basic categories *t* and *e*, and allowed each category to contain only items that make contributions of a fixed logical type (predictable by general rule from the category name) to semantic interpretations. This credit is balanced by an important thing to his debit, namely, that, as in early transformational grammar, he treated morphology

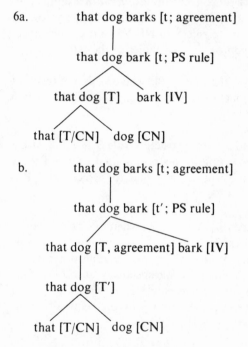

6a.        that dog barks [t; agreement]

that dog bark [t; PS rule]

that dog [T]     bark [IV]

that [T/CN]     dog [CN]

b.        that dog barks [t; agreement]

that dog bark [t'; PS rule]

that dog [T, agreement] bark [IV]

that dog [T']

that [T/CN]     dog [CN]

as if it were a part of syntax with no autonomous status of its own (compare the agreement rule given as transformation 15 in *Syntactic Structures* p. 112). In both traditions, this policy has given rise to 'syntactic rules' that get the right inflectional morphemes in the right places but embody no particular insight.

The application of syntactic rules in deriving any expression can be represented in an 'analysis tree', which indicates the category of each constituent expression and the syntactic rule by which it is derived from its constituents:

7.

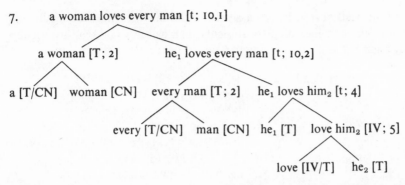

As Partee (1975) has observed, the information given in a Montague analysis tree is comparable to that given in the 'T-marker' of early transformational grammar, which indicated the kernel phrase markers of the constituent sentences of a given complex sentence, plus the transformations that deform and combine them. The principal difference between the Montague analysis tree and the T-marker is that in Montague grammar the category 'S' (Montague's t) does not have the privileged role that it has always played in transformational grammar, and thus the inputs to the Montague analogue to a transformation may be of categories other than S. The mode of interaction of the 'transformations' embodied in Montague's rules can be characterized as cyclic, with every constituent serving as a domain for the cycle, and with an especially strict principle of strict cyclicity: in effect, as each syntactic rule applies, the constituents to which it applies lose their identity as constituents (i.e., 'brackets are erased'), and thus all inputs to a syntactic rule are strings and all figure in the effect of the rule.

The remaining two parts of a classical Montague grammar are a system of intensional logic and a set of translation rules, which associate every derived expression with a translation into a formula of intensional logic. The translation rules are semantic counterparts of the various syntactic rules: to every syntactic rule there corresponds a translation rule, which provides a way of combining the translations of the constituents of the derived expression, as in the translation rule corresponding to 5:

5'. If A translates $\alpha$ and B translates $\beta$, then A $[(\lambda x_n)B]$ translates $F_{10,n}(\alpha,\beta)$.

The translation of a complex expression into intensional logic is illustrated in 9 (simplified in some details; see note 6).[5] Note that the translation of each derived constituent is obtained by putting together in some fashion the translations of the constituents from which it is constructed. The eventual result of $\lambda$-conversion is the formula you were taught to come up with in your elementary logic course; the $\lambda$-notation allows you to come up with it on the basis of translations assigned to the various syntactic constituents of the sentence, including constituents such as *every dog* that are usually not regarded as corresponding to a constituent of logical structure.

9.

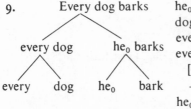

$he_0 \Rightarrow x_0$; $bark \Rightarrow (\lambda x)bark'(x)$

$dog \Rightarrow (\lambda x)dog'(x)$

$every \Rightarrow (\lambda P)(\lambda Q)(\forall x)(Px \supset Qx)$

$every\ dog \Rightarrow$

   $[(\lambda P)(\lambda Q)(\forall x)(Px \supset Qx)](\lambda y)dog'(y)$

   $\rightarrow (\lambda Q)(\forall x)(dog'(x) \supset Qx)$

$he_0\ barks \Rightarrow (\lambda x)bark'(x)(x_0)$

   $\rightarrow bark'(x_0)$

$every\ dog\ barks \Rightarrow$

   $(\lambda Q)(\forall x)(dog'(x) \supset Qx)[(\lambda x_0)bark'(x_0)]$

   $\rightarrow (\forall x)(dog'(x) \supset bark'(x))$

The first parallel with early transformational grammar that I wish to discuss in detail is that both classical Montague grammar and early transformational grammar allowed morphemes to be either 'base generated' or 'transformationally derived' and provided no clear grounds for choosing the one sort of analysis or the other. For example, in "English as a Formal Language" Montague (1974: 196) treated *not* as 'base generated': it has the category IV/IV (essentially, 'VP modifier') and has a specific translation which, though not provided by Montague, can easily be supplied:[6]

10. *not*   IV/IV
   $(\lambda P)(\lambda x) \sim (^{\text{ex}}P(x))$

However, *not* could as easily be 'transformationally introduced', that is, introduced by a special syntactic rule that combines it with a VP, with a corresponding semantic rule that translates the derived VP as $(\lambda x) \sim P(x)$, where the translation of the original VP was $(\lambda x)P(x)$. In contrast, Montague treated coordinating conjunctions as transformationally introduced (Montague 1974:252):

11. Syntactic rules: if $\phi$, $\psi \in P_t$, then $\ulcorner\varphi\ and\ \psi\urcorner \in P_t$, $\ulcorner\varphi\ or\ \psi\urcorner \in P_t$.
   Semantic rules: If A translates $\varphi$ and B translates $\psi$, then
      A $\wedge$ B translates $\ulcorner\varphi\ and\ \psi\urcorner$;
      A $\vee$ B translates $\ulcorner\varphi\ or\ \psi\urcorner$.

An alternative analysis is available in which coordinating conjunctions are base-generated members of category (t/t)/t (i.e., things that combine with a sentence to yield something that combines with a sentence to yield a sentence):

12. *and*   $(t/t)/t$

$(\lambda q)(\lambda p)(^{ex}p \wedge {}^{ex}q)$

The analyses and translations under the two approaches are illustrated in 13, which shows that both approaches ultimately yield the same translation of the sentence:

13.  John screamed and Mary wept [t; 11]

John screamed        Mary wept

John screamed $\Rightarrow$ A

Mary wept $\Rightarrow$ B

John screamed and Mary wept $\Rightarrow$ A $\wedge$ B

John screamed and Mary wept [t; new rule a]

John screamed        and Mary wept [t/t; new rule b]

and [(t/t)/t]   Mary wept

and Mary wept $\Rightarrow$ $(\lambda q)\,\lambda p)\,{}^{ex}p \wedge {}^{ex}q)\,{}^{in}B$

$\rightarrow (\lambda p)\,(^{ex}p \wedge {}^{ex\ in}B) \rightarrow (\lambda p)\,(^{ex}p \wedge B)$

John screamed and Mary wept $\Rightarrow$

$(\lambda p)\,(^{ex}p \wedge B)\,{}^{in}A \rightarrow {}^{ex\ in}A \wedge B$

$\rightarrow A \wedge B$

Montague (1974:251) indeed introduced quantifiers transformationally (14); Thomason (1976:81), in contrast, treated them as base generated (15):[7]

14.  S2. If $\zeta \in P_{CN}$, then $F_0(\zeta)$, $F_1(\zeta)$, $F_2(\zeta) \in P_T$, where

$F_0(\zeta) = every\ \zeta$

$F_1(\zeta) = the\ \zeta$

$F_2(\zeta)$ is *a* $\zeta$ or *an* $\zeta$, according as the first word in $\zeta$ takes *a* or *an*.

15. If $\alpha \in P_{T/CN}$ and $\beta \in P_{CN}$, then $F_9(\alpha, \beta) \in P_T$, where

$F_9(\alpha,\beta) = \alpha\beta$ if $\alpha \neq a$ or $\beta$ begins with a consonant,

$= an\ \beta$ if $\alpha = a$ and $\beta$ begins with a vowel.

The grounds on which a Montague grammarian will prefer a 'transformational' or a 'base-generated' treatment of a given morpheme are not clear, though there appears to be some reliance on a 'free ride principle' (Zwicky 1970a): analyses are preferred to the extent that they allow one to utilize existing descriptive or logical machinery. Montague's choice of whether to treat a given element as base generated appears to be pretty haphazard, in much the same way that there was no particular reason for

Chomsky (1957) to take *not* as transformationally introduced and progressive *be* as base generated, rather than vice versa. Thomason appears to take virtually everything to be base generated, though he has not to my knowledge offered any explicit rationale for this policy. One ground that could be offered in some cases for a base-generated treatment has to do with the fact that, in classical Montague grammar, transformationally introduced elements do not belong to *any* syntactic category. Thus, if a category exists, as evidenced by its playing a rule in some syntactic rule, its atomic members would have to be base generated; to my knowledge, it is only this consideration which rules out a Montague analysis in which all nouns are transformationally introduced. Of course, this rationale for a particular analysis is exactly parallel to the popular rationale for base-generated passive *by* phrases on the grounds that transformational introduction of the *by* phrase allegedly would fail to assign it to the proper category (Chomsky 1965:104). In both cases, in my opinion, the argument rests on a lousy theory of syntactic categories: a theory that incorrectly makes category membership of items depend only on their real or potential 'source' in derivations.[8]

I note also that Thomason's policy can be viewed as a step in the direction of making transformations (or at least, the Montague analogs to them) 'meaning preserving'. The Montague analog to a 'meaning preserving transformation' is a syntactic rule for which the corresponding semantic rule simply concatenates the translations of the operands (while prefixing [in] to the argument) to yield a translation of the derived constituent. The resulting syntactic rules in Thomason are 'meaning preserving' in this sense, whereas many of Montague's rules are not.

I turn now to a second parallel: in both classical Montague grammar and early transformational grammar, the operands of syntactic rules are officially taken to be strings rather than trees. This policy is quite explicit in Montague's work, in which the syntactic rules are literally presented as recursive definitions of various sets of strings. Interpreting Montague literally, when one of his rules refers to, say, an operand containing a member of $P_{CN}$ (i.e., a common noun expression), what it means is that some substring of the operand belongs to that category, whether or not it figured as a member of that category in the given derivation. This policy comes to grief when applied to examples such as Lees's (1960) celebrated pair:

16a. Drowning cats are/*is hard to rescue.
  b. Drowning cats is/*are against the law.

According to Montague's formulation of agreement in terms of 'the first member of $B_{CN}$' (i.e., the first atomic common noun) in the subject NP, both sentences ought to get plural number agreement. Just as transformational grammar in the middle 1960s rapidly developed formulations of rules in which explicit note was taken of constituent structure, so too, recent works by Thomason (1975, 1976) refer not to mere membership of strings in categories but to the way those strings are analyzed in the given sentence; thus, the version of Montague grammar that Thomason employs is able to distinguish correctly between 16a and 16b for the purposes of number agreement, whereas Montague's original framework is not.

Or at least, it is not unless you claim that the subjects of 16a and 16b are of different categories and are combined with the VP's by different rules, which incorporate separate agreement rules. This latter approach figures in work by Michael Bennett (1976), who notes that it is similar in content to Emonds's 1970 treatment of complements, in which *that* and *for-to* complements are not NP's, though for Bennett, even Poss-*ing* complements (which are NP's for Emonds) would have to be treated as not being NP's. Bennett adopts such an analysis in order to rule out analyses such as

17.   *That no man walks is believed by him

  no man    that $he_0$ walks is believed by $him_0$

Bennett's solution to the problem presented by 17 was to have a special rule for forming sentences with sentential subjects (comparable to the 'anti-extraposition' rule of Emonds (1970), and to restrict that rule so that it would not apply when the complement contained a variable, thus ruling out *that $he_0$ walks is believed by $him_0$* and hence making the derivation in 17 impossible. An alternative approach to 17 not considered by Bennett, would be to change the rule (given above as 5) for forming quantified sentences: to have the rule not simply substitute the (quantified) NP for the first occurrence of the corresponding variable, as Montague's rule did, but instead substitute it for an occurrence of the variable that commands all other occurrences of the variable and precedes those that are in the same clause. With this revised version of the rule, the derivational step in 17 would lead to *That he walks is believed by no man.* I conjecture that one of the reasons why Bennett did not adopt that alternative is that the variety of Montague grammar with which he was operating was formulated entirely in terms of strings rather than in terms of trees, and thus formulations in terms of notions like 'command' were not available but only formulations in terms of string-based notions like 'first occurrence of $he_n$'.

Montague's works contain several instances where the string-based nature of his descriptive system lead him to formulate rules in terms of fudge-factors that serve only to circumvent any reference to essentially structural notions such as 'head noun'. Thus, in his relative clause rule and the part of the quantification rule that does pronominalization, Montague took the choice of pronoun as determined by 'the first member of $B_{CN}$', that is, the first atomic common noun, in the antecedent NP. That formulation amounts to an algorithm for finding the head noun. The algorithm works in those cases that figure in Montague's fragmentary grammars but fails when additional syntactic phenomena are admitted; thus, Montague's rules would generate the starred versions of 18 but not the unstarred versions, since *brick* is the first member of $B_{CN}$ in the NP *the bricklayer*:

18. the bricklayer such that Mary loves $\begin{cases} \text{him/*it} \\ \text{that bricklayer/*brick} \end{cases}$

I turn now to the notion of 'grammaticality' and the way that conception of it have changed as both transformational grammar and Montague grammar have evolved. In both early transformational grammar and classical Montague grammar there was a relatively tight conception of grammaticality; grossly aberrant sentences were considered ungrammatical, and the grammar was constructed in such a way that those sentences would have no derivations. Thus, for Montague, verbs that take sentential complements and verbs that take ordinary objects were assigned to different categories (IV/t and IV/T, respectively), and thus no derivations were available for sentences such as:[9]

19a. *John alleged the teapot.
  b. *John slapped that God is dead.

This policy resulted in large-scale proliferation of categories within what would normally be called verbs, much as in Lees 1960. Thus, in 4, Montague's statement of agreement involves a list of different types of verbs, all of which must undergo agreement, and that list would have to be much longer if the description of English were less fragmentary. Recently, Thomason (1976) has presented an alternative analysis of object complements in which he took complementizers to be of the category T/t; this means that *that* complements are now the same category as ordinary objects (T), *allege* and *slap* are now both of category IV/T, the sentences in 19 that Montague insured would have no derivation do have a derivation (i.e., both count as grammatical), and their oddity is accounted for purely semantically, namely through meaning postulates that allow one to derive blatant contradictions from them.

The rationale for Thomason's revision of Montague applies with equal force to the question of how to treat sentences that violate strict subcategorization conditions:

20. *John put.
   *John slept three teapots Ray's clarinet that Lenin is gay.

There is nothing to prevent one from setting up syntactic rules that ignore the distinctions among 'intransitive verb', 'transitive verb', and 'doubly transitive verb' (say, by assigning all verbs to the category IV, and having a syntactic rule that forms derived IV by combining an IV with a T or a prepositional phrase), giving such analyses as[10]

21.

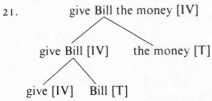

Since the translation of any verb into intensional logic must indicate the number of arguments that it combines with (it will have that many $\lambda$'s prefixed to it), the oddity of 20 can be regarded as semantic rather than grammatical: they will be syntactically well-formed sentences, but their translations into intensional logic will not be of the type that corresponds to sentence.[11]

In the various comparisons that I have drawn in this paper, I have treated Montague grammar in its various versions as a linguistic theory. While Montague himself might have balked at considering his scheme of linguistic description as embodying a theory of natural language, it at least can serve as such a theory and has to some extent been so interpreted by Montague grammarians, at least to the extent that their system of description is subject not only to logical constraints but also to linguistic constraints (such as the 'local well-formedness' requirement that Montague abided by: the constituents in the analysis tree must all be possible surface expressions in the given natural language). Montague grammarians, especially those whose background is primarily in philosophy rather than in linguistics, have generally given little attention to the problem of developing their approach so that it provides a detailed and specific set of answers to such questions as 'What is a possible human language?' and 'What features of human languages are language universal and which ones language-particular?' but there is no particular reason why such questions could not be asked and answers given to them within a Montague framework as well as within a transformational framework. Important questions have been brushed aside in Montague grammar that would have been impossible to brush aside had the respective authors been more concerned with providing as tight a characterization as possible of what is a natural language. To take one example, Montague (1974:263–64) gives a list of meaning postulates containing the following:

22a. $(\exists S_\delta)$ $(\forall x)$ $(\forall P)$ $\Box$ $[\delta(x,P)\leftrightarrow({}^{ex}P)^{in}(\lambda y)S_\delta({}^{ex}x, {}^{ex}y)]$ where $\delta$ translates *find, lose, eat, love,* or *date* (i.e., where $\delta$ translates any transitive verb in Montague's fragment, other than *seek*).

  b. $\Box$ $[seek'(x,P) \leftrightarrow try\text{-}to'(x, {}^{in}[find'(x,P)])]$

Montague failed to raise the important question of whether the disjunctive relation between 22a and 22b (i.e., the fact that the verb that is 'decomposed' in 22b is excluded from the postulate 22a saying that object NP's are 'extensional') is 'accidental'—could there be a lexical item that was decomposed by a meaning postulate of the form of 22b but nonetheless figures in a meaning postulate such as 22a that made its object 'extensional'? If not, then 22a should be stated in completely general form and its inapplicability to *seek* predicted metatheoretically.

The precise and tightly organized model-theoretic semantics that forms the most attractive feature of Montague's work is independent of most details of Montague's approach to syntax; in particular, it can be combined with a tree-based syntax in which morphology and morphophonemics are separated from syntax proper. I regard it as unfortunate that Montague's syntax retains as much of the status of a paradigm among Montague grammarians as it does, and I will be pleased when references to S4 and S14 have become as rare among Montague grammarians as references to kernel sentences have among transformational grammarians.[12]

# III    The Lexicon

# 15    Verbs of Bitching

Fillmore's "Verbs of Judging" is subtitled 'an exercise in semantic descrip-tion'. It is only to avoid compounding the chutzpah that I have not added the same subtitle to this paper. I will be concerned here with the semantic structure of the verbs that Fillmore investigated, roughly those that relate to guilt and virtue, and will operate within a descriptive framework not much different from Fillmore's. Fillmore presents his analyses in the form of a list of atomic formulas, segregated into a 'meaning' part and a 'presupposition' part, for example,

1. ACCUSE [Judge, Defendant, Situation (*of*)]
   Meaning: SAY [Judge, '*X*', Addressee]
   *X* = RESPONSIBLE [Defendant, Situation][1]
   Presupposition: BAD [Situation]

Each atomic formula consists of a predicate followed by a sequence of arguments, each of which is either the name of a 'role' (Judge, Defendant, Affected, . . . ) or the name of a lower formula. Since each named formula is referred to in exactly one higher formula, Fillmore's analyses are mechanically convertible into diagrams such as 2, in which the meaning (in the narrow sense) and the presuppositions are represented as trees and presupposed material is connected by dotted lines to the constituent it is presupposed by, as in the diagram at the top of the following page. I will henceforth use the latter format for the presentation of Fillmore's analyses and alternate analyses. I will also assume that the analyses are to function as the logical structures of corresponding sentences (i.e., they are what can appear in the input and output of rules of inference) and that they constitute the deepest level of a syntactic derivation.[2]

Reprinted by permission from *Contemporary Research in Philosophical Logic and Linguistic Semantics*, ed. Hockney et al. (Dordrecht: Reidel, 1975), pp. 313–32. Copyright © 1975 by D. Reidel Publishing Co., Inc.

2.

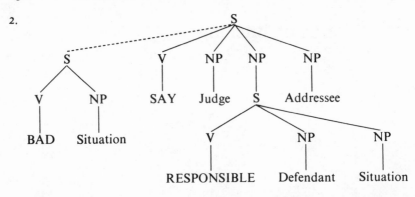

This paper is concerned particularly with (i) whether the items that Fillmore treats as presuppositions really are presuppositions, (ii) whether the various roles in his analyses can be filled by the same kinds of things for the various verbs under consideration, and especially whether the role Fillmore calls 'Situation' is always filled by the same kind of things, and (iii) the extent to which syntactic characteristics of these verbs are idiosyncratic, as opposed to being related in a systematic way to their meanings.

Let me begin by playing around a little with the first verb that Fillmore discussed, namely *accuse*. It is not clear whether Fillmore would take the 'Situation' in 3 to be the proposition that Agnew wants to end the war or the propositional function '*x* wants to end the war', to mention the two most obvious possibilities.

3. Nixon accused Agnew of wanting to end the war.

Neither of those possibilities works if 'presuppose' is understood in the usual way, since to say sentence 3 felicitously it is not necessary that the speaker believe that it would be bad for Agnew to want to end the war nor that he believe that it is bad to want to end the war. For example, Fulbright could perfectly well use 3 in the middle of an anti-war speech. One possible correction in Fillmore's analysis to bring it into conformity with this observation would be to change the presupposition from BAD [Situation] to THINK [Judge, BAD [Situation]], that is, the presupposition of 3 would not be that it is bad to want to end the war but that Nixon thinks it is bad to want to end the war. However, that doesn't work either, in view of the fact that saying 4 does not commit the speaker to the proposition that it is bad to offer Officer O'Reilly a bribe and bad not to offer him one, nor to the proposition that Officer O'Reilly thinks both that it is bad to offer him a bribe and bad not to offer him one.

4. Officer O'Reilly accused me of not offering him a bribe and threatened to take me to the police station and accuse me of offering him a bribe.

Indeed, one could utter 4 in good faith even under the belief that Officer O'Reilly considers the offering of bribes morally neutral. His belief that offering him a bribe is bad is certainly a condition for his being sincere in accusing you of offering him a bribe, but an insincere accusation is still an accusation.

Example 4 brings into prominence an important characteristic of accusations which is not mentioned in Fillmore's analysis, namely, that an accusation creates some kind of 'jeopardy' (using that word fairly loosely). When someone is accused of something, he must successfully defend himself against the accusation or suffer the consequences. The consequences may be quite trivial, for example, the accuser being annoyed at the accused; but unless there are some such undesirable consequences, a statement cannot constitute an accusation. This is illustrated by the difference in normalness between[3]

5. Officer O'Reilly$_i$ took Susan $\left\{ \begin{array}{c} \text{before the judge} \\ \text{?to Tiny Tim} \end{array} \right\}$ and accused her of offering him$_i$ a bribe.

If Susan is a normal person, she would care about the possibility of the judge fining or jailing her, but she shouldn't care a hoot whether Tiny Tim shakes his finger at her and says 'Naughty, naughty'.

As Fillmore's formulas would predict, saying that a person did some foul act may constitute an accusation, that is, it is possible for an occurrence of the sentence *Last night while you were drunk, you stabbed your mother to death* to be correctly reported by saying *Mary accused Bill of stabbing his mother to death while he was drunk the previous night*. However, such a report is not always correct. An occurrence of the sentence *Last night while you were drunk you stabbed your mother to death* is an accusation if uttered by a policeman who is going to cart you off to jail unless you come up with a good alibi quick, or if uttered by your mother's lover, who wants vengeance, but is not an accusation if uttered by a friend who is informing you of the danger of your being arrested and wants to help you escape. Note also that in a trial the prosecutor accuses the defendant of the crime, but the foreman of the jury, in reporting a guilty verdict, is saying that the defendant committed the crime but is not accusing him. The prosecutor's action creates the situation of jeopardy, whereas the foreman's action brings an existing situation of jeopardy to culmination. I thus conclude that the meaning of *accuse* includes the information that the linguistic act which it reports creates a situation of jeopardy, that is, that the logical structure of 6a is along the lines of 6b:

6a. John accused Sam of breaking the window.
  b. John said that Sam broke the window and thereby put Sam in jeopardy.

This actually is inadequate, since an accusation has to be made with the intention of creating jeopardy. Thus, if someone in a group which includes an FBI undercover agent discusses the group's plans to bomb the Treasury Building, he hasn't accused his friends of planning to bomb the Treasury Building, even though he has (inadvertently) put them into some kind of jeopardy. The logical structure of 6a must indicate not merely that jeopardy results from the act, but that the creation of jeopardy is indeed part of the act. It is evidently this characteristic of the meaning of *accuse* which is responsible for the possibility of using it as a performative verb: its logical structure is in this respect like the large subset of Austin's 'exercitives' (Austin, 1962) which Vendler (1972) calls 'operatives': verbs such as *appoint*, *decree*, and *excommunicate* which refer to an act of making something the case by saying that it is to be the case (under appropriate circumstances).

Let me now take up *criticize*, which Fillmore has claimed contrasts almost minimally with *accuse* with respect to the assignment of various parts of its content to 'presupposition' and 'meaning' in the narrow sense:

7.

Since in this structure and the one for *accuse* the same predicates are predicated of 'Situation' (save for the additional occurrence of ACTUAL [Situation] in 7), and likewise the same predicate is predicated of 'Defendant', there is nothing in the two structures which would imply any difference between what can fill these two roles in sentences with *accuse* and what can fill them in sentences with *criticize*, other than what can be attributed to the presence of ACTUAL [Situation] in 7. It turns out, however, that there are differences which cannot be ascribed to 'ACTUAL [Situation]'. *Accuse* but not *criticize* requires the 'Defendant' to be a person:

8a. Mencken criticized act 2 of *Lohengrin* for being too long.
  b. *Mencken accused act 2 of *Lohengrin* of being too long.

9a. The principal criticized Rocky's hair for being untidy.
  b. *The principal accused Rocky's hair of being untidy.

Here 'person' must be taken in the extended sense which includes corporate persons:

10. Nader accused General Motors of dumping mercury in the Detroit River.
    Nixon accused Tanzania of endangering American interests in Antarctica.

Not quite anything is possible as the 'Defendant' with *criticize*:[4]

11a. *John criticized wisdom for being hard to achieve.
  b. *Arthur criticized 17 for being an unlucky number.
  c. *Sam criticized the Mississippi River for being too wide.

To get a better idea of what 'Defendant' *criticize* allows, consider the following sentences, which differ only slightly from 11c but are much more normal:

12. Sam criticized the Cuyahoga River for being too filthy.
    Sam criticized the Erie Canal for being too narrow.

What appears to make these sentences better than 11c is that the filthiness of the Cuyahoga River and the narrowness of the Erie Canal are the result of the decisions and actions of people, whereas the width of the Mississippi is not. Where the object of *criticize* is not a person, it is something for which a person or persons are responsible, and the criticism of the object is at least by implication a criticism of the person(s) responsible. Actually, 11c is perfectly good if taken as a criticism of God for a lousy job of creation.

Let us now take a look at some differences in what *accuse* and *criticize* allow in the role of 'Situation'.

13a. McGovern criticized Nixon for $\begin{cases} \text{*irresponsibility.} \\ \text{his irresponsibility.} \\ \text{?Mitchell's irresponsibility.} \end{cases}$

  b. McGovern criticized Nixon for the fact that he puts ketchup on his cottage cheese.

  c. McGovern criticized Nixon for $\begin{cases} \text{what he said to the Knights of} \\ \quad \text{Columbus} \\ \text{the basis on which he fills court} \\ \quad \text{vacancies.} \\ \text{the way in which his economic} \\ \quad \text{policy has failed.} \end{cases}$

14a.  McGovern accused Nixon of {
irresponsibility.
*his irresponsibility.
*Mitchell's irresponsibility.

b.  *McGovern accused Nixon of the fact that he puts ketchup on his cottage cheese.

c.  McGovern accused Nixon of {
*what he said to the Knights of Columbus.
*the basis on which he fills court vacancies.
*the way in which his economic policy has failed.

Certain of the above facts are accounted for by the presence of ACTUAL [Situation] in Fillmore's analysis of *criticize*. For example, *his irresponsibility* involves a presupposition that he is irresponsible (e.g., neither *McGovern discussed Nixon's irresponsibility* nor *McGovern didn't discuss Nixon's irresponsibility* is appropriate unless the speaker believes that Nixon is/was irresponsible). It may be used with *criticize*, which for Fillmore has a presupposition that the 'Situation' is 'actual'. Similarly with the expression *the fact that he puts ketchup on his cottage cheese*, which involves the presupposition that he puts ketchup on his cottage cheese. It is not completely clear to me why *accuse* not only allows NP's which do not carry a presupposition that the situation is actual, but indeed excludes NP's which do carry such a presupposition. One possible answer would bring in the idea that 'jeopardy' is a situation which one can get out of by defending himself successfully against the accusation, and that if you presuppose the truth of the charge, as opposed to asserting it, you are ruling out the possibility of defense.

The items in 13c have peculiar properties that will have to be discussed before the significance of those examples can be determined. Note that the inferences in 15 are valid and those in 16 invalid:

15a.  The length of the Bible exceeds the length of *Tropic of Cancer*.
The length of the *Tropic of Cancer* is 287 pages.
Therefore, the length of the Bible exceeds 287 pages.

b.  Many people believe what Nixon said to the Knights of Columbus.
What Nixon said to the Knights of Columbus is that Mao is a yellow aryan.
Therefore, many people believe that Mao is a yellow aryan.

16a.  Schwartz criticized *Tropic of Cancer* for its length.
The length of *Tropic of Cancer* is 287 pages.
*Therefore, Schwartz criticized *Tropic of Cancer* for 287 pages.
(grammatical only in an irrelevant sense)

b. McGovern criticized Nixon for what he said to the Knights of Columbus.

What Nixon said to the Knights of Columbus is that Mao is a yellow aryan.

Therefore, McGovern criticized Nixon $\left\{\begin{array}{l} \text{*for that Mao is a yellow aryan.} \\ \text{*that Mao is a yellow aryan.} \\ \text{*for the proposition that Mao is a yellow aryan.} \end{array}\right.$

The only appropriate inferences from the premises of 16 involve an expansion of the first premise:

17a. Schwartz criticized *Tropic of Cancer* for $\left\{\begin{array}{l} \text{having a length of 287 pages.} \\ \text{being 287 pages long.} \end{array}\right.$

b. McGovern criticized Nixon for saying to the Knights of Columbus that Mao is a yellow aryan.

I suggest that the difference between 15 and 16 is the result of the first premises of the inferences in 16 being abbreviated forms, that is, that the extra material which appears in 17 is present in the logical structure of the first premises of the inferences of 16. Rules of inference, of course, apply to the logical structures of sentences and not to their surface forms. I thus maintain that the sentences in 13c have the same logical structure as the following sentences and have undergone an optional deletion:[5]

18. McGovern criticized Nixon for saying to the Knights of Columbus what he said to them.

McGovern criticized Nixon for filling court vacancies on the basis on which he fills them.

McGovern criticized Nixon for his economic policies failing in the way in which they have failed.

I am not in a position to state exactly what this deletion rules does. The rule, which I will refer to as TELESCOPING, applies to certain structures in which a clause contains, roughly speaking, a nominalization of itself, and deletes all of that clause but the nominalization. Telescoping has also been noted by Elliott (1971) who observes that it is involved in exclamatory sentences such as

19a. It's amazing the books that John has read. (= . . . that John has read the books that he has read)

b. It's absurd the kind of things that I'm forced to put up with.
(= . . . that I'm forced to put up with the kind of things that I'm
forced to put up with).[6]

It is important to note that the possibility of Telescoping depends on the
linguistic context in which the clause in question is embedded:

20. I'm angry at Nixon because he said what he said.
   I'm angry at Nixon despite his saying what he said.
   I'm angry at Nixon as a result of his saying what he said.
   I got angry at Nixon before/after he said what he said.
   I was angry at Nixon until he said what he said.
   I will be angry at Nixon as long as he makes appointments on the basis
   on which he makes them.

21. I'm angry at Nixon because of what he said.
   I'm angry at Nixon despite what he said.
   I'm angry at Nixon as a result of what he said.
   *I got angry at Nixon before/after what he said.
   *I was angry at Nixon until what he said.
   *I will be angry at Nixon as long as the basis on which he makes
   appointments.

Both *criticize* and *accuse* allow complements such as *Nixon said what he
said*:

22a. McGovern accused Nixon$_i$ of saying what he$_i$ said.
   b. McGovern criticized Nixon$_i$ for saying what he$_i$ said.

Therefore, the problem which sentences 13c and 14c present is that of why
only one of the two verbs allows Telescoping. Examples 20 and 21 suggest a
conjecture: that Telescoping is permissible in a reason clause and that the
complement of *criticize* (but not that of *accuse*) is a reason clause in logical
structure, that is, that the logical structure of 22b is along the lines of
'McGovern said that Nixon is bad because Nixon said what Nixon said'.[7]
I have at the moment no really strong support for this conjecture, but I
note that Telescoping is possible in other complements which require an
analysis as reason clauses,[8] for example,

23. I'm happy about what Nixon did. (= . . . about Nixon's doing what
   he did)
   I'm annoyed at the attention you pay her. (= . . . at your paying her
   the attention that you pay her)
   I'm distressed at the amount of time Harry spends in the pool hall.
   (= . . . at Harry's spending the amount of time in the pool hall that
   he does).

I thus have arrived at conjectures about the logical structures of clauses with *criticize* and *accuse* which appear to explain certain differences between those verbs which are not explained by Fillmore's analyses:

24a. $x$ criticize $y$ for $S$ = $x$ say ($y$ is bad because $S$)
　　b. $x$ accuse$_z$ $y$ of $S$ = ($x$ say$_z$ $S$) and (become$_z$ ($y$ in jeopardy))

(the subscript denotes the event in question; the double occurrence of $z$ on the right side of 24b means that the event of $x$'s saying $S$ is the same as [or includes] the event of $y$'s coming to be in jeopardy). I do not mean to suggest that these formulas constitute a decomposition of the meanings of *accuse* and *criticize* into semantic primes; 'jeopardy', at least, is surely further decomposable. The fact that 'in jeopardy' is predicated of $y$ in the decomposition of *accuse* but not that of *criticize* accounts for the restriction that the 'Defendant' of *accuse* but not of *criticize* must be a person: only a person (in the extended sense noted above) can be in jeopardy. One respect in which the above formulas may be inadequate is that they do not in themselves impose any restriction on the $S$. For example, there is nothing in 24b which would rule out such nonsentences as

25. *McGovern accused the Republican Party that Nixon is irresponsible.
　　*McGovern accused the Republican Party of Nixon's being irresponsible.

However, I am not sure that the ungrammaticality of 25 is due to characteristics of the meaning of *accuse* rather than to purely grammatical restrictions on what *accuse* may appear in combination with in surface structure. Note that *accusation* does not combine with the same material as does *accuse*, the verb that it apparently is a nominalization of:

26a. McGovern's accusation that Nixon is irresponsible (is well founded).
　　a′ *McGovern accused that Nixon is irresponsible.
　　b. McGovern accused Nixon of being irresponsible.
　　b′. *McGovern's accusation of Nixon of being irresponsible (is well founded).

Note also that the accusation reported in 26a need not be directed at Nixon but can perfectly well be directed at the Republican Party (which McGovern is accusing of nominating someone irresponsible). The discrepancy between what can appear in combination with *accuse* and what can appear in combination with its action nominalization, *accusation*, evidently involves an idiosyncratic restriction on one or the other or both of *accuse* and *accusation*, and the ground covered by the two of them appears to correspond to 24b without any restriction such as that $y$ be the subject of $S$.

I turn now to some of the other verbs that Fillmore discussed. Fillmore states that *credit* and *praise* are positive counterparts of *accuse* and *criticize*, respectively, that is, that they have the same semantic structure as *accuse* and *criticize* except for having 'GOOD' where *accuse* and *criticize* have 'BAD'.[9] If that is the case, then to the extent that syntactic properties of words are predictable from their semantic structure plus general rules of grammar, *credit* and *praise* should behave syntactically like *accuse* and *criticize*. It in fact is the case that much of what I said above about *accuse* and *criticize* is also true of *credit* and *praise*, respectively. For example,

27. Nixon praised Agnew$_i$ for
$$\begin{cases} \text{*wisdom} \\ \text{his}_i \text{ wisdom} \\ \text{?Laird's wisdom} \\ \text{the fact that he}_i \text{ has threatened} \\ \quad \text{reporters} \\ \text{what he}_i \text{ said to Queen Elizabeth} \\ \text{the basis on which he}_i \text{ picks his} \\ \quad \text{speech writers.} \end{cases}$$

28. Nixon credited Agnew$_i$ with
$$\begin{cases} \text{wisdom} \\ \text{*his}_i \text{ wisdom} \\ \text{*Laird's wisdom}^{10} \\ \text{*the fact that he}_i \text{ has threatened} \\ \quad \text{reporters} \\ \text{*what he}_i \text{ said to Queen} \\ \quad \text{Elizabeth} \\ \text{*the basis on which he}_i \text{ picks} \\ \quad \text{his speech writers.} \end{cases}$$

Also, *praise* is like *criticize* and *credit* like *accuse* with respect to the interpretation of a sentence lacking an overtly expressed 'Situation'. Fillmore has noted that 29a is normal even in a context which does not specify any grounds for the criticism, but 29b is normal only when it refers to a specific offense already under discussion:

29a. Max criticized Arthur. (= Max criticized Arthur for something.
　　　　　　　　　　　　　≠ Max criticized Arthur for it.)
　b. Max accused Arthur. (= Max accused Arthur of it.
　　　　　　　　　　　　≠ Max accused Arthur of something.)

The same is true, mutatis mutandis, of 30a and 30b:

30a. Max praised Arthur. (= Max praised Arthur for something.
　　　　　　　　　　　　≠ Max praised Arthur for it.)
　b. Max credited Arthur. (= Max credited Arthur with it.
　　　　　　　　　　　　　≠ Max credited Arthur with something.)

If the conjectures I made above about the semantic structure of *criticize* and *accuse* are to be consistent with the claim that they are the negative counterparts of *praise* and *credit*, then 'BAD' must appear in the semantic structure of 'jeopardy' and the logical structure of clauses with *praise* and *credit* must be roughly

31a. $x$ praise $y$ for $S = x$ say ($y$ is good because of $S$).
  b. $x$ credit$_z$ $y$ with $S = (x$ say$_z$ $S)$ and (become$_z$ ($y$ in schmeopardy)).

In 31b 'schmeopardy' is what results from replacing 'BAD' by 'GOOD' in the logical structure of 'jeopardy'. I find this highly implausible. The closest thing to a positive counterpart to 'being in jeopardy' that I can think of is a situation where you are assured of receiving some blessing if you don't screw up, for example, you will get tenure if you don't offend any administrators. However, crediting you with something does not normally put you in that sort of situation.

I am accordingly led to inquire whether *credit* behaves like a positive counterpart to *accuse* with respect to the examples which were supposed to show that the notion of 'jeopardy' had to be part of the analysis of *accuse*. Here the two verbs turn out to differ. *Credit*, unlike *accuse*, does not require that the 'Defendant' be a person:

32a. *Mencken accused *Lohengrin* of being too long.
     Shaw credited *Lohengrin* with having beautiful choruses.
  b. *Tom accused the number 17 of having brought him bad luck.
     Tom credited the number 28 with having brought him good luck.
  c. *Max accused his belief in Taoism of breaking up his marriage.
     Max credited his belief in Jainism with improving his golf score.

This means that *credit* isn't quite a positive counterpart to my analysis of *accuse*.[11] However, it isn't quite a positive counterpart to Fillmore's analysis of *accuse* either, since it can be shown not to have a presupposition that the 'Situation' is good, in just the same way that *accuse* was shown not to have a presupposition that the 'Situation' is bad:

33. Mayor Daley$_i$ credited me with saving his$_i$ life and promised to reward me by taking me to Mike Royko and crediting me with refusing to save his$_i$ life.

I have not as yet isolated the respect in which the meaning of *credit* fails to be a positive counterpart to the meaning of *accuse*. I have a gut feeling that the answer is intimately connected with the analysis of the notion of 'jeopardy', but I have not yet got any concrete results out of that gut feeling.

I now turn to the three senses of *blame* which Fillmore discusses, namely *blame*₁ 'shift the blame onto', *blame*₂ 'hold culpable', and *blame*₃ 'think guilty', as illustrated by

34a. Phil put a bomb in the governor's office and then blamed₁ it on mé.
   b. Jack blámed₂ me for writing that letter.
   I don't bláme₂ you.
   c. Bert blamed₃ mé for what had happened.

I will henceforth ignore *blame*₁ and concentrate on *blame*₂ and *blame*₃. Fillmore's analyses of *blame*₂ and *blame*₃ are as follows:[12]

35a.

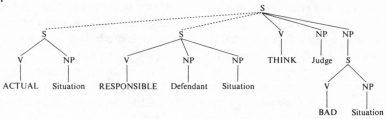

b.

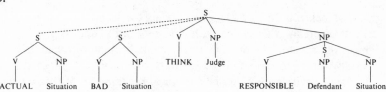

For Fillmore *blame*₂ and *blame*₃ thus differ only with respect to which clauses are assigned to 'presupposition' and which to 'meaning' in the narrow sense. There is thus nothing in these analyses which would imply any difference between *blame*₂ and *blame*₃ as to what can function as the 'Situation'. It turns out, however, that there is considerable difference as to what they allow as 'Situation':

36. Do you { bláme₂ me / *blame₃ mé } for {
  killing/murdering Sally?
  drinking all the beer?
  saying something nasty to Kissinger?
  getting angry at Spiro?
  being angry/disappointed?
  wanting to kill Nixon?
}

37. Do you $\left\{\begin{array}{l}\text{blame}_3\text{ mé}\\[1mm]\text{*bláme}_2\text{ me}\end{array}\right\}$ for $\left\{\begin{array}{l}\text{the/Sally's murder?}\\\text{Sally's death?}\\\text{the predicament that we're in?}\\\text{Cuba's going communist?}\\\text{the fact that Cuba went}\\\quad\text{communist?}\\\text{John's killing Sally?}\end{array}\right.$

*Blame*₃ is indeed the only verb I have discussed so far whose 'Situation' really has to be a situation (as opposed to, e.g., an action), and indeed allows a NP whose head is the word *situation*:

38. $\left\{\begin{array}{l}\text{I don't blame}_3\text{ yóu for}\\\text{*I don't bláme}_2\text{ you for}\\\text{*I accused him of}\\\text{?*I criticized him for}\\\text{?*I praised him for}\\\text{*I credited him with}\end{array}\right\}$ the situation that we're in.

Also, *blame*₂ but not *blame*₃ requires that 'Defendant' be a person:

39a. I blăme₃ the high cost of líving for Max's suicide.

*I bláme₂ the high cost of living for $\left\{\begin{array}{l}\text{causing Max to commit}\\\quad\text{suicide.}\\\text{driving many shops out}\\\quad\text{of business.}\end{array}\right.$

   b. Nixon blămes₃ the lack of support from the Démocrats for the failure of his fiscal policy.

   *Nixon blámes₂ the lack of support from the Democrats for causing his fiscal policy to fail.

The facts given so far are perfectly consistent with Fillmore's analysis of *blame*₃, provided 'RESPONSIBLE' is taken in the sense of *responsible for* which is the converse of *attributable to*. Note that sentences with *blame*₃ appear to have exact paraphrases with *responsible for*:

40a. Janet blames₃ the high cost of living for Phil's suicide.
   Janet thinks that the high cost of living is responsible for Phil's suicide.

   b. Sam blames₃ the steel plant for the dirt on his windows.
   Sam thinks that the steel plant is responsible for the dirt on his windows.

With *blame₂*, there is a restriction which does not follow from Fillmore's analysis, namely, that the 'Situation' must be an act or a controllable state on the part of the 'Defendant'. One revision in Fillmore's analysis which would account for that restriction is to replace BAD [Situation] with the semantic material that corresponds to a sentence like *It was bad of you to drink all the beer* or *You were bad to drink all the beer*. Note that the *bad* of *bad of* or *bad* + infinitive allows the kinds of items that appear with *blame₂* in 36 and excludes items corresponding to those which *blame₂* excludes in 37:

41a. It was bad of Tom
  to drink all the beer.
  to get angry at Spiro.
  to want to kill Nixon.
  *for Sally to die.
  *for us to be in this predicament.
  *for Cuba to go communist.

b. Tom was bad
  to drink all the beer.
  to get angry at Spiro.
  to want to kill Nixon.
  *for Sally to die.
  *for us to be in this predicament.
  *for Cuba to go communist.

Furthermore, sentences with *blame₂* appear to be paraphrasable by sentences with *bad of* but not by sentences in which *bad* is predicated of a 'Situation': for example, 42a is paraphrased by 42b, but is not even implied by, let alone paraphrased by, 42c:

42a. Sheila blámes₂ Tom for drinking all the beer.
  b. Sheila thinks it was bad of Tom to drink all the beer.
     Sheila thinks Tom was bad to drink all the beer.
  c. Sheila thinks it is/was bad that Tom drank all the beer.

She can think *it* was bad without thinking that *he* was bad. I thus maintain that 43 is a closer approximation than 35a to the meaning of a clause with *blame₂*, where BAD′ is the binary relation between a person and an act or controllable state of his which is expressed by *bad of* or by *bad* + infinitive:

43.

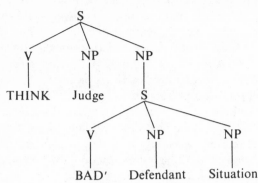

BAD' is of course surely decomposable into more basic elements, but I
do not yet have a decomposition that I am happy with. Since it is BAD'
that is responsible for the presuppositions that the 'Situation' is actual and
that the 'Defendant' is responsible for the 'Situation', the omission of
those presuppositions from 43 is justified, though they may well have to
appear explicitly in the decomposition of BAD': until I have a viable
analysis of BAD', I cannot tell whether those presuppositions are predictable from the 'meaning' in the narrow sense or are idiosyncratic
additions to the latter.

Since I have little in the way of conclusions, let me conclude this paper
with a pep talk instead. The most widely quoted point in Fillmore's
paper is the claim that verbs can differ as to whether semantic material
that they contain is a presupposition or part of the 'meaning' in the narrow
sense. I have shown above that the supposed examples of such differences
given in Fillmore's paper really differ in some respect(s) other than that of
which part of their content are assigned to presupposition. They thus
do not show presuppositions to be as idiosyncratic a part of meaning as
they had initially appeared to, but they still leave quite open the important
question of the extent to which presuppositions can constitute differences
among words of a language. Certain presuppositions are predictable from
other parts of the meanings of sentences in which they are involved; this,
for example, is the case with those presuppositions whose violation constitutes a 'category mistake', for example,

44a. *I poured sesame oil over August 13. [presupposition that locus of
pouring is a physical object]
  b. *Gödel has proved the universal quantifier. [presupposition that
what is proved is a proposition]

On the other hand, it is clear that some presuppositions are distinctive parts of the meaning. For example, the difference between *blame*₃, the mental-state sense of *credit* mentioned in note 9, and *attribute* seems to be the presence of a presupposition that the thing in question is bad, a presupposition that it is good, or neither of those presuppositions. Similarly German *schwanger* and *trächtig* appear to have the same meaning, ('pregnant') and to differ in that *schwanger* carries a presupposition that the subject is human and *trächtig* a presupposition that the subject is not human. However, I am willing to wager that a huge range of conceivable presuppositions cannot function distinctively in lexical items, for example, that no language can have word meaning 'pregnant' which carries a presupposition that the subject is dark-haired or a word meaning 'praise' which carries a presupposition that the subject is of the same sex as the speaker. I thus am fairly convinced that the possibility of words in a language having distinctive presuppositions exists but is fairly heavily restricted. I have looked in sufficient depth at so few words that I have no hint to offer as to what those restrictions are. Finding out something about them will be an important step toward understanding the role which presuppositions can play in the lexicon of a language and in logical structure in general.

# 16 Remarks on the Lexicography of Performative Verbs

At several places in *How to Do Things with Words*, Austin (1962) speaks of the importance of compiling a comprehensive list of performative verbs, or alternatively, of illocutionary forces,[1] and in his twelfth lecture he sets up a five-way categorization of performative verbs and gives long lists of representatives of each category. Austin evidently regarded the tabulation and classification of performative verbs and illocutionary forces as important principally because of the inherent interest of the question, what can people do with words? I regard such tabulations as important because of their relation to a somewhat different question: what determines which verbs are or can be performative, and what determines what illocutionary forces are possible? My concern is not for tests to determine whether, for example, the verb *criticize* can be used performatively (Austin provided an excellent treatment of that problem) but rather with determining, for example, what it is about *accuse* that makes it possible to use it performatively and what it is about *know* that makes it impossible to use it performatively. Why is it that verbs such as *shout* and *whisper*, which can be used to report speech acts, cannot be used performatively?[2] Is it possible for two verbs to have the same meaning but for only one of them to be used performatively? Or can one predict from the meaning of a verb whether it can be used performatively? As one learns one's native language, does one have to learn separately for each verb whether it can be used performatively, or does one automatically know whether he can use a verb performatively once he has learned what it means? I am fairly convinced that the meaning of a verb does in fact completely determine whether it can be used performatively; however, I am much less sure of

Reprinted by permission from *Proceedings of the Texas Conference on Performatives, Implicature, and Presupposition*, ed. A. Rogers, R. Wall, and J. Murphy (Washington, D.C.: Center for Applied Linguistics, 1977), pp. 13–25. Copyright © 1977 by the Center for Applied Linguistics.

what the relationship between semantic structure and performativity is. Are there, for example, a small number of 'basic' performative predicates, such that the meaning of any performative is one of those predicates combined in various ways with other elements of meaning? If so, then what is it about those predicates which makes them bearers of performativity?

I am also interested in the relationship, if any, between Austin's classification of performative verbs and the conception of lexicon which figures in the linguistic theory which I will assume in this paper, generative semantics. Austin's informal characterizations of the various classes of performative verbs can in some cases be interpreted as references to the logical structure of sentences involving those verbs, as, for example, when he states that an exercitive is the giving of "a decision that something is to be so, as distinct from a judgement that it is so"; this can be interpreted as a distinction between the kind of complement clauses that appear in the semantic structure of verdictive clauses and exercitive clauses.

Austin's five categories of performatives, with his informal characterizations of them, are as follows:

1. *Verdictives*: "Verdictives are typified by the giving of a verdict" (1962: 150); "Verdictives consist in the giving of a finding, official or unofficial, upon evidence or reasons as to value or fact" (p. 152).
2. *Exercitives*: "Exercitives are the exercising of powers, rights, or influence" (p. 150); "an exercitive is the giving of a decision in favour of or against a certain course of action, or advocacy of it" (p. 154).
3. *Commissives*: "Commissives are typified by promising or otherwise undertaking" (p. 150); "the whole point of a commissive is to commit the speaker to a certain course of action" (p. 156).
4. *Behabitives*: "Behabitives are a very miscellaneous group, and have to do with attitudes and social *behaviour*" (p. 151); "behabitives include the notion of reaction to other people's behaviour and fortunes and of attitudes to someone else's past conduct or imminent conduct" (p. 159).
5. *Expositives*: "[Expositives] make plain how our utterances fit into the course of an argument or conversation, how we are using words" (p. 151); "expositives are used in acts of exposition involving the expounding of views, the conducting of arguments, and the clarifying of usages and of references" (p. 160).

None of these passages just quoted comes close to being a real definition, and in some cases they clash sharply with his evident intention; for example, most of the verbs that he lists as exercitives have nothing to do with 'advocacy of a course of action', for example, *appoint*, *baptize*, and *excommunicate*. Only ironically could one say that Nixon 'advocated a certain course of action' by appointing Rehnquist to the Supreme Court. Nevertheless, the examples that Austin gives of each category, plus his comments on the distinctions among the five categories, makes pretty clear what the basis of the categorization is.

Vendler (1972) argues convincingly that 'exercitives' include two clearly distinct subclasses, one of which he calls 'operatives' and the other of which he retains the name 'exercitives' for. 'Operatives' refer to acts by which the speaker makes something the case, for example, appointing Gene Autry ambassador to France brings it about that Gene Autry is ambassador to France, and excommunicating Bing Crosby brings it about that Bing Crosby is not a member of the Catholic Church. Vendler's subclass 'exercitives' refers to acts by which one orders, requests, advises, and so on, a person to do something. Separating out the operatives makes Austin's characterization of 'exercitive' less glaringly inadequate, though these characterizations do not really fit Vendler's exercitives either: ordering someone to shine your shoes can hardly be described as 'giving a decision in favor of . . . or advocacy of' his shining your shoes.

The following lists illustrate Austin's other four categories, plus the two categories into which Vendler divided Austin's 'exercitives'. I have subdivided Vendler's exercitives still further, for reasons to be given below. I have supplemented Austin's lists with extra verbs, deleted some items which are clearly not performative, and shifted around some items which I think he misclassified.

*Verdictives*: accuse, acquit, analyze, appraise, ascribe, calculate, call, characterize, charge (a person with a crime), convict, credit, date, denounce, describe, diagnose, estimate, evaluate, find, grade, guess, hold, interpret as, locate, make it, measure, place, put (it) at, rank, rate, read (it) as, reckon, rule, take it, understand, value.
*Operatives*: abdicate, accept (an application), adjourn, annul, appoint, authorize, award, baptize, bequeath, call to order, cancel, charge (a person with a task), choose, christen, claim, concede, condemn (to death, etc.), countermand, declare (open, closed, the winner, . . . ), decree, dedicate, degrade, demote, deputize, dismiss, disown, dub, enact, enter (a plea of insanity), excommunicate, exonerate, fine, forgive, give, grant, levy, name, nominate, offer, ordain, overrule (an objection), pardon, permit, proclaim, pronounce (man and wife), quash, reinstate, release, repeal, reprieve, rescind, sentence, sustain (an objection), veto, vote.
*Exercitives*:
1. *Imperatives*: admonish, appeal, ask, beg, bid, call on, caution, command, demand, direct, enjoin, entreat, forbid, implore, insist, instruct, order, petition, plead, pray, request, solicit, supplicate.

2. *Advisories*: advise, advocate, counsel, exhort, propose, recommend, suggest, urge, warn.

*Commissives*: adopt, agree to, accept, apply for, assure, bet, bind myself, challenge, condemn (someone's actions), consent, contemplate, contract, covenant, dare, it's a deal, defy, declare for, declare my intention, dedicate myself to, embrace, engage, envisage, espouse, express my intention/ support/opposition, favor, give my word, guarantee, intend, invite, mean to, offer, oppose, order (food, etc.), plan, plead (guilty), pledge (myself), promise, propose to, purpose, shall, side with, surrender, swear, undertake, volunteer, vow, warn.

*Behabitives*: apologize, applaud, approve, bid farewell, blame, bless, commend, commiserate, complain of, compliment, condole, congratulate, curse, don't mind, drink to, express my regrets/gratitude/admiration/ (and so on), felicitate, forgive, greet, overlook, protest, salute, sympathize, thank, toast, welcome, wish (a happy birthday, and so on).

*Expositives*:

1. admit, affirm, announce, characterize, claim, class, declare, deny, describe, guess, identify, insist, maintain, predict, state, submit, suggest.

2. interpose, mention, note, observe, remark.

3. answer, apprise, inform, rejoin, remind, repeat, reply, respond, tell, warn.

3a. ask, inquire, query, wonder.

4. confess, conjecture, report, swear, testify.

5. accept, admit, agree that, concede, demur to, disagree, object to, protest, recognize, repudiate, retract, take back, withdraw.

5a. correct, revise.

6. argue, assume, conclude that, deduce, emphasize, neglect, postulate, stipulate.

7. begin by, conclude by, digress, first (second, third, and so on), in conclusion, turn to.

7a. analyze, define, distinguish, interpret.

7b. explain, formulate, illustrate.

7c. call, refer, regard as, understand.

Austin's classification would receive strong support if it could be shown that membership in each category corresponded to a specific pattern of syntactic behavior. The following are the principal syntactic phenomena that I know of on which performative verbs differ from one another.[3] In some cases practically all of the things assigned by Austin to a particular class behave alike and the exceptions are things which on other grounds might be held to belong to another category; for example, *acquit*, which Austin calls a verdictive, might be held instead to be an operative, and indeed it is similar to operatives and unlike vedictives in that it cannot be used performatively with *would*: saying 1a cannot be an act of acquitting, though saying 1b can be an act of estimating:[4]

1a. I would acquit Dean of the charge.
 b. I would estimate that the repairs will cost $200.

However, in some cases the test cuts across one of Austin's (or Vendler's) categories, as indicated in the table.[5]

|  |  | in passive | *would like to* | with *would* | with *will* | with *let me* |
|---|---|---|---|---|---|---|
| can be used performatively with | | | | | | |
| Verdictive |  | */OK | * | OK | OK | ? |
| Operative |  | OK | * | * | * | * |
| Imperative |  | OK/* | * | * | * | * |
| Advisory |  | OK | OK | OK | OK | OK |
| Commissive |  | */OK | OK | * | * | OK |
| Behabitive |  | * | OK | * | * | OK |
| Expositive | 1 | * | OK | OK | * | OK |
|  | 2 | * | OK | OK | OK | OK |
|  | 3 | * | OK | OK | OK | OK |
|  | 3a | * | OK | OK | OK | OK |
|  | 4 | * | OK | OK | OK | OK |
|  | 5 | * | OK | OK | OK | OK |
|  | 5a | * | OK | OK | OK | OK |
|  | 6 | * | OK | OK | OK | OK |
|  | 7 | * | OK | * | OK | OK |
|  | 7a | * | OK | OK | OK | OK |
|  | 7b | * | OK | OK | OK | OK |
|  | 7c | * | OK | OK | OK | * |

The possibility of using a passive performatively apparently hinges on a characteristic that is irrelevant to Austin's classification, namely, whether the act can be performed as an 'official', 'impersonal' act. It is probably that characteristic which makes it impossible to use a behabitive performatively[6] (* *You are hereby thanked for the lovely dinner you cooked last night*). Regarding the other phenomena, the only category of Austin-Vendler's in which there is a great amount of nonuniformity is the exercitives. One subset of exercitives consists of acts of advising and is almost exactly singled out by the property of allowing both *would* and *would like to* when used performatively, though that property is shared by *request*. One systematic difference between what I have labeled as 'Advisories' and 'Imperatives' above, and one for which even *request* behaves like an imperative rather than like an advisory, is that *ask* can be used to report imperative acts[7] but not advisory acts. If someone orders you to shine his shoes or begs you to shine his shoes, he asks you to shine his shoes. If he forbids you to shine his shoes, he asks you not to shine his shoes. While it might be more usual to report the latter as his having *told* you not to shine his shoes the following shows *ask* to be applicable:

2. Did he ask you not to shine his shoes?
   a. Yes, indeed he forbade me to shine them.
   b. *No, (but) he forbade me to shine them.

However, advising, recommending, and the like, are not asking:

3. Did he ask you to shine his shoes?
   a. *Yes, indeed he advised me to shine them.
   b. No, but he advised me to shine them.
   c. Yes, and he also advised me to shine them.

I wish now to take up the question of whether the seven classes of performative verbs that I have arrived at each examplify some general semantic structure, and more importantly, whether such a semantic structure also provides a *sufficient* condition for a verb to be of the class in question. I note that both Austin and Vendler have provided necessary conditions on the semantic structure of verbs of various categories, for example, that verdictives must have a complement that is in the indicative mood; this must be interpreted as a condition on semantic structure rather than on surface structure, in view of verbs such as *value*, for example, *I value this vase at $300*, which do not have a surface complement but correspond to a semantic structure such as 'I state that this vase is worth $300'.

The class for which it is most obvious what the verbs have in common and what makes them performative is the operatives. An operative speech act is an act in which the speaker makes something the case by saying that it is to be the case, for example, make Gene Autry ambassador to France by saying that Gene Autry is to be ambassador to France or makes Bing Crosby cease to be a member of the Catholic Church by saying that Bing Crosby is no longer a member of the Catholic Church. In almost all cases, the operative verb incorporates part of the meaning of a complement clause; *decree* is the only one for which the complement appears intact in surface structure. To a large extent, felicitous utterances in which *decree* is used performatively can be reported using more specific operatives, for example, a felicitous utterance of 4a can be reported by 4b:

4a. I decree that Bing Crosby is no longer a member of the Catholic Church.
  b. The Pope excommunicated Bing Crosby.

However, decrees (and operative acts in general) form a proper subset of acts in which something is made the case by saying that it is to be the case. A person who possesses magic powers may be able to cause Richard Nixon to have two heads by saying 'Richard Nixon has two heads' or 'Let Richard Nixon have two heads', but such an act is not an operative act, nor any other kind of illocutionary act, nor is the appearance of a second head on Nixon's shoulders a perlocutionary effect,[8] even though it conforms to definitions of 'perlocutionary effect' that are sometimes offered. It will not do just to say that an operative act is an act of making something the case by saying that it is (to be) the case. The relationship of the act of saying the sentence and the event of Gene Autry becoming ambassador to France, or of your nephew ceasing to be your heir, or of Mr. Birnbaum ceasing to have a job in your firm is not one of mere causation but of inclusion, perhaps even of identity. At the moment, I have thought of no better way of representing this relationship than in terms of referential indices, where event verbs have referential indices and the predicate of saying has the same index as does the verb of becoming for example,[9]

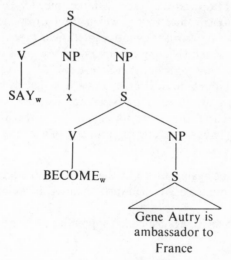

Imperatives and commissives also make something the case by saying that it is to be the case, though what they make the case is not something that is describable by the apparent complement sentence. When you order someone to shine your shoes, you are not causing him to shine your shoes; however, you are causing him to owe you a shoeshine. Assuming that the order is felicitous (i.e., that you are in a position to issue orders to that person and that he hears and understands the order), he is in debt to you and will remain in debt until either he discharges the obligation by shining your shoes or you relieve him of the obligation by canceling your order. If you promise someone to mow his lawn on Saturday, you bring it about that you owe him an act of mowing his lawn on Saturday and, as before, you remain in his debt until either you discharge the obligation or he relieves you of the obligation. Imperatives and commissives do not always create debts, but they create some kind of commitment, either on the part of the speaker or on the part of some affected person, or on both. Imperatives divide into two types: those which cause the person to whom they are addressed to owe the speaker an act of the type in question (*admonish, caution, command, direct, forbid, order*), and those which commit the person to whom they are addressed to considering the request and commit the speaker to being grateful if the request is complied with (*beg, entreat, implore, plead, pray, request, supplicate*). There are in addition two verbs which do not really fit into either class (*demand* and *insist*) and which have to do with the interesting case where the speaker believes the addressee to be unwilling to do what he ought to do.

I propose that the logical structure of imperative and commissive clauses is similar to that of operative clauses, with the embedded clause specifying the debt, commitment, and so on, which the corresponding act would bring about, for example, the semantic structure of *I promise to mow your lawn on Saturday* would be along the lines of 'I say$_w$ that it comes$_w$ about that I owe you mowing your lawn on Saturday'.

I should now talk about advisories, but I have hardly anything to say about them. There are three really hard-core advisories: *advise, counsel,* and *recommend.* These three verbs (though not the other verbs that I have called advisories) have the interesting property of allowing the preposition *against*:

5a. Bill advised me against bombing the Treasury Building.
 b. The lawyer counseled Mrs. Schwartz against demanding custody of the pelican.
 c. Spiro recommended against Nixon appointing Gene Autry ambassador to France.

This might be taken as suggesting that these verbs involve advocacy; however, as Searle (1969) has pointed out, they do not involve quite that since they refer to acts in which the speaker takes the addressee's point of view: 'If I were you, I wouldn't bomb the Treasury Building'. There is nothing insincere about advising a person to do something that the giver of the advice wants him not to do. Good advice is advice which would benefit the recipient if followed, not the giver of the advice. *Urge* and *advocate*, on the other hand, take the speaker's point of view. The appropriate semantic structure may very well be something like 'I tell you that for you to do X would be good for you' in the case of *advise, counsel,* and *recommend,* and 'I tell you that for you to do X would be good for me' or just plain ' . . . would be good' in the case of *advocate* or *urge.* However, I can offer nothing of substance to back up this suggestion.

It is interesting to ask whether Austin and Vendler were simply in error when they lumped advisories and imperatives together. Do those classes have any more in common with each other than with commissives or expositives? One important thing, not to my knowledge so far noted, which they have in common and share with nothing else is that they can be used as parentheticals with sentences that are grammatically imperative:

6a. Shine my shoes, I command you.
  b. Please raise my pay, I implore you.
  c. Don't ask for custody of the pelican, I advise you, Mrs. Schwartz.
  d. Appoint Frank Sinatra director of the FBI, I urge you, Mr. President.

The discussion in Searle 1975 makes clear what is are the bottom of the similarity between advisories and imperatives: they are the kinds of speech acts where the 'point' of the act is to get the addressee to do the thing in question. When successful, an imperative act gets the addressee to do the thing in question because it is the speaker's desire, and an advisory act gets him to do it because it is good (for him or for the speaker, or just plain good). However, at the moment I do not see how to incorporate Searle's notion of 'point' into the system of semantic representation that I have been using.[10]

I now turn to behabitives. Surface appearances to the contrary, wishing a person a happy birthday does not consist in expressing a wish that his birthday will be happy. Indeed, telling a person that you hope he will enjoy his birthday does not really constitute wishing him a happy birthday.[11] In wishing a person a happy birthday, one is acknowledging that it is (or soon will be) that person's birthday and that one owes the person that acknowledgment. Likewise, congratulating a person on his promotion does not consist in telling him that you are glad that he was promoted; for example, you don't congratulate a person by saying, 'I'm glad that you were promoted, since that means that you will be able to pay me the money you owe me'. On the other hand, saying 'I'm delighted that you were promoted' *can* be an act of congratulating if it is done for the right reason. In congratulating, as in most behabitive acts, the speaker is not simply informing the addressee of his feelings but is expressing those feelings (or feigned facsimiles of feelings) as an act of homage to the addressee. To congratulate a person for something is not to inform him that you are glad about it, and to thank a person for something is not to inform him that you are grateful for it, since to inform a person of something it is necessary that he not yet know it, whereas to congratulate or thank a person it is irrelevant whether he already knows that you are glad or that you are grateful. Indeed, if a person says 'I'm very happy that you were promoted', meaning to congratulate you, it would be not merely rude but a non sequitur for you to reply 'I already know that'.

My best guess as to the semantic structure of behabitives is that they are benefactive constructions, for example, that 'I thank you for helping me' means something like 'I offer to you my statement that I am grateful to you for helping me'. This would make behabitives a special case of whatever class of performative verbs *give* and *offer* (as in *I offer you these flowers as a token of my esteem*) belong to. Operative and commissive are the only obvious possibilities, and I think *give* and *offer* make clear that no real line can be drawn between operatives and commissives: acts of giving and offering bring about something which is only in part a commitment on the part of the speaker (namely, the commitment to give up any claim on the disposition of the gift; in the case of *offer*, this commitment is contingent upon the beneficiary's accepting it).

The above sketch will not fit some verbs which Austin included, to my mind incorrectly, under 'behabitives': *challenge, dare, defy*. Those three verbs should perhaps be called commissives, since they amount to bets ('I bet that you won't have the guts/ability/chutzpah/ . . . to X').

Austin's observations about verdictives  as contrasted with exercitives and commissives, amount to saying that in semantic structure verdictives involve a complement in the indicative mood (i.e., something which purports to be true or false) whereas exercitives and commissives involve some other kind of complement. For example, *I diagnose Mrs. McGonigle's disease as cirrhosis of the liver* has a semantic structure involving the proposition that Mrs. McGonigle's disease is cirrhosis of the liver, and it is appropriate to respond to a verdictive utterance by expressing agreement or disagreement with that proposition. This constrast can be seen in adjuncts which modify the embedded clause:

7a. Harry estimated that the repairs would cost $200, which was true/ correct.

b. *Harry ordered Susan to kiss him, which was true/correct.[12]

This characteristic is shared with expositives (except for subclasses 3a and 7), and the question arises whether there is a systematic difference between verdictives and expositives. That there is a systematic difference is suggested by the fact that, quite generally, verdictives do not allow *would like to* or *let me* when used performatively, whereas expositives do allow them. I think the following fact gives a clue as to the difference. It is much easier to imagine a situation in which 8a would be appropriate than a situation in which 8b would be:

8a. Since Mrs. McGonigle was admitted to the hospital, Dr. Novotny has stated fifty times that she is suffering from cirrhosis of the liver.
 b. Since Mrs. McGonigle was admitted to the hospital, Dr. Novotny has diagnosed her ailment fifty times as cirrhosis of the liver.

Example 8a suggests that Dr. Novotny has held a single opinion steadfastly since he first examined Mrs. McGonigle; 8b suggests that he has recurring doubts or that the other doctors keep challenging him and that he keeps reexamining her, only to keep arriving at the same diagnosis. When a doctor diagnoses a patient's ailment, he puts his judgment of the patient's ailment into the record. He can make a new diagnosis only when his previous diagnosis has been rendered no longer part of the record (for example, because of his coming to doubt his earlier judgment) and there is again an empty space in 'the record' for his judgment. But one can state something regardless of whether he is already on the record as holding the view which he states. In this respect, assuming that *diagnose* is typical of verdictives and *state* of expositives, then verdictives behave like operatives, imperatives, advisories, and commissives, whereas expositives behave like behabitives. I can thank you for you helping me even if I have already thanked you (indeed, one often says *Thanks again for helping me*). However, the Pope can excommunicate Bing Crosby again only if Crosby has in the meantime made amends and become a Catholic in good standing again; I can order you again to shine my shoes only if the earlier order is no longer in force (through your having discharged it or my having withdrawn it or the deadline for your obeying it having elapsed); I can advise you again to change all your dollars into yen only if either I have withdrawn my earlier advice or the situation has changed so as to render my earlier advice inapplicable; I can promise you again to proofread your article only if you have relieved me of the obligation which I had originally contracted.

This suggests that verdictives have a semantic structure along the lines of 'I say$_w$ that it comes$_w$ about that it is on the record that I believe that S'.[13]

My remark that Dr. Novotny can state fifty times that Mrs. McGonigle is suffering from cirrhosis of the liver, without his having changed his mind or anything else having happened, implies that expositives, at least, insofar as *state* is typical of them, are not causatives, whereas verdictives, operatives, imperatives, advisories, and commissives are. Actually, there are some verbs which Austin classes as expositives which appear to be causatives, particularly in his subclasses 5 and 5a. *Correct, repudiate, retract, revise, take back,* and *withdraw* are of interest because of their relationship to illocutionary acts of other types: you can correct an estimate or repudiate a diagnosis, for example. These verbs all mean something like 'cause oneself to cease to be on record as holding that S' (or in the case of *correct* and *revise*, 'cause oneself to be on record as holding that $S_1$ instead of being on record as holding that $S_2$'). However, this leaves a mystery: if they have semantic structures like verdictives or operatives, why do they allow *would like to* and *let me* when used performatively, which expositives normally allow but verdictives and operatives do not?

There are two other subclasses of Austin's expositives which are grossly different from the rest: the interrogative verbs (group 3a) and the discourse structure verbs (group 7). Other expositives take indicative declarative complements. However, group 3a take dependent questions as complements and group 7 take performative complements (indeed, generally expositive or behabitive complements), except for *turn to*, which takes not a complement but a NP that describes the next point on the 'agenda':

9a. I would like to begin by asking whether you subscribe to *Screw*.
  b. Let me conclude by expressing my gratitude to the wonderful people who invited me here.
  c. I now turn to the question of whether performative deletion involves an essential variable.

I take it as obvious that the items in group 7 are the same ones which appear in such sentences as

10a. Dr. Novotny began the operation by making an incision in Mrs. McGonigle's right earlobe.
  b. John Cage concluded his performance by pouring coffee into a cello while four nude women turned the pegs and plucked the strings.

Sentences such as 9b have a deleted object which refers to whatever undertaking the utterance is being conceived as part of (a speech, an argument, etc.). I conjecture that these sentences have the same semantic structure as sentences with nonrestrictive clauses, as in

11. Dr. Novotny made an incision in Mrs. McGonigle's right earlobe, which [= Dr. Novotny's making the incision] was the beginning of the operation.

This proposal is attractive in that at least allows one to say that in semantic structure the embedded performative in 9b is not embedded, that is, that 'My expressing gratitude . . . is the beginning (of this talk)' would be external to 'I express gratitude . . . ' in the semantic structure of 9b. The exact details of this proposal would depend on an account of nonrestrictive clauses, a topic which is of considerable relevance here since, as has been pointed out many times, a nonrestrictive clause has its own illocutionary force, over and above whatever illocutionary force the sentence to which it is adjoined has.

There is reason to propose a similar analysis for *answer, rejoin, reply*, and *respond* (group 3). Note that these verbs can also be used with embedded performatives:

12a. I would reply by stating that political offices in Chicago are hereditary.
  b. Let me respond by asking whether your premises are consistent.
  c. I'd like to answer by denying that I have ever supported minimum wage laws.

I conjecture that in sentences like 13 an embedded performative has been deleted:

13a. I would reply that political offices in Chicago are hereditary.
  b. I'd like to answer that I have never supported minimum wage laws.

Putting this conjecture together with that of the last paragraph, I would conjecture that *X reply to Y that S* would have a logical structure along the lines of 'X say$_w$ to Y that S, and X's doing w is a reply to (what Y asked)', or whatever analog to this best fits what is known about nonrestrictive clauses. The deletion of an embedded performative that I conjecture for 13 may also be involved in such a sentence as 14, though *repeat* evidently involves a different semantic structure from that of *reply*:

14. I repeat that I have to leave by 11:30.

I have so far been commenting on relatively atypical expositives and have had hardly anything to say about such garden-variety expositives as *state, declare,* and *remark*. In fact I have very little to say about garden-variety expositives. Their meanings all seem to involve 'I say that S', but I have no clear picture of what else they involve and how they differ from one another, except that it is clear that they differ in all sorts of ways. For example, when used nonperformatively, *mention* is factive but *state* is not, as the following examples illustrate:[14]

15a. Did Prof. Schwartz state/mention that the moon revolves about the sun?
  b. Prof. Schwartz didn't state/mention that the moon revolves about the sun.

In any event, it appears that the performativity of garden-variety performatives belong to the 'say' part of their meanings. Further investigation of what else may be involved in the meaning should also take into account

Austin's important observation that expositives 'make plain how our utterances fit into the course of an argument or conversation', a point that I have not done justice to here.

I have given a rambling and less than fully coherent sketch of performative verbs here, in the course of which I have largely ignored the many questions with which this paper began. However, I think that in the course of it I have got a lot closer to the answer to one of those questions, namely that of what makes performative verbs performative. Specifically, the performativity seemed to be attributable in each case to one of two things. Verdictives, operatives, imperatives, advisories, and commissives all refer to a linguistic act and something that comes about as part of that act. Most behabitives and most expositives refer to acts of saying that S, with the meaning of the verb being allowed to incorporate motives, and the like. Verbs such as *begin* and *conclude* were suggested to be not really performative themselves but to originate in nonrestrictive clauses which can combine with a wide range of performatives. I regard it as fairly plausible that these two characteristics are the only bearers of performativity, though it will take a lot of serious and detailed lexicography to establish that. It is of interest that I have ended up with two sources of performativity rather than one, since the two kinds of illocutionary acts that they correspond to are fairly close matches to what Austin called 'performative' and 'constative'.[15] The performative-constative distinction thus may be alive and well after all, though taking a quite different form from what Austin considered, since, for example, my analysis allows for the possibility of a clause being both constative and performative at the same time, as in the case of behabitive acts, in which one is generally both stating something and offering the act of stating it.

# 17 Lexicography and the Count-Mass Distinction

To my knowledge, the only published dictionary of English which explicitly indicates whether each noun is a count noun or a mass noun is Hornby, Gatenby, and Wakefield's *Advanced Learner's dictionary of Current English* (1963). This paper is concerned with issues raised by the question of whether a dictionary in fact *should* indicate explicitly whether a noun is count or mass, that is, the question of whether counthood or masshood is predictable from the meaning of the word.

I emphasize that I am speaking of the meanings of the words and not about characteristics of the entities that can be described using those words. There is clearly no difference between noodles and spaghetti that can be held responsible for *noodles* being a plural count noun and *spaghetti* a mass noun (in English, this is, not in Italian), nor is there any such difference between garlic and onions or between rice and beans, or between the data that are referred to by a plural count noun and the data that is referred to by a mass noun. The same entities can be described as footwear or as shoes; as furniture or as chairs. However, this does not rule out the possibility that the words *garlic* and *onion* or the words *footwear* and *shoes* or the plural count noun *data* and the mass noun *data* differ in meaning in a way that allows one to infer that the one is a mass noun and the other a count noun. The most obvious aspect of meaning to examine is individuation, and the obvious hypothesis to try is that the meaning of a count noun specifies an individuation but that of a mass noun is neutral as to individuation.

The fact that a particular type of thing always comes in individual quanta does not imply that the meaning of a word describing those things has to make reference to that individuation, for example, from the fact that rice comes in grains or that footwear comes individuated the same way

Reprinted by permission from *Berkeley Linguistics Society* 1 (1975): 314–21. Copyright © 1975 by Berkeley Linguistics Society.

165

that feet are, nothing follows about the meanings of the words *rice* and *footwear*.[1] Actually, I am not completely sure that my claim that the meanings of count nouns but not of mass nouns specify an individuation has any content. In fact, I am encountering head-on Quine's (1960) problem of 'radical translation'. In a language such as Japanese, in which nouns are normally unspecified as to grammatical number and a classifier must be used both in expressions of cardinal number and expressions of quantity, do I have any basis for deciding whether a given noun is a count noun or a mass noun? For example, do I have any basis for treating Japanese *hito'tubu no mu'gi* 'a grain of barley' as semantically like English *a grain of barley* rather than like English *a bean*? If Japanese conceive of beans the way that we conceive of barley, how could we tell?

There is an area of research that may eventually provide the basis for solid answers to such questions, namely, the logic of mass expressions. However, at present that area is grossly underdeveloped.[2] The few existing treatments of quantification of mass expressions (e.g., Parsons 1970) reduce it to quantification over individuals by interpreting an expression such as *all gold* as if it were an abbreviation for *all objects that result from partitioning a mass of gold*. I feel strongly that this approach is misguided and is doomed to failure when any attempt is made to apply it to such expressions as *most gold* or *much gold*. However, until I put my typewriter where my mouth is and produce a (to me) satisfactory account of the logic of mass terms, I will have to content myself with an expression of my visceral feeling that there is a content to the claim that the words *rice* and *bean* differ in meaning by more than just information as to the biological species.

I should at this point also observe that when the meaning of a word does not specify an individuation, it is not necessarily the case that what it refers to is indefinitely divisible. It has occasionally been objected (Antley 1974) against the claim that mass nouns are unspecified as to individuation that many mass nouns cannot be combined with measure expressions that refer to minute quantities, for example,

1. *a molecule of footwear/rice.

However, all that that shows is that there can be a lower limit to the quantity of matter that can possess a given property. There are impeccable mass nouns which refer to mixtures or suspensions rather than to chemically pure substances and which thus cannot be combined with *molecule*:

2. *a molecule of $\begin{cases} \text{Irish coffee.} \\ \text{butter pecan ice cream.} \end{cases}$

If, as I conjecture, the meaning of *footwear* is simply 'to be worn on the feet', the oddity of *a molecule of footwear* will come from the fact that a single molecule is too little to be worn. There is in fact a gradient as to the smallest quantity that is describable by a given mass noun:

3a. an atom of sodium/*water.
  b. a molecule of water/*ice.[3]
  c. a milligram of ice/??garbage/*excelsior.
  d. an ounce of excelsior/?garbage/?ballast.

Excelsior is wood shavings used as a packing material, and you can't call something excelsior unless there is enough of it to use as packing material. Ballast is anything used to weigh down the bottom of a floating object and thus cause it to float upright, and unless you have enough to lower the center of gravity of the object, it isn't ballast.[4]

It is quite easy to find dictionary definitions in which a count noun is defined in terms of an individuation and a semantically similar mass noun is defined without reference to an individuation, for example,[5]

4. *noodle*. A thin strip of food paste, usually made of flour and eggs.
   *pasta*. Paste or dough made of flour and water, used dried, as in macaroni, or fresh, as in ravioli.

The definition of *noodle*, on the one hand, specifies an individuation: a noodle is a strip, two noodles is two such strips, and so on. The definition of *pasta*, on the other hand, indicates no individuation: it indicates what pasta is made of, what its texture is, and how it is used, but it does not indicate any quantum of pastahood.

It is also quite easy to find pairs of words that differ as to counthood but as defined by a dictionary in a way that provides no information from which that difference could be predicted:

5. *rice*. 1. A cereal grass, *Oryza sativa*, . . .
         2. The starchy edible seed of this grass.
   *bean*. 1. Any of several plants of the species *Phaseolus*, . . .
          2. The edible seed or pod of any of these plants.

In either case, the definition amounts to 'the edible seed of X', which provides no hint of the fact that one seed of *Phaseolus vulgaris* is *a bean* whereas one seed of *Oryza sativa* is not *a rice* but rather *a grain of rice*. In this case, the failure of the lexicographer to provide the information is partly due to the fact that he chose to include a nonrestrictive modifier ('edible') in the definitions, which forces a definite article on him and thus robs him of the possibility of using an indefinite article as a means of indicating the individuation of beans ('A seed or pod of any of these plants').[6] It is less clear how the definition of *rice* could be fixed up as to make it clear from the definition that *rice* is a mass noun. If the predicate use of nouns is taken to be the basic use, a definition of *rice* (that is, of *is rice*) could be given along the lines of 'consists of seed(s) of *Oryza sativa*', where 'seed(s)' is intended to be unspecified as to number. I offer this definition only to show that it is possible (albeit by brute force) to cast a definition of *rice* into a form that makes it refer not to grains of rice but to the substance of those grains.

Before leaving *rice* and *beans*, I should touch on the senses listed as '1' in these definitions. In what sort of sentences does sense 1 appear? Perhaps in sentences like 6?

6. We grow beans in this field.
   A lot of rice is grown in Southeast Asia.

While both of these sentences are used with reference to the planting and cultivation of whole Phaseolus or Oryza plants, and in large numbers at a time, the grammatical number of the noun is still singular in the case of *rice* and plural in the case of *bean*. Thus, even when the cultivation of whole plants is referred to, the choice of number is made as if it were the food for which that plant is grown that was being referred to. This fact leads me to conjecture that, contrary to the apparent opinion of the lexicographer responsible for the definitions (5), sense 2 is more basic than sense 1, if sense 1 is even a real sense of the words *rice* and *bean*. In fact, a case can be made that the object of *grow* can just as easily refer to the product that the plant yields as to the plant itself and thus that *rice* and *bean* in 6 are really used in sense 2. For example, in 7 the object NP clearly refers to the vegetable (in the culinary sense) that results, not to the whole plant or to the biological species, since parsley and parsnips are two parts of the same plant but the sentences of 7 differ in meaning:

7. I always grow my own parsley.
   I always grow my own parsnips.

The nouns *cold* and *headache* are clear cases of count nouns whose countness can be attributed to an individuation specified in their meanings, as contrasted with *flu*, *diarrhea*, and *tuberculosis*, which have meanings that are neutral as to individuation. Colds and headaches can be counted:

8. I had two colds last winter.
   I've had two headaches within the last three days.

A cold is a 'case' of a particular infection. A 'case' must be distinguished from an 'attack': the attack is the onset of the disease, whereas the 'case' endures from onset to cure. The observation that a cold is a case of something is supported by the fact that *cold* appears to pattern exactly the way that *case of X* does:

9.  I have a cold.

I have $\begin{Bmatrix} \text{a case} \\ \text{*an attack} \end{Bmatrix}$ of the flu.

Do you have the same cold/*flu that you had last week?

Do you have the same case of the flu that you had last week?

I had a sudden $\begin{cases} \text{attack of the flu.} \\ \text{*case of the flu.} \\ \text{*cold.} \end{cases}$

There are ambiguous words whose different meanings correspond to different individuations. *Job* has the three senses illustrated in the following sentences:

10a. Let me finish this job, and then I'll join you in the bar.
  b. Harry and I have the same job—we're both file clerks.
  c. They not only fired me, they abolished my job.

In 10a, the job is a specific piece of work, and the job ceases to exist when that work is completed. In 10b, the job is an ongoing activity which the agent does as a profession or means of livelihood, and two persons who are hired to perform the same activity have the same job, in this sense. In 10c, the job is an institution, which comes into being when the employer creates such a position in the organizational structure of his firm, and the job continues in existence, regardless of who is employed in the job (or even whether anyone is) and regardless of any changes that are made in the duties that the holder of the job must perform, until either the job is abolished by the employer or the firm ceases to exist. In this sense of *job*, the job you have today in which you are paid $15,000 a year to teach Montague grammar may be the same job in which 30 years ago someone else was paid $5,000 a year to teach freshman German and coach the squash team. Different words may share just one of these individuations. For example, *task* has only a sense parallel to the *job* of 10a, *profession* only a sense parallel to the *job* of 10b, and *chairmanship* only a sense parallel to the *job* of 10c. And the most common sense of *work* involves no individuation at all. The individuation is part of the meaning of all of these nouns (except *work*), and their countness is predictable from the presence of the individuation in the meaning.

Let us now turn to *footwear*, which Katz (1970) has held to have the same meaning as *articles of apparel to be worn on the feet*, that is, to have the same meaning as a count expression. One can of course claim (as I have, in McCawley 1971*b*) that *footwear* rather has the meaning of the mass expression *apparel to be worn on the feet* and that *articles of apparel to be worn on the feet* makes reference to an individuation but *apparel to be worn on the feet* does not. But because of the fact that the apparel that people wear on their feet is as individuated as their feet are, it is not easy to come up with evidence that shows whether any of these expressions differ in meaning. Relevant facts might be sought in an imaginary situation in which, through the miracles of modern technology, nonindividuated footwear is put on the market, for example, socks that you can spray on your feet, in the fashion of the spray-on bandages that have been developed in recent years. However, it is not clear that it is the liquid inside the aerosol can that constitutes footwear, rather than just the socklike units that are formed as it is sprayed on the feet. A similar situation prevails in the case of *furniture*, though the possibility of nonindividuated furniture is less fanciful; indeed, there are dozens of stores where you can buy crates full of modules that can be assembled to fit your fancy into one gigantic structure or several small ones. To the extent that 11 is a normal thing to say with reference to such modules, *furniture* will have to be taken to be unspecified as to any individuation:

11. I've just ordered two crates of furniture.

However, there is great variability among informants as to the extent to which they are happy in applying 11 to modular furniture.

There are in fact sentences that might be taken to show individuation lurking in the meaning of *furniture*. While 12b would be true in a situation where Fred has one 2000-foot-long piece of rope, 12a is not true in a situation in which Fred has one 40-foot-long sofa but no other furniture:

12a. Fred has a lot of furniture.
  b. Fred has a lot of rope.

Example 12a seems to imply that Fred has at least several pieces of furniture,[7] despite that fact that a single piece of furniture, unlike a grain of rice, can be enormous. Likewise, *furniture* admits adjectives referring to the size of the piece much more readily than do more hard-core mass nouns such as *rice*, and even *footwear* is not outlandish in such a usage:

13a. large furniture
  b. ?large footwear (accepted by some informants as a way of referring to ski boots, etc.)
  c. *large rice (cf. long-grained rice)
  d. **large sand[8]

However, *a lot* in 12a does not just mean 'a large number' though it appears to imply it. Example 14 does not allow the interpretation that the number of pieces of furniture that Fred has exceeds the number that I do.

14. Fred has more furniture than I do.

It is easy to come up with situations in which 14 would be judged false even though Fred has more pieces of furniture than I do; for example, if Fred has 4 chairs, 3 magazine racks, 2 coffee tables, and 1 lamp, and I have 2 chairs, 1 desk, 1 bed, 1 sofa, and 1 table, my six pieces of furniture would constitute more furniture than Fred's ten pieces do.

The situation is similar with

15. Fred has more clothes than I do.

If Fred's wardrobe consists of 2 pairs of shoes, 2 pairs of socks, 1 pair of swimming trunks, and 4 T-shirts, and mine consists of 1 pair of shoes, 1 pair of socks, 1 pair of levis, 2 shirts, and 1 jacket, it would be strange to say that Fred has more clothes than I do, even though Fred has 9 or 13 articles of clothing (depending on whether a pair of shoes or of socks counts as 1 or as 2 articles of clothing) but I have only 6 or 8. I conjecture that the reason for this is that Fred's 9 or 13 articles of clothing don't clothe him as fully as my 6 or 8 articles clothe me; likewise, Fred's 10 pieces of furniture don't furnish his apartment as fully as my 6 pieces furnish mine. I thus maintain that the reason that 12a is not true unless Fred has a large number of pieces of furniture is that a really small number of pieces of furniture is not enough to make an apartment fully furnished. Or at least, that is the case with regard to conventional furniture. George Williams informs me that modular furniture has been taken to such extremes in West Germany that one can purchase modules from which one can construct a 'Wohnungslandschaft', which may be a continuous structure constructed out of modules and incorporating sleeping space, sitting space, work space, and so on. I do not find 12a odd if it is used with reference to a single very elaborate Wohnungslandschaft which furnishes the apartment as thoroughly as would a large number of pieces of conventional furniture.

I thus conclude that the meanings of *furniture*, *clothing*, and presumably also *footwear*, though that is a less clear case, are not of the form 'articles for doing X' but are rather simply 'for doing X', for example, *clothing* would be 'for wearing' or 'to be worn', *footwear* would mean 'to be worn on the feet', and *furniture* would mean something like 'to support persons and objects', supplemented by additional conjuncts such as 'is moveable', and these words thus do not conflict with the claim that a noun is a mass noun if and only if its meaning does not provide an individuation for the things that it describes.

But wait a minute—in the above argument, specifically, in 15, the noun involved was not *clothing* but *clothes*. I could just as well have used *clothing* instead of *clothes* in that argument, and nothing would have been any different. But what about *clothes*? Is it a mass noun? The fact that it takes plural agreement might suggest that it is really a count noun:

16. My clothes are/*is in this locker.

However, other facts show more clearly that it isn't a count noun; for example, it can't be combined with cardinal number expressions:

17. *I've just bought several/five clothes.
    *Many clothes are too expensive for me to buy.

*Clothes* evidently is a plural mass noun, as are such words as *brains*, *guts*, and *intestines*:

18. His guts were splattered over the wall (, *all five of them).

So we have plural mass nouns, a fact that we'll have to live with, just as we have to live with the fact that there are count nouns with only a plural form, due to either pure idiosyncrasy (as with Russian *časy* 'clock') or to a minor regularity (as in the case of *trousers*, *tweezers*, and *goggles*).

But then what about some of the count nouns that I talked about at the beginning of this paper? Is there any way of telling whether the plural forms *noodles* and *beans* are ambiguous between a plural count sense, as in 19a, and a plural mass sense, as in 19b?

19a. How many noodles did you eat?
  b. How much noodles did you eat?

I am at a loss as to how to tell whether these are distinct senses. If this is a real ambiguity, it can be incorporated into a grammar in the form of a redundancy rule which would predict the mass sense from the count sense, for example, it would predict a sense 'food consisting of seeds of X' for any noun which has a sense 'seed of X' (though this extra sense would be in use only for those species whose seeds were used as food). But that raises the question, why should the prediction go in that direction rather than the opposite? Why not take the mass sense as basic, recognize a lot of mass plurals, and have a redundancy rule predicting a count sense for the singular of any mass plural with a meaning 'consisting of X's of Y'?

Offhand, I can't think of any solid reason for preferring either analysis over the other. However, either way, the counthood or masshood of a noun will still be predictable from its meaning. But also, either way, my hope expressed above that the logic of mass expressions might provide a basis for setting up a semantic distinction between *rice* and *beans* would be shattered: it could at best provide a basis for a distinction between *rice* and one sense of *bean*, but it would not help answer the question of which sense of *bean* is more basic nor, thus, the question of whether *bean* basically differs from *rice* in more than the difference between *Phaseolus vulgaris* and *Oryza sativa*. Answers to those questions would be available if someone could show that *beans* really is not ambiguous between a count sense and a mass sense. A way of telling whether it has that ambiguity ought to be lurking in any theory of grammar and lexicon that is worth *Phaseolus vulgaris*.[9]

# 18    Review of R. Lakoff, *Language and Woman's Place*

Feminist activists have devoted an unusually large amount of their energies to matters of language: to publicizing respects in which language as it exists (especially the English language) allegedly fosters sexism, and to promoting reforms that are supposed to purge English of its sexism. Indeed, one of the most tangible effects that the feminist movement has had on American society so far is linguistic: the widespread adoption of *Ms.* before women's names.

Language reform is in many respects like urban renewal. It is easy for people to find causes for dissatisfaction both in cities as they are and in languages as they are, and to come up with ideas about how they would like things to be; and in both cases, those who clamor for change usually have little understanding of how the thing that they want to change really works (in particular, they view it as far more static than it really is), have badly misidentified problems, and have given little thought to what would happen if things were as they say they want them. Before there can be intelligent feminist language reform, there must be serious studies of the area that is to be reformed. Robin Lakoff's *Language and Woman's Place* is a major step in that direction.

*Language and Woman's Place* is an extremely perceptive and well-informed work and, equally importantly, one that displays a refreshing sense of proportion. Lakoff, who is associate professor of linguistics at the University of California at Berkeley, waits until page 40 before touching on any of the more celebrated areas of feminist agitation about language, having chosen wisely to concentrate on points that are much less widely known (many of which she was evidently the first to notice) but which are of more importance in understanding how language affects women and how the status of women is reflected in language. When she gets to the much-discussed matter

Reprinted by permission from *Reason*, August 1976, pp. 40–42. Copyright © 1976 by Reason Enterprises.

of English pronouns (both the fact that English distinguishes a masculine pronoun and a feminine pronoun and the fact that the masculine pronoun is used in sentences like *Everyone should take his seat*, in which persons of both sexes are referred to), Lakoff says that she feels that "the emphasis upon this point, to the exclusion of most other linguistic points, by writers within the women's movement is misguided. . . . My feeling is that this area of pronominal neutralization is both less in need of changing and less open to change than many of the other disparities that have been discussed earlier, and we should perhaps concentrate our efforts where they will be most fruitful."

The "disparities" to which Lakoff refers include pairs of words that are generally thought to differ only in the sex of the person referred to (*bachelor* vs. *spinster*; *widow* vs. *widower*; *gentleman* vs. *lady*) but in fact have additional differences which reflect and perhaps reinforce respects in which women are at a disadvantage. Take the fact that you can refer to a woman whose husband has died as *John Smith's widow* but you cannot refer to a man whose wife has died as *Mary Smith's widower*: he is only a widower, not *her* widower. This, of course, is a reflection of the fact that in this society we assign women a name and a status through their husbands (she is Mrs. John Smith, and when you are introduced to her, one of the first things you ask is "What does your husband do?"), but we don't assign men a name and a status through their wives (he stays Mr. John Smith, just as he was before his marriage, and you don't ask him "What does your wife do?" unless you have been told that she "does" something). Here the sexism of the language goes a step beyond that of the culture: you can't refer to Arthur Miller as *Marilyn Monroe's widower*, regardless of your views of the status of husbands and wives.[1]

Lakoff's discussion of the word *lady* is masterful.[2] She shows that *lady* is not just a "more polite" word than *woman*: note the difference in meaning between *She's a real lady* and *She's a real woman*, and how ludicrous it would sound to say *Ladies' Lib* or *Ladies' Strike for Peace*. *Lady* means not "woman" but "woman in a standard feminine role." This is why it is even more insulting to a female M.D. to speak to her as a *lady doctor* than as a *woman doctor*: it implies that her medical practice falls into the area of triviality that is the stereotype of proper activities for women and thus implies about the same estimate of her medical skills (though not of her bedside manner) as would *girl doctor*. Similarly, a serious art gallery may hold a *one-woman show*, but never a *one-lady show*.

The differences between how men speak and how women speak that Lakoff discusses are much less striking than those between words referring to men and words referring to women. Aside from a couple of usages that are pretty well confined to the speech of women (such as *divine* and *adorable* in exclamations like *What a divine idea!*), the differences she cites are things that occur in the speech of both sexes but which one sex is freer to use, in the sense of being less open to ridicule or censure, or open to less severe censure. Women are free to use highly specific color terms (*magenta, heliotrope*, etc.) which men are "permitted" to use only when they are "specialists," such as a stamp collector talking about stamps or an interior decorator talking about paint. (The laughter aroused when a man speaks of magenta drapes is comparable to the irritation a dentist feels when a nondentist patient speaks of the buccal surface of the upper right lateral incisor: in either case the speaker's language expresses intimacy with a subject that he is not "entitled" to treat with familiarity—it's as if he had said *tu* to someone he ought to address as *vous*; but why is it that just being a woman entitles you to say *tu* to the world of colors?) If a 10-year-old boy calls you a motherfucker, he may get spanked, but he won't be sent to a psychiatrist; however, if a 10-year-old girl calls you a motherfucker, . . .

Lakoff indeed attempts to relate the fact that far more women than men are psychiatric patients to the "double bind" that she sees male/female language differences putting women in: women are expected to "talk like ladies," but a person who talks like a lady removes herself from serious competition for respect as a person. The term "double bind," referring to a situation in which an authority imposes a requirement on someone but will punish him if he complies with that requirement, is from Gregory Bateson, who sees double binds as a cause of schizophrenia. Lakoff doubts that the double bind of male/female language differences leads to real schizophrenia, but she sees it as a respect in which "society is putting a far greater strain on its women than on its men;" she holds that "fighting the paradoxes a woman necessarily faces tends to break down a woman's mental resources; therefore a woman is more apt to run into mental difficulties and, when she faces real stress, to have fewer inner resources left to overcome her problems."

Lakoff could have made a better case for these points if she had widened her perspective here. The differences that she cites between male and female speech are much smaller in scale than those between ghetto black English and "standard" white English, or between many regional dialects and the more prestigious dialects, and it might seem at first glance as if her position implies that blacks and Appalachian whites should have 10 times the psychiatric problems that women do. There is, however, an important difference, namely, that when a black or an Appalachian white wants to become a part of urban white society, acquiring urban white English will help him to do so and will not cause him to be ridiculed behind his back (or at least, not by urban whites). Learning a prestige dialect may cause him problems by antagonizing or alienating his relatives and old friends, but those problems aren't a double bind; whites may penalize a black for being black, but they don't penalize him for trying to talk and look like a white. Moreover, as Breggin (1974) has emphasized, women who visit a psychiatrist for help in replenishing their "mental resources" are likely instead to be administered a mental coup de grace; women, particularly those whose problems are connected with an attempt to break out of a stereotyped female role, have far more to fear from male psychiatrists than from male gynecologists.

One major gap in Lakoff's book is comparison between English and other languages. While she includes a little material about Japanese, she does not get into much detail, which is a pity, since Japanese has much more striking differences between male and female language than English does (for example, only women may omit the verb *to be*) and thus provides an excellent opportunity for testing hypotheses about how language is related to sexism in the culture. (Do women form the majority of psychiatric patients in Japan too?) Some popular beliefs collapse in the face of facts about other languages; for example, Hungarians and Turks don't appear to be less sexist than Americans despite the fact that their languages don't distinguish between *he* and *she*. However, doing a solidly based crosslinguistic study would take a long time, and Lakoff probably has done the best thing by publishing her fairly extensive observations about English now and thus making other investigators aware now of questions that they should raise in investigating other languages.

I will close this review by calling the reader's attention to an interesting point of contact between feminist language reform and a libertarian author who is not normally associated with feminism. A potent way of defusing any sexism in the use of *he* as a "common gender" pronoun is to be found in Harry Browne's *How I Found Freedom in an Unfree World*. Browne adopts the policy of *consistent* use of *he* as a common gender pronoun: he uses *he* whenever there is any chance that persons of both sexes might be included. Most persons use "common gender *he*" inconsistently, by switching to *she* when "typically" a woman is referred to (as in *A teacher should respect her pupils' intellects*) that is, they switch to *she* when a "literal" interpretation of *he* would conflict with stereotypes of sexual roles. Browne's consistent use of common gender *he* results in sentences where an interpretation of *he* as "that male person" would either conflict with the stereotypes (*A teacher should respect his pupils' intellects*) or impose a female point of view (*You shouldn't worry if your spouse spends a lot of time with his parents*), which means that male chauvinists can't maintain their chauvinism and still interpret all "common gender *he*" as implying "typically male." By contrast, saying *he or she* (as some feminists have recommended) fosters the standard sexual stereotypes in a way that saying *he* does not: if you say *he or she,* you imply that women aren't included unless they are specially mentioned, and you make it easier to talk about cases where only one sex is included than where both are.[3] Browne's solution to the problem of sexism in common gender *he* amounts to an application of Gresham's law. A *he* that is really unspecified as to sex would drive out of circulation a *he* that meant "typically male," because it would be "on a par" with it but would have less content; the more that people are confronted with instances where *he* has to be interpreted as covering both sexes, the harder it will be to convey "typically male" by using *he.*

Lexicographic Notes
on English Quantifiers

Textbooks of formal logic can easily give the casual reader the impression
that there are only two quantifiers: 'the' universal quantifier and 'the'
existential quantifier. This paper is an attempt to do some of the lexicographic work that is needed to bridge the gap between the spartan conception of quantifier that is current among logicians and the profusion of
words found in natural language that are quantifiers both syntactically and
semantically: syntactically in that they occur in the same position as words
such as *every* and *some* that correspond directly to the logicians' quantifiers
and semantically in that they express the amount or proportion of some
domain for which a given propositional function is true.

While there is a huge literature on the question of how quantifiers fit into
underlying linguistic structure, there has been remarkably little work done
on identifying the contribution of each quantifier to the semantic interpretation of sentences. One particularly outstanding study in this area[1] is Zeno
Vendler's "Each and Every, Any and All," in which Vendler (1967:70–96)
shows that the four English words that are generally held to represent 'the'
universal quantifier are in fact semantically distinct from one another. I
will begin my discussion of English quantifier words by recapitulating and
elaborating on Vendler's observations and conclusions.

If the words *each, every, any, all* were merely surface realizations of 'the'
universal quantifier, the logical formula given in 1 ought to be expressible
by any of the sentences that follow it, and the incoherence of the formula
in 2 (it is incoherent because *similar* cannot be predicated of an individual)
ought to prevent any of the sentences in 2 from being acceptable:

1. ($\forall$x: x is one of the blocks) (x is yellow)
    a. All (of) the blocks are yellow.
    b. Every one of the blocks is yellow.

Reprinted by permission from *Chicago Linguistic Society* 13 (1977): 327–83.
Copyright © 1977 by Chicago Linguistic Society.

    c. ?Each of the blocks is yellow.

    d. *Any of the blocks is yellow.

2. *($\forall$x: x is one of the blocks) (x is similar)

    a. All (of) the blocks are similar.

    b. *Every one of the blocks is similar.

    c. *Each of the blocks is similar.

    d. *Any of the blocks is similar.

However, *each* and *any* are not acceptable expressions of the universal quantifier in 1, and *all* is acceptable in 2 even though the sentence expresses something other than a universal quantification of what you get by replacing the quantified NP by a variable.

The acceptability of 2a leads Vendler to the conclusion that *all* involves reference to a totality (either a set or a mass; he notes that *all* combines with mass terms as well as with individual terms, while *every* and *each* do not combine with mass terms) and he analyzes 2a as involving simply that totality but not a quantifier ranging over the set of blocks. Vendler's discussion suggests that he takes 1a and 1b to involve distinct but equivalent logical forms, with the *all* of 1a providing the set formation operation and the quantifier being 'understood' rather than supplied by *all*:

1a'. ($\forall$x: x $\in$ {y: y is one of the blocks}) (x is yellow)

1b'. ( $\forall$x: x is one of the blocks) (x is yellow)

It is easy to find sentences that are ambiguous between the use of *all* exhibited in 1a, in which the sentence expresses a universal proposition, and that of 2a, in which it does not. For example, G. Lakoff's (1972) example, 3a, can be interpreted either like 1a (implying that each boy individually carried the piano upstairs) or like 2a (implying that there was an act in which all the boys participated jointly); 3b by contrast allows only the former interpretation:

3a. All of the boys carried the piano upstairs.

   b. Every one of the boys carried the piano upstairs.

I interject here the remark that the contrast between *every* and *all* is neutralized in the words *everyone, everybody, everything,* and so on. There are no such words as *allone, *allbody, *allthing,* and the words of the *every* series take over the work of the missing *all* series, as in 2a' and 3a':

2a'. Everyone here is similar.

3a'. Everyone carried the piano upstairs.

Note that 3a' has the same ambiguity as does 3a.

The difference Vendler finds between *all* and *every* is confirmed by the examples in 4:

4a. Köchel compiled a catalog of all of Mozart's works.
  b. ??Köchel compiled a catalog of every one of Mozart's works.
  b'. Köchel compiled a catalog of everything that Mozart wrote.
  c. Imagine all the castles in Spain.
  d. Imagine every castle in Spain.

Example 4a refers to a single catalog that lists all of Mozart's works and does not imply, for example, that Köchel compiled a catalog of *The Magic Flute*. The expression 'a catalog of *The Magic Flute*', of course, is not normal English, though one could easily supply an interpretation of it as, say, a catalog that lists all editions of or recordings of or publications about *The Magic Flute*. While 4c does imply that one is to imagine the castle at Segovia, it does so only because imagining the whole involves imagining the parts; 4c directs the addressee to engage in a single act of imaging in which all the castles in Spain are projected together on his mental screen, whereas 4d suggests that he is to imagine them one by one.

However, it is not quite correct to say that in the 'group' use of *all* the expression *all N* simply refers to a set. Note the difference in meaning between a sentence involving 'group' *all* and a corresponding sentence involving a simple plural NP that presumably refers to the same set:

5a. All of the boys carried the piano upstairs.
  a'. The boys carried the piano upstairs.
  b. It took all of the boys to carry the piano upstairs.
  b'. It took the boys to carry the piano upstairs.

Example 5a implies that all the boys participated in the carrying, but 5a' leaves open the possibility that some of them did not participate. This difference is even clearer in 5b and b': 5b implies that if less than all of them had participated, it would not have been possible to carry the piano upstairs, whereas 5b' implies only that the boys were the only ones who could or would carry the piano upstairs, though it leaves it open whether all of them participated. Thus, group *all* appears to involve a universal quantifier, but applied to a different propositional function than what one might expect: not 'x carried the piano upstairs' but 'x participated in carrying the piano upstairs' (with the subject of *carry* unspecified).

I turn now to *each*. Vendler notes that sentences involving *each* are often odd by virtue of being 'incomplete'. For example, 6c is quite peculiar but becomes normal when an appropriate conjunct is added, as in 6c'; by contrast, the other universal quantifier words do not suffer from this incompleteness:

6a. Take all of the apples.
  b. Take every one of the apples.

c. ?Take each of the apples.
c′. Take each of the apples and weigh it.
d. Take any (one) of the apples.

Whether a simple sentence with *each* will suffer from this sort of incompleteness depends on the choice of lexical items:

7a. Susan admired each of her husbands.
 b. ??Susan admired each of her uncles.
 b′. Susan admired each of her uncles in a different way.

The difference in acceptability between 7a and 7b can be attributed to the fact that in our society women have their husbands in succession but have their uncles at the same time. Example 7a implies that in each period in which Susan was married, she admired the husband she had at that time, whereas no such interpretation is open for 7b. Compare the difference in acceptability of 8a and 8b:[2]

8a. Two secretaries assist each executive.
 b. *Susan assists each executive.
 b′. Susan assists each executive on a different day of the week.

 *Each* involves some pairing of two domains: times with husbands, executives with pairs of secretaries, uncles with ways of admiring them, or acts of selecting an apple with associated acts of weighing the apple. Note the difference between *Five boys wrote a poem*, which refers to a single jointly authored poem, and *Five boys each wrote a poem*, which refers to five different poems. A similar pairing of domains is found with *respective* and *respectively*, an observation that will not surprise those who know Japanese, where the same word, *sorezore*, is used both for *each* and for *respective(ly)*. In many cases, the same idea can be expressed in English using *each* (*Each of the students carved his name on the tree*) or *respective* (*The students carved their respective names on the tree*), though in many cases only one of the two devices is available; for example, there is no alternate form of 6c′ or 7a involving *respective*. The noninterchangeability of *each* and *respective* in English reflects first the fact that *respective* is restricted to definite NP's but *each* does not require that the 'matching' NP be definite and, second, the fact that *respective* is an anaphoric device and thus must appear in an acceptable position relative to its antecedent.

9a. Each of the boys repaired a bicycle.

 b. The boys repaired $\begin{cases} \text{their respective bicycles.} \\ \text{*respective bicycles.} \\ \text{*a respective bicycle.} \end{cases}$

However, I am not yet able to offer a statement of the structural restrictions on the occurrence of *each* and *respective* that is detailed enough to yield a conclusive argument that *each* is or involves what otherwise goes into *respective*.

Consider now *any*. Quine (1960:138–41) has proposed that *any* is a conditioned variant of *every*, specifically that *any* is a universal quantifier with 'wide scope', as in 10a and b, whereas *every* is a universal quantifier with 'narrow scope', as in 10c and d:

10a. If anyone objects, I'll leave.    $(\forall x) [(x \text{ objects}) \supset (I \text{ leave})]$
  b. John didn't see anyone.    $(\forall x) \sim (\text{John saw } x)$
  c. If everyone objects, I'll leave.    $[(\forall x) (x \text{ objects})] \supset (I \text{ leave})$
  d. John didn't see everyone.    $\sim (\forall x) (\text{John saw } x)$

Quine appears to have held the *any* of examples like 11 to express a universal quantifier and thus to have accepted an analysis in which *any* always expresses a universal quantifier:

11. Any two-year-old can assemble this cabinet.

The question of whether *any* can be given a uniform analysis remains a matter of controversy among linguists. Klima (1964) and Horn (1972) have analyzed the *any* of 10a and b as an existential quantifier that is commanded by an element triggering a rule of *some–any* conversion, thus assigning to 10a and b the logical forms in 10a′ and b′:

10a′. $[(\exists x) (x \text{ objects})] \supset (I \text{ leave})$
10b′. $\sim (\exists x) (\text{John saw } x)$

LeGrand (1975) defends Quine's analysis against Horn.[3]

Sentences such as 6d present an important problem for the uniform analysis of *any*. The only way to treat 6d so that it differs from 6b only in the scope of a universal quantifier would be to invoke the performative analysis and treat them as differing with regard to whether the quantifier is above or below the performative verb:

12a. $(\forall x: x \text{ is one of the apples}) (I \text{ request you } (\text{you take } x))$
  b. I request you $((\forall x: x \text{ is one of the apples}) (\text{you take } x))$

The analysis of 6b as 12b is perfectly adequate, but 12a appears to embody more generosity than can be found in 6d: for each apple, it invites the addressee to take that apple, and it thus does not preclude the possibility that he might accept all of those invitations and take all of the apples, which would be availing himself of more than the speaker in uttering 6d had entitled him to.

For clarity's sake, I will replace 6d by examples that will let me circumvent an irrelevant problem. Note that 6d is really two examples, one with *one* and one without it, and the version without *one* is ambiguous as to whether *any* is singular or plural. Let us accordingly shift to examples that are unambiguous as to the number of the NP in question:

13a. Order any dish you think you'd like.
  b. Order any dishes you think you'd like.

The more generous of these two offers is 13b: it places no limit on the number of dishes the addressee may order (though it need not override other restrictions that may be in force that would limit the quantity, for example, that the food ordered is to comprise a meal that is appropriate to the time of day). Example 13b involves the generosity that we found in 12a: the invitation to order beggar's chicken is independent of the invitation to order red-cooked bear's paw or the invitation to order fish lips in oyster sauce, and accepting one of these invitations does not nullify the other invitation except insofar as other constraints come into the picture (e.g., the constraint that one must not order two sweet-and-sour dishes). Example 13a, by contrast, allows the addressee to make only one choice: once he has decided on red-cooked bear's paw, he is no longer authorized to order tea-smoked duck.[4]

The difference in generosity between 13a and 13b is connected with the fact that, while singular is the unmarked number morphologically and plural the marked one, semantically the situation is reversed: where there is a singular/plural opposition, plural is unspecified as to whether one object or more than one is involved, whereas singular specifies that only one is involved. (See in this connection McCawley 1968c:568–69, where it is noted, e.g., that the plural is used in NP's that are meant to cover both the case of 'one' and that of 'more than one', as in questions on forms: 'schools attended', 'previous positions', 'names of children'. I would argue, though I decline to do it here, that the relationship between singular number and the proposition that one object is involved is a case of conventional implicature, in the sense of Grice 1975, whereas that between plural number and the proposition that more than one object is involved is conversational implicature, i.e., if you know that only one object is involved, cooperativity demands that you use the singular, since otherwise you do extra morphological work only to be less informative.)

My understanding of how conventional implicature interacts with logical structure is not sufficient to tell me whether the restricted generosity of 13a can be explained by combining an analysis of 13a along the lines of 12a with the proposal that distinctive singular number conventionally implicates that exactly one object is involved. If that is possible, and surely it ought to be, then 13 (and 6d) presents no obstacle to Quine's analysis.

Vendler analyzes *any* in terms of the notion of choice: according to Vendler, 14 authorizes the addressee to pick a doctor and guarantees that whichever doctor the addressee has picked, that doctor will say that Stopsneeze helps:

14. Any doctor will tell you that Stopsneeze helps.

This informal analysis fits 11 and 13 perfectly well: pick a two-year-old, and I guarantee you that he will be able to assemble the cabinet; choose an apple, and I invite you to take that apple. It is least plausible in the cases where it is controversial whether *any* is a universal quantifier with wide scope or an existential quantifier with narrow scope (10a and b). Vendler, through remarkable oversight, says nothing about *any*'s that are commanded by negatives (*John didn't see anyone*). He provides the following statement of why *any* is unacceptable in affirmative nongeneric sentences such as 15: "*Any* calls for a choice, but after one has been made, *any* loses its point" (1967:81):

15a. *Any of those blocks is yellow.
   b. *Any of Beethoven's symphonies was first performed in Vienna.
   b'. *Any Beethoven symphony was first performed in Vienna.
   c. *I opened any of the windows.
   d. *Bill took any of the apples.

If the *any* of *John didn't see anyone* were the same *any* that Vendler's remark applies to, that sentence ought not to be possible: choice is as irrelevant to negative past tense clauses as it is to affirmative ones. Thus, Vendler's analysis of *any* can be upheld only if 'negative polarity' *any* is derived differently from the *any* of affirmative clauses. (The *any* of conditional clauses could be identified with either of these *any*'s.)

The failure of the uniform analysis of *any* to provide an explanation of the oddity of 15 is in my opinion its greatest failing. It also encounters difficulty in explaining which occurrences of universal quantifier words can be modified by *almost* (a point first made by Horn 1972):

16a. Almost all of the blocks are yellow.
   b. Almost every student here smokes hash.
   c. *Almost each lecture was followed by a discussion.
      *Two secretaries assist almost each executive.
   d. Almost any two-year old can assemble this cabinet.
   d'. *John didn't talk to almost anyone.

LeGrand (1975) attempts to explain the oddity of 16d' as a violation of a constraint against crossing quantifiers (here, *almost*) across negatives, a constraint that *any* is specifically exempted from (or in LeGrand's formulation: a constraint that can be violated by converting into *any* a quantifier that would otherwise surface as *all* or *every*). However, I doubt the correctness of this constraint; note the acceptability of *John didn't answer almost 50/half of the questions*. While I find these arguments strong enough to lead me to prefer a nonuniform analysis of *any* along the lines of Horn 1972, I emphasize that the uniform analysis has borne up remarkably well against objections that have been raised against it (LeGrand 1975 shows how an impressive number of objections to it can be disposed of and provides penetrating discussion of serious problems with both Quine's analysis and the alternatives to it) and thus still deserves to be regarded as a serious contender for the title of the correct analysis of *any*.[5]

I will conclude my discussion of the universal quantifier words by citing two further differences among them that ought to be explainable on the basis of an adequate analysis of the semantics and syntax of those words. First, there is the impossibility of combining *almost* with *each* (16c), which may fall out of the relationship between *each* and *respective* that I attempted to establish above, though I did not arrive at anywhere near a precise enough statement of how *each* works to be able to demonstrate why it fails to combine with *almost*. Second, there is the often-remarked difference in existential commitment: *every* and *all* carry an existential commitment but *any* does not, for example, 17a does not commit the speaker to the proposition that there are philosophers who accept Meinong's theory of reference, whereas 17b and c do:[6]

17a. Any philosopher who accepts Meinong's theory of reference is insane.
   b. Every philosopher who accepts Meinong's theory of reference is insane.
   c. All philosophers who accept Meinong's theory of reference are insane.

I turn now to nonuniversal quantifiers. Whether a given subject NP allows *there*-insertion depends on its determiner: some quantifiers, including the universal quantifier words, the hedged universals such as *almost all*, and the problematic quantifier *most*, do not allow it, whereas existential quantifiers and their negations (such as *no = not any*, *few*, and *not many*)[7] do allow it:

18. There are some people who think Daley was a saint.

There are $\begin{cases} \text{many} \\ \text{a lot of} \\ \text{a large number of} \\ \text{a great many} \end{cases}$ Americans who like baseball.

$$\text{There are} \begin{cases} \text{a few} \\ \text{a couple/number of} \\ \text{several/three} \\ \text{at least/most 30} \\ \text{few} \\ \text{not many} \\ \text{(almost) no} \\ \text{*most} \end{cases} \begin{matrix} \text{books that I'd never} \\ \text{recomment to a student.} \end{matrix}$$

There aren't any hangers in the closet.
*There are (almost) all of the books on the table.
*There is every book by Chomsky in our library.
*There is each person in his own room.
*There is any two-year old capable of solving this problem.

These data pose the problem of how to analyze *most* in such a way as to predict the nonapplicability of *there*-insertion without simply marking *most* a lexical exception. Note that the most obvious analyses of *most* provide no basis for classifying it as nonexistential. For example, just as a logician who was forced at the point of a gun to give an analysis for *Many Americans like baseball* would probably come up with something like 19a, a logician who was forced at the point of a gun to give an analysis of *Most Americans like baseball* would probably come up with something like 19b, a formula that is in no way less 'existential' than the formula for *many*:

19a. $(\exists M: M \subseteq \{x: x \text{ is an American}\} \land M \text{ is large})$
$(\forall x: x \in M)(x \text{ likes baseball})$
  b. $(\exists M: M \subseteq \{x: x \text{ is an American}\} \land M \text{ is more than half of}$
$\{x: x \text{ is an American}\})(\forall x: x \in M)(x \text{ likes baseball})$

Moreover, *most* does not behave the same as all of its synonyms—except for *the majority*, the apparent paraphrases of *most* allow *there*-insertion:

20.
$$\text{There are} \begin{cases} \begin{Bmatrix} \text{more than} \\ \text{over} \end{Bmatrix} \begin{Bmatrix} \text{half} \\ 50\% \end{Bmatrix} \text{of all Americans} \\ \text{a/*the majority of (all) Americans} \\ \text{*most Americans} \end{cases} \begin{matrix} \text{who oppose} \\ \text{abortion.} \end{matrix}$$

I wish to suggest that *more than half* and *over 50%* are not as good paraphrases of *most* as they are generally held to be. There are cases of clear contrast between *most* and *more than half*, for example, "Most of the ladies and more than half of the gentlemen wore evening clothes" (Sinclair Lewis, *It Can't Happen Here*). A particularly interesting case where they contrast is where the domain is infinite, as on the following page.

21a.  Most positive integers are greater than $10^{80}$.
  a'.  More than half of all positive integers are greater than $10^{80}$.
  b.  Most positive integers are composite.
  b'.  More than half of all positive integers are composite.

Of the four sentences, only 21b is a fairly normal use of English. Moreover, while 21b can reasonably be held to express a true proposition, 21b' is clearly false, whereas 21a' is more clearly true than is 21a. These differences could be accounted for in the following fanciful but still fairly natural procedural semantic treatment: the procedure for evaluating *most* begins with the instruction 'look' and the procedure for evaluating *more than half* begins with 'count'. Since both the primes and the composites are infinite in number, neither set comes out as 'more than half' of the positive integers, and thus 21b' comes out false; but since primes are always outnumbered locally by composites, (i.e., primes are always surrounded by composites, but composites are rarely surrounded by primes), 'inspection' tells you (albeit, wrongly) that composites outnumber primes. The Sinclair Lewis example can be interpreted similarly: the ladies wearing evening clothes outnumber the other ladies everywhere in the hall, whereas you have to count the gentlemen to tell that more than half of them are wearing evening clothes.

This suggestion as to how *most* and *more than half* are evaluated can be reworked into a proposal that makes *most* nonexistential while allowing *more than half* to be existential. In the proposal of the last paragraph, the procedure for *most* involved comparing a set directly with its complement, whereas with *more than half* a set was counted and compared with the cardinal number of the whole domain. This can be reinterpreted as an analysis in which *many* and *more than half* are analyzed along the lines of 19, while 'Most A's are B' is analyzed as 'the set of A's which are not B is smaller than the set of A's which are B', or even as 'The set of A's which are not B is small'. The latter suggestion is essentially what is proposed by Peterson (1978), who analyzes *most* as *few not*, that is, as *not many not*. Peterson's analysis solves the problems with which I am grappling. First, it explains the impossibility of *there*-insertion with *most*: *there*-insertion requires that the existential quantifier be immediately above the clause into which *there* is to be inserted, and Peterson's proposal has *not* intervening between the existential quantifier and the host clause.[8] Second, this proposal allows one to build the vagueness of *large* into the analysis of *many* and thus allows subjective factors to affect whether a particular subset is viewed as most of the whole. The dividing line between large and not large can be below, at, or conceivably even above 50%.[9] It is only because 50% is such a natural dividing line between small and large that *most* often conveys the same thing as *more than half*.

I turn finally to a problem in pinning down the differences among certain existential quantifiers. *Several* differs from *a few* in that *several* refers to a fixed though vague range[10] (typically, from about 4 to about 10), whereas *a few* refers to a number that is small relative to the domain in question but may be large in absolute terms. For example, someone wishing to denigrate the Libertarian Party 1976 presidential campaign could truthfully say 22a but not 22b:

22a. A few people voted for Roger McBride, namely about 180,000.

b. Several people voted for Roger McBride (*, namely, about 180,000).

Since *a few* can thus refer to numbers much larger than *several* can, it is perplexing to find that *a few* can be used to convey the smallness of the number and *several* to convey its largeness, as in 23a, where a person sympathetic to the author would use *a few* to indicate that the analysis was basically right, though flawed, compared with 23b, where a person antagonistic to the author would use *several* to suggest that the analysis was riddled with errors:

23a. There are a few errors in his analysis.

b. There are several errors in his analysis.

This difference might be explained by analyzing *a few* as 'a small number', in which case in 23a the speaker would be asserting that the number was small whereas in 23b he would be merely putting the number into a range that is in fact small. The difficulty with that suggestion is that there are sentences in which *a few* appears not to be analyzeable as 'a small number'. If *a few* meant 'a small number', then *quite a few* should mean 'a quite small number'. However, it in fact means a reasonably large number, certainly more and not less than what you would describe as *a few*.[11]

*A number* is a near synonym of *a few*. By judicious invocation of conversational implicature, *a number* can be taken to mean quite literally 'a number': if the number is zero or very small, cooperativity would demand that one say something more specific than just *a number*. *Quite a number* is close to interchangeable with *quite a few*. I use the hedge 'close to', since I am not completely sure about the appropriateness of either expression when the numbers are really large. Example 24a may be more of an understatement than 24b:

24a. Quite a few Americans eat hamburgers.

b. Quite a number of Americans eat hamburgers.

However, I find that judgment somewhat unclear. At least, in both cases, *quite* implies 'more of a number', that is, a large number. The one way that I can think of to at least achieve consistency in the description of *a few* is to invoke a common practice of lexicographers to make a semantic element 'peripheral' and define *a few* as 'a number, especially a small number'. Modifiers such as *quite* would then modify 'a number', thus making *a few* then refer to relatively large numbers and weakening the effect of 'especially a small number' so that it makes *quite a few* inappropriate only for really enormous numbers.

# IV    Foundations of Linguistics

# 20 Statement versus Rule in Linguistic Description

A grammar of a language is viewed by many linguists as consisting of statements, that is, of assertions about the language and about the units involved in it.[1] In the view of other linguists, the pieces of which a grammar is composed are not statements but rather rules, that is, abstract formulas consisting of a left half, which specifies a configuration of items, and a right half, which specifies an operation which may or must be performed on structures containing such a configuration.

Let me at this point digress briefly into a rapid survey of some notions about rules that will figure prominently in my later discussion. A set of rules may apply either simultaneously or sequentially. In the case of sequential application, the input to the rules is converted into the output through a series of stages: first some rule applies to the input, creating a new structure, then some rule applies to that structure, yielding something else, and so on, until a condition is reached where no more rules may be applied. In the case of simultaneous application, on the other hand, the input passes directly to the output without going through any intermediate stages; the effect of the rules on any individual item in the input depends only on its environment *in the input* and not in the environment that it comes to be in after the application of rules, the way it generally could with sequential application. 'Allophonic statements', which list the allophones of each phoneme in terms of its *phonemic* environment, can be interpreted as a set of simultaneously applying rules that convert a string of phonemes into a string of phones without passing through any intermediate stages.

As regards sequential rules, two situations must be distinguished: ordered rules and unordered sequential rules. Ordered rules have a pre-assigned order: first rule, second rule, third rule, and so on. The first rule is applied to all configurations in the input which meet the conditions of the rule; then the second rule is applied to all configurations in the resulting structure which meet the conditions of the rule; then the third rule is applied, until one finishes applying the final rule, at which point the application of the rules terminates. Unordered sequential rules have no preassigned order. At each point of the derivation, any rule may apply, just as long as the previous rule applications have yielded a structure containing the configuration that the rule affects; the derivation terminates when a structure is obtained which contains no configuration of elements which any of the rules would have any effect on. As examples of ordered rules, I can cite both the transformational component and the phonological component of a transformational grammar; as examples of unordered sequential rules, I can cite Yngve's (1961) phrase structure grammars,[2] the formulas of Harris (1946), and the constituent structure component of at least one version of transformational grammar.

Another distinction that must be drawn is that between rules of *construction* and rules of *conversion*, the former exemplified by phrase-structure rules, the latter by transformations and phonological rules. The phrase-structure rules of a transformational grammar assemble the deep structure of an utterance by a series of steps, each of which serves partially to complete an incomplete tree structure; for example, a phrase-structure rule NP → Det N will apply to a tree structure which is incomplete by virtue of having a node labeled NP that has no nodes under it; its effect will be to introduce under it two nodes labeled Det and N, respectively, as in the conversion of 1a into 1b:[3]

1a.

```
              S
          /   |   \
        NP   Aux   VP
                  /  \
                 V    NP
```

b.

```
                 S
             /   |   \
           NP   Aux   VP
          /  \       /  \
        Det   N     V    NP
                        /  \
                      Det   N
```

The distinguishing characteristic of construction rules is that the input to each rule is in some sense contained in the output, as here, where the input is a subtree of the output. Conversion rules, on the other hand, operate on structures that are already complete in the sense that they can be said to be representations of specific sentences; the effect of a conversion rule is to convert one representation of a sentence into a different representation of the same sentence.[4] For example, the transformation 2a would convert 2b into 2c:

2a.

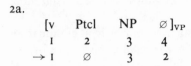

b.

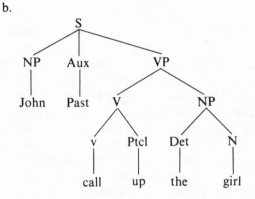

c.

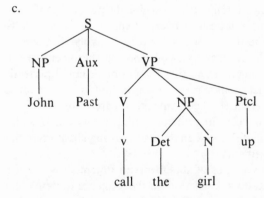

Both 2b and 2c are representations of the sentence *John called the girl up*, 2b being a 'deeper' representation than 2c. In a transformational grammar, the phrase-structure rules are construction rules, whereas the transformations and the phonological rules are conversion rules.

One obvious difference between statements and rules is that while a statement has a truth value, that is, can be said to be 'true' or 'false', depending on whether the language does or does not possess the characteristic which the statement asserts of it,[5] a rule does not have a truth value. A rule cannot be said to be 'true' or 'false', since it embodies no assertion about the language: the only assertion contained in a grammar of rules is the assertion that the structures which can be derived by admissible sequences of rule applications are identical with the structures actually present in the language, and thus truth or falsehood can only be ascribed to the entire body of rules as a whole rather than to individual rules.[6]

Nonetheless, there are numerous instances in which a grammar of statements can be translated into a grammar of rules or vice versa by, for example, translating a statement "/p/ takes the form [p$^h$] in initial position" into a rule "/p/ $\rightarrow$ [p$^h$] in environment #——". The remainder of this paper will deal with the conditions under which a set of statements can be translated into a system of rules or vice versa.

I consider first the question of translating from statements into rules. I will base my results on the "item-and-arrangement" model of description elucidated in Hockett 1954, which I consider (I hope correctly) to be typical of grammars of statements. Hockett's item-and-arrangement model assumes each utterance in a language to have representations on several different 'levels': a phonetic representation, a phonemic representation, a syntactic representation in terms of morphemes and immediate constituent structure, possibly also a morphophonemic representation. His item-and-arrangement grammar consists of inventories of the items involved on each 'level', plus statements concerning the possible configurations on each level and the relations between items on different levels. Since the items listed in the inventories will each be involved in one or other of the statements, the information contained in the inventories is already contained in the statements, so that the grammar could perfectly well be considered to consist of statements alone, without any inventories of items. I will thus assume that Hockett's inventories are merely an aid to the reader's memory and at least in principle could be dispensed with.[7] Thus, for the purposes of what follows, an item-and-arrangement grammar will be simply a set of statements.

The grammar contains two types of statements: a statement is either a 'tactic statement', which states a restriction on the sequence of items that can occur on some level of representation, or a 'representational statement', of which there are two kinds: one, which I will call a 'constituency statement', is found only in syntax and is an assertion that some syntactic category can be filled by some sequence of syntactic categories, say, that the category 'Noun phrase' can be filled by the sequence of categories 'Determiner'–'Noun'; the other kind of representational sttaement, which I will call an 'emic-etic statement', is a statement that an item on one level corresponds to some item or sequence of items on a 'lower' level, for example, a statement that /p/ is realized as [pʰ] in initial position or a statement that the morpheme *go* is realized as the sequence of morphophonemes /wend/ when followed by the morpheme 'Past Tense'.[8]

The grammar will contain one class of constituency statements plus several classes of emic-etic statements: there will be a class of emic-etic statements for every pair of adjacent levels. These statements can be translated into rules in a very natural fashion: the constituency statements correspond to an unordered sequential set of phrase-structure rules, and each class of emic-etic statements corresponds to a set of simultaneous rules:

3.

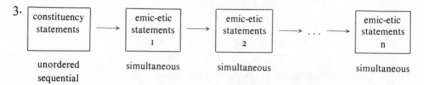

The rules corresponding to constituency statements are construction rules and the rules corresponding to the emic-etic statements are conversion rules. These considerations show that except possibly for tactic statements, which I have yet to discuss and will return to later, a grammar of statements can be translated into an equivalent grammar of rules.

Not only can it be translated into a grammar of rules, but it indeed can be translated into a very special kind of grammar of rules, namely, one which consists of a set of construction rules, within which rule application is unordered sequential, and any number of sets of conversion rules, within each of which the application of rules is simultaneous. What then of grammars of rules that are not of this very restricted type? Is there anything which they can do but grammars of statements cannot? Or is it possible to translate rule grammars of a more general type into equivalent grammars of the restricted type that corresponds to statement grammars? To attack this question, one must first note that what will be crucial is the possibility of having sets of sequentially applying conversion rules, since in the rule grammar corresponding to a statement grammar, each set of conversion rules is simultaneous. Especially crucial will be the possibility of ordered conversion rules, such as comprise the transformational component and phonological component of a transformational grammar and have also figured in earlier works such as Bloomfield's treatments of Menominee (1939) and Tagalog (1933). The earliest instance I know of in which the question of whether ordered rules can be translated into simultaneous rules is treated is Harris (1951a:237–38). Harris concludes on the basis of an example from Bloomfield's Menominee rules that ordered rules can indeed be translated into simultaneous rules. However, his argument is unconvincing, since the example on which it is based involves exactly two rules from the grammar of Menominee; Harris does not indicate whether he attempted to translate any larger body of ordered rules into simultaneous rules. A more recent discussion of the problem is found in Hockett (1966:229). Hockett reports having attempted to translate sets of ordered phonological rules for Potawatami and for Yokuts into simultaneous rules and states that for Potawatami he found the translation fairly difficult and for Yokuts the results became so complicated that his patience wore out before he got very far.

To see why the results would become so complicated, consider the following set of three ordered rules taken from a grammar of Yokuts:

4. A.
$$\begin{bmatrix} - \text{cns} \\ \alpha \text{ dif} \end{bmatrix} \rightarrow [+ \text{ flat}] \text{ in env.} \begin{bmatrix} - \text{cns} \\ \alpha \text{ dif} \\ + \text{ flat} \end{bmatrix} C_0 \underline{\quad\quad}$$

(A vowel becomes rounded if preceded by a rounded vowel of the same height, e.g., hubiş → hubuş)

B.
$$\begin{bmatrix} - \text{cns} \\ + \text{ long} \end{bmatrix} \rightarrow [- \text{ dif}]$$

(A long high vowel becomes mid, e.g., k'ili:y → k'ile:y.)

C. $[- \text{cns}] \rightarrow [- \text{ long}]$ in env. $\underline{\quad\quad} C \begin{Bmatrix} C \\ \# \end{Bmatrix}$

(A vowel becomes short before two consonants or before a word-final consonant, e.g., k'ile:y → k'iley.)

Suppose that the grammar contained only rules A and B. Then they could be replaced by the statements[9]

5. /u:/ becomes [o:]
   /i:/ becomes [e:] if not preceded by /u/ or /u:/
   /i:/ becomes [o:] if preceded by /u/ or /u:/
   /u/ becomes [u]
   /i/ becomes [i] if not preceded by /u/ or /u:/
   /i/ becomes [u] if preceded by /u/ or /u:/

Now consider the system of rules A, B, C. In place of the six statements needed to account for the effect of just rules A and B, a total of nine statements would now be needed:

6. /u:/ becomes [o:] if followed by CV or #
   /u:/ becomes [o] if followed by CC or C#
   /i:/ becomes [e:] if followed by CV or # and not preceded by /u/ or /u:/
   /i:/ becomes [e] if followed by CC or C# and not preceded by /u/ or /u:/
   /i:/ becomes [o:] if followed by CV or # and preceded by /u/ or /u:/

/i:/ becomes [o] if followed by CC or C# and preceded by /u/ or /u:/
/u/ becomes [u]
/i/ becomes [i] if not preceded by /u/ or /u:/
/i/ becomes [u] if preceded by /u/ or /u:/

The number of statements for the long vowels has doubled, since the environments of the earlier statements have to be split in two, corresponding to the instances of the segment which are affected by rule C and those that are not. As more and more rules are added to the three given, the environments would have to be subdivided still further, and the end product would be a set of statements that contained bits and pieces of virtually every rule that affects the segments in question. (For example, one Yokuts rule that I have not brought in is a syncope rule that deletes a short high vowel in the environment VC–CV; all the statements involving a clause 'followed by CV' or 'followed by CC' would have to be replaced by pairs of much more complicated statements since the syncope rule, which precedes rule A, would determine whether a vowel will or will not be 'followed by CV' or 'followed by CC'.)

There are two diametrically opposed interpretations that one could put on this argument, depending on what one means by 'translating a system of ordered rules into a set of statements'. If one were to apply the word 'translation' in the narrow sense in which the translation must contain some isolable analog of each rule, the above statement would indicate that ordered rules cannot in general be translated into statements, since a statement that contains fragments of half a dozen rules cannot be considered a translation of any one of them. However, the above discussion could also be interpreted as showing that one can always translate ordered rules into statements just as long as one has a mechanical procedure for turning a set of rules into a set of statements that convert the same inputs into the same outputs. In that sense, the scheme that I was using for replacing ordered rules by statements would indeed yield a set of simultaneous rules that, fantastically complicated as each might be, still would convert each input into exactly the same output as did the original set of ordered rules.

I propose now to show that there is an important class of grammars of rules that cannot be translated into grammars of statements even in the extremely broad sense of translation that I have just mentioned. Recall the translation procedure that I used above. I first selected a segment and wrote down two statements, one stating what it is converted into in the environments in which a certain rule is applicable, the other what it is converted into in environments where that rule is not applicable. I then subdivided those environments (thereby doubling the number of statements) by bringing in some other rule and separating the cases in which that rule is applicable from those in which it is not. The process would continue until all possible combinations of environments had been exhausted for each possible input segment. For this procedure to yield a result, it is necessary that the possible combinations of environments actually be exhausted by the procedure in a finite number of steps. That condition will be met if there is a limit to the number of rule applications in the conversion, as will be the case in a simple ordered set of rules, where the maximum number of rule applications will equal the number of rules. However, there is no upper limit to the number of rule applications in a grammar with a cyclically applied block of rules.

Cycles of rules have been used extensively to describe situations where the behavior of composite forms is determined by the behavior of their components, as in English stress, where the stress pattern on an involved compound is determined by the stress patterns of its immediate constituents, which are in turn determined by the stress patterns of their immediate constituents, and so on. Such a situation is formalized by having a block of rules apply to the innermost constituents, then reapply to the next larger constituents, until the nodes of the immediate constituent structure have been exhausted.[10] For example, the English stress rules would first apply to the encircled constituents of 7a, yielding the stress assignment in 7b:

7a.

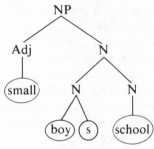

b.

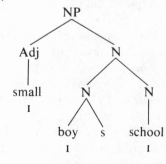

The rules would then apply to the next larger constituent (encircled) and finally to the largest constituent (the whole phrase), yielding 8c:[11]

8a.

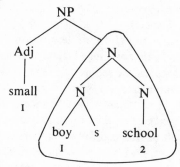

b.

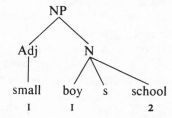

c.

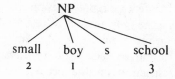

Since there is no syntactic limit to the depth to which structures can be embedded within structures, there will be no limit to the number of rule applications, that can result from applying a cyclic block of rules. Consequently the above procedure for translating rules into statements will never terminate and thus will never yield any translation. Now, I actually made a stronger statement above: I said not merely that *this* method will not translate a cycle into a set of statements but that indeed, *no* method of translating rules into statements would yield a result for all cycles. However, this stronger claim follows from the fact that the method of translation that I have given is essentially the only method there could be, since the result of translation must be a set of statements that enumerate the different environments in which different combinations of rule applications occur.

Since, according to the current theory, the transformational component and the phonological component of a transformational grammar each involve a cyclically applied block of rules, neither transformational syntax nor transformational phonology is translatable into statement grammar (although there will of course be cases of particular cycles that happen to be equivalent to sets of statements).

I now return to the notion of 'tactic statements'. In his description of an item-and-arrangement grammar, Hockett calls for a set of tactic statements for each level, which state the restrictions on the sequence of elements on that level. But note that the tactic statements for some levels will be completely superfluous, since they will be automatic consequences of the tactic statements for higher levels. For example if the grammar contains a 'morphophonemic' level, then there will be no need for statements giving the restrictions on sequences of phonemes, that is, for 'phonotactic statements' as normally understood, since the possible phoneme sequences will be fully determined by what morpheme sequences are possible.[12] The superfluous classes of tactic statements are the one part of a statement grammar that cannot be translated into rules, since they are involved neither in the construction of a representation of an utterance nor in the conversion of a higher-level representation into a lower-level one; in relation to a grammar of rules, their function would not be as part of the grammar itself, but rather merely as data that are used in setting up higher-level representations and the relevant conversion rules. The nonsuperfluous classes of tactic statements in Hockett's framework could be replaced by context-sensitive phrase-structure rules; in a feature representation such as that found in transformational grammars, the only analogs to tactic rules are rules that fill in redundant feature specifications; this takes in both morpheme-structure rules and rules relating to selectional restrictions between morphemes; note that any restriction on the occurrence of feature complexes implies that fewer contrasts than are theoretically possible can actually occur, so that the feature specifications corresponding to the nonoccurring contrasts are redundant.

Finally, I wish to comment on an unfortunate piece of terminology that has become rather prevalent, namely, the use of the word 'knowledge' for what a person has learned in acquiring a language.[13] The term suggests that what a person carries around in his head corresponding to his linguistic competence is identifiable with a set of 'facts' or 'statements' about his language. If that were the case, one would be forced to ascribe to the speaker a power that verges on the magical, namely, the power of taking a large body of statements and synthesizing arbitrary structures that are consistent with all of those statements. To describe the behavior of speakers in terms only of natural and not supernatural powers, I believe it to be necessary to suppose that a speaker's linguistic competence is stored in his head not in the form of a set of facts but rather as something like a map, whose form can presumably be represented abstractly by a system of rules, and that the brain in applying this competence acts as a glorified map-reading device rather than as a device for deducing the implications of a huge set of facts.

# 21 On the Role of Notation in Generative Phonology

This paper is concerned with the kinds of arguments that can be given for or against notational systems in phonology. Such arguments as have been given are of three types: those relating to evaluation measures, those relating to 'insufficient power', and those relating to 'excessive power'. The classic argument relating to evaluation measures is that given by Morris Halle (1964a: 337) for a feature notation rather than an alphabetic notation in phonology. Halle points out that an evaluation measure which counts feature specifications in rules written in a feature notation evaluates a rule that fronts [a] to [æ] before all front vowels as less costly than a rule that fronts [a] to [æ] before [i] and evaluates the latter rule as in turn less costly than a rule which fronts [a] to [æ] before [i, p, z] (see table). Halle claims that this is in fact the correct ordering of the 'complexity' of the rules and that there is no apparent way in which to set up an evaluation measure based on alphabetic symbols which would yield this ordering: "It is, of course, conceivable that a simplicity criterion may be formulated that yields the proper results even when segments are represented as indivisible entities. The burden of proof, however, is clearly on those who reject the view that segments are complexes of distinctive features."

An important unstated step of this argument is Halle's rejection of the alternative proposal that both rules and 'items' are represented in an alphabetic notation but the evaluation of rules is done by translating them into a feature format and counting the feature specifications in the translation. Halle rightly rejects that proposal on (I gather) the grounds that the alphabetic symbols which it involves are completely dispensable: that at the one place where he has shown it to matter whether one has a feature representation or an alphabetic notation, the feature representation is

Reprinted by permission from *The Formal Analysis of Natural Languages*, ed. M. Gross et al. (The Hague: Mouton, 1973), pp. 51–62. © Copyright 1973 in the Netherlands, Mouton & Co., N.V., Publishers.

necessary. To read more into Halle's remarks than he actually says, Halle is rejecting the free use of 'secondary concepts' defined in terms of 'primary concepts': while one could take either 'feature' or 'atomic segment' as basic and define the other in terms of it, a symbol defined in terms of the 'basic' symbols is for Halle an "unofficial circumlocution . . . lacking all systematic import" (p. 336). He evidently regards his notational system not merely as a device for expressing what happens in a language but as a hypothesis as to what entities are present in linguistic competence. It is this exclusion of 'secondary concepts' from the theory which makes Halle's argument for a feature representation in rules also an argument for a feature representation for 'items'.

Effect of the rule        Formulation of the rule according to notation of
                                    Chomsky and Halle 1968

$a$ becomes $æ$ before $i, e, æ$ $\begin{bmatrix} + \text{syll} \\ + \text{low} \end{bmatrix} \rightarrow [- \text{back}]/ \underline{\hspace{1cm}} \begin{bmatrix} +\text{syll} \\ -\text{back} \end{bmatrix}$

$a$ becomes $æ$ before $i$ $\begin{bmatrix} + \text{syll} \\ + \text{low} \end{bmatrix} \rightarrow [- \text{back}]/ \underline{\hspace{1cm}} \begin{bmatrix} +\text{syll} \\ -\text{back} \\ +\text{high} \end{bmatrix}$

$a$ becomes $æ$ before $i, p, z$ $\begin{bmatrix} + \text{syll} \\ + \text{low} \end{bmatrix} \rightarrow [- \text{back}]/ \underline{\hspace{1cm}} \left\{ \begin{matrix} \begin{bmatrix} +\text{syll} \\ -\text{back} \\ +\text{high} \end{bmatrix} \\ \begin{bmatrix} +\text{obst} \\ -\text{cont} \\ -\text{voice} \\ +\text{anterior} \\ -\text{coronal} \end{bmatrix} \\ \begin{bmatrix} +\text{obs} \\ +\text{cont} \\ +\text{voice} \\ +\text{anterior} \\ -\text{coronal} \\ +\text{strident} \end{bmatrix} \end{matrix} \right\}$

It is not the case that Chomsky and Halle exclude 'secondary concepts' entirely; but I will argue that the 'secondary concepts' which they do admit are either not secondary or not justified. Their conception of 'evaluation measure' involves a number of notational devices which they refer to as 'abbreviatory conventions' and which they treat as defining a 'rule' in an expanded notation as a sequence of rules in a more restricted notation. I maintain that with one exception, these so-called 'abbreviatory conventions' are not 'abbreviatory', that is, that they do not really 'define' a composite rule as a sequence of other rules, and that the one 'abbreviatory convention' which is truly abbreviatory, namely, curly brackets, is wrong in the sense that when combined with an adequate system of phonological features the only instances in which it would be applicable are instances of consecutive rules in a grammar which have purely accidental similarities and which can in no sense be said to act as a unit.[1]

However, I wish first to say something about the other type of argument that has been used in choosing between notational systems, namely, arguments relating to 'excessive' or 'insufficient' power. Arguments based on 'insufficient power' often crucially involve the notion of 'significant generalization'. Assuming that a feature system allows one to distinguish among all the segments types that are involved in phonological derivations in a language,[2] the effect of almost any[3] putative phonological rule can be brought about by simply listing its inputs and outputs, expressed in the given feature system, and putting arrows in between. However, in that case, one has not written a rule but a sequence of rules. If it can be established that there is a single phenomenon here rather than several disparate phenomena (evidence that there is a single phenomenon rather than several would include, for example, evidence that in language acquisition or aphasia the various effects of the putative rule are acquired together or lost together, evidence that in language change the whole rule is modified or generalized rather than just special cases of it, or evidence that dialects differ by the ordering of the putative rule with respect to other rules but do not differ by the ordering of the special cases which the 'list' alluded to above would distinguish), then it is correct to argue that a grammar must have a single rule to cover the various special cases and that a notational system which does not make it possible to formulate such a single rule is inadequate on grounds of 'insufficient power'. As an example, consider the argument which I have offered (1967) against the Jakobsonian feature 'diffuse' on the grounds of both excessive and insufficient power. High vowels and alveolar, dental, and labial consonants are [+ diffuse) and velar and palatal consonants and mid and low vowels are [− diffuse]. I argued that no language has rules in which diffuse vowels and diffuse consonants are treated alike (although Jakobson's feature system would allow the formulation of such rules, so that it has 'excessive power') whereas there are a number of rules (e.g., the Sanskrit retroflexion of [s] before [i, u, r, k]) which treat 'diffuse vowels' and 'non diffuse consonants' alike (although the Jacobsonian feature system does not group them together and thus has 'insufficient power').[4]

Arguments on the grounds of 'excessive power' crucially involve the notion of 'possible rule', which in turn crucially involves the notion of 'significant generalization'. One who takes 'excessive power' arguments seriously has as his goal characterizing 'phonological rule' so as to include all and only the phonological rules that the phenomena of a natural language could demand, and the mere fact that a certain putative rule would give correct answers if incorporated in a grammar of some language does not justify calling it a 'possible rule'. For example, the fact that the shortening of vowels in my dialect could be described by three rules, one which shortens vowels before (oral) stops, one which shortens vowels before nasals, and one which shortens vowels before [l], does not mean that those three rules must be included in the set of possible rules: here there is a single rule that shortens vowels before segments with closure, and the fact that the three rules mentioned could duplicate the effect of that single rule does not justify admitting them as 'possible rules'. An example of an 'excessive power' argument to which I will return below has to do with Chomsky and Halle's use of numerical subscripts (meaning 'that number or more') in rules like the following:

1a. Penultimate stress: $[+syll] \rightarrow [1\,stress]/\!\!-\!\!-\!\![-syll]_0\,[+syll]\,[-syll]_0\,\#$.

Chomsky and Halle's conception of numerical subscripts as an 'abbreviatory convention' abbreviating a (potentially infinite) set of rules, each of which calls for a specific number of segments of the type in question (e.g., one rule is 'vowel is stressed before zero consonants plus one vowel plus zero consonants plus word boundary', another is 'vowel is stressed before one consonant plus one vowel plus zero consonants plus word boundary', another is 'vowel is stressed before three consonants plus one vowel plus two consonants plus word boundary', etc.), forces one to include among rules supposedly abbreviated by the numerical subscripts rules which in fact are not possible: for example, no language could have a stress placement rule which applied *only* to words ending in a vowel plus three consonants plus a vowel plus two consonants. The statement that a rule is impossible crucially involves the notion of 'significant generalization': while there are hundreds of languages in which all words ending in vowel plus three consonants plus vowel plus two consonants have penultimate stress, the placement of stress in those languages always goes under some generalization such as that the penultimate syllable is stressed (regardless of how many consonants or vowels each syllable contains) or that stress is put two moras before the last syllable (as in Latin).

I now return to the status of the so-called 'abbreviatory conventions' of Chomsky and Halle (1968). Regarding curly brackets, which Chomsky and Halle use to combine into a single rule consecutive rules are partially identical, I maintain that all cases where linguists have used this device fall into the following categories: (1) one of the rules supposedly abbreviated gives wrong outputs (e.g., the second environment of Chomsky and

Halle's vowel shift rule, which is supposed to account for height alternations in strong verbs, gives the right alternation in verbs with an underlying high or low vowel but not in verbs with an underlying mid vowel),[5]
(2) the convention is not applicable, since (contrary to the claim of their
author) the rules are not consecutive in the grammar (e.g., the lowering of
[u] to [ʌ], which Chomsky and Halle make the third environment of the
vowel shift rule, is not adjacent to vowel shift in the rule ordering, since the
rule which laxes the vowel of *says*, *said*, and *does* must apply after vowel shift
and before [u] into [ʌ], (3) the rule presupposes something incorrect which,
if corrected, would eliminate the occasion for using curly brackets (e.g.,
many rules in Chomsky and Halle 1968 and earlier works involve {+cons,
−voc}; the feature system which those rules presuppose must for various
reasons be rejected in favor of one containing the feature of 'syllabicity',
and the rules should all have [−syll] in place of the material in the curly
brackets), and (4) the curly brackets are applied to consecutive rules which
only accidentally have identical parts and which in no way act as a unit. I
thus propose abolishing curly brackets from linguistics as serving no
function other than the pernicious one of making it easy for the linguist to
ignore defects in his analysis.[6]

The remaining abbreviatory conventions used by Chomsky and Halle
are: 'variable coefficients', which mark sameness or difference between
feature coefficients, for example,

2. Progressive voicing assimilation: $[-\text{syll}] \rightarrow [\alpha \text{ voice}] \Big/ \begin{bmatrix} -\text{syll} \\ \alpha \text{ voice} \end{bmatrix}$ ——

numerical subscripts (described above); and parentheses, which Chomsky
and Halle use to indicate what might best be called 'semiobligatory
material'; for example, I said that the Latin stress rule (following Jakobson)
inserts stress two moras before the last syllable; but a Latin word which
contains only one mora before the last syllable gets stressed one mora
before the last syllable (e.g., *ibō*), and a monosyllable gets stressed on its
single syllable (e.g., *res*), so that the rule should put stress on a mora
which is followed by a mora (if one is available) followed by a syllable (if
one is available) followed by word boundary:

3a. Latin stress: Insert [ 1 stress]/ <u>mora</u> (mora) (syll) #

(I am prepared to argue that it must be possible to state rules in terms of
such units as syllables and moras as well as segments, but do not choose to
go into that question here). Similarly, the penultimate stress rule, if
formulated in terms of segments rather than syllables would have to be

3b. penultimate stress: $[+\text{syll}] \rightarrow [1 \text{ stress}]/$——$([-\text{syll}]_0 [+\text{syll}]) [-\text{syll}]_0 \#$

so as to cover monosyllables also. Chomsky and Halle treat all three of these devices as abbreviating sequences of rules: in the first case, two rules of which one has a + in place of the variable and the other a − ; in the second case, an infinite set of rules, one calling for $n$ segments, where $n$ is the subscript, one calling for $n+1$ segments, one calling for $n+2$, and so on; and in the third case, two rules, one calling for the parenthesized material and one not calling for it. There are two main reasons for withholding the term 'abbreviatory' from these notational devices. First, the rules they supposedly abbreviate are often not 'possible rules'. For Chomsky and Halle, the nasal assimilation rule

4. nasal assimilation: $[+ \text{nasal}] \rightarrow \begin{bmatrix} \alpha \text{ anterior} \\ \beta \text{ coronal} \end{bmatrix} / \underline{\quad} \begin{bmatrix} - \text{ syll} \\ \alpha \text{ anterior} \\ \beta \text{ coronal} \end{bmatrix}$

is an abbreviation for four rules, each assimilating nasals to a specific place of articulation. However, not all of those four rules are possible; for example, no language has a rule assimilating nasals to the place of articulation of labials and only labials. An example of an impossible rule included in what is supposedly abbreviated by the subscript convention was given above. And I conjecture that a rule assigning stress to the second mora before the last syllable and only there (thus leaving the possibility for another rule to assign final stress to two-syllable words whose first syllable has only one mora) is not a possible rule either. Second, as Chomsky and Halle point out, the sets of rules supposedly abbreviated by these devices do not stand in the same kind of ordering relations that rules normally do. Whereas rules normally are 'conjunctively ordered', so that the output of one rule is the input to the next rule, Chomsky and Halle must say that the rules 'abbreviated' by these devices are 'disjunctively ordered' with respect to each other, that is, if one of the rules applies, then the others are inapplicable. This interpretation is necessary, since if the two rules which Chomsky and Halle say are abbreviated by rule 4 were 'conjunctively ordered', any word of at least two syllables in length would receive two stresses: one from the one rule and one from the other.

I thus conclude that the types of rules which Chomsky and Halle express using the above devices are in fact not definable in terms of the other devices of the theory (+ and − feature specifications and [conjunctive] rule ordering) and that, assuming that the kinds of rules which Chomsky and Halle express using those three devices are in fact necessary in phonology, phonological theory must have more 'first order concepts' relating to rules than Chomsky and Halle proposed. For representing items, it suffices to specify what segment follows what segment and which value (+ or −) each segment has for each feature. Rules may call for one segment to follow another or to be + or − for a certain feature, but they may equally well call for one segment to be the closest segment of a given type before or after a given segment (e.g., the penultimate stress rule calls for the last vowel before a word boundary and for the last vowel before that vowel) and may call for one segment to agree (or disagree) with another on a certain feature. I propose the following notation for rules as something which at least makes clear the primitive notions involved:

5.  nasal assimilation: If 1 impr 2          (impr = 'immediately
　　　　　　　　　　syll (1) = −            precedes')
　　　　　　　　　　nasal (1) = +
　　　　　　　　　　syll (2) = −
　　　　　　　　　　Then coron (1) → coron (2)   (i.e., the coronality
　　　　　　　　　　　　　　　　　　　　　　　specification of 1
　　　　　　　　　　　　　　　　　　　　　　　becomes whatever the
　　　　　　　　　　　　　　　　　　　　　　　coronality specification
　　　　　　　　　　　　　　　　　　　　　　　of 2 has been)

　　　　　　　　　　anterior (1) → anterior (2)

6a. penultimate stress: If seg (1) = −        (i.e. 1 is a non-segment,
　　　　　　　　　　　　　　　　　　　　　i.e. a boundary)

　　　　　　　　　　2 is last [+syll] before 1
　　　　　　　　　　3 is last [+syll] before 2
　　　　　　　　　　then stress (3) → 1.

'Excessive power' arguments are arguments that a notational system is wrong because it allows one to express impossible rules. One can reasonbly ask whether it makes sense to demand that a notational system be solely responsible for distinguishing between possible rules and impossible rules. Such a demand of course unheard of outside of linguistics—no mathematician criticizes a notation on the ground that it allows one to write the sentence 2+2 = 59. The following extremely interesting suggestion by Quine (discussion at a conference in Palo Alto, August 1969)[7] was intended as a *reductio ad absurdum* of the position that one should except a notational system to do all the work of separating the 'possible' from the 'impossible'. Quine points out that one could give an 'excessible power' argument against the traditional notations of symbolic logic and in favour of the following notation, which allows the formulation of fewer contradictions.[8] Suppose that *and, or, all,* and *some* are represented by the symbols ∧, ∨, ∧, ∨ (which are the symbols used anyway by many logicians), predicates are represented by symbols which do not look the same when turned upside down (e.g., *p, q, f, g*), individuals are represented by symbols which look the same when turned upside down (e.g., ×, o), and the negation of a formula represented by writing each of its symbols upside down, for example, the negation of $\bigwedge \times (f\times \vee g\times)$ would be $\bigvee \times (f\times \wedge \mathcal{S}\times)$. The formulas which are contradictory by virtue of the law of double negation or de Morgan's laws cannot even be stated. Moreover, it is unnecessary to state either of those two principles as postulates: no law of double negation is needed, since inverting a symbol twice restores it to its original form, and de Morgan's laws (which say that the negation of a conjunction is equivalent to the disjunction of the negations of the terms, and the negation of a disjunction is equivalent to the conjunction of the negations of the terms) would be unnecessary since negating a conjunction would involve turning the symbol for *and* into the symbol for *or* and the symbols for the conjuncts into the symbols for their negations.

Of course, Quine's proposed notation does not make the law of double negation and de Morgan's laws unnecessary: it merely shifts them from postulates which one expresses in the notational system to postulates which one assumes in accepting the notational system (or rather, consequences of such postulates). The relation as described by Quine relies heavily on the type face used: type faces differ as to whether $x$, $o$, $D$, and $B$ are changed into something different by turning them upside down. In using the notation system one assumes that every symbol has an 'inverse', that 'inverse' is a 'symmetric relation', and that the symbols divide into two types: those which are their own inverses (individual constants and variables) and those which are distinct from their inverses (predicates, conjunctions, and quantifiers). If the negation of a formula is defined as the formula obtained from it by replacing each of its symbols by its inverse, the law of double negation and de Morgan's laws become theorems deducible from the assumptions just listed.

The point of the above example is that in any notational system, certain typographical characteristics of the formulas are treated as 'significant' and others not. Specifying what characteristics are significant amounts to giving postulates which are really not postulates about the notational system but about the entities in the description of which the notational system is employed. A choice between two notational systems is really a choice between two alternatives for what entities are to be hypothesized and what properties are to be postulated of them. A postulate for which it is possible to set up a notational system that exactly 'fits' that postulate should not thereby be accorded any special status. This has the unhappy consequence of making it much less clear than it previously seemed how to choose between alternatives, since there is no obvious criterion for choosing between alternative postulate systems that are 'deductively equivalent'. The only criterion I can think of that will ever go beyond esthetic reactions in the viscera is the criterion that a system of postulates must be wrong if it lists separate cases that clearly belong under a generalization. I conclude that an 'excessive power' argument, if taken literally, is as nonsensical as Quine suggested but in many cases can be replaced by an argument about alternative postulates which some sense can be made of.

Having, I hope, clarified the status of 'excessive power' arguments, let me turn to one in particular which I have recently given, an argument against the position generally accepted by generative phonologists that all phonological features are binary and in favor of the position that at least vowel height and pitch should be represented by single nonbinary features rather than by combinations of binary features (e.g., that high, mid, and low vowels be represented as [2 high], [1 high], and [0 high] rather than as $\left(\begin{bmatrix} +\text{high} \\ -\text{low} \end{bmatrix}, \begin{bmatrix} -\text{high} \\ -\text{low} \end{bmatrix}, \begin{bmatrix} -\text{high} \\ +\text{low} \end{bmatrix}\right)$.

Several examples exist of phonological rules which raise low and mid vowels to mid and high, respectively, or which lower high and mid vowels to mid and low, respectively; as examples of the former I can cite the vowel shift rule in English (see McCawley 1974*a* for justification of this version of vowel shift and criticism of Chomsky and Halle's) and the rule in Eastern Finnish dialects which converts *ee, öö, oo, ää, aa* into *ie, üö, uo, eä, oa*, respectively; as an example of the latter, I can cite a rule in a Southern Lappish dialect (Ove Lorentz, personal communication) which lowers the second element of long high and mid vowels, so that *ii, üü, uu, ee, oo* become *ie, üö, uo, eä, oa*. To express such a rule using exclusively binary features (e.g., Chomsky and Halle 1968 feature system), it is necessary that the rule involve a change of two features and a variable which connects a feature in the 'structural change' to a different feature in the 'structural description':

6b. part of English vowel shift: $\begin{bmatrix} +\text{syll} \\ -\text{high} \\ \alpha\,\text{low} \\ +\text{tense} \end{bmatrix} \rightarrow \begin{bmatrix} -\alpha\,\text{high} \\ -\text{low} \end{bmatrix}$

However, the only well-founded rules that are of the form

7. $\begin{bmatrix} \alpha F \\ -G \end{bmatrix} \rightarrow \begin{bmatrix} -\alpha G \\ -F \end{bmatrix}$

are rules in which *F* and *G* are binary features used to split up a domain such as vowel height or pitch height[9] which the alternative under consideration would represent in terms of a nonbinary feature which could be incremented in a phonological rule, for example,

8. vowel shift revised:
$$\begin{bmatrix} + \text{syll} \\ n < 3\,\text{high} \\ + \text{tense} \end{bmatrix} \rightarrow [n + 1\,\text{high}]$$

The binary proposal thus requires a notion of 'possible rule' in which symbol combinations are allowed that in fact do not correspond to possible phenomena of real languages, for example, a rule of the form 7 in which $F$ was 'low' and $G$ 'rounded', which would have the effect of rounding $i$ and $e$ to $ü$ and $ö$ while raising $æ$ and $a$ to $e$ and $ʌ$. To translate the above from a nonsensical argument about notation into a possibly meaningful argument about alternative sets of postulates, the choice is between a set of postulates like the following:

9. Every feature has the two values $+$ and $-$.
   Each line in the 'then'-part of a rule has one of the forms

   $F(n) \rightarrow +$
   $F(n) \rightarrow -$
   $F(n) \rightarrow G(m)$
   $F(n) \rightarrow - G(m)$, where $F$ and $G$ are features.

   If a rule has an 'if'-part containing $F(n) = -$ and a 'then'-part containing $F(n) \rightarrow - G(n)$ and $G(n) \rightarrow -$, then $F$ and $G$ are either high and low (tongue position) or high pitch and low pitch.

and a set of postulates like the following:

10. (Tongue) height and pitch have the values 0, 1, 2, and all other features have the values 0 and 1.[10]
    Each line in the 'then'-part of a rule has one of the forms

    $F(n) \rightarrow a$, where $F$ is a feature and $a$ is a value of $F$
    $F(n) \rightarrow F(n) + 1$
    $F(n) \rightarrow F(n) - 1$
    $F(n) \rightarrow G(m)$, where $F$ and $G$ are two features with the same set of values
    $F(n) \rightarrow - G(m)$, where $F$ and $G$ are both 'binary' features.

    A rule cannot have an 'if'-part containing $F(n) = 0$ and a 'then'-part containing $F(n) \rightarrow - G(n)$ and $G(n) \rightarrow 0$.

Or at least, that would be choice if the last line in 9 or 10 was to be the extent of restrictions on the use of 'variables' in rules. But these restrictions are clearly insufficient to characterize the set of possible rules, since they do not exclude such impossible rules as $[\alpha\,\text{high}] \rightarrow [\alpha\,\text{nasal}]$ (which would make velar consonants and high vowels nasal and make everything else nonnasal). It will not do simply to exclude rules in which a 'variable' links two different features, since there are fairly clear cases (at least, among redundancy rules) of rules that make rounding agree with backness (back vowels become rounded and front vowels unrounded) or make voicing disagree with obstruence (obstruents become voiceless and sonorants voiced). Rather than all rules of a certain format being possible, it appears that there are only a small number of pairs of features that may be linked by such a rule. If this is so, then a set of postulates correctly characterizing the set of possible rules would presumably have to have a postulate that simply listed the formulas of the type $F(n) \rightarrow (-) G(n)$ that could appear in the 'then'-part of a rule. The postulate for the binary proposal would involve a longer list than the corresponding postulate for the nonbinary proposal, and the former list would also have to have a qualification that when the 'then'-part contained high $(n) \rightarrow$ low $(n)$, the 'if'-part would have to contain high $(n) = -$ and the 'then'-part would have to contain low $(n)$ $\rightarrow -$ (and a similar condition on a rule that lowered tongue height or a rule that raised or lowered pitch height).

This leaves the postulates for the binary proposal looking somewhat messier than those for the nonbinary proposal. More importantly, it can reasonably be argued that the side conditions mentioned two sentences back are not randomly distributed among the rules in question but go only with those pairs of features which divide up some multivalued domain, that is, the binary proposal necessarily involves postulates which miss a valid generalization as to why some rules but not others are possible. While this is something of an argument, it does not give a really crushing case one way or the other. What would give a really crushing case for the nonbinary proposal would be to show some major restriction on rules which could be imposed under the nonbinary proposal but not under the binary proposal. Since the binary proposal requires rules which make two changes (see 6) where the corresponding rule under the nonbinary proposal would make only one change (see 8), the case for the nonbinary proposal would be really clear if it could be shown that it allowed all rules to be 'one-change' rules.[11] There are some obvious objections to raise to a proposal that all rules are 'one-change' rules, note for example, the extremely common nasal assimilation rule cited earlier (which makes the nasal agree in both coronality and anteriority with the following segment; here a rule making only one of the two changes would not be possible, it effects being to turn [ŋ] into [m] before [t], and [n] into [ñ] before [k]) and 'compensatory lengthening' rules, which simultaneously lengthen the vowel on one side of a consonant and shorten or delete the vowel on the other side of it.

It is in fact possible to treat these rules as 'one change' rules, though doing so involves two important additions to phonological theory, which however, I maintain are necessary anyway. The first is the principle that rules may have 'side effects' beyond the change that the rule specifically mentions; specifically, any additional changes are made that are necessary in order that the output of the rule contain only possible combinations of features; for example (see McCawley 1967), the rule in Korean that makes all syllable-final consonants unreleased has the side effect of giving them a closure, since only a segment with a closure can be unreleased, and also has the side effect of making them unaspirated, since only a released segment can be aspirated. The second addition to phonological theory is the recognition of the distinction between 'states' and 'events' and the recognition of rules whose effect is to change the timing of an event. For example, it is necessary to distinguish between 'closure', the state of there being a total occlusion, and 'closure', the event of an active articulator entering into an occlusion with a passive articulator. In the case of the nasal assimilation rule, the rule can be stated as the shift of the closure event (or more generally, the 'onset') of the second consonant to the beginning of the preceding segment. The fact that the first segment acquires the coronality and anteriority of the second can be said to be a 'site effect': a segment which begins with a certain closure event must have the place-of-articulation features of that closure. Similarly, many cases of 'compensatory lengthening' are the delay by one segment of the onset of a consonant, and the rule found in many Bantu languages whereby a nasal prefix is realized as prenasalization of the following consonant plus lengthening of the preceding vowel (e.g., $\ldots a\,N\text{-}la\ldots \rightarrow \ldots a\cdot{}^{n}da\ldots$) is a postponement by one segment of the onset of the nasal (including the lowering of the velum). If stated in feature notation without the aid of the two theoretical innovations referred to above, these rules would involve wholesale changing of features—note that the Bantu rule would involve simultaneous changes in three segments. A theory of 'possible rules' must characterize which wholesale changes of features are possible; the theory that I am proposing here says that wholesale changes of features only arise as side-effects of atomic changes, where the atomic changes include anticipation or postponement of phonological events. Obviously, what I have presented falls far short of a complete demonstration that phonological rules can be restricted to making a single change (which may then have predictable side-effects); however, I think it has disposed of the most formidable objections that might be presented against that conclusion. The conclusion, if established, would then provide strong evidence that the binary treatment of vowel height was wrong, since it would require two-change rules, and that vowel heights should be represented in terms of a single nonbinary feature. It should be noted, incidentally, that within the approach that I am taking here, the behavior of Bantu prefixes has a bearing on how one is to formulate the English vowel shift rule.

The main moral that I want to draw from the above discussion is that except for arguments relating to evaluation measures, which in my opinion can never be put on a sound footing, all arguments about the correctness of a system of phonological description revolve about the notion often called 'linguistically significant generalization' and perhaps better called 'unitary linguistic phenomenon'. I mentioned earlier several kinds of evidence that can be offered (but rarely are) for concluding that there is or is not a single 'piece of linguistic competence' reflected in a set of facts. Much of my argument is weak because of lack of such evidence, especially for the language universals that I have stated. However, I would at least claim that these statements are not incorrigible, whereas such statements as Halle's assertion about the relative complexity of the rules of the table probably *is* incorrigible. The notion of 'linguistically significant generalization' is much more pervasive in recent transformational linguistics than an examination of the available literature would suggest. It deserves much more attention than the complete barren notion of 'evaluation measure', which, regrettably, a tremendous fuss is made over in most of the works that students are given to read in courses of transformational grammar.

# 22    On Interpreting the Theme
of This Conference

The announced theme of this conference, 'On Limiting the Domain of
Linguistics', is ambiguous. The interpretation that I conjecture was intended
by its organizers is 'How ought we to limit the domain of linguistics?',
which involves the presupposition that the domain of linguistics should be
limited. The other interpretation that it allows is one in which 'limiting the
domain of linguistics' is the subject matter rather than the goal, and the
discussion is to be about the consequences and implications of limiting the
domain of linguistics. There is a similar ambiguity in such titles as On
Bombing Villages in Vietnam or the title which that of this conference
originally suggested to me: On Fighting Obscenity.[1]
    Whether I will have the chutzpah to present a paper in which I interpret
the conference theme in a way which I know damn well is not what the
organizers intended, as I would of course do if invited by the YMCA to
speak at a conference on fighting obscenity, will depend on another
ambiguity or perhaps vagueness in the theme, namely that of the word
'domain'. 'Domain' might be taken as referring to the class of facts that a
linguist should or may pay attention to; with 'domain' interpreted that
way, I think 'limiting the domain of linguistics' is something really
pernicious and guaranteed to cause one the loss of at least some contact
with reality. An alternative interpretation of 'the domain of linguistics'
would take 'domain' to mean the kinds of things that a linguist ought to
be attempting to provide an account of, and I find a limitation of the
'domain' in this sense at least somewhat less pernicious. It is not surprising
that many linguists do not distinguish between these two notions of
'domain': in the schools of linguistics that have been most influential in
this country, namely, Bloomfieldian structuralism and the varieties of
transformational grammar found in Chomsky's *Syntactic Structures* (1957)

Reprinted by permission from *Limiting the Domain of Linguistics*, ed. David
Cohen (Milwaukee: University of Wisconsin at Milwaukee, 1972), pp. vi–xi.

217

and *Aspects of the Theory of Syntax* (1965), the things that the linguist is to account for are precisely the facts that he is allowed to look at, namely, distributional facts about the phonological and syntactic constituents of sentences. While *Syntactic Structures* and *Aspects* are full of references to 'linguistic competence' as being what a grammar is to provide an account of, the notion of 'competence' actually employed in *Aspects* is so closely tied to the distributional facts that it is no exaggeration to say that distributional facts are all that a grammar according to *Aspects* is supposed to account for: 'competence' is taken to be the knowledge on the basis of which the speaker is able to distinguish 'grammatical sentences' from everything else, and, subject to a qualification about evaluation measures which I will mention later, the only evidence concerning that knowledge which one is allowed to bring in is facts about what is or is not grammatical.

While I oppose any limitation on the class of facts that a linguist may bring into his arguments, there are a number of possible pursuits concerned with language which I would not label as linguistics. Let me first give a couple of such examples and then attempt to formulate a proposal for limiting 'the domain of linguistics' in the latter of my two senses. The first example is quite trivial: one would not be doing linguistics if he confined his attention to the third formant of possible utterances in some language and took his goal to be the writing of a system of rules that specified the class of functions F(t) that express the third formant of a possible utterance in terms of time. This would not be linguistics, since it would not be the study of language but only of one extremely peripheral aspect of language without reference to its role in language. A second example is a somewhat less trivial one, though not in principle a great deal different from the first: one would not be doing linguistics if one were to confine his attention to the sequences of morphemes that can occur in possible utterances of some language and to take for his goal the writing of a set of rules that specifies the class of all strings of morphemes that are 'grammatical'. One reason for hesitating to call that pursuit linguistics is that the data that it is supposed to account for is not elicitable from informants. Heringer (1970) has presented facts that confirm a long-held suspicion of mine, namely, that (contrary to claims by Chomsky, Katz, and others) native speakers of a language are not capable of giving reliable judgments as to whether a particular string of morphemes or words is possible in that language.[2] When they appear to be giving such a judgment, what they generally are really reporting is that they have succeeded or have not succeeded in thinking of a meaning that it would be a normal way of expressing and a context in which it could express that meaning, subject to constraints on the meaning and context that they take the linguist to have been imposing. This means that informants' judgments that some string of words is possible are more reliable than their judgments that it is not possible. Heringer has shown that informants who in fact can perfectly well say some sentence will fail to think of the meaning that they could express by it or judge that meaning irrelevant and will report the sentence as ungrammatical. For example, he presented the sentence *John left until 6 P.M.* out of context to one group of informants and was told by 90% (18 out of 20) that it was ungrammatical; he presented the same sentence to another group with the information that it was supposed to mean 'John left and is to come back at 6 P.M.' and was told by only 60% (24 out of 39) that it was ungrammatical.

A more striking example of this phenomenon is provided by sentences discussed in Morgan 1973 such as *Spiro conjectures Ex-Lax*. Few persons would realize that that sentence is possible if they were presented with it in isolation; however, I am sure that hardly anyone would find the sentence strange if presented with it as an answer to the question *Does anyone have any idea what Pat Nixon frosts her cakes with ?*. It has indeed been claimed (Makkai 1971) that for essentially any sequence of words that meets gross restrictions on well-formedness (e.g., the word order and agreement are right), a context can be found in which it is appropriate. While I think that Makkai's claim is an exaggeration, it is nonetheless not far off the mark. To the extent that it is correct, writing rules to specify what strings of words are grammatical is pointless and in particular, irrelevant to the study of linguistic competence. Of course, Makkai's conclusion would not be accepted by those linguists who maintain that one should only treat as 'fully grammatical' those sentences which can be understood without reference to 'strange' factual situations and without interpreting any of the words metaphorically (cf. Katz and Fodor 1963, Katz 1964; Makkai's argument for his conclusion rests heavily on the possibility of using words metaphorically).[3] Such a conception of 'grammaticality' is highly suspect, since (1) what constitutes a 'strange' factual situation is surely a matter of the informant's imagination and experience and not of his linguistic competence, (2) it is doubtful that any sharp line can be drawn between metaphoric and nonmetaphoric use of language, and (3) such an approach sabotages its own goals, since it in effect makes 'grammaticality' not a property of strings of words or morphemes in themselves but a property of them in relation to what they can mean. Furthermore, if one attempts to rule out sentences like *Spiro conjectures Ex-Lax* as ungrammatical by the most obvious tactic, namely, by excluding those sentences that are appropriate only in some larger linguistic context, it would be necessary also to declare ungrammatical such sentences as

*The cat sat on the mat.
*The farmer killed the duckling.
*Did he leave any message?
*John forced the doctor to examine Bill.

which contain anaphoric devices (such as the past tense marker) that must have antecedents in an earlier sentence of the discourse[4] and are bizarre if used in any other context. Note, incidentally, that this observation suggests another side to Makkai's 'contextual adjustability principle': not only can just about any string of words be good in an appropriate context, but also just about any string of words can be bad in an (in-?) appropriate context.

I maintain that a linguist's concern should be with describing and explaining competence and that, despite claims of Chomsky and Katz to the contrary, the linguistic theories of *Syntactic Structures* and *Aspects* have little to do with linguistic competence. This is an appropriate place for me to bring up the qualification that I mentioned above regarding what Chomsky allows one to bring in in deciding among alternative grammars, namely, that for Chomsky the decision is made on the basis not only of grammaticality facts but also of an evaluation measure. I have argued elsewhere (McCawley 1968c)[5] that there is no reason for accepting the relationship between evaluation measures and acquisition that Chomsky sees; that if any kind of numerical evaluation of alternatives plays a role in language acquisition, it is not the evaluation of alternative entire grammars but the evaluation of alternative *revisions* in an already acquired grammar, that is, that acquisition proceeds by a principle of least effort; and that the grammar which has resulted from successive applications of a least-effort principle will generally not be 'optimal' in a way that would correspond to the kind of evaluation measure that Chomsky has proposed. A useful analogy here is the fact that the meandering of rivers has been shown (Leopold and Langbein 1966) to be the result of a least-effort principle. In addition, Peters has shown that, contrary to Chomsky's claims, the choice of an evaluation measure is not an empirical matter unless heavy a priori constraints are placed on what is allowed as a possible evaluation measure: given any set of facts and any grammar of the *Aspects* type consistent with those facts, it is possible to set up an evaluation measure which rates that grammar as less costly than any other such grammar.[6]

Taking 'domain' in the second sense considered above, I would propose a rather sharp limitation on the domain of linguistics, namely, that it be linguistic competence, both in itself and in its interaction with everything that it interacts with. I take 'linguistic competence' here as referring to a speaker's internalized system for relating meanings to possible ways of expressing them and the characteristics of linguistic and extralinguistic contexts under which particular ways of expressing them are appropriate. It should be clear that I reject the widespread idea that one is not doing linguistics if one is studying how language is used in reasoning, telling jokes, writing poetry, or persuading people to buy Volkswagens or vote for Eugene McCarthy, or how language malfunctions when one has a bullet in one's brain or is high on hash. I find the idea that such studies are not linguistics as peculiar as the (fortunately not very popular) idea that one should study the physiology of the digestive tract without reference to food and drink. One striking manifestation of the position that linguistics must be isolated from everything else to really be linguistics is found in Chomsky (1970b:186), where Chomsky states that one gives up the notion of any linguistic level of 'semantic representation' if one accepts the position of Grice (1957) and Dennis Stampe (1968) that meaning must be analyzed in terms of the relation 'speaker $x$ means/meant $y$ by sentence $z$ (in speech act $w$)'. The $y$'s of such formulas would seem to me to be necessarily some kind of 'semantic representation'; however, Chomsky evidently demands that they be ruled no part of linguistics if they can only be related to sentences by means of considerations of what speakers of the language do in using it. Another striking illustration of this position is Chomsky's (1970b:191) insistence that an analysis of a sentence may involve the information that two NP's are coreferential but may not involve information as to what a NP refers to. To continue the analogy with physiology, that is comparable to allowing a description of the digestive tract to mention sameness and difference between chemical constituents present in the digestive tract but not allowing reference to hydroxyl ions or to the COOH radical.

I said that I have proposed a sharp limitation on the domain of linguistics. It is a sharp limitation in that it rules out of linguistics a lot of the favorite pursuits of linguists of many theoretical persuasions. It of course does not involve any limitation on the 'domain' in the first of the two senses that I discussed at the beginning of this paper, the class of facts that a linguist may look at in the course of his duties. I think that my recurrent analogy of a language to a digestive tract is apt: either can be understood only in terms of its interaction with things that are not part of it. I suspect that the widespread failure of linguists to think of a language in that way is due to a belief that every fact 'belongs to' one and only one science and that if a linguist brings into a linguistic argument such distinctions as[7]

Five crooks joined forces with three others to murder a ninth/*tenth.
Five crooks joined forces with three other to murder a ninth and a tenth/
    *sixth.

he is provoking a border dispute with arithmetic which carries with it the grave danger that linguistics might win the dispute and be left possessing an enormous piece of territory that it does not have the forces necessary to police or defend. That, however, isn't the way things are: facts don't belong to anybody.[8]

# 23   ¡Madison Avenue, Si, Pennsylvania Avenue, No!

This paper deals with scientific revolutions and their relation to advertising, a subject that was touched on in Makkai 1975.

The notion of scientific revolution, popularized particularly by Thomas Kuhn (1962), has figured in much discussion of the recent history of linguistics. Kuhn's ideas, however, have often been grossly misunderstood; for example, there is a deplorably common tendency to form an unholy synthesis of Kuhn's notion of revolution with the previously standard view that science develops cumulatively, which yields the popular but totally unwarranted view that scientific revolutions are always for the better. I note in passing that Chomsky's conception of the history of linguistics commits him to the view that there have been scientific revolutions for the worse in linguistics and psychology (e.g., the 'neogrammarian revolution' and the 'behaviorist revolution'). Since the notion of scientific revolution and other notions with which Kuhn works have been subject to a wide variety of interpretations, many of which Kuhn has explicitly repudiated (1970, 1974), it would be worth my while to begin with a brief sketch of the conception of 'scientific revolution' which I will assume below. The reader is cautioned that what follows may not be exactly what Kuhn had in mind.[1]

Kuhn (1962) devotes little explicit discussion to what is perhaps the most fundamental notion in his conception of the history of science, namely, the notion of scientific community.[2] A scientific community is first of all a community: it is a body of persons which is potentially immortal, in that new members can enter it without its losing its identity, and its members communicate with each other (often via highly indirect paths of communication) and have some awareness of the identity of this body to which they belong and some concern for the future of the body and of their

Reprinted by permission from *The Second LACUS Forum*, ed. Peter Reich (Columbia, S.C.: Hornbeam Press, 1976). Copyright © 1976 by the Linguistic Association of Canada and the United States.

relationship to it. What distinguishes a scientific community from other kinds of community, such as a religion or an artistic clique, is that the activity relevant to the identity of the community is the acquisition and refinement of knowledge. I emphasize that the *refinement* of knowledge is essential to the status of a community as a scientific community: the life of the community must include not only the accretion of new knowledge but the replacement of existing knowledge by better knowledge and the purging of old 'knowledge' that has been found to be in error. (Found by whom? Read on for an eventual answer.) According to this highly informal characterization, Catholic theologians might form a scientific community, but the Catholic religion would not. I am not disturbed to have a community of theologians coming out to be a 'scientific community': the term ought to be broad enough to include freakish and nonproductive scientific communities as well as scientific communities such as we would be likely to approve of, since, following Kuhn, I want to separate clearly the question of how scientific communities do in reality develop over the course of time and the question of what are valid grounds for accepting a scientific theory. My characterization allows for the possibility of a community becoming a scientific community, or of a scientific community losing the status of a scientific community though still remaining a community, or of a scientific community splitting into two or more separate communities, all or some or none of which constituted scientific communities. For example, I would hold that the community of historians has gradually been turning into a scientific community over the last century.

Kuhn (1962) used the term 'paradigm' in a bewildering range of ways, as has been noted by critics (Shapere 1964, Masterman 1970) and admitted by Kuhn himself (1970, 1974). The sense of 'paradigm' that will be most important in the discussion below is what a linguist might describe as a set of 'markedness principles'. At any time, in any scientific community, there are certain factual and theoretical claims and approaches to the solution of problems which have acquired such prestige and/or wide acceptance that members of the community feel free to employ them without offering further justification for them; these ideas and approaches will generally be what appear in textbooks and courses that are intended for elementary instruction in the subject that the scientific community is concerned with. These claims and approaches are 'unmarked', as contrasted with 'marked' claims and approaches, which students will be exposed to (if at all) only after they have a background in the unmarked approaches; a person presenting a paper at a meeting cannot just assume 'marked' claims or approaches but must also defend them, or at least, he must if he is to retain his standing as a member of the community and not acquire the reputation of a gate-crasher or a crackpot. Note that a member of a scientific community can contradict claims of the community's paradigms and still remain a member in good standing of the community; however, to do so, he has to exert the effort of offering (rather than presupposing) justification. A paradigm need not even be consistent: several mutually inconsistent approaches may each have achieved sufficient status within a scientific community that any may be adopted without further ado.

Within any scientific community there are likely to be subcommunities which have different markedness principles than the whole community does. This will almost certainly be the case whenever the large community has an inconsistent paradigm; for example, within the community of physicists, among which several conceptions of atomic structure are 'paradigmatic', there are subcommunities whose paradigms include only one conception of atomic structure. A similar situation prevails in linguistics; for example, in a presentation at an LSA meeting one could assume without further ado the interpretive-semantic version of transformational grammar presented in Jackendoff 1972, but one would be obliged to offer some justification for it in presenting a paper in that framework at a meeting of the Chicago Linguistic Society. A person can thus recognize a proposition as part of the paradigm of a community to which he belongs even though he does not accept that proposition himself.

How can a situation such as this come about or prevail more than briefly? Wouldn't a proposition of the paradigm have to have been refuted before a subcommunity that accepted a conflicting proposition came into being? Once a proposition of the paradigm has been refuted, won't all reasonable persons recognize that it has been refuted, and won't it thus lose its status immediately as part of the paradigm? And won't a new analysis that works where the existing paradigm has failed rapidly become accepted as a component of a new paradigm?

Far from it. The grounds on which it is appropriate for one to reject or to accept a proposition or a theory or an approach are nowhere near as clear-cut as they are often held to be. There can be reasonable disagreement among individuals as to what putative facts should count as facts and what facts should be regarded as having relevance to the given scientific discipline. For example, the followers of Velikovski accept ancient myths as providing reports (albeit, distorted reports) of actual cataclysms and take the agreements among myths of different cultures as facts that require explaining and which bear on geology and astronomy; but 'mainstream' geologists and astronomers do not feel obliged to account for these putative facts. In this and many similar cases, there are no clearcut grounds for agreeing with one group against the other. There can also be reasonable disagreement as regards what features of a scientific theory are grounds for harboring doubts about it. For example, many first-rate physicists have viewed with great suspicion the 'action at a distance' which is central to Newton's theory of gravitation; indeed, Newton himself accepted it only with grave misgivings. But there are also many first-rate physicists who aren't bothered a whit by action at a distance. Further, as Feyerabend (1970) has argued, the fact that a theory has been refuted does not mean that it will stay refuted for all time. Supposed refutations of a theory generally rest on auxiliary theories and factual claims, some of which might well be wrong. Feyerabend notes that the heliocentric theory of the planets, which has been kicking around since antiquity, stood as refuted until around 1600, when a new theory of motion was developed that allowed the heliocentric theory to be reconciled with the facts.

An adherent of a theory that has been refuted has several honorable alternatives available to him. If there is an alternative theory available that works where his theory fails, he may simply junk the one theory in favor of the other. Or he might attempt to construct a variant of his theory which accords with the facts, by pinpointing some aspect of that theory that can be held responsible for the discrepancy with the facts and revising that particular point of the theory so as to eliminate the discrepancy. Or one might identify a particular area that an as yet nonexistent auxiliary theory might cover, and act under the assumption that an auxiliary theory will eventually be forthcoming which will bring his theory into line with the facts.[3] This last alternative amounts to issuing a promissory note on behalf of the theory, and it is not wise to do that unless the theory's credit rating is good,[4] that is, unless the theory's value as a tool of explanation and prediction has been sufficiently high as to warrant confidence in it. But of course members of a scientific community can be in reasonable disagreement as to the credit ratings of various theories. And one generally cannot be sure which of these alternative responses to a supposed refutation is the right one until long after the fact.

Thus, at any moment in its history, a scientific community may have a 'paradigm' and yet harbor considerable disagreement among its members not only about matters on the 'frontiers' of the science, but even about points of the paradigm itself, and these disagreements need not reflect any ignorance or moral turpitude among the parties to the disagreement. These observations set the stage for what Kuhn calls 'paradigm shift', which is the essence of a scientific revolution. Paradigms change in the course of a scientific community's history, sometimes in minor ways and sometimes drastically. In the case of a major shift, the change in the paradigm of the larger community begins with the development of a subcommunity which accepts the new paradigm (or some embryonic form of the new paradigm) and culminates when that subcommunity has swelled in numbers to such an extent that it is hard to distinguish between the subcommunity and the whole community.

The full story of scientific revolutions will then have to cover both how subcommunities come into being and how subcommunities can grow (or diminish) in importance within the larger community. This is where advertising starts to raise its head. Journals and professional meetings provide forums that are an essential part of the business of extending and refining knowledge. Since a paper that merely reiterates points of the paradigm will be a waste of time for all concerned, a large proportion of the papers presented in journals and at meetings will contain ideas which are not part of the paradigm, and which may perfectly well conflict with the paradigm. Meetings and journals facilitate the formation of sub-communities: they allow holders of nonparadigm positions to identify others of like mind, and they expose the readers and participants to presentations of ideas or viewpoints that they previously had not been aware of or had not attached much importance to, possibly influencing some members of the audience to accept those ideas or at least to take an option on them and invest some of their intellectual capital in exploring their consequences.

Such presentations, whatever else they are, certainly constitute adver-tising. They present the audience with grounds for adopting the ideas in question, by illustrating what can be done with them and by pointing out advantages of those ideas over other ideas that might be harnessed to do the same work. When the new ideas conflict with a person's current ideas, selling him the new ideas will be difficult in proportion to the use that he gets out of his present ideas, since "as in manufacture, so in science— retooling is an extravagance to be reserved for the occasion that demands it" (Kuhn 1972:76). To put it on a more mundane level, if you want to sell can-openers to people that already have can-openers, you aren't going to succeed just by telling them that your can-openers open cans. You will have to convince them that your can-openers have advantages over their present can-openers, and not just any advantages, but advantages that they care about or that you can make them care about. A person might junk his present can-opener in favor of one of yours because yours makes it harder for him to cut his fingers, but not because it plays *The Star-spangled Banner* while he turns the handle. In summary, to win an adherent to a new idea, you must convince him that the expenditure of intellectual capital that is involved in his adopting the idea will pay off in things that matter to him.

Let's turn now to advertising in general. Makkai compares advertising with witchcraft and sees a need for exorcists to free the victims of adver-tising from its spells. He accuses transformational grammarians of recruiting adherents to their paradigm through the practice of this black art. By contrast, he says proudly of stratificational grammar, "We do not advertise" (1975:207).

This last claim is just as much nonsense as was Newton's claim that he didn't construct hypotheses. Of course, stratificational grammarians advertise their theory, and Makkai's paper is a perfect example of advertising on the part of stratificational grammar. This doesn't mean that Makkai and Lamb are practicing a black art; they are engaging in a perfectly ordinary activity that is practiced by everyone from the pros on Madison Avenue to the pastor announcing next Sunday's sermon. In treating professional advertising as witchcraft, Makkai is grossly overestimating the power of advertising and grossly underestimating both the intelligence and the inertia of the audiences at whom advertising is directed.[5] As an illustration of this point, consider what effect the cigarette commercials that Makkai describes with great indignation have actually had. From 1961 to 1970, the per capita consumption of tobacco by adult U.S. residents decreased steadily, and the per capita consumption of cigarettes also decreased, though somewhat more erratically:

| Year | Consumption per U.S. Resident ≥ 18 Years Old | |
| | Pounds of Tobacco | Number of Cigarettes |
|---|---|---|
| 1925–29 | 9.68 | 1285 |
| 1930–34 | 8.80 | 1389 |
| 1935–39 | 9.22 | 1779 |
| 1940–44 | 10.88 | 2558 |
| 1945–49 | 12.46 | 3459 |
| 1950–54 | 12.61 | 3695 |
| 1955–59 | 11.71 | 3806 |
| 1960 | 11.82 | 4171 |
| 1961 | 12.00 | 4266 |
| 1962 | 11.80 | 4265 |
| 1963 | 11.78 | 4345 |
| 1964 | 11.54 | 4194 |
| 1965 | 11.51 | 4258 |
| 1966 | 11.12 | 4287 |
| 1967 | 10.70 | 4280 |
| 1968 | 10.59 | 4186 |
| 1969 | 10.04 | 3993 |
| 1970 | 9.68 | 3985 |

In the early 1970s, while per capita consumption of tobacco as a whole continued to drop, per capita consumption of cigarettes increased to a figure approaching that of the early 1960s:

| Year | Consumption Per Capita (U.S. Adult) | |
| --- | --- | --- |
| | Pounds of Tobacco | Number of Cigarettes |
| 1970 | 9.68 | 3985 |
| 1971 | 9.54 | 4042 |
| 1972 | 9.46 | 4080 |
| 1973 | | 4100 (estimate) |

SOURCE: *Tobacco Situation*, Washington, D.C.: U.S. Dept of Agriculture, March 1971, p. 5, and Sept. 1972, p. 6; *New York Times Index 1973*.

January 3, 1971 is an important date in this story, since that was the last day on which cigarette commercials could legally be shown on American television. The above figures show that while television viewers were being exposed daily to these diabolical cigarette commercials, their average consumption of tobacco in general and cigarettes in particular was decreasing, but as soon as the commercials were taken off the air, they started smoking more cigarettes. These figures suggest two things to me. First, that cigarette commercials in the 1960s led very few people to start smoking and led very few smokers to break a resolution to stop smoking: Rather, their principal effect was on *what brands* smokers smoked.[6] Their effect is thus something of no consequence to me. While I consider smoking to be about as polite as farting, I couldn't care less whether the noxious fumes that my neighbors are forcing me to breathe come from a Marlboro or from a Salem. Second, the figures suggest that antismoking ads that viewers saw only once in a rare while were more effective at turning people off of smoking than the cigarette commercials that they were deluged with night after night were at turning people on to smoking.

More generally, I conjecture that people are a damn sight more rational in their responses to advertising than they are often given credit for being. In particular, they are aware of the implications of Grice's (1975) 'conversational maxims', that is, they draw conclusions not only from what the advertisement says but also from the fact that it doesn't say other things that it might have said. If someone is trying to sell you something, it is in his interest to give you reasons why you should buy it: "If you've got it, flaunt it," as the National Airlines ads used to say. Using Grice's principles, one can infer that if an ad doesn't flaunt anything, it must because there isn't anything for it to flaunt. The cigarette ads that Makkai cited didn't flaunt anything, and the most that any of them was able to bring about was that a significant number of smokers happened to think of that brand when their regular brand was sold out or when they for some reason felt they would rather switch than fight.

I've been talking about advertising which is merely vacuous; let's now turn to advertising that is deceitful or irresponsible. I maintain that irresponsible advertising is far more common in amateur advertising than in professional advertising. To illustrate this point, let's look at something that isn't generally thought of as advertising but which obviously is if you just think about it, namely, university course catalogs. Course catalogs constitute advertising fully as much as the Sears-Roebuck catalog does: they are distributed to prospective customers and provide information about the seller's products that the prospective customers use in deciding what, if anything, they will buy from the seller.[7] Viewed as advertising, course catalogs are often disgracefully irresponsible. They are often prepared far in advance and based on guesswork as to what faculty members will be around three or four years hence and what courses they will be offering, but only rarely do they contain any indication of the tentative nature of their listings. If, as is often the case, many of the superstars on the university's faculty spend much of their time away from the university, that fact is not noted in the catalogs. A department's course listings often reflect the chairman's wishful thinking about courses that he'd like to see offered if he could get a new position budgeted and could find the right person to fill it. Catalogs often list obsolete degree requirements which no one on the faculty took the trouble to read and correct.

Universities are able to get away with irresponsible advertising simply because the people concerned, both purveyors and consumers, do not think of it as advertising and do not demand of it the standards that they would demand of advertising by a mail-order house or an insurance company; for example, students don't bring lawsuits against universities whose catalogs have led them to waste time and money on courses that were not what was advertised. I enter a cautionary note here: to say 'We do not advertise' is to court disaster; to keep from producing irresponsible advertising, one must make an effort to recognize his advertising as such and to impose on it the standards that he would impose on advertising in general. In fact, Makkai's paper contains many irresponsible claims and suggestions about the theories he is arguing against and how they differ from his theory, as when he cites as an advantage of stratificational grammar the fact that "we do not make the mistake of deriving the participial interpretation [of *Visiting relatives can be a nuisance*] from the gerundival one, or vice versa" (p. 202). To my knowledge, no one has ever made that mistake, least of all his antagonists, who are unanimous in deriving the two interpretations from two distinct underlying structures.[8] Shades of the Lucky Strike ads that said "It's toasted," when in fact all cigarette tobacco is toasted.

In this attack on Makkai, I have espoused propositions that seem to be leading me toward Makkai's conclusion that advertising in scientific communities may be particularly pernicious and may result in scientific revolutions for the worse: I've agreed that advertising plays an important role in scientific revolutions, and I've maintained that amateurs are more irresponsible advertisers than professionals are. Let's then see to what extent perversions of advertising can be expected to occur and to have pernicious effects in scientific communities.

Deceitful or irresponsible advertising can gull suckers into buying an inferior product; however, it is powerless to lead a sucker to buy the same product a second time. A corollary to this observation is that deceitful or irresponsible advertising can be of more than transitory benefit to the advertiser only if the product is something that one doesn't buy very often. Even here, the incidence of irresponsible advertising is kept fairly low by the fact that the bilked or injured customer is often in a position to bring a lawsuit against the offending company and win it, and it is in the company's interests to keep from losing lawsuits. Another corollary: irresponsible or deceitful advertising is potentially most effective in the case of products which a consumer buys only rarely and where his dissatisfaction with a particular product does not provide grounds for a lawsuit. It now looks as if Makkai is onto something: scientific theories *are* something that one doesn't buy very often (remember Kuhn's remark about avoiding the expense of retooling) and furthermore, no one could sue a scholar for having sold him a lousy theory, since the transactions in the market for ideas do not involve the transfer of money. The market for ideas thus seems to have all the characteristics of a market where irresponsible or deceitful advertisers could have a field day. And in fact, the market for ideas has a pretty bad record as far as markets go. It is much easier to find revolutions for the worse in the market for ideas than in the markets for more mundane things like writing instruments; there is no instance that I know of in which one type of writing instrument has supplanted another in which the new writing instrument did not enable people to do more writing, do it faster, and do it more cheaply.

I think that suckers do get fleeced worse in the market for ideas than in the market for writing instruments. However, most of the wrath that this idea stimulates in me is directed not against the swindlers but against the suckers. Scientific communities get the scientific revolutions that they deserve. The members of a scientific community are in the business of acquiring and refining knowledge, and they thus ought to be adept at evaluating claims. If the community is filled with persons who have little awareness of the implications of their supposed knowledge and little concern with the critical evaluation of other ideas, people who are willing to invest their intellectual capital on a scientific vehicle that they haven't given a thorough test-drive, then the community is in bad shape: it is in serious danger of mass investment of its collective intellectual capital on worthless projects. However, if a community is in that bad shape, its members can't have all that much intellectual capital to be bilked out of. If anything, a scientific revolution, regardless of the relative merits of the new and old paradigms, is likely to do good for that kind of scientific community, since any kind of scientific revolution would be likely to stimulate some members of the community to the critical thinking that the community has been lacking in. In the case of a healthy scientific community, irresponsible advertising is likely to be ineffective, since the community will be full of people adept at detecting its irresponsibility. Indeed, the only real danger of irresponsible advertising in a healthy scientific community is that if a good theory is irresponsibly advertised, it will become a laughingstock and not be given as serious an examination as it deserves. Thus, my impression of advertising in science is that it is the lifeblood of scientific communities, and that even irresponsible advertising does as much good as it does harm.

So far, I have said nothing about the other thoroughfare that is mentioned in my title, Pennsylvania Avenue. I will conclude by rectifying that omission and in the process relate the anarchistic philosophy of science that I have been working with to anarchist political philosophy. When a subcommunity develops within an existing scientific community, it is impossible to determine whether that subcommunity forms the vanguard of a scientific revolution. In its early stages, a subcommunity will have only a fragmentary paradigm, and its members will have extended more credit to that paradigm than its credit rating really warrants; their membership in the subcommunity will to a certain extent represent a speculative investment of their intellectual capital.[9] The subcommunity's paradigm may become more highly articulated and may provide solutions to important problems, and the auxiliary hypotheses needed to pay its debts may be developed, so that its credit rating improves and it attracts investment of a less speculative character, possibly culminating in its paradigm becoming the paradigm of the larger scientific community. The subcommunity's paradigm may, however, just go deeper into intellectual debt without ever developing beyond mere fragments, and it may lose all power to attract additional investment. If the investors are rational and well informed (of course they won't all be), a subcommunity's paradigm will become that of the larger community only if it has shown itself over a period of several years to be a worthwhile investment.

Now let's see how government spending on research and education alters the picture. I maintain that government subsidization of research and education, regardless of how benevolently and fairly it is administered, increases the likelihood of scientific revolutions for the worse, since it makes it possible for a subcommunity to increase its membership drastically without demonstrating that its intellectual credit so warrants. The kind of development that I have in mind is illustrated by the rapid growth of American universities during the late 1950s and the 1960s, stimulated by massive spending by the federal government. This spending made it possible for many universities to start linguistics programs that otherwise would not have been started or would not have been started so early, or to expand existing programs much further than they would otherwise have been expanded. Given the situation of the early 1960s, it was inevitable that a large proportion of the new teaching jobs in linguistics would go to transformational grammarians. In the case of new programs, since at that time transformational grammar was the kind of linguistics in which it was most obvious that new and interesting things were going on, many administrators would prefer to get a transformational grammarian to organize the new program; in the case of expansion of existing programs, even when those who had charge of the new funds would not speculate their personal intellectual capital on the new theory, it was to their advantage to speculate their newfound monetary capital on it, since if the new theory was going to become influential, a department would have to offer instruction in it if the department was to attract students in numbers that were in keeping with its newfound monetary riches. And with the first couple of bunches of students turned out by the holders of these new jobs, the membership of the transformational subcommunity swelled greatly.

In saying this, I am not saying that it is a bad thing that the transformational paradigm acquired its position of eminence in linguistics. What I am saying is that it acquired that position faster than it deserved to and that the mechanism which speeded up its achievement of that position could equally well have done the same for a paradigm that was headed for intellectual bankruptcy but which, at the time when the manna was raining down from heaven, looked like the safest investment.[10]

# 24     Some Ideas Not to Live by

This paper will consist of commentary on a number of widely accepted ideas about the nature of language and the relation of language to language acquisition which I hold to be pernicious in that they have retarded our development of an understanding of how language functions and is acquired and have led to the waste of countless hours on pointless controversies. I apologize in advance for the anomaly that in a paper which will criticize linguists for failing to provide a foundation in psychology for their psychological claims, my arguments will rest heavily on mere conjecture about the acquisition and perception of language.

Pernicious idea number 1 is the idea that a language is a set of sentences, and the concomitant idea that the linguist's principal or even only goal in describing a language should be to specify what are and what are not possible sentences of that language. This idea, which is generally assigned major importance in transformational grammarians' statements of policy, though it in fact plays much less of a role in transformational grammarians' actual practice, has its roots in the extremely antipsychologistic point of view which prevailed in American linguistics from the 1930s until about 1960: linguists were supposed to concern themselves only with linguistic data and not to indulge in speculation about the relation of the linguistic data to the minds of the speakers of the language. That point of view entails an extremely narrow conception of 'linguistic data': the fact that certain utterances occurred, the fact that certain conceivable utterances did not occur, the fact that certain utterances 'counted as' identical or as different; any other data were considered 'extralinguistic'.

There is only one significant respect in which this latter conception of 'linguistic data' differed from that of early transformational grammarians, namely, that whereas the American 'descriptivists' accorded a more important place to 'positive' data than to 'negative' data (i.e., they

Reprinted by permission from *Die neueren Sprachen* 75 (1976): 151–65.

regarded the failure of a grammar to account for an occurring form as a more serious defect than its failure to account for the nonoccurrence of a nonoccurring form), transformational grammarians from the very beginning have accorded the same importance to negative data as to positive data.[1] This difference will naturally make transformational grammarians more receptive to introspective data than were the 'descriptivists': positive data can be gathered passively—you hear someone utter a sentence, and you've got yourself a positive datum; but to get yourself negative data, you have to either have some way of extrapolating from nonoccurrence in your positive data to nonoccurrence in general (which would mean giving positive data a place of priority relative to negative data) or rely on negative judgments that speakers make about putative sentences, those judgments necessarily being based on introspection. Since a subject may reject as 'unacceptable' or 'odd' a sentence that has occurred (even in his own speech), one is then forced to rely on introspection in one's positive data as well as in one's negative data.

The shift to introspective data, in my opinion, has considerably narrowed the previously huge gap between linguistics and language. A language is something that one learns, and what one learns is not just a set of linguistic data. One learns how to do things with words, and the learning involves the whole gamut of interactions among one's goals, the objects of one's experience and imagination, and the words and structures of the language that one is learning. Without bringing in introspective data, it is hard to imagine how any insight could be gained into the relationship between 'linguistic data' and language. However, it is not at all obvious that the specific distinction that transformational grammarians have been concerned with, that between 'grammatical' and 'ungrammatical' strings of words (or between 'acceptable' and 'unacceptable' strings),[2] is even a real distinction, let alone a distinction that is open to introspection. The judgments of 'grammaticality' or of 'acceptability' that have figured in the transformational literature are, I maintain, judgments of something else: perhaps that the speaker has thought of an appropriate use for the sentence,[3] or has judged it an acceptable way of expressing the meaning that he takes it to be supposed to express, or perhaps that he has failed to see any reason why it could not be used, or why it could not express the meaning that he takes to be at issue. That is, the actual judgments that a person makes are judgments not about the sentence itself but about specific uses of the sentence, or about his ability to find a use for it. My impression is that the ability to judge accurately whether a given string of words has a use is closely related to the ability to construct good puns and is about as rare.

It is quite easy to construct sentences that sound incoherent when presented out of context but which are quite normal in specific contexts. For example, Morgan (1973) has noted that sentences such as 1a make no sense in isolation but are perfectly normal when used as the answer to a question such as 1b:

1a. Kissinger conjectures poached.
  b. Does anyone know how President Ford likes his eggs?

The question whether 1a is grammatical has no substance. The closest that one can come to answering that non-question is to reply that 1a is a possible way to say that Kissinger conjectures that Ford like his eggs poached, when it is used in a context that allows for the ellipsis of 'President Ford likes his eggs . . .'. Those sentences which are universally judged as 'grammatical' are simply those for which no one has any difficulty in thinking of uses.

A further respect in which 'grammaticality judgments' fail to be judgments of any property of the given string of words is that the informant (particularly if he is identical to the investigator) tends to 'cooperate' with the investigator by ignoring meanings and uses that he assumes are irrelevant to the investigator's concerns. This point was brought out well by Heringer (1970), who found that 40% of his informants judged 2 grammatical when told that it was supposed to mean 'John left and is to return at 6 P.M.', but none of a second group of informants, who were not told what it was to mean, judged it grammatical:

2. John left until 6 P.M.

In the discussion after the presentation of his paper, Heringer mentioned that he later asked the informants of the second group whether they had realized that 2 might be used to mean 'John left and is to return at 6 P.M.' and found that several had realized that fact and found 2 acceptable with that meaning, but assumed that such an interpretation was irrelevant to Heringer's concerns.

It thus appears as if speakers of a language can make introspective judgments about their language that are reasonably accurate and consistent but that these judgments are generally not about a sentence itself but rather about that sentence relative to uses and contexts. This point is of importance in connection with language acquisition, since it shows that the 'negative data' that influence a child's acquisition of his language cannot be 'ungrammaticality data'. When a child is corrected, or is laughed at, or is not understood, he is not thereby informed that he has uttered an ungrammatical sentence. The reactions of those around him may inform him that what he has said is not a normal way of saying what he wants to say in the given context, but they give him no information about whether it is a normal way of saying something else or whether it would be normal in some other context. Much of the 'positive data' that he receives could be said to inform him that the sentences in question are grammatical.[4] However, that fact is incidental to something more important, namely, that the 'positive data' provide him with the information that those sentences are an acceptable way for the speaker to do whatever he is doing. I conclude that the data that a child is presented with in the course of his language acquisition do not provide him with a basis for distinguishing the supposed set of all grammatical sentences of his language from the set of ungrammatical strings of words of that language (assuming here, for sake of argument, that the notion 'grammatical' makes sense), and even if it did enable him to draw such a distinction, it is not clear that the distinction would play any role in his acquisition of language.

Pernicious idea number 2 is the idea that 'the data determine the grammar'. Actually, this is two pernicious ideas, one relating to linguistic analysis (the idea that a linguist can determine whether a given grammar of a certain language is correct by checking whether it generates the right sentences, associates the right meanings to each sentence, etc.) and one relating to language acquisition (the idea that what grammar a child internalizes is determined by the set of 'linguistic data' that he has been confronted with); the narrower the conception of 'data' that these ideas are combined with, the more pernicious they are.

The pernicious nature of these ideas becomes most evident from a consideration of the problem of determining what morphemes the language has. Propositions of morphemic identity form most of the factual basis of arguments that generative phonologists have offered in support of specific analyses, for example, the proposition that *righteous* consists of *right* plus a suffix is crucial to Chomsky and Halle's (1968:233–34) argument that *right* derives from underlying /rixt/. However, little attention has been paid to the problem of justifying these morpheme identifications and to distinguishing between them and other, clearly incorrect identifications; what basis could we provide for saying that *right* is related to *righteous* but not to *rich*? or that *duchess* is a derivative of *duke* and not of *duck*? or that *lawyer* is a derivative of *law* but *mother* is not a derivative of *moth*? The criteria for morpheme identity that are found in works by 'descriptivist' linguists are not up to drawing these distinctions. For example, Harris' procedures (1951a: chaps. 12, 13) of dividing utterances into morphemic segments and grouping those segments into morphemes so as to minimize the inventory of morphemes and regularize the distributions of each, appear to be just as easily applicable to *moth/mother* as to *right/righteous* or *berry/cranberry*. Since different morphemes rarely if ever have exactly the same distributions, Harris's procedures have to be interpreted loosely if they are to ever be applicable, and there is no obvious basis for allowing a loose interpretation which would accommodate *berry/cranberry* but not *moth/mother*. To my knowledge, no generative grammarian has ever proposed any criteria for morpheme identity. Someone might interject at this point that no criterion is necessary: that the evaluation measure, which is to serve as the basis for choosing the 'least costly' of all the grammars that are consistent with the given facts, will solve the problem by giving you the optimal grammar, and with it, whatever morphemic analysis it happens to involve. (The notion of 'evaluation measure' constitutes pernicious idea number 4, and I will discuss it later in this article.) I will confine myself at this point to noting that, given the general form that proposed evaluation measures have taken, it is hard to believe that any evaluation measure could justify either the morpheme identities that have been accepted by linguists or those that ordinary speakers will assent to. If an evaluation measure evaluates cost by counting symbol occurrences in some standard notation for grammars, it will be possible to reduce the cost of a grammar by making the morpheme divisions and morpheme identifications in such a way that the distributions of the morphemes are given by maximally general rules and one is thus able to exchange costly repetition of lexical material for relatively 'cheap' rules.[5] But a large proportion of psychologically real morpheme identities (to say nothing of morpheme identities that are accepted by linguists) involve combinations for which no particular general rule can be given (e.g., what rule would cover *right/righteous* or *bomb/bombard*, or even such more obviously psychologically real identifications as *egg/eggnog* or *lady/ladybug*?) and thus would not be distinguished from pairs like *moth/mother*.

I propose the following alternative to pernicious idea number 2: For any given speaker, the morpheme identifications that are psychologically real to him are determined not by the set of data that he has been exposed to but by the specific history of his own personal language acquisition. The acquisition of morpheme boundaries and morpheme identities is non-deterministic. Whenever a child learns a word, he has an opportunity to divide it into pieces and to identify those pieces with other morphemes that he has learned. Various factors affect the probability of his making particular divisions and identifications. Among the factors that increase the likelihood of his making a particular division and identification are: (i) that one of the pieces is phonetically similar to a morpheme that he already knows, (ii) that he can relate the meaning of that other morpheme to the meaning of the new word, (iii) that the remainder of the word can be identified with morphemes that he already knows, (iv) that the phonetic relationship between the old morpheme and the 'related' part of the new word is parallel to that between other pairs of 'morphs' that he has identified. The reason that most persons identify the first syllable of *eggnog* with *egg* but do not identify the first syllable of *mother* with *moth* would then be that when one learns the word *eggnog* one already knows the word *egg* and one is generally told that eggnog contains eggs, whereas when one learns the word *mother*, one does not yet know the word *moth*, and even if one did, one has no reason for associating mothers with moths; it has nothing to do with the distributions of morphemes.

In many cases, it will be of no consequence whether a given division and identification is made. For example, whether you relate *gap* and *gape* or *fuzz* and *fur* or *wild* and *wilderness* will have no particular bearing on your ability to speak and understand English. There is in fact considerable individual variation with regard to what morpheme identifications different speakers make. These differences lie buried within the minds of the individual speakers except at odd moments when one person expresses surprise at learning that some pair of words are related that another person 'knew all along' to be related, or when a spelling error reveals an unconventional morpheme identification (for example, the fact that I have been caught writing *higherarchy* shows that I have identified the first syllable of *hierarchy* with *high*). Note that nondeterministic acquisition of morphemics is perfectly consistent with there being total agreement among adult speakers as to much of morphology. If a child acquiring English has not yet learned a rule for forming plurals, each regularly formed plural which he identifies as a plural will provide him with an opportunity to divide it correctly into morphemes and to learn the plural marker of that noun as the plural marker in general. There is no fixed number of plural nouns that he must learn before he learns an adequate rule of plural formation; however, the more plural nouns that he has learned, the greater the likelihood that he will have learned such a rule, and when the number of plurals that he can 'handle' is sufficiently large, the probability of his not having learned a rule that covers regular plurals adequately will be vanishingly small.

In the last couple of sentences, I have spoken of learning a rule for English plural formation and have thus left it open whether everyone learns the same rule. Recent studies by Haber (1975) have shown that there is appreciable variation as to what rules of plural formation different speakers have, the variation being manifested in such things as the handling of novel words that an investigator has presented his subjects with, in the context of a task that will force them to use the word in the plural. For example, many of the responses given by Haber's subjects had the [iz] allomorph in words where 'normal' English rules predict [s] or [z] as the plural marker. Haber suggests that her subjects, rather than having a uniformly applicable process of plural formation, each have a 'core' system, which covers a wide range of cases, but not necessarily everything, plus strategies ('patches') for handling cases that are not covered by the 'core' system.[6] That would mean that the subjects had learned less general rules of plural formation than what an evaluation measure such as is envisioned in Chomsky and Halle 1968 would pick as the 'optimal' rules. In addition, Haber argues that the 'patches' that a person employs largely reflect rules which he had in his 'core' grammar at some earlier stage of his development (false generalizations that he had made) but which were rendered 'dormant' when other rules took over their work. Haber's data suggest that speakers of what are to minutest details 'the same dialect' often have acquired grammars that differ in far more respects than their speech differs in.

Pernicious idea number 3 is the idea that the 'data' that influence a child's language acquisition are things outside him (such as the actual sounds that persons around him are making) rather than his percepts of such things. A child (like an adult) perceives language in terms of his own linguistic system (the system as it exists in his mind, that is, which need not be manifested directly in his speech). Since the child's linguistic system changes frequently, the 'data' that he perceives at one stage of his development and those that he perceives at a later stage are really not data of the same language (even though the people around him were speaking the same language, perhaps even uttering the same sentences, at both times). For example, in early stages of acquisition he will not even perceive articles, though later he will be able to identify them; at the earlier stage, *Dish on table* will not only be what the child himself says but will in his perception be what his mother is saying to him (though he may be dimly aware that nonspeech sounds such as [ðə] and [iz] occur frequently in adult speech).

This observation has two important consequences for the conception of language acquisition that is outlined in several works by Chomsky (e.g., 1965, 1966). Chomsky proposes an idealized 'language acquisition device' which takes as input a set of 'primary linguistic data' and gives as output a grammar:

The 'evaluation measure' is to provide the basis for the choice of a particular grammar from among those that are consistent with the 'primary linguistic data'. The most radical 'idealization' in this scheme is that it treats acquisition as if it were instantaneous: it ignores all intermediate grammars that a child might go through in the course of acquisition, and simply sets up a correspondence between the whole set of data and the final grammar that is to result from exposure to those data. It is not clear that a model with this idealization could have any relationship to real language acquisition. since in real acquisition the child never has available to him the supposed input to the acquisition device, namely, the whole set of data that he has 'processed'; at any time he has only a much more fragmentary set of data stored as such in his brain, plus a grammar, with the grammar being his only link to most of the data that he has processed. If 'data' is to be taken in the realistic sense of the facts that impinge on the child's brain, the total set of data would not be an appropriate input to the acquisition device, since it is inconsistent: it would include both the 'fact' that *Dish on table* is grammatical and the fact that it is ungrammatical. If a grammar were to be constructed on the basis of the total set of data that a child had processed up to say, age six, it would be a grammar not of normal English but of a mixture of adult English and babytalk. Each step in acquisition both refines the gammar that the child is in the process of constructing, and renders the 'data' on which he based earlier grammars irrelevant to his subsequent development.[7]

Second, the observation that the child perceives speech in terms of his current linguistic system removes much of the mystery from Chomsky's puzzle as to how a child can acquire 'normal' language despite the fact that he is continually exposed to 'degenerate data', that is, utterances which contain hesitations, false starts, and miscellaneous muddles and incoherencies. For a 'degenerate' utterance to play any role in the child's language acquisition, he must understand it. (He isn't learning to make Englishlike sounds, but to speak English. Note in this connection how totally irrelevant to language acquisition the memorization of things which the child does not understand, such as prayers, is.) If he does understand the utterance, it will be because he has been able to interpret it in terms of his existing linguistic system, supplemented by his ability to fill in gaps plausibly. The resulting percept will in most cases be the same as if the speaker had produced a 'normal' sentence: the child has the task of forming both a linguistic percept and an interpretation and making them match, and both the percept and the interpretation can be altered in the process of making them match. This, of course, is exactly like the perception of speech by adults: most speech errors aren't even perceived. False starts and hesitations also lose much of their mystery when one notes that such things are found not only in speech but in all activities (walking, buttoning one's shirt, as well as more elaborate activities like carving a turkey or playing the piano). Identifying false starts and hesitations as such is a trivial task in comparison to many tasks that children's minds can cope with. And if the child fails to perceive a hesitation or a false start as such, he will not understand what was said, and thus the processing of the utterance will not proceed any further.[8]

The above discussion may suggest one flagrantly wrong assumption, namely that a child's perception of language is always entirely within his current linguistic system, which would have the absurd consequence that he would then retain that linguistic system for the rest of his life. To make a coherent theory out of the ideas just sketched, it will be necessary to bring in the fact that perception takes place on many levels: there are things that you are acutely aware of, things that you are only subconsciously aware of, and many gradations in between. This is just as true in the perception of language as elsewhere; for example, you normally are much more aware of what someone is saying than of phonetic details of his pronunciation, though under some circumstances you will be much more aware of phonetic details. (See Turvey 1975 for a survey of experiments demonstrating 'levels of awareness'.) Presumably, language acquisition must involve shifts of attention and awareness; for example, a child who at one stage is only dimly aware of articles and auxiliary verbs in adult speech (and who hears them as extraneous sound rather than as real language) may increase his awareness of them later, allowing him to incorporate them into his 'data', in which they have hitherto played no role. And presumably such shifts of awareness are constrained by limits on the number of things that one can pay attention to at a time.[9] It would be counterproductive for a child to pay much attention to articles until he has acquired a good deal of syntax and vocabulary. I thus feel that an incorrect interpretation has often been placed on the celebrated mother-child interchange which McNeill (1966:69) cites:

> CHILD: Nobody don't like me.
> { MOTHER: No, say 'nobody likes me'.
> CHILD: Nobody don't like me. }     repeated 8 times
> MOTHER: No, now listen care-fully; say 'Nobody likes me'.
> CHILD: Oh! Nobody don't likes me.

This example has often been taken as showing that corrections do not influence language acquisition, sometimes even that 'negative' data play no significant role in language acquisition. However, all that is shows is that at that point in his development the child could not accurately perceive that particular correction. It says nothing about whether the same correction would have been effective at another time or other corrections would have been effective at that time. In addition, since the 'positive' aspect of the correction (i.e., the information that *Nobody likes me* is grammatical) is even more ineffective than its 'negative' aspect (the information that *Nobody don't like me* is 'ungrammatical'; after all, the child does for the moment stop saying it), the interchange no more shows that 'negative' data are irrelevant than that 'positive' data are.

I now reach pernicious idea number 4, the idea that a numerical measure of the 'cost' or the 'complexity' of a grammar makes sense, together with the pernicious subidea that such a measure of complexity has something to do with language acquisition. I am concerned here especially with evaluation measures of the type that has figured in much generative grammatical (particularly, generative phonological) work, in which the 'cost' of a grammar is measured by counting symbol occurrences when the grammar is formulated in some fixed standard notation.

The notion of 'evaluation measure' has a history that extends back to Panini and the ancient Sanskrit grammarians. Panini's notational conventions were, if anything, even more precise than Chomsky and Halle's, and involved a convention for the omission of repeated elements that is quite similar to Chomsky and Halle's use of curly brackets in abbreviating sequences of rules that have shared elements. The notational practices of Chomsky's M.A. thesis (1951) are particularly close to Panini's, though I do not know whether there was any Paninian influence on it (perhaps via Harris from Bloomfield, who was familiar with the Sanskrit grammarians).

The well-articulated notion of evaluation measure that appears in Chomsky 1955 (and in better-known later works) was developed in the context of a major problem that occupied linguists in both America (Harris, Twadell, Bloch) and Europe (Hjelmslev) namely, that of avoiding arbitrariness in linguistic description, for example, the problem of justifying the choice of /p/ (or of /b/ or of an archiphoneme) as the second segment in the phonemic transcription of *spy*, *spin*, and the like. The evaluation measure was intended to replace by something more precise such vague concepts as 'simplicity', 'generality', and 'symmetry', which had figured in previous attempts at justification of previous analyses, and thus to provide a general nonarbitrary basis for choosing among alternative analyses.

Or at least, a procedure whose application to any case is nonarbitrary. However, the choice of the particular procedure remained arbitrary. It was not until the 1960s that Chomsky came to grips with the question of the choice of an evaluation measure from among the infinite range of conceivable evaluation measures. To provide any substance to that question, it is necessary to relate the evaluation measure to phenomena of some kind, and Chomsky did that by making an evaluation measure part of a model of language acquisition: it is to serve as the basis for the particular choice that the child makes among all of the grammars that are consistent with the data that he has processed.[10] He was thus able to say

such a measure is not given a priori, in some manner. Rather, any proposal concerning such a measure is an empirical hypothesis about the nature of language . . . Given primary linguistic data D, different choices of an evaluation measure will assign quite different ranks to alternative hypotheses (alternative grammars) as to the language of which D is a sample, and will therefore lead to entirely different predictions as to how a person who learns a language on the basis of D will interpret new sentences not in D'. [Chomsky 1965:37]

However, considerations of the latter type have been conspicuously absent from arguments about the details of the evaluation measure. For example, the section of Chomsky and Halle 1968 that deals with details of the evaluation measure does not appear to be based on any facts at all (cf. McCawley 1974a:53). The most obvious prediction that would follow from an evaluation measure of the type generally considered is that all rules of a language must be learned, since extra rules will mean extra cost, if cost is measured by a symbol count.[11] The position argued for in Stampe 1969 implies that that prediction is false. Stampe holds that a child is innately equipped with strategies for avoiding 'difficult' sounds and combinations and that a major part of learning the phonology of a language is learning to suppress and restrict those strategies. The strategies cover much of the ground of the generative phonologist's rules (e.g., a rule making final obstruents voiceless in German). Stampe's approach predicts that if the language that the child is learning does not force him to suppress a given strategy (i.e., if the language does not contain the 'difficult' item that the strategy provides a way of avoiding), he will retain it in his adult grammar. However, according to the 'standard' generative grammatical conception of evaluation measure, a grammar not having a rule for devoicing final obstruents will be 'cheaper' than a grammar with such a rule, and thus the adult grammar should not contain such a rule unless the language has underlying final voiced obstruents for the rule to affect. Stampe argues that facts such as those of second-language acquisition support his prediction: the learner applies all sorts of rules which, according to Chomsky's theory, he ought not to have in his grammar.[12]

I indeed find it highly implausible that an evaluation measure that measures the cost *of grammars* could play a role in acquisition, even evaluation measures that were not of the 'standard' form and not open to Stampe's objection. In any step in which a child is to change his grammar, the problem confronting him is not 'which grammar shall I pick from among those consistent with all the available data?' but rather 'How shall I modify my present grammar so as to bring it into conformity with such-and-such data?' Unless strong reasons should be found for holding otherwise, we should operate under the assumption that the child does not undertake drastic revision of his grammar: all he needs to do is to change his grammar so that it will do something for him that it does not now do; whether it is also optimal, in any sense other than 'easiest to get to *from where he is now*', is immaterial. The closest analog to an evaluation measure which I find at all plausible as part of an acquisition model is a measure of 'distance' between grammars.[13] Note, though, that if that sort of 'evaluation measure' were what determined the course of acquisition, there would be no reason to expect that the eventual result would be 'optimal' in any sense. Acquisition would be proceeding according to a principle of 'least effort'; however, the result of successive applications of a least-effort principle typically involve 'detours' that have served to minimize effort but which add up to a convoluted path; in fact, the meandering of rivers has been shown to be a consequence of the least-effort principle that determines how water flows.

The results of Haber 1975 also suggest that acquisition leads to 'non-optimal results': recall her conclusion that false generalizations that the child has made in acquiring morphology remain part of his linguistic competence, though they play no role in normal linguistic behavior because other rules have taken over their 'work'. In addition, it seems reasonable that compound and derived forms which a child learned as units before he learned a productive process that derives them will be retained in his lexicon even though they are now superfluous.

To some extent, pernicious idea number 4 is reinforced by number 1. If what the child is learning is not the distinction between 'grammatical' and 'ungrammatical' but how meanings are associated with surface structures, he is in a better position to separate factors and learn separately how to deal with each, for example, he is able to learn that putting an auxiliary verb at the beginning of a sentence signals that it is a question, regardless of whether any of the sentences that he is able to form with an auxiliary at the beginning are grammatical in adult speech. This means that in any particular step of acquisition, the alternatives that the child is presented with are narrowly circumscribed (namely, alternatives as to what exactly the semantic correlate is of the syntactic and lexical material that he is acquiring and as to how general the correlation is), and incorrect learning is either easily corrigible (i.e., if the acquired item does not mean what he thinks it does, or if the correlation is less general than he thinks, he will have access to information showing that to be the case) or not in need of correction (i.e., if he learns an insufficiently general correlation between meaning and form, he is not prevented from later learning the more general correlation *in addition*).

The four ideas discussed in this paper have held linguistics back from developing into what Chomsky (1968) has described it as: a 'branch of cognitive psychology'. Chomsky has correctly identified the subject matter of linguistics as psychological in nature, but he has failed to provide psychological substance for most of his theory and has taken positions (including the four ideas discussed above) which presuppose an autonomy for linguistics which it cannot have if it is to be a 'branch of cognitive psychology'. You can't draw psychological conclusions from nonpsychological premises, notwithstanding the apparent belief of most descriptivists and most transformationalists that you can.[14] The four pernicious ideas all constitute excuses for the linguist to confine himself to 'linguistic data' even when questions arise that can only be answered on the basis of details about how language is used, perceived, and acquired, and to shirk his responsibility to provide empirical content for his claims about language.[15]

# Notes

*Preface*

1. The reader should thus not be puzzled to find a reference to 'McCawley 1973a' in a paper written in 1971 and published in 1972: the original citation as 'in press' or 'to appear' has been replaced by a reference to the actual publication date.

*Chapter 1*

1. At least, not within the works of Sapir that Chomsky refers to. In very late works, such as Sapir 1939, however, the texts are written in what appears to be an 'intermediate' phonemic representation.

2. Lamb (1966) argues that 'neo-Bloomfieldian' linguists did not impose a condition of linearity on phonemic transcriptions, citing as evidence the fact that they virtually all recognized phonemes of stress and pitch which occurred simultaneously with 'segmental phonemes' and did not set up phonemes of 'high-pitched primary-stressed /a/', 'high-pitched secondary-stressed /a/', etc., as would be required by adherence to strict linearity. While Lamb's observation is correct, it is incomplete. The 'neo-Bloomfieldian' linguist typically separated segmental phenomena from one or more types of suprasegmental phenomena (stress, pitch) and required his phonemicization of each of these classes of phenomena to meet some criterion of linearity, albeit often one much weaker than that which Chomsky (1964) attributes to them. Deviations from strict linearity within segmental phenomena were countenanced only to the extent of allowing a single phonetic segment to be phonemicized as a sequence of phonemes which occur elsewhere in the language (e.g., by representing a phonetic nasal flap as /nd/; cf. the passage by Bloch cited in Lamb's n. 21). Each phoneme type appearing in the 'segmental part' of these transcriptions will correspond in at least some environments to a phonetic segment rather than to a feature of a neighboring segment. Such an element as the 'phoneme of devoicing' which Lamb introduces later in the same paper is totally foreign to the notion of 'phoneme' in the authors such as Bloch whom he cites; it may be described as a prosody in the sense of Firth (1948) which Lamb treats as if it were a sound in the sense of Firth.

3. It should be noted that the conception of 'phoneme' in Bloomfield's *Language* is a departure from earlier works of his such as the *Tagalog Texts* (1917), which use a conception of underlying representation like Sapir's without any additional 'phonemic' representation.

4. I replace Bloomfield's square brackets by slashes in accordance with modern practice.

5. Bloomfield also cites /pɛrot/, although here I suspect that orthographic rather than linguistic reasons prompted him to represent the reduced vowel as /o/.

6. In the reprinting of this paper in his *Selected Writings*, Jakobson has added minus signs at various places in the table of segments.

7. This work was actually written in 1917.

8. Harms (1966) has shown that Sapir's other two 'process markers' are also unnecessary.

9. [Kenstowicz (1973) argues that there is an additional systematic discrepancy between Sapir's phonological practice and classical generative phonology: while the rules of classical generative phonology are 'local' (i.e., they refer only to the state of affairs in the input that they affect, not to what that input may have been derived from) and apply according to a preassigned ordering, Sapir (according to Kenstowicz) allowed rules to apply in 'random sequential' fashion but constrained their application by incorporating global restrictions into their formulation.]

*Chapter 2*

1. [This paper, like the preceding one, originated in a course on the history of phonological theory that I taught at the University of Chicago in 1965; in McCawley 1973c I provide a discussion of Whitney's conception of syntax that originated in a similar course on the history of syntactic theory. In the 1965 course I made a point of seeking precursors of generative phonology not only among earlier linguists that were held in high regard by generative grammarians but also among those who for some reason were held in low regard, such as Whitney, who was disdained by generative grammarians for the way that he had disparaged Steinthal, a disciple of Humboldt's and thus a good guy. I do not mean by my choice of words to suggest that seeking precursors was a major goal of these courses; my attitude rather is and was that precursors are a dime a dozen unless one has very stringent criteria for what is to count as a precursor. In my 1965 course, I asked a great many questions about phonological structure, attempted to find various linguists' explicit or implicit answers to those questions, and found (to no one's surprise) that virtually all earlier linguists were precursors of generative phonology in some respects. I now recognize that I misrepresented those other linguists by failing to inquire what questions *they* thought it important to answer.]

In this article, for reasons of legibility I write cited segments and combinations of segments within slashes (Whitney used boldface); the slashes do not imply that the transcription is in any sense "phonemic." I have modified Whitney's transcriptions to the extent of writing /ś/ instead of /ç/ and writing aspirates with a raised h, both in accordance with modern practice.

2. The forms cited are Vedic Sanskrit. In later Sanskrit, /dipsati/ was replaced by /dʰipsati/, and, indeed, the distinction between CʰVCʰ and CVCʰ stems seems to have been lost entirely.

3. Cyclically applied rules figure in much recent work in generative phonology; see Chomsky and Halle 1968 for discussion.

4. Note that the notion of "inadmissible sequence" involved here requires attention to boundary symbols (# denotes word boundary, % denotes phrase boundary): /nt/ is perfectly admissible, but /nt#/ is not.

5. This term is introduced in McCawley 1965, where "unordered sequential" application is compared with other possible modes of rule application.

6. This term was applied to Boas's grammars by C.F. and F. M. Voegelin (1963). Postal (1964) criticizes their use of the term on the grounds that Boas clearly used both "underlying" and "phonetic" representations. Postal's factual observation is quite correct; however, it is possible to interpret the Voegelins' remark as meaning that Boas's phonological rules did not convert high-level "abstracts" into low-level "concretes" but merely converted elements of a single formal type into other elements of the same formal type, in which case their observation is correct and in no way conflicts with Postal's.

7. I am grateful to David L. Stampe for his contribution to my understanding of some of the points treated in this paper.

## Chapter 3

1. In this paper I use square brackets to enclose all segmental transcriptions, phonetic or not, and slashes only to call special attention to the fact that a representation is the underlying representation. Slashes here thus do not indicate "phonemic" representation, which never figures in my examples and which I indeed reject completely. Note that in a system of ordered rules the input to and output from a rule are generally neither "underlying" nor "systematic phonetic" representation but something intermediate.

2. [The second of these two features corresponds to nothing in Chomsky and Halle 1968, despite my footnote in the original version of this paper to the effect that these two features were introduced in (the then still forthcoming) *Sound Pattern of English*. In *The Sound Pattern of English* (p. 313), Chomsky and Halle suggest that a contrast between dental and alveolar articulation is always accompanied by a difference between greater and lesser length of constriction ([+distributed] vs. [−distributed]), though one language can differ from another as to whether the dental is [+distributed] and the alveolar [−distributed] or vice versa, and they provide no direct means in their feature system for distinguishing between alveolar and dental place of articulation.]

3. [Zwicky (1970b) expresses doubts that the retroflexion after /k/ is the same rule as the retroflexion after /i, u, r/, in that there are no instances where an /s/

after /k/ irregularly fails to retroflex but there are several instances of irregular failure of /s/ to retroflex after /i, u, r/.]

4. I am grateful to Lester Rice for formulating this definition.

5. E.g., "These two extremes of vocal tract shape, the horn and the Helmholtz resonator, are taken as the defining characteristics of the features *compact–noncompact* (horn shape or not), and *diffuse–nondiffuse* (Helmholtz resonator shape or not)" (Halle 1957:71). This definition would make not only [p, t] but also [č] "diffuse."

6. E.g., "Diffuse sounds are produced with a narrowing which in degree exceeds that of a constriction and is located in the front part of the vocal tract; ... The dividing line between *front* and *back* is further retracted for vowels than for other sounds: for the vowels, *front* includes almost the entire oral cavity, while for other sounds, the dividing line between *front* and *back* runs between the alveolar and palatal regions" (Halle 1964b:327).

7. A feature of laterality is required in an adequate phonological theory, since in most Athabascan and Salishan (N.W. United States and S.W. Canada) languages there are minimal contrasts between laterally released and apically released segments, many of the languages having a full series of lateral obstruents exactly paralleling the apical obstruents.

*Chapter 4*

1. [Among the participants in the session on Uto-Aztecan languages at the 1969 Chicago Linguistic Society annual meeting, at which I read this paper, was Carl Voegelin, whose masterful analysis this paper constitutes a commentary on. I am grateful for the informative and sympathetic comments that he made on my paper at the meeting, particularly the reminiscences that they contained about Edward Sapir, whose guidance appears to have had considerable influence on Swadesh and Voegelin's eventual analysis. Further discussion of Swadesh and Voegelin's analysis of Tübatulabal and of my reanalysis appears in Lightner 1971.]

2. [The discussion of rule-ordering in this paper rests on an assumption that I no longer subscribe to, namely, that rule interaction is governed by a fixed preassigned ordering of the rules. I have not yet attempted to redo the analysis given here in such a way as to make rule interactions wholly or largely predictable from the content of the rules and their relation to surface phonotactic constraints. Kenstowicz (1973) presents convincing arguments that Edward Sapir's conception of rule interaction involved 'random sequential' rule application and 'global' conditions on individual rules, i.e., rules would apply in sequence as long as the conditions on the application of the rule were met, but the conditions in some cases related not to the input to the rule but to the underlying forms from which the input was derived. A clear example of a global rule in Swadesh and Voegelin is quoted below in my discussion of my rule 3: their rule for the contraction of VʔV sequences refers both to the ultimate underlying vowel length (the rule is applicable only when both vowels are 'light', that is, underlying short) and to derived vowel length (the resulting vowel is long if either of the two input vowels is long, that is, has been made

long by the lengthening rule). Similar examples, cited from Meeussen's work on Bantu tone systems, are taken up in "Some Tonga Tone Rules" (in this volume).]

3. I suspect that there may be more than pure exceptionality here, since an unusually high fraction of nondeletable final vowels are underlyingly long. However, there are examples of both deletable long vowels and nondeletable short vowels (e.g., pɔlɔːla).

4. A convincing case that at least some phonological rules operate in left-to-right fashion is given in L. Anderson 1967. [Extensive discussion of how different potential applications of a rule interact with one another can now be found in Johnson 1972, Howard 1972, and Kenstowicz and Kisseberth 1977, chaps. 5 and 6. Howard presents convincing examples of self-bleeding rules (as here, where the application of the rule to one vowel will inhibit its application to the next vowel), of self-feeding rules (where the application of the rule to one segment will make it possible for it to apply to another segment), of rules that must apply in left-to-right fashion, and of rules that must apply in right-to-left fashion. He argues that the direction of application is normally predictable from the form of the rule (rules apply left-to-right except when the conditioning factor is to the right of the affected segment) but admits exceptional cases in which rules apply in a direction counter to that predicted by his generalization. Kenstowicz and Kisseberth argue that the problem of predicting the interactions between different applications of the same rule is no different in principle from that of predicting the interactions of different rules.]

5. ɘ is voiceless ʔ. The example should have an underlying final vowel, but I have not been able to determine what it is.

6. Voegelin (1958) uses a phonemic transcription in which initial ʔ's are written.

7. Gaberell Drachman has provided an appropriate slogan with which to characterize this position: 'Write every rule as if it were your last.''

8. [Lightner (1971:233) points out that there are consonant clusters before which vowels are always short, clusters before which vowels are always long, and one cluster [yʔ] before which both long and short vowels are found. The clusters in the first group consist of 'true consonants', and all but one of those in the second group involve a semivowel as either first or second member; however, the remaining cluster in the second group, [nc], prevents the writing of a neat rule for vowel shortening that would cover clusters as well as geminates.]

## Chapter 5

1. [This paper constitutes a less simple-minded version of the typology of tone and accent that I presented in McCawley 1964a; I provide a more up-to-date treatment of this topic in McCawley, in press a and give a more thorough presentation of the facts of Japanese (standard language, dialects, and history) in McCawley 1977a. In the examples below, ` indicates low pitch and ´ high pitch; ' indicates the place of 'accent' (here, the place where pitch drops), although later in the paper it will be used to indicate 'downstep'. There should

be no confusion between the two uses of ', since it can indicate downstep only in expressions in which it is combined with pitch marks (specifically, it only occurs at a syllable boundary that intervenes between two occurrences of '), whereas when it indicates 'accent', only accent marks and not pitch marks will appear elsewhere in the expression.]

2. Here the slightly more conservative Hyōgo dialect is substituted for Kyoto, since in Kyoto oo'o has become o'oo, whereas o'oo and oo'o are kept distinct in Hyōgo. There is no low-initial counterpart of o'oo in modern Kyoto-Hyōgo–type dialects, though such an accentual type is recorded in the Ruijum-yōgisho (ca. A.D. 1100).

3. The accent reduction rule in Ịjọ to which I allude differs in an important respect from the Japanese rule that makes the first accent in a phrase pre-dominate: in Japanese, if the first element of a phrase is unaccented, the accent (if any) on the second element is pronounced (as in *hana ma'de*), whereas in Ịjọ, even if the first element of a phrase is of the type that in the Kyoto-ized representation looks 'unaccented', any underlying accent on the second element is eliminated: diri + 'gụọ → diri gụọ.

4. This is something of an exaggeration. In addition to there being Ganda nouns having a fixed drop in pitch and nouns having no drop in pitch, there is a class of nouns that have a drop in pitch after the third mora of the prefix-noun combination: mù-wàlâ, ù-mù-wálà 'girl' (Cole 1967:80–86).

5. I know of no way of stating this rule other than in terms of a global derivational constraint that is sensitive to the state of affairs at an earlier point of the derivation. The dissimilation rule must apply before the rule that raises final lows, even though lows created by dissimilation are not subject to raising (Stevick 1969).

6. [Downstep in fact does not always arise from underlying HLH. Awobuluyi (1973) points out that in Owon Affa, downstep occurs at the boundary between a word ending on a high pitch and a word beginning on a high pitch. He notes that the downstep cannot be accounted for by setting up a segmentless low (or mid) tone at such boundaries, since a high after a low or mid tone is not any lower than a high before the low or mid tone, i.e., the surface realization of HLH and HMH sequences in Owon Affa is such that elimination of the low or mid tone would not yield downstep].

7. [For reasons beyond my comprehension, when I wrote this sentence I did not think of checking it against the precise pitch measurements given in Weitz-man 1969. For his four informants, the respective average pitch drops between the second and fourth syllables of an unaccented phrase were 4.7, 2.1, 5.9, and 3.7 semitones. The average drop in pitch after an accented second syllable (8.0, 6.8, 5.6, and 6.2 semitones for the four informants) is close to this figure only for the third informant, though for the first and fourth informants it is in the range of the pitch drops after other accented syllables, which range from 4.5 to 8.1 semitones for the first informant and 4.5 to 6.2 for the fourth informant.]

8. [Each word is given both in isolation and with the nominative marker *ga*]. 'Falling' and 'level' are reflexes of initial high pitch and initial low pitch. The proto-Japanese accentual system was of the same general type as that found in modern Kyoto dialect.

9. Here % indicates phrase boundary and 'Falling' is a morpheme feature. See Edmondson and Bendor-Samuel 1966 for a proposal in which melodies are assigned to Etung words as wholes. Similar ideas can be found in American structuralist work on intonation, e.g., Stockwell, 1962.

## Chapter 6

1. The underlying forms, though not (except in the Twi example) the intermediate stages, are quoted directly from the respective authors. The superscript numerals indicate relative pitch levels, higher numbers corresponding to higher pitches. I follow the standard practice of using ´ for high tone, ` for low, ^ for a high-low fall, and ˅ for a low-high rise. [For downstep, ' is substituted for the ¹ that originally appeared in this paper and in the study by Arnott from which the data are taken.]

2. [This paper appears to have started the current popularity of Tiv among generative phonologists. Tiv has been treated in some detail in Leben 1973 and Goldsmith 1976, both of which offer reanalyses of the treatment presented here. Goldsmith, for reasons that I do not find convincing, rejects the analysis of downstep as a reflex of a low tone. The idea of autonomous melodies whose notes are associated with words of arbitrarily many syllables figures in Edmondson and Bendor-Samuel 1966 and Hirayama 1960, both of which I was familiar with when I wrote this paper. Goldsmith develops that idea into a more general theory that allows phonological representations to involve two or more 'tiers' of units, with the association among the units of different tiers generally being many-to-many.]

3. Except, of course, that for syntactic reasons certain items such as /kâ/ 'it is' can never occur in phrase-final position.

## Chapter 7

1. The reason for taking phrase boundary to be the relevant environment rather than word boundary will be given at a later point.

2. Parentheses have been added so that the rule will cover isolated determinants, as in *balamulanga*.

3. I note in passing that "determinant" corresponds to proto-Bantu high, not low.

The possibility of global rules should not be dismissed lightly. See McCawley (1973b) for a demonstration that global rules rather similar to those just mentioned here are necessary in a description of tone in Bangubangu.

[Bangubangu provides a less clear case of global rules than I thought at the time I wrote this note. It seemed so clearly to demand global rules only because of the restricted range of possibilities that I had considered for the way that rules might interact. I would now analyze Bangubangu in the same way that Pratt (1972) treats Kikuyu: in terms of tone copying or shifting rules that apply right-to-left (and thus have a global flavor: the left environment refers to the state of affairs before tone shifting, the right environment to the state of affairs afterwards), Ganda (see chap. 5, n. 5), provides a more solid example of global rules in a Bantu tone system.]

4. [Dissimilation and Terminal Lowering provide an interesting argument against random sequential application of rules: if rule application were random sequential, the derivations would never terminate, since each of the two rules creates a combination of segments to which the other rule is applicable. To insure that the derivations terminate, something besides the two rules (as formulated here) must come into the picture: either an ordering restriction, requiring Dissimilation to apply before Terminal Lowering, or a global condition on one of the rules (such as a restriction that Dissimilation affect only basic and not derived L's), or some overall constraint on derivations such as a prohibition against what Pullum (1976) calls 'Duke of York derivations' (derivations in which A changes into B and then back into A again) or the constraint (attributed to Panini by Kiparsky 1977) that a rule may not affect the same segment twice.]

5. Bantuists use "tense" to refer to a combination of mood, tense proper, positive/negative, strong/weak, predicative/attributive, and so on and thus do not hesitate to speak of "tense number 65," for example. Since I know of no standard term which corresponds to the Bantuists' "tense" I have adopted their usage within this paper.

6. By "primary" determinant, Meeusen means a determinant that has not become neutral through the dissimilation rule.

7. Meeussen notes that the same tones result in this tense regardless of what underlying tone one assumes for the agreement marker. It is put into category b here because all other preinitials impose a tone on the agreement marker and because there are otherwise no examples of N = N.

8. The indirect relative contains a concord marker (determined by the noun that it modifies) followed by a (subject-)agreement marker (determined by the verb's own subject). Both morphemes come out on a high tone except in the present tense, where an -o- appears between the concord marker and the subject-agreement marker and the latter has low tone (or downstep arising from low tone on it): $n\text{-}c\text{-}ó = {}'tú\text{-}láng\text{-}a$ ( $< n\text{-}c\text{-}ó = tù\text{-}láng\text{-}à$ ) 'which we do not look at', $n\text{-}c\text{-}ó = tu\text{-}ta\text{-}bon\text{-}i$ 'which we do not see'. Meeussen treats $n\text{-}c\text{-}ó$ as arising from $n\text{-}cí\text{-}ò$, in which case -o- would belong to group c.

9. I have treated $í\text{-}má\text{-}kani$ as underlying LH rather than LL since in the one case I have found where a noun of this tonal shape is directly followed by a determinant, its final syllable fails to cause dissimilation: $í\text{-}cí\text{-}'fúmó\text{-}fumo$ 'morning', compare $í\text{-}cí\text{-}fumo$ 'tomorrow'. Assuming that 'morning' is a case of simple reduplication, /fùmò/ would yield *$í\text{-}cí\text{-}fumo\text{-}fumo$.

I have been unable to formulate underlying forms for infinitives which adequately cover infinitives with incorporated object and negative infinitives. The interested reader may attempt to grapple with the following data:

| 'to V' | 'to V him' | 'to V them' |
|---|---|---|
| i-ku-lang-a | í-kú-mu-lang-a | í-kú-ba-lang-a |
| í-kú-bon-a | í-kú-mu-bon-a | í-kú-ba-bon-a |
| 'not to V' | 'not to V him' | 'not to V them' |
| í-kú-ta-lang-a | í-kú-tá-mu-lang-a | í-kú-tá-ba-lang-a |
| í-kú-ta-bon-a | í-kú-tá-mú-bon-a | í-kú-tá-bon-a |

10 There is no downstep in the second word because the HLH sequence is within a single syllable; compare the preceding example.

11. The output in 25 must still undergo the "downstep" rules discussed in connection with 8 for the appropriate representations to be achieved.

12. Meeussen's analysis has an infix -áà- in the indicative affirmative hodiernal past tense (tense number 15). However, since all other past tenses (all 35 of them) have an infix -à- instead, it seems preferable to treat the peculiar tonal behavior of this tense by means of some minor rule(s) rather than a difference in underlying form.

13. The unmarked vowels in the underlying forms are those whose underlying tone I have been unable to determine.

14. Data on compounds might force one to distinguish between these possibilities; see also note 9.

15. The data are from Hirayama 1960.

16. Both the isolation form and the form with nominative case marker *ga* are given.

17. This restriction has the same effect as the extra clause of contraction which made V́V̀ high if the preceding syllable was low.

18. [I regret that I have not had an opportunity to adequately assimilate Carter's more recent study (1971–72) of Tonga tone and rethink this paper in light of her conclusions.]

## Chapter 8

1. [The % that appears in 3c is a symbol devised by Larry Horn and Paul Neubauer (ca. 1970) to indicate that there is dialectal or idiolectal variation in the acceptability of the example. In the original of this paper, I omitted the %, thereby ignoring the many speakers for whom 3c sounds odd.]

2. [Morgan (1972b:49–50) observes another case in which the applicability or nonapplicability of Comparative reduction distinguishes between comparatives and an extended use of a comparative construction. Specifically, when comparatives are used as exaggerations, Comparative reduction is obligatory: while *George is bigger than a house* and *John runs as fast as a deer* can be exaggerated ways of saying that George is very big or that John runs very fast, *George is bigger than a house is* and *John runs as fast as a deer does* allow only a literal interpretation (George's size exceeds that of a house; John's speed exceeds that of a deer). Note that while semicomparative *before* fails to behave like a comparative with regard to Comparative reduction, exaggerations behave more like comparatives than do ordinary comparatives themselves: the normally optional deletion that typifies comparatives is obligatory.]

3. [Bresnan (1973:316ff) has independently adopted an analysis in which *taller man*, *better lawyer*, etc., are comparatives of *tall man*, *good lawyer*, etc., rather than being nouns modified by the comparative of an adjective.]

4. This choice of words should not be taken as implying that I believe in such a category as verb phrase. See McCawley 1970b for some discussion of the superfluousness of such a category, first noted by G. Lakoff. Formulating

Adjective-preposing without recourse to VP would take me too far afield here to be worth the trouble.

## Chapter 9

1. In this connection, see McCawley 1972a.

2. This means that Davidson presumably would take 2 as an abbreviation for (∃x) [Fly(Amundsen, x) & To (x, the North Pole) & In (x, 1926)]. I have ignored, as did Davidson, the question of what relationship there may be between the transitive *fly* of 4a and the intransitive *fly* of 3.

3. There is great reluctance on the part of philosophers to speak of anything as being predicated of a proposition. Items of the Lukasiewicz category s/s are most often spoken of as 'operators' or 'connectives' rather than as 'predicates'. However, that terminological practice leads to absurdity when applied to elements such as *believe*, which combine with not just a proposition but an individual *and* a proposition. Treatments of *believe* by those who refuse to allow anything to be predicated of a proposition range from the devious practice of writing the 'believer' as a subscript and thus making it not appear typographically like the first argument of a two-place predicate, to Prior's schizophrenic judgment (1971:19) that *fear* and *think* are 'predicates at one end and connectives at the other'. Setting up a logical semantics for predicates with propositional arguments appears not to present any insuperable problem, provided that the set of all propositions can be enumerated. A grammar which purports to specify what logical structures are possible can be taken as defining the set of 'all propositions'.

4. I reject the distinction between syntax and (linguistic) semantics which Fodor assumes, and likewise the notion of 'deep structure' which goes along with that distinction; the closest analogue to Fodor's and Chomsky's 'deep structure' which I accept is 'logical structure'. See McCawley 1972a and G. Lakoff 1972 for exposition of the conception of grammar which Lakoff and I subscribe to. Within our theoretical framework, incidentally, there appears to be no reason to recognize 'verb phrase' as a syntactic category. Those constituents which linguists such as Fodor label 'VP' are simply sentences which have lost their subjects through deletion or 'subject-raising' (in the case of a 'simple' sentence such as *Dick likes scallion cakes*, the tense is the predicate of a higher clause: [Present (like Dick scallion cakes)], and raising of the subject of the 'subordinate' clause into the 'main' clause leaves *like scallion cakes* as a constituent of the sentence).

5. In saying this, Fodor repeats his earlier error of treating sentential modifiers as if they were predicated of the action (if any) rather than of the proposition. The standard formalisms in fact do not cover *Clearly, John spoke*.

6. The supposed examples of 'constituent negation' that I have seen do not establish the need for recognizing any such entity. For example, the sense of *They were arguing about nothing* which can be paraphrased as 'They were arguing about something trivial' (discussed in Jackendoff 1969) allows an analysis as 'They were arguing about something which was not anything (important)', which involves sentence negation. (One unexplained puzzle about

this use of *nothing* is that it is impossible as the subject of the clause, e.g., *Nothing was being discussed* cannot be interpreted as 'Something trivial was being discussed'.)

7. To represent definite descriptions, I use a formula like $(\iota x: Fx)Gx$ rather than the more traditional $G((\iota x)Fx)$, or $((\iota x)Fx)G((\iota x)Fx)$, rejecting the former as (at least sometimes) ambiguous and the latter as redundant.

[A more detailed treatment of some of the matters dealt with here relating to adverbs is given in a paper by George Lakoff (1973) that appears in the same issue of *The Monist* in which this paper was first published. See Heny 1973 for a perceptive and thorough survey of the literature on the syntax and logic of adverbs.]

8. Note by contrast that *for two minutes* gives not the length of time *elapsed* from start to stop but rather the total amount of time *taken up* by the (possibly interrupted) activity. If a person runs half a mile in two minutes, then stops for a minute to drink some coffee, and then runs another half mile in two minutes, it is appropriate to say that he ran a mile in five minutes but not that he ran a mile in four minutes, that he ran for four minutes but not that he ran for five minutes.

9. *Aimed at* makes implicit reference to the path of a projectile and is thus not logically equivalent to *pointed at*: bullets do not always travel in a straight line. An analysis of *aim* and *point* (as in *He aimed/pointed the gun at my head*) as causative structures provides the solution to the 'worry' which Fodor discusses in the last paragraph of the long footnote which concludes his paper: how can we analyze adverbs in such a way as to insure the validity of i and the invalidity of ii?

i. He pointed the stick.
Therefore, he pointed the stick at something.
ii. He waved the stick.
Therefore, he waved the stick at something.

*Point* is a causative of 'is pointed at'; transitive *wave* is a causative of intransitive *wave* (e.g., *The branches were waving in the breeze*). Thus, *point* is three-placed and transitive *wave* two-placed.

10. [See Chomsky 1970b for criticism of Lakoff's analysis of instrument adverbs and McCawley 1975b:240–42 for rebuttal of Chomsky's criticism.]

11. Since Fodor is concerned with *typical* and not with *Georgian*, I have not bothered to analyze the role of *Georgian* in *Georgian house*.

12. For discussion of the syntactic and semantic intricacies of generic sentences, see Lawler 1972 and R. Lakoff 1972. [For a highly insightful analysis of generics in which it is argued that they have no direct relation to quantification but instead make direct reference to 'kinds', see Carlson 1977.]

13. I have no explanation for the ungrammaticality of many sentences involving *well* for which paraphrases involving *do a good job of* are grammatical:
John did a good job of shooting his mother-in-law.
*John shot his mother-in-law well.

14. For example, the logical structures proposed here are inadequate if they plus the rules of grammar which they necessitate and those which are otherwise

necessary do not explain why the adverbs of 9a–h, as Fodor pointed out, cannot be moved to the beginning of the clause (e.g., *At the target, John aimed the gun* cannot have the sense of 9d but only a sense in which the target is the place where the aiming is carried out.) In McCawley 1973g, I sketch a possible explanation of the nonpreposability of the adverbs of 9c–d on the basis of logical structures such as are presented above.

### Chapter 10

1. [Ross (1976) argues independently for the analysis of *want* as having a sentential object in examples such as 1c; the publication dates notwithstanding, Ross's paper was written about a year before mine.]

2. This example was brought to my attention by Masaru Kajita.

3. It is far from clear that *all* nonreferential NP's can be taken as originating in subordinate clauses. Such an analysis is particularly hard to justify in such cases as *John imagined a polar bear*, which Richard Montague (1974:168) indeed took as reason for rejecting Quine's account of nonreferential NP's.

[See Dougherty 1970b for criticism of the decomposition of *look for* into 'try to find' and McCawley 1973d:165–66 for a reply to Dougherty in which I argue that some of his objections are irrelevant to the actual analyses proposed, but that one class of arguments that he offers (those relating to differences in potential for collocation with adverbs, e.g., *He looked high and low for a goat* versus *\*He tried high and low to find a goat*) are real counter-examples to the 'try to find' analysis, though they are consistent with an alternative decomposition, namely 'look (in the sense of 'examine') in order to find'. I now accept the latter analysis rather than the 'try to find' analysis, since it not only solves the problems raised by Dougherty but also allows a uniform treatment of the *for* or *listen for, watch out for*, etc.]

[My attribution of 8a to Quine may appear to be a gross misrepresentation, in view of his repeated objections to formulas in which quantifiers outside the scope of a "modal operator" bind variables within its scope. For example (1960: 167), he rejects $(\exists x)$ (Tom believes that $x$ denounced Cataline) as not making sense, though admitting $(\exists x)$ (Tom believes $x$ to have denounced Cataline), in which he takes the $x$ to be a constituent of the main clause, i.e., he takes *Tom believes x to have denounced Cataline* as involving a 3-place predicate, with *Tom* and $x$ filling the first two places and $(\lambda y)$ ($y$ denounced Cataline) in the third place. This is not too implausible in light of the apparently 3-place *believe* in *Tom believes of Cicero that he denounced Cataline*. However, most verbs for which Quine's policy would demand such an analysis have no extra-place variants; e.g., there is no *\*John tried of Oscar to find him*. I maintain that the extra place is unnecessary: all that Quine's 3-place *believe* buys him is already provided by the formulas like 8a that he rejects, namely, that it insures that the values of the variable are objects of the real world rather than of some alternative world. In saying this, I am taking a quite different position from Quine on a number of issues; for example, I accept *de re* propositions as such, rather than trying to analyze them away in *de dicto* terms, and I assume that the rule of "existential generalization," which is centrally involved in Quine's rationale for his policy on bound variables, is formulated in *de re* rather than *de dicto* terms: rather than sanctioning the inference from $F(a)$ to $(\exists x)\, F(x)$, where $a$ is a referring expression and F meets the criteria for being a "transparent context," I take the rule as sanctioning the inference from $F(u)$ to $(\exists x)F(x)$, where $u$ is an object (not the name of the object) of the world in which the expression is being evaluated.]

4. Kenny (1963:122) observes that these two senses correspond to quite different states of affairs.

5. See McCawley 1972*a* for arguments in support of this claim.

6. I owe this argument to Judith N. Levi.

7. It will undoubtedly be of interest to investigate how this state of affairs came about. Since *want* originally meant 'lack', i.e., 'not possess', English quite likely went through a stage in which *X wants Y* meant 'X wants to have (= possess) Y'. If that is the case, then it appears that the older deletion rule has been generalized in two ways: by being allowed to cover not only 'possess' but also 'come to possess' and by being allowed to cover uses of *have* which do not express its core meaning of 'possess'. I would be interested in finding out whether this conjectural history is correct and, if so, whether the two generalizations of the deletion are independent and whether such generalizations are attested in other languages.

[A fascinating, though highly programmatic, account of linguisitic rules in terms of 'cores' of applicability combine with strategies for extending their applicability to broader classes of cases is given in Lakoff 1977; the historical development that I suggest above fits very well into Lakoff's general approach.]

8. I intend here the adjective *closed*, not the passive participle.

9. Many details will have to be added to this decomposition. Robin Hood is not merely in a jail but is confined there against his will, and for many speakers the sentence does not imply that Robin Hood spent four years in a jail (it does not preclude his having escaped or his having been released early for good behavior) but only that he was required to be there for four years.

## *Chapter 11*

1. [The assignment of modal auxiliaries to a syntactic category has been discussed subsequently by Pullum and Wilson (1977), who argue from within a theory of 'autonomous syntax' for an analysis of auxiliaries as main verbs, and by Akmajian, Steele, and Wasow (1977) who argue for a syntactic category that they call 'AUX' (misleadingly, since it has little relationship to what Chomsky (1957) called 'AUX') that is filled in English by the first auxiliary verb and the *n't* (if any). To my knowledge, nothing in Akmajian, Steele, and Wasow's paper provides any reason for preferring their analysis, in which modal auxiliaries are deep structure daughters of the AUX node but other auxiliary verbs appear as the V of a deep structure $[V \ V^n]_{V^{n+1}}$ combination (where superscripts correspond to the number of bars in the 'X-bar notation'), to an otherwise identical analysis in which a model auxiliary verb is treated like the other auxiliaries and gets to be a daughter of the AUX node the same way that a *have* or a *be* would, namely, by a movement transformation.

In a subsequent paper (McCawley 1977c) I have dealt in some detail with an important question that I sidestepped here despite its centrality to the matter under discussion, namely, the question of what it means to say that two items belong to the same syntactic category.]

2. Some modals do not even have that: *must*, which is historically a past tense form, has no past tense in modern English. *Shall*, *should*, and *ought* likewise have only present tense forms, except to the extent that *should* can function as a past tense of *shall* in clauses involving sequence of tense. [Here and elsewhere, I have ignored the many dialects and idiolects in which *must* is used as both a past tense and a present tense.]

3. In the interests of maximizing comparability of analyses, I have given a derivation which agrees with Jackendoff's analysis in all respects except those directly relevant to this note. I in fact contest several details of the derivation given here; for example, I maintain (McCawley, 1970b) that 'VP's' are simply S's that have lost their subjects and that there is thus no need for such a node label as VP. See McCawley 1971c for arguments supporting the analysis of tenses and auxiliary verbs as 'V'.

4. Jenkins (1972) adds a further difference: that modals do not have nominalizations (other than the highly idiosyncratic ones found in *John has a strong will* and *This dishwasher is a must for every housewife*). But if modals undergo raising out of a subject complement (i.e., [*John play tennis*] *may* → *John may play tennis*), the absence of nominalizations is actually a similarity between true verbs and modals, since, as noted by Chomsky (1970a), there are no nominalizations of structures to which Raising has applied (e.g., *\*The happening of/by John to run into Marcia*). See however, Postal 1974 for discussion of possible counter-examples such as *John's tendency to yell at me*.

5. These rules are inadequate since they fail to distinguish those uses of *have* which undergo Subject-auxiliary inversion, etc. from those which do not.

6. [Two facts indicate that the defective morphology of modals does not provide an adequate explanation of why they come first among the verbs of a clause. First there are dialects of English (described in Pampell 1975) in which certain combinations of two modals are permitted, e.g., *might could*. There is no difference in morphology between these dialects and standard English that can be held responsible for this difference in the occurrence of modals. For example, it is not the case that in these dialects certain modals have infinitive forms and accordingly can follow all modals; rather, *might* can precede most modals and a couple of additional combinations like *shouldn't oughta* are permitted. Second, *is to*, as in *John is to have finished the laundry by noon*, appears only in present and past tense forms, preceding any other auxiliary verbs. Since it clearly involves the same morpheme *be* that is used as a copula and an existential verb, with the same suppletive present and past tense forms, there is no morphological reason for the nonoccurrence of such sentences as *\*John is believed to be to go to Cleveland next week* or *\*Susan's being to arrive soon is a welcome development*. Note, incidentally that Jackendoff's criteria for modalhood give conflicting results for *is to*: it has only finite forms but also shows agreement with its subject.]

## Chapter 12

1. Shibatani's example of this type of causative was the sense of *John made Mary cry* that allows the paraphrase *John did something* (e.g., *slapped Mary*) *which directly caused her to cry*. However, an example in which the "caused phase" is agentive is more relevant here, and indeed, it is not clear that Shibatani's example should not simply be classed as "ballistic causation."

[There are also examples in which *chase* is clearly not causative: *Fido always chases cars*. I do not have evidence that the *chase* of this example has a different sense from that of 9c.]

2. The only clear cases that I have seen where *have* refers to a coercive act are those where previous context establishes that the *have* clause refers to part of a larger coercive act, e.g.: *The bandit took the passengers' money and then had them lie face down on the floor while his partner tied them up.*

3. I have ignored one important factor, namely, quantitative relations between the cause and effect. For example, *Minimum wage laws cause unemployment* cannot be analyzed as *There are frequently cases in which someone is unemployed and if there were no minimum wage laws he would be employed*, since the first sentence has implications about the quantity of unemployment but the second does not. If the speaker believes that there will be the same number of jobs whether or not there are minimum wage laws, though with different people holding them, the second sentence would be a more truthful thing to say than the first.

4. [Dowty has since repudiated this proposal.]

5. I owe this reference to Hospers (1967).

6. This analysis has the defect of not distinguishing normal causal sentences from odd-sounding sentences in which the analog to 14b is equally true but irrelevant material is present in the statement of the cause, e.g., *The roses died because the gardener didn't water them and Rome is in Italy* or *The roses died because either the gardener didn't water them or 12 is a prime number*. The closest worlds in which the gardener watered the roses are the closest worlds in which either he watered them or Rome is not in Italy, since in the closest worlds in which he watered the roses, Rome is still in Italy.

[The problem mentioned here is spurious. The examples are odd since they are blatant violations of Grice's (1975) maxim of relevance. There is nothing to prevent one from taking these examples to express true propositions but to be misleading because they mention things that are irrelevant to why the roses died.]

7. Obviously, two worlds cannot differ in just one proposition—there have to be additional differences in order for each world to be consistent (e.g., if *w* differs from the real world to the extent that Evel Knievel is not mortal, then *All men are mortal* will be false in *w* though true in the real world). Thus working out the details of this proposal would require one to adopt something like the proposals of Goodman (1947) and Rescher (1964), according to which one gets a consistent description of an alternate world out of a description of the real world by eliminating those real world propositions to which one is least "attached" that are inconsistent with the counterfactual "defining

property" of the alternative world (as where my description of *w* indicates that I am more attached to, i.e., less willing to reject, the proposition that Evel Knievel is a man than the proposition that all men are mortal).

8. "Minimal" here means "smallest number of arcs." Counting arcs can give only a first approximation to the relevant notion of distance. Note that "distances" between worlds have to be proportional to differences in physical variables; e.g., a world in which Dick Cavett's height is 5′9″ is closer to the real world than one in which his height is 5′9.1″.

## Chapter 13

1. [At the time I wrote this, transformational grammarians had not neglected morphology quite as badly as I made it sound here: Halle 1973 was readily available and I was familiar with a prepublication version of Jackendoff 1975, though I was not yet aware of the existence of three dissertations that take up questions of morphology in considerable depth: Siegel 1974, Rardin 1975, and the 1974 dissertation published in revised form as Aronoff 1976.]

2. I include person in this list, since 'full NP's' are not restricted to third person: witness *we linguists, you Republicans,* which can themselves serve as antecedents of (first and second person) pronouns: *We linguists love our profession; You Republicans should be ashamed of yourselves.*

3. For other speakers, corresponding pronoun forms in the two VP's must be the same for the two VP's to count as identical (but see n. 4), and thus 6b is unacceptable for them if the neighbor is female.

4. Interestingly, this deletion is allowed even by speakers who supposedly 'require morphological identity' between the deleted VP and the antecedent VP, i.e., speakers who can only interpret *John loves his wife and so do I* as meaning that I love John's wife, not that I love my own wife.

5. In McCawley 1968*b*, I claimed to have an analysis that did without conjunction reduction. However, the discussion in that paper is extremely faulty, since I paid no attention to those examples (such as *Sam is both friendly and easy to please*) in which a transformationally derived constituent appears as a conjunct of a coordinate structure; those are of course the examples which yield the strongest case for a rule of conjunction reduction.

[Dougherty (1970*a*: 865–66) derives a sentence with an *n*-term conjoined VP from a coordinate S containing the same *n* conjuncts that would be there under the usual Conjunction reduction treatment, except that one of the conjunct S's is represented as having a deep coordinate VP with *n*-1 empty conjuncts and one 'full' one; a transformation copies material from the other *n*-1 S's into the *n*-1 empty VP's and throws away the originals. This approach does not do away with Conjunction reduction but merely conceals it beneath baroque trappings.]

6. The idea that I am proposing here is an outgrowth of a proposal made in an unpublished paper on presupposition by Östen Dahl, in which Dahl argued that the 'pragmatic presupposition' that an individual referred to with *she* is female is not part of the meaning of the sentence but is only a condition for its felicitous use.

7. My saying this should not be taken as a full endorsement of 1, which I would claim fails to account for some of the more interesting examples of *each other*, such as *Those boys have a tendency to gang up on each other* and *They spent the day taking group photographs of each other*. (Or do these examples illustrate a further dimension of indeterminacy, namely, indeterminacy as to whether the x and y of the 'fxy' that *each* is combined with range over individuals or over sets?). In any event, the objection to 1 that I am about to discuss provides an interesting example of an objection that has less substance than it appears to have.

8. [I have substituted the term 'reduced passive' for the more standard 'agentless passive', since the omitted NP need not strictly speaking be an agent, e.g., it is not an agent in *It is known that most Congressmen are power-hungry*.]

9. This dual function of indefinite NP's is discussed insightfully in Karttunen 1976.

## Chapter 14

1. Montague used primes to indicate the predicate corresponding to (the relevant sense of) a given lexical item; e.g., walk′ is the predicate corresponding to the word *walk*.

The syntactic categories are derived from two basic categories *t* (standing for 'truth value') and *e* (standing for 'entity') through the formation of complex category names of the form A/B ('combines with category B to yield category A'). The following gives a rough correspondence between Montague category names and more familiar syntactic categories:

| Montague | Transformational grammarians |
|---|---|
| t | S |
| e | (a very special kind of NP: Russell's 'logically proper name') |
| t/e (= IV) | VP or Intransitive verb |
| t/IV (= T) | NP |
| t // e (= CN) | N̄ |
| T/CN | Determiner |
| IV/T (= TV) | Transitive verb |
| IV/t | Verb with sentential object |
| IV/IV | VP-modifier |

(when two or more categories 'combine with category A to yield category B', they are distinguished arbitrarily by number of slashes, as above, where 'IV' and 'CN' both 'combine with a logically proper name to yield a truth value').

Since the λ-notation, which figures in 1, will recur in many places below, a brief explanation of it had best be given here. The λ-notation allows one to form a function from an expression containing a variable. Thus, $(\lambda x)$tall′$(x)$ is tall′$(x)$ viewed as a function of $x$, i.e., the function that maps Jimmy Carter into the proposition that Jimmy Carter is tall, maps Norman Mailer into the proposition that Norman Mailer is tall, etc. The bound variable need not be an individual variable; thus, $(\lambda P)P$(Napoleon) is the function that associates to each predicate P the proposition that P applies to Napoleon. This feature of the λ-notation makes it possible to provide semantic representations for syntactic constituents that a linguist would otherwise be hard put to find a semantic representation for. Montague grammar exploits this property of λ-notation fully. As an illustration of the way in which λ-notation can be used in representing the content of sentences, consider the sentence *Being stubborn was one of Napoleon's properties*, which could be symbolized as $[(\lambda P)P(\text{Napoleon})]\ (\lambda x)\text{stubborn}'(x)$. Such expressions can be simplified by the process of 'λ-conversion' (indicated here, following Partee 1975, by a single-shafted arrow), in which the bound variable of the λ-expression is replaced by the item of which the λ-expression is predicated:

$$[(\lambda P)P(\text{Napoleon})]\ (\lambda x)\text{stubborn}'(x)$$
$$\rightarrow (\lambda x)\text{stubborn}'(x)\ (\text{Napoleon})$$
$$\rightarrow \text{stubborn}'(\text{Napoleon})$$

2. A syntactic rule for Montague need not derive an expression from exactly *two* expressions, though most of Montague's rules were in fact 'binary'. A more general schema for a Montague syntactic rule is: 'If $\alpha_1 \in P_{A_1}$, $\alpha_2 \in P_{A_2}$, ... and $\alpha_n \in P_{A_n}$, then $f(\alpha_1, \ldots, \alpha_n) \in P_C$'.

3. The fragmentary grammar of "The Proper Treatment of Quantification in English" allowed only for third person singular NP's, and thus Montague formulated it so that it gave third person singular agreement. In a more complete description, the agreement marker would have to be chosen on the basis of the person, number, and gender of the subject NP; compare the way that the form of the pronoun is chosen in the rule quoted in 5.

4. I ignore here the head noun, which in most generative semantic treatments of quantified NP's gets to its surface position by a step distinct from quantifier lowering (see, e.g., Keenan 1972).

5. Following Partee 1975, I use a double-shafted arrow for 'is translated as'. The reason for constituents such as $he_1$ *loves* $him_2$ (rather than simply $x_1$ *loves* $x_2$, with variables in both NP positions) in Montague's analyses was Montague's adherence to a principle of 'local well-formedness' (Bach 1976): the constituents of the syntactic analysis have to be well-formed surface representatives of the category in question, with deviation only to the extent that phonologically unrealized diacritics such as the subscripts on the *he's* were permitted. Since you don't say $x$ in English but you do say *he*, subscripted *he*'s were available to Montague in his syntax but subscripted $x$'s weren't.

6. It would of course be necessary to alter the syntactic rule for combining IV/IV with IV, so as to accommodate the different surface position of *not* and of other VP modifiers:

John did   not/*quietly   walk away.
John   quietly/*not   walked away.

In 10 and subsequent formulas, [ex] and [in] stand for 'extension' and 'intention' (Montague's ˇ and ^, respectively). The reason for [ex] in 10 is that Montague took all predicates as predicated of intensions, and here as in many other cases, and [ex] must be supplied in the translation so as to cancel out the (in this case) unwanted [in]:

$$(\lambda P)(\lambda y) \sim (^{ex}P(y))^{in}(\lambda x)walk'(x)$$
$$\rightarrow \quad (\lambda y) \sim (^{ex\ in}(\lambda x)walk'(x)\ (y))$$
$$\rightarrow \quad (\lambda y) \sim walk'(y)$$

The [ex]'s and [in]'s that would have to be included in 5' and 9 in conformity with this policy have been omitted for expository convenience.

7. Note that in both cases the choice between *a* and *an* is built into the rule for forming quantified NP's. This is because, as in the matter of agreement discussed above, there could not be a separate obligatory rule turning *a* into *an* before a vowel.

8. For an alternative approach to syntactic categories, see Anderson 1976, where it is argued that the assignment of constituents to syntactic categories should be on the basis of (largely universal) definitions of the categories; such definitions are distinct from the rules specifying what combinations of elements the language allows in deep structure.

[I have subsequently given a programmatic sketch of an approach to the notion 'syntactic category' in which syntactic categories as such are dispensed with: references to syntactic categories are replaced by references to other things, such as logical categories, morphological categories, dependency relations, and topological details of syntactic structures (McCawley 1977*c*).]

9. Montague actually treated *believe that* rather than *believe* as a member of $B_{IV/t}$; thus *\*John alleged that the teapot*, rather than 19a, is the sentence ruled out by the category assignment. Besides implying a bizarre derived constituent structure, this policy would complicate any general statement of where the inflectional morphemes are to be suffixed.

10. [While the syntactic rule alluded to here can be formulated in a trivial fashion, the corresponding semantic rule(s) may not be so trivial; see in this regard the careful and insightful study of 'Dative movement' phenomena by Dowty (in press), in which relatively trivial syntactic rules change a verb from one category to another (e.g., there is a rule changing a certain class of verbs from the 'double object' category to the 'object plus PP' category) and fairly involved semantic rules insure that the various NP's are associated with the right arguments of the propositional functions that the verbs denote.]

11. My purpose in referring to the 'grammaticality' of 19 and 20 is not to ridicule Thomason; in fact, I agree with Thomason that the oddity of 19 (and presumably also 20) is due to semantic incoherence. My quarrel with the use of the term 'grammatical' in such works as Chomsky 1972 and Jackendoff 1972 is not with the authors' identification of the oddity of the various sentences as with the proposition that the notion of 'grammaticality' with which they work is of any relevance to linguistic research; see McCawley 1976*a* for arguments that there are no such things as 'grammaticality facts'.

12. [Further remarks by me on the relationship between Montague grammar and transformational grammar can be found in McCawley, in press *b*.]

*Chapter 15*

1. I have put 'Defendant' before 'Situation' in accordance with the other occurrences of RESPONSIBLE in Fillmore's formulas. I take it that the reverse order of 'Defendant' and 'Situation' in the formula that he gave for *accuse* is a mistake.

2. See McCawley (1972*a*) and G. Lakoff (1972) for elaboration of the conception of grammar and logic to which this sentence refers.

3. When necessary I will use paired subscripts to indicate the intended antecedent of a pronoun.

4. There actually is a case in which 11a–c could be used in normal discourse, though one which is irrelevant to the question under discussion, namely that they could be used to report criticisms of the choice of wisdom, 17, etc., for some purpose, e.g., criticizing the choice of 17 hexagons as part of the design of a flag on the grounds that 17 is an unlucky number. In this case it is in the act of choosing 17 rather than the number 17 itself which is the 'Defendant'.

5. The examples under 18 are ambiguous as to the scope of the definite description. The interpretation of 18 which is relevant here is that in which the definite description has the whole sentence as its scope, i.e., roughly 'the $x$ for which Nixon said $x$ to the Knights of Columbus is such that McGovern criticized Nixon for saying $x$ to the Knights of Columbus'.

6. Telescoping is also relevant to a current controversy about the syntax of nominalizations. Chomsky (1970*a*:217) finds implausible any derivation of *Einstein's intelligence* from a source containing the sentence *Einstein is/was intelligent*. He does not state his objections explicitly, but what he says suggests the objection that the most obvious sources, namely *the fact that S* and *the extent to which S*, are not synonymous with the nominalization under discussion, i.e., i and ii are not paraphrases of iii:

i. The fact that Einstein was intelligent was his most remarkable property.
ii. The extent to which Einstein was intelligent was his most remarkable property.
iii. Einstein's intelligence was his most remarkable property.

The following, however, appear to be exact paraphases of (iii):

iv. The fact that Einstein was as intelligent as he was was his most remarkable property.

The fact that Einstein was intelligent to the extent that he was was his most remarkable property.

Actually, ii can be used with this sense. Chomsky's discussion assumes a really literal reading of ii, in which it is the extent or degree of intelligence possessed by Einstein (e.g., 210 IQ points, if you accept that as an extent of intelligence) of which *his most remarkable property* is being predicated, and he accordingly marks it as ungrammatical. I can see no objection to deriving iii from a structure which combines factive nominalization and extent nominalization, as in iv, by steps one of which is Telescoping.

[I hang my head in shame for having completely forgotten that what I have here dubbed Telescoping had already been proposed in Kuroda 1970. See McCawley 1975b for further discussion of Telescoping.]

7. This proposal obliterates the distinction between *criticize* and *denounce* Since *denounce* and *criticize* are syntactically identical as far as I can determine, I conjecture that the difference between their meanings is simply the kind or degree of 'badness' that is attributed to the 'Defendant'.

8. See Akatsuka 1972 for reasons why the complement of *happy*, etc., must be analyzed as an underlying reason clause.

9. *Credit* is ambiguous between a sense referring to a linguistic act and a sense referring to a mental state:

Every time Nixon makes a speech, he credits Agnew with being a great statesman.

I have always credited Agnew with being a great statesman, but this is the first time I have admitted that I feel that way about him.

That these are two distinct senses (as opposed to two situations in which a single sense of *credit* is applicable) is shown by the fact that syntactic phenomena such as pronominalization with *so* or deletion of repeated verb phrases respect this difference:

*Secretly I have always credited Agnew with being a great statesman, and I am delighted that Nixon did so in his speech last night.

In what follows, I have restricted my attention to the 'linguistic act' sense of *credit*.

10. The asterisk refers only to the intended interpretation, in which the NP can be paraphrased '(the fact) that Laird is wise'. It is grammatical with another interpretation, namely 'Nixon credited Agnew with having the (degree/kind of) wisdom that Laird has'. This last fact brings out a difference between *credit* and *accuse* for which I have no explanation, namely that *credit* much more easily allows the deletion of *have* before objects like *Laird's wisdom* than *accuse* does, i.e., only marginally can I admit a sentence like *Chomsky accused Nixon of Hitler's inhumanity* with the interpretation 'Chomsky accused Nixon of having the (kind/degree of) inhumanity that Hitler had'.

11. In addition, there is no nominalization of *credit* which works anything like *accusation*: *Nixon's credit that Agnew is a great statesman is well founded.

12. [Important points about *blame* are made in Jackendoff 1974.]

## Chapter 16

1. These two tasks do not differ greatly, since to every performative verb there corresponds an illocutionary force which utterances in which the verb is used performatively have. The two tasks differ principally in that (i) distinct performative verbs may be synonymous and thus correspond to the same illocutionary force, and (ii) there can be illocutionary forces to which no performative verb corresponds, as in the case of 'echo-questions' (*You tried to burn down what?*) and exclamations (*Boy, am I hungry!*; see N. McCawley 1973), which are speech act types to which no performative verb corresponds.

2. I owe this observation to Zwicky (1971).

3. See Fraser 1974 for a more detailed treatment of syntactic differences among performative verbs.

4. That saying 1b can be an act of estimating is shown by the fact that it can be reported as 'He *then* estimated that the repairs would cost £200', with the reference of *then* being the time of the speech act.

5. Since this table purports to summarize over a thousand grammaticality judgments, it should not be taken too seriously.

6. Other than *forgive*, which might anyway be held instead to be an operative.

7. In the discussion below, I will not only refer to verdictive verbs, commissive verbs, etc., but also to verdictive speech acts, commissive speech acts, etc., by which I will mean illocutionary acts which can be described by a verdictive verb, by a commissive verb, etc. Actually, this is upside down: I should define 'verdictive act' directly and define 'verdictive verb' as a verb which describes a verdictive act.

8. Or at least, I take Austin to have intended his term 'perlocutionary effect' only to cover effects in the addressee which come about as a result of his understanding what was said.

9. One important respect in which this approximate semantic structure is inadequate is that it fails to indicate any relationship of the speech act to 'the record'. Nixon cannot appoint Autry ambassador to France simply by saying to him in private 'I hereby appoint you ambassador to France': the act of appointing him must involve somehow making the President's decision a matter of record. This is true even in the bizarre case of the Pope creating cardinals *in pectore*. What makes Bishop X a cardinal is not the Pope's decision that he should be a cardinal but his incorporating that decision into the celestial record by communicating it to the celestial record-keeper, God himself.

10. Another important class of sentences which are imperative in form and whose point is to get the addressee to do the thing in question is printed instructions such as 'Just add water and mix to a creamy consistency' (see Sadock 1974:140–41 for discussion). However, not all sentences of imperative form have the point of getting the addressee to perform the action in question, e.g., 'Take one more step and I'll shoot'.

11. Nor, indeed, does saying 'I wish you an enjoyable birthday'.

12. This example refutes the occasionally encountered proposal that the complement of *order* is simply a future indicative clause. If such were the case, there would be no obstacle to deriving 7b from a structure that contained two occurrences of *Susan will kiss Harry*, since *It is true that Susan will kiss Harry* is grammatical. Note that the infinitive form poses no obstacle to a non-restrictive clause: *Napoleon claimed to be a great general, which was true*.

13. One important verb which Austin classes as a verdictive but probably should be considered an operative is *accuse*. I argue in "Verbs of Bitching" (chap. 15) that an accusation is not simply a statement that someone did some evil deed but is rather a use of such a statement that serves to put that person in a state of jeopardy.

14. Curiously, there are acts of mentioning which do not allow performative uses of *mention*. For example, if the point of your argument is that taxation is immoral, you cannot conclude the argument by saying *I mention that taxation*

*is immoral.* However, in stating your conclusion in any normal way, you do mention that taxation is immoral, and if someone asked me whether you had mentioned that taxation was immoral, I would have to answer that you had.

15. This is essentially the same distinction that Fraser (1974) draws between 'verbs changing the world' and 'verbs describing the world'.

## Chapter 17

1. [A striking example of a mass noun referring to something that normally comes in a very specific individuation is *toast*. Toast comes in slices (*\*a loaf of toast*), yet one cannot use *toast* to refer to the normal quantum of toasthood (*two slices of toast*, not *\*two toasts*, except in the derived sense of 'two orders of toast'; cf. *two spaghettis*). At least *toast* behaves semantically like a mass noun to the extent that it can still be used in cases where the standard individuation has been destroyed, e.g., a recipe that calls for slices of toast to be cut into cubes can contain the instruction *Cover the bottom of the pan with toast.* Interestingly, there is a type of toast that is referred to by a count noun: *rusk*.]

2. [With the appearance of Bunt 1976 and Pelletier 1978, this state of deprivation has been alleviated significantly.]

3. Do these facts imply that *water* is ambiguous between the sense '$H_2O$' and the sense 'liquid $H_2O$'? Any of the molecules in a block of ice is 'a molecule of water'. The fact that the whole block cannot be described as water is probably due to considerations of cooperation: you could be more informative by using the word for 'solid $H_2O$'.

[It is doubtful that *water* can be taken to mean simply '$H_2O$' or even 'liquid $H_2O$', since the presence of impurities is far less of an obstacle to calling a sample of liquid 'water' than to calling it '$H_2O$'. The relationship of impurities to the applicability of mass terms is discussed insightfully in Sharvy 1978.]

4. [The same point is made by Quine (1960:98): "In general a mass term in predicative position may be viewed as a general term which is true of each portion of the stuff in question, excluding only the parts too small to count. Thus 'water' and 'sugar', in the role of general terms, are true of each part of the world's water or sugar, down to single molecules but not to atoms; and 'furniture', in the role of general term, is true of each part of the world's furniture down to single chairs but not to legs and spindles."]

5. The definitions in 4 and 5 are quoted from *The American Heritage Dictionary of the English Language* (New York, 1966).

6. This definition ought also to incorporate the fact that whether the pod is regarded as edible determines whether it is the seed or the pod that is called a bean: when the pod is normally eaten, it is the pod what is called a bean, whereas for those kinds of beans whose pods are not normally eaten, it is the seed that is called a bean.

7. Lurking individuation may also be seen in the fact that *a piece of furniture* can refer to a chair or a magazine rack but not to a leg of a chair or a drawer of a cupboard, let alone to a chip off of a table.

8. I have not investigated the consitions under which spatial adjectives can

be combined with mass nouns in such expressions as *thick cloth*, *long hair*, and *deep mud*.

9. [In Lingala (Mufwene 1978), and presumably in other Bantu languages, mass nouns normally take prefixes that, in combination with count nouns, yield plural forms. I conjecture that the reason for this difference between Lingala and English is a consequence of the fact that in English one number is morphologically unmarked, whereas in Bantu languages, usually both numbers are equally marked morphologically. In English, plural is morphologically marked but semantically unmarked (as witness its use when a NP is to cover both one entity and more than one, as in headings on forms: 'Schools attended', 'Names of children', and the like). Reasons of efficiency dictate that if one number is to be morphologically unmarked, it will be the singular: the occasions on which one is talking about one object outnumber occasions on which one is either talking about more than one or talking in general terms that cover both one and more than one, and thus, fewer morpheme tokens will be used if singular is morphologically unmarked and plural marked rather than vice versa. Since there is no singular-plural opposition in mass nouns, they will normally take the morphologically unmarked number, if there is one (as in English), and the semantically unmarked number if there is no morphologically unmarked number (as in Lingala).]

## Chapter 18

1. [Another asymmetry is illustrated by the word *priest* and *priestess*. If the Catholic Church changed its position on the ordination of women, the female priests that would then be ordained would not be priestesses: a priestess is not a female performer of priestly duties but rather a performer of female priestly duties. There could not be Catholic priestesses unless the Church created priestly duties that had to be performed by women.]

2. [In looking over the manuscript of this review before submitting it for its original publication, I noticed that it was ironic that *masterful* should have been the word that came into my mind here. But I let the word stand, because what else could I say? *\*Mistressful*? *\*Expertful*?]

3. [Miller and Swift (1976:29) criticize a letter by me that appeared in the *New York Times Magazine*, 10 November 1974, in which I make this point about *he or she*. They paraphrase my conclusion as 'In other words, never, never, never qualify the generic pronoun and you will always be understood to include both sexes'. That was not my point at all—it was rather that if you use *he or she* you are likely to be interpreted as including only males when you say just plain *he*, whereas if you use common gender *he* even in instances where an interpretation including only male referents would clash with stereotypes and male viewpoints, your use of common gender *he* in other contexts will be less likely to be understood as referring to males only. I realize now, however, that it is possible to alternate between *he or she* and common gender *he* in such a way as to gain the potential advantages of both; for example, in *Any Ph.D. candidate who completes all of his or her degree requirements by the fifth week of*

*the term will receive a 50% refund of the fees that <u>he</u> has paid that term*, the *he or she* gets it across that women are included and the subsequent use of *he* will help get it across that the author does not exclude women when he says *he*. I will take this opportunity to recant an erroneous view that I have occasionally expressed about another widely proposed alternative to common gender *he*, namely, *they*; e.g. *the act of suggesting contains a fundamental dichotomy between the speaker claiming the suggestion as <u>their</u> idea, and <u>their</u> holding up the idea to the addressee for approval.* This example is taken from a paper by Don Forman (1974:168), who uses *they* consistently in place of common gender *he*. I have occasionally objected that *they* cannot do the full duty of common gender *he* because it sounds relatively natural only when it has a generic antecedent and sounds quite bizarre when used to refer to a specific individual whose sex one simply does not know (e.g., *\*I hear that Bill's lawyer has just broke their leg*). However, I now think that that is no objection, in that there is no reason to expect problems of generality and problems of ignorance to have a common solution. For example, while the plural serves as a 'common number' in sentences that are general with regard to whether one or more than one individual is involved (as in questions on application forms where entries such as *Schools attended* and *Names of children* do not presuppose that the applicant attended more than one school and has more than one child), it cannot be used to cover up ignorance as to whether more than one individual is involved (thus, it is bizarre to say *John's children are smart* when you aren't sure whether he has one child or more than one).]

## Chapter 19

1. Another important contribution, Peterson 1978, will be taken up briefly below.

2. Note that, contrary to the usual tendency to assign the first quantifier in each clause higher scope than subsequent quantifiers, 8a must be interpreted with *each* having higher scope than *two*.

3. The Klima-Horn position requires one to go beyond the bounds of classical logic in analyzing sentences such as i, since the anaphoric device is outside the scope of the quantifier binding the variable it involves, which forces on the analysis a formula that is generally regarded as incoherent (ii). There is no such difficulty with the Quine proposal, which yields the perfectly coherent formula iii. See, however, Karttunen 1976 for a proposal according to which formulas such as ii would be acceptable.

i. If anyone asks, I'll tell him the answer.

ii. $[(\exists x) (x \text{ asks})] \supset (\text{I tell } x \text{ the answer})$

iii. $(\forall x) [x \text{ asks} \supset \text{I tell } x \text{ the answer}]$

[In McCawley, to appear *c*, I elaborate on Karttunen's proposal and develop from it an analysis of pronouns and definite descriptions that can cope with such problematic cases as *If we have a son, we'll name him Oscar* and *George thinks a unicorn has been eating his geraniums and intends to catch the unicorn by throwing a rope around its horn.*]

4. [My discussion of this point is modeled after Kamp's (1974) discussion of sentences involving the *may* of permission.]

5. The impossibility of *Take almost any of the apples* can be attributed to non-cooperativeness: if there are restrictions on your generosity, you must indicate what they are in order to make clear what you are offering.

6. This existential commitment is relative to the world in which the quantifiers range. While i and ii say nothing about the existence of real-world messages, ii commits the speaker to the proposition that, in the hypothetical situation under discussion, the addressee would have sent messages:

i. Any message you sent would have been intercepted.

ii. Every message you sent would have been intercepted

7. The possibility of *there*-insertion with *not . . . any* confirms the claim that this use of *any* is a narrow-scope existential quantifier and not a wide-scope universal.

8. It will be necessary either to weaken this statement of the conditions for *there*-insertion so as to allow the rule to ignore the ∀ that appears in 19 or to revise 19 so as to avoid the ∀.

9. The one case I know of where something greater than 50% could count as 'not large' and thus something below 50% count as 'most' is that in which more than 50% of something is spread out over time in such a way as to be of relative insignificance. For example, *You have to pay most of the money in advance* is not outlandish as a description of an arrangement where you pay 40% down and the remainder over the next 10 years.

10. The range is fixed for the individual speaker, not for the whole speech community. Speakers differ considerably from one another as to how many each is willing to see described as *several*.

11. The impossibility of *quite several* and *quite a couple* follows from the fact that they refer to fixed numerical ranges: they are as incoherent as *quite between 4 and 10*. There is dialect variation for the acceptability of *quite many* and *quite few*, which is puzzling in that there are obvious meanings for them to express ('a quite large number' and 'a quite small number') and they are interpreted with those meanings even by speakers who would not say them. Note that *quite few* poses a problem for the analysis (assumed here) of *few* as 'not many': *quite not many* makes no sense.

*Chapter 20*

1. [This paper was read at the annual conference of the New York Linguistic Circle on March 13, 1965; it is published here for the first time. The discussion of rule interaction that it contains overlaps portions of my dissertation, written in 1964 and published as McCawley 1968a. This paper constituted one of the earliest deviations from the remarkably uniform position on rule interaction that was held by early transformational grammarians, in which, as in a computer program, rules applied sequentially, in a preassigned order of application. There is now a quite extensive literature on the question of how the different applications of the different rules fit together in a derivation, some of the most important works being Chomsky and Halle 1968, Johnson

1972, S. Anderson 1974, Howard 1972, Kenstowicz and Kisseberth 1972, and Koutsoudas, Sanders, and Noll 1974.]

2. [An important respect in which Yngve's grammars deviate from the account given above of random sequential application is that for Yngve the rules must apply 'left-to-right': at each step you do not just apply any rule whose conditions for application are met but must process the leftmost item that can be affected by a rule. Given the nature of Yngve's rules, the same language is generated under left-to-right application as under purely random sequential application. However, Matthews (1963) has shown that context-sensitive grammars generally generate a smaller language if only left-to-right derivations are permitted than if all the possibilities of random sequential application are allowed.]

3. [In this sentence I confound two conceptions of phrase-structure rule that were first explicitly distinquished in McCawley 1968d. The conception described here, which I later dubbed 'tree formation rules', corresponds to what many early transformational grammarians actually intended but not to what they said they were doing: with to my knowledge the sole exception of Stockwell, Bowen, and Martin 1965, which operated explicitly in terms of tree formation rules, early transformational grammarians took the 'official' position that phrase structure rules were *rewriting rules*, i.e., rules for converting a string into a string (e.g., an application of NP → Det N would not convert 1a into 1b but would rather convert the string NP Aux V NP into the string NP Aux V Det N or into Det N Aux V NP), and the labeled trees that figured in most discussions of syntactic analyses were officially taken to be graphic representations of derivations that operated in terms of strings. In McCawley 1968d (which relied heavily on unpublished work by Richard Stanley), a third conception of phrase-structure rules was presented, namely, *node admissibility conditions*. If interpreted as a node admissibility condition, NP → Det N is not an instruction to replace a symbol by a string or to add nodes to an incomplete tree but is a condition on the well-formedness of complete trees, namely, that a node labeled NP is well formed if what it directly dominates is two nodes, labeled Det and N, in that order; an entire tree is well formed according to a given set of node admissibility conditions if every nonterminal node is well-formed according to some condition of the given set and all the terminal nodes are labeled by terminal symbols. See McCawley 1968d for arguments that many pseudo-problems are avoided and nothing of value is lost if the base rules of a transformational grammar are interpreted as node admissibility conditions rather than as rewriting rules.]

4. This is strictly true only of the recent (post-1963) version of transformational grammar, in which there are no two-base transformations (what was done by two-base transformations in the earlier theory is now accomplished by phrase-structure rules that produce structures with sentences embedded in them, plus one-base transformations that operate on such composite structures) and in which optional transformations are restricted to creating 'stylistic variants'. A 'deep structure' will then underlie not just one but a certain finite number of sentences, any two of which are stylistic variants of one

another, and will be 'a representation of' all of those sentences (Chomsky 1965). In the earlier theory, a transformation could convert a representation of one sentence into a representation of a different sentence, e.g., its negation.

5. I emphasize that I am using the term 'statement' here in such a way that not everything having the form of a declarative sentence will be a 'statement'. For example, the sentence "The phonemes of Russian are /p/, /t/, /č/, /k/, . . ." and "Rule 21 voices intervocalic obstruents" are not statements, since they embody assertions not about the language but about the analysis that the linguist has chosen to make of the language. The first sentence, for example, simply means "I have chosen to represent Russian utterances by phonemic transcriptions involving elements that I indicate by /p/, /t/, /č/, /k/, . . ." Such an assertion is to be distinguished sharply from a real statement such as "/i/ is a high central vowel when preceded by a nonpalatalized consonant", which asserts that all things occurring in the language that are represented as /i/ in the system of transcription are pronounced as high central vowels when a nonpalatalized consonant precedes.

6. [One should not confuse the notions 'true' and 'false' that appear here with the more general notions of 'right' and 'wrong': a rule need not have a truth value in order for it to be 'wrong'.]

7. [In saying this, I overlooked the important point that the inventories might be involved in evaluating alternative descriptions. American descriptivist linguists in fact often argued for one description over another on the basis of characteristics of an inventory of units, e.g., that the inventory of phonemes in analysis 1 was more symmetric than that in analysis 2.]

8. [The description of a 'grammar of statements' given here is quite similar to that found in a work that was in press at the time I wrote this, namely Lamb's *Outline of stratificational grammar* (1966b), with the 'emic-etic statements' of this paragraph corresponding exactly to Lamb's 'realizational rules'. I am at a loss to see why I did not regard 'constituency statements' as a special type of 'tactic statements': they obviously are exactly that. Lamb, of course, allowed tactic statements for all of the n + 1 levels rather than for just the first one. Contrary to what I say below, tactic statements for levels after the first are not superfluous, since they serve to restrict the correspondence among items on different levels (an expression on one level can only be realized on another level by a combination of elements that conforms to the tactics of the latter level). This idea has been taken up belatedly by transformational grammarians under the name of 'output constraints', first discussed in Ross 1967, later expanded in Perlmutter 1971 and subsequent works.]

9. [The remainder of the discussion of this problem is largely a non sequitur, since it confuses two separate issues: whether the rules apply simultaneously or sequentially and whether the units in terms of which the rules are formulated and of which the relevant structures are composed are features or are segment types. There is in fact nothing to prevent vowel harmony, lowering, and shortening, all stated in their pristine form in terms of features, from applying simultaneously. A much better case for sequential application can be made on the basis of the syncope rule that I gloss over in the parenthetical remark at

the end of this paragraph: vowel harmony cannot be simultaneous with syncope, since the effect of vowel harmony depends on what the immediately preceding vowel is after any syncope has taken place (i.e., if the second of three vowels is syncopated, the third vowel will harmonize with the first vowel, not the second), and syncope cannot be simultaneous with shortening, since syncope creates some of the consonant clusters that trigger shortening (i.e., syncope *feeds* shortening). At the time I wrote this paper, I was not yet familiar with Kiparsky's (1965) notions of 'feeding' and 'bleeding' rule interaction.]

10. A particularly clear discussion of cycles is given in Kiparsky 1966.

11. [In drawing these trees, I followed a peculiar policy that was in vogue during the 1960s, namely, that at the end of each application of the cycle, the constituent structure of the affected constituent is destroyed ('brackets are erased'). That policy undoubtedly owed its popularity to the fact that transformational grammarians in the 1960s formulated theories in terms of strings (including labeled brackets) rather than in terms of trees, and the policy of 'erasing brackets' at the end of each application of the cycle made it easy to locate in string terms the domain to which the cycle would next apply. In one respect 7a misrepresents the generative phonological tradition: while I have encircled the plural marker /s/, indicating that the stress rules apply to it, generative phonologists have generally taken affixes not to constitute 'cyclic domains'.]

12. [What sequences of phonemes are possible will obviously depend both on what morpheme sequences are possible and on what morphophoneme sequences are possible within each morpheme. I have already remarked that when I wrote this passage, I held the peculiar belief that constituent structure rules were not 'tactic statements'. I note also that it was sheer arbitrariness on the part of generative phonologists in the mid 1960s that they never considered anything but the deepest phonological level to be the one to which their analog of tactic statements (morpheme structure rules) applied. Certain more recent varieties of generative phonology (see Stampe 1969, Hooper 1976, Leben and Robinson 1977) take something comparable to the sort of phonemic representation that figures in Sapir's work as the level of phonological structure that is most relevant to the formulation of the combinatory possibilities of segments.]

13. [I have since rejected the narrow conception of 'knowledge' that I assumed here; see McCawley 1974b for remarks on different kinds of knowledge, including such nonpropositional sorts of knowledge as knowing how pineapple tastes or knowing how tennis balls bounce. I no longer think that the 'power' described in the next few sentences is very supernatural; indeed, I think that regardless of whether one's knowledge of one's language is in the form of 'rules' or of 'statements', one is continually assembling linguistic structures so as to fit constraints imposed by that knowledge and by a variety of external factors; if one's linguistic competence can be likened to a machine, it is not to a computer or a robot but to a machine like an automobile or an electric organ, which functions only through continuous intimate interaction with the user.]

*Chapter 21*

1. [In one respect I would now weaken this statement. There are cases in which it is plausible to conjecture that a child acquires phonological alternations by first observing that strange things happen in a certain context and later learning the details of what it is that happens in that context, without necessarily learning a single generalization that will cover all of the things that happen. I suspect that this is the case with Finnish consonant gradation, for example, and that attempts to give a uniform gradation rule (e.g., a rule that voices a stop at the beginning of a non-initial short closed syllable, with subsequent rules deleting, spirantizing, or assimilating the resulting voiced stop under various conditions) are misguided. While I thus now find plausible a treatment of consonant gradation that would be formalizable using curly brackets, the curly brackets would not serve the function of 'abbreviation': if my conjecture about the acquisition of consonant gradation is correct, the child would never have the rules that are supposedly abbreviated by the curly brackets, since he would have 'learned the curly brackets' (i.e., internalized a rule that allows for a list of disparate subcases) before he learned what was to go inside the curly brackets.]

2. Of course, many 'insufficient power' arguments have been arguments that this condition was not met by a certain feature system and that therefore a different system was necessary (e.g., McCawley 1967, Chomsky and Halle 1968, Postal 1968a).

3. This qualification is necessary because of putative phonological rules that would exchange segment types, e.g., Chomsky and Halle's (1968) proposed rule that makes tense high vowels mid and tense mid vowels high. I have argued (McCawley (1974a) against the supposed examples of rules of that type but do not wish to exclude them from the present discussion.

[Here and in the next sentence of the text, I have gratuitously assumed that rules must apply sequentially. On the issue of how rules interact, see note 9 to "Statement versus Rule in Linguistic Description" (chapter 20 of this volume) and note 9 to "Sapir's Phonologic Representation" (chapter 1).]

4. [See note 3 to "The Role of a Phonological Feature System in a Theory of Language" (chapter 3 of this volume).]

5. [I give detailed justification of this claim and the next one in McCawley 1974a]

6. [This function is not as pernicious as I made it sound here: to get anything done, you *have to* ignore some defects in your analysis, at least until you have enough hindsight to be able to judge what would be an improvement. What is pernicious about Chomsky and Halle's policy on curly brackets is that it gave a major role in a linguistic theory to something that should have been only a temporary makeshift. Perhaps this is what is liable to happen to you if your office is in a building that was erected in 1942 as a temporary structure.]

7. [The conference referred to here is the one that gave rise to Davidson and Harman 1972.]

8. For the purposes of this discussion I assume that this notation is being used as a language for formulating propositions of some science, so that all

contradictions would be wrong. The fact that certain contradictions cannot be formulated in this notation is actually a defect of it if it is being used not to state propositions about the world but to represent the meaning of sentences. Contradictory sentences can be perfectly grammatical and meaningful, and a linguist must be able to describe their meanings.

[Quine's notation does not so much make contradictions unstateable as it makes tautologies unstateable. The only unstateable contradictions are indeed the negations of unstateable tautologies.]

9. [There is a well-known counterexample to this sweeping claim: the weakening of stops in Danish, which can plausibly be formulated as

$$\begin{bmatrix} -\text{ cont} \\ \alpha\,\text{voice} \end{bmatrix} \rightarrow \begin{bmatrix} +\text{ voice} \\ \alpha\,\text{cont} \end{bmatrix}$$

10. I have chosen o and 1 rather than + and − to avoid making the difference between binary and ternary features appear greater than it is. A much more satisfactory treatment of nonbinary features than is given here is found in unpublished work by Martin Minow.

11. [I am embarrassed to acknowledge having suggested that this putative universal could provide "a really crushing case" for anything. Here, as earlier in "English as a VSO language" (1970b) where I also based an argument on the possibility of enforcing this universal, I was following the prevalent custom of constructing cheap arguments by presenting one's favorite conclusions as part of the ongoing war on excessive power. In fact many of the universals that linguists have proposed in doing their bit in the war effort are propositions that I find it hard to imagine a sane linguist wanting to be universal, e.g., the often proposed constraint against quantifiers in the formulation of rules (which would exclude conditions like 'where X contains no V'). That constraint excludes rules that pick out the first or last occurrence of something in a domain, which is a bizarre thing to want to exclude, in that virtually all perception and cognition involves searches through structured domains (Miller and Jonson-Laird 1976). To adopt that constraint is to say that language is impoverished in comparison with most cognitive domains. The 'one change' universal is not as bizarre as this, but it does not have much plausibility: if 'changes' correspond in any sense to things that speakers or hearers do in using language, what could possibly prevent one from doing two such things together? The other arguments for nonbinary vowel height are really much better arguments.]

## Chapter 22

1. [The editor of the symposium proceedings in which this paper appeared made it the preface to the volume rather than including it among the other papers because, in his opinion, "its topic appears to be *about* the symposium rather than *in* it." Similar views about the domain of linguistics appear in the interviews with me and with George Lakoff that appear in Parret 1974. To a certain extent the views attributed below to Chomsky (e.g., "the position that

linguistics must be isolated from everything else to really be linguistics") are a caricature, in the sense of a coarse sketch that exaggerates prominent features (here, the centrality that Chomsky gives to the notion of 'grammatical' and his insistence on the 'autonomy' of syntax); readers should consult Chomsky's more recent works (e.g., 1975, 1977) for a fuller and more accurate picture of what he means by 'autonomy'.]

2. [I do a better job of making this point in "Some Ideas Not to Live By." See Martin, Bradac, and Elliott 1977 for a careful and impressive statistical analysis of the factors that affect informants' 'grammaticality judgments'.]

3. [Chomsky (1965:148–53) and Katz (1964) have expounded a notion of 'degrees of grammaticality', according to which knowledge of the rules generating the 'fully grammatical' sentences provides a basis for assigning degrees of grammaticality to morpheme strings that are not 'fully grammatical'. I find such a conception of degree of grammaticality implausible, in that it is doubtful that a speaker could tell what sentences are 'fully grammatical' until he had developed a fairly rich knowledge of the factors that can make sentences not fully grammatical and thus already had a conception of 'grammaticality' that would not be in terms of a simple dichotomy grammatical/ungrammatical; I see no reason why he would need to develop such a dichotomy.]

4. [See now Hankamer and Sag 1976 for valuable discussion of the distinction between anaphoric devices that require a linguistic antecedent and those that allow 'pragmatic control'.]

5. [Further criticism of the notion of evaluation measure is given in McCawley 1976a, 1977b.]

6. It is trivial to extend Peters's result to the following: for any set of languages $L_1, \ldots, L_n$, any sets of facts $F_1, \ldots, F_n$ about $L_1, \ldots, L_n$, respectively, and any *Aspects*-type grammars $G_1, \ldots, G_n$ that are consistent with $F_1, \ldots, F_n$, respectively, there is an evaluation measure which for every $i$ rates $G_i$ the least costly of all the grammars of $L_i$ that are consistent with $F_i$.

7. These example are suggested by Postal's (1968b) example *Five Arabs beat up a sixth/*seventh.

8. I should say here a little about what I think a linguistic analysis of the above examples should involve. I take the examples as showing that the logical structure of a sentence of the form '*m* crooks joined forces with *n* others to murder a *p*-th' somehow involves the proposition that $p = m + n + 1$, presumably as some kind of presupposition. It takes more than linguistic knowledge to know that the presupposition of one version of the sentence ($9 = 5 + 3 + 1$) is true and that of the other ($10 = 5 + 3 + 1$) false. However, one is copping out if one declares all such sentences grammatical and declines to identify what makes speakers accept some such sentences and reject others. Worse than copping out, he would be destroying the empirical basis for his notion of 'grammaticality', since informants will reject sentences like *Four crooks murdered a ninth* as unhesitatingly as they will reject *To bomb the White House is wanted by John.*

*Chapter 23*

1. [Percival (1976) argues that Kuhn's notion of paradigm "cannot be applied either to the history or the present state of linguistics." However, Percival's arguments are concerned with two features of Kuhn's conception of paradigm that I regard as peripheral to Kuhn's main claims, namely, Percival's view of a paradigm as "(1) resulting from an outstanding scientific achievement on the part of a single innovator, and (2) commanding uniform assent among all the members of the discipline" (Percival 1976:285). The question of where the ideas embodied in a paradigm come from is clearly immaterial to the question of how a set of ideas and approaches acquires the status of a paradigm. The existence of a single innovator (or of someone who can be palmed off as a single innovator) is a propagandistic asset that has undoubtedly helped various paradigms to acquire paradigm status faster than they otherwise would have, but Percival's first point is at best a side issue. Furthermore, uniform assent among the members of a discipline is neither necessary nor sufficient in order for an idea to be part of a paradigm for that discipline. An idea or approach is part of the paradigm of a discipline if it is uniformly regarded as the 'standard' answer to certain questions or the standard way of dealing with certain kinds of problems, even by members of the discipline who regard the answer as wrong or the method as unsound. See the introduction to McCawley 1976*b* for further remarks on scientific revolutions in linguistics and Laudan 1976 for arguments that in the respects in which Percival sees linguistics deviating from Kuhn's conception of a 'mature science', the physical sciences also deviate from it.]

2. Kuhn makes up somewhat for this omission in Kuhn 1970, 1974.

3. This alternative is not radically different from the 'puzzle-solving' that Kuhn takes to be a major part of 'normal science'. Putnam (1974) describes 'puzzle solving' as finding the auxiliary hypotheses which, in conjunction with the assumed theory, will imply given facts, that is 'solving the syllogism for A':

Theory T (given)

Auxiliary hypotheses A (to be found)

Facts F (given)

A promissory note is issued when the community does not quickly come up with a solution to the syllogism.

4. [Feyerabend (1975, 1976) would dispute the claim that this is not wise.]

5. For many valuable comments on the lack of power of advertising to engage people's attention, let alone to sell them something, see Cone 1973.

6. Things were different in the 1920s, when many cigarette advertisements were concerned with popularizing smoking in a previously untapped market, namely, women. The ads popularized both the idea that women had just as much right to smoke as did men and the idea that smoking could serve a useful purpose ("Reach for a Lucky instead of for a sweet"). Given that in the 1920s the connection between sweets and fatness was more widely recognized than the connection between smoking and cancer, these ads were not at all objectionable: they helped wipe out a stupid reason for not smoking and helped spread

something that, relative to the time, was a good reason (albeit not an overwhelming one) for smoking.

7. It is unfortunate that people in academia, whether students, faculty, or administration, rarely think of a university's students as its customers. Greater awareness of the buyer/seller relationship would be advantageous to, if not all, at least most of those concerned. Students at present do not give enough thought to the question of how best to get full value for their (or their benefactors') money, and faculty members think very little about the question of whether their students are getting their money's worth. Much student unrest could be avoided by judicious application of the principle that the customer is always right, i.e., by recognizing that the university in accepting the student's money is entering into a contract with him and the student has the right to decide for himself whether he is getting what he paid for and to cancel the contract and get a refund if he isn't.

8. Here are more misrepresentations from Makkai's paper: (1) Makkai indicates (p. 201) that transformational grammarians accept the proposition "Surface structure is to deep structure as performance is to competence." However, the notions of competence and performance are applicable with reference to *any* level of linguistic structure. (It is especially clear that 'competence' has to do with all levels, since a grammar is supposed to be a formal account of competence, and a grammar includes rules relating to all linguistic levels.) (2) Makkai applies the term 'publicly verifiable' to Lamb's 'complexity count' in such a way as to suggest that he is citing a difference between stratificational grammar and transformational grammar. There is in fact no dearth of 'publicly verifiable' methods of measuring 'complexity' of the grammars of a given theory. What is lacking is a 'publicly verifiable' basis for choosing among the possible 'evaluation measures' or for deciding whether the notion of 'evaluation measure'/'complexity count' is even of any relevance to a linguist's concerns (see McCawley 1977b for arguments that it isn't). Makkai's aversion to first-order arbitrariness is coupled with a willingness to accept second-order arbitrariness, much in the same way that Immanuel Kant (Kaufmann 1973:239–41) lived the minutest details of his life according to universal maxims but was quite arbitrary in his choice of maxims to live his life by (for example, he adopted the maxim that one must not smoke more than one pipe of tobacco per day).

9. There is nothing to prevent the investigator from spreading his intellectual capital among several speculative ventures. The more speculative a venture is, the wiser it is not to risk everything on it.

10. At this point, one might ask whether I should be condemning just *government* subsidies for education and research, rather than subsidies from any source, public or private. I in fact maintain that private support for education and research is far less likely to cause undesirable or premature scientific revolutions, since the mechanics of private subsidy produces a tendency toward diversity, whereas the mechanics of government subsidy produces a tendency toward uniformity. When a government subsidy program goes into effect, all universities have potential access to the funds, the same

kinds of uses are made of the funds in different places, and the same ideas will influence the recipients of the funds with regard to how they should spend them. By contrast, private subsidies are more sporadic as regards who gets them and when they are available, are distributed and used in a great variety of ways, and the individual donor, even if he is H. L. Hunt, has nothing near the funds to pour into a single project that the federal government does.

## Chapter 24

1. This difference may reflect a hitherto unnoticed respect in which mathematical studies of formal 'languages' have influenced the development of transformational grammar. The less constraints there are on how the symbols of a formal language may combine, the simpler the grammars that generate that language. Thus, the crucial data in showing that no grammar of such-and-such type generates a given language will always be negative data: you need high-powered descriptive devices to exclude things, not to include them.

2. The distinction that Chomsky draws between the grammatical/ungrammatical dichotomy and the acceptable/unacceptable dichotomy appears to be that sentences which are unacceptable only for reasons that are extraneous to Chomsky's concerns are to count as grammatical, whereas those that are unacceptable for reasons that are within his area of concern are ungrammatical. (In certain places, e.g., Chomsky 1970a:194, he appears to also allow an acceptable sentence to count as ungrammatical if a factor extraneous to his concerns impairs the speaker's ability to perceive some characteristic that otherwise renders sentences ungrammatical.) Note that under this conception of 'grammaticality', to tell whether an unacceptable sentence is grammatical, you have to identify why it is unacceptable. It is not clear to me why, if one can identify why a given string of words is unacceptable as a sentence, there is any point to further classifying it as 'grammatical' or 'ungrammatical'. The division of sentences into 'grammatical' and 'ungrammatical' is not so much a distinction among sentences as a distinction among sources of unacceptability, a distinction which seems to me to tell one more about the linguist (what factors determine the sources of unacceptability that a given linguist is willing to disregard?) than about the language.

3. Or at least, an appropriate use of it *as* a sentence *of* the language or dialect in question. The fact that any noise could be used as a signal, or that certain nonsensical strings of English words are homophonous with normal sentences of Swahili, is irrelevant.

4. However, 'positive data' about his own speech do not inform him that his sentences are 'grammatical': the people around him may be used to the way he speaks and may understand him despite marked differences between his speech and theirs.

5. This, of course, is essentially what Harris said about morpheme identity.

6. The terms 'core' and 'patch' are taken from Morgan 1972a. Morgan argued that number agreement rules in English do not cover all the cases that actually arise and that individuals develop 'patches' to provide them with a

way of saying things that go beyond the bounds of their grammars (as in *Either he or I ?is/ ?am sure to be elected*).

7. More extensive discussion of the material of this paragraph appears in McCawley 1977*b*. [The publication dates notwithstanding, the present paper is the sequel to McCawley 1977*b*.]

8. I owe much of the content of this paragraph to discussion with William Labov. [Language acquisition is also made to seem more mysterious than it is by the false assumption that the samples of language that children are exposed to are as 'degenerate' as those that adults are exposed to. See Snow and Ferguson 1977 for discussion of respects in which the language that adults (especially mothers) speak to children may facilitate language acquisition.]

9. Compare the fact that second-language learners will often display excellent pronunciation in language-laboratory drills but wretched pronunciation when they are actually speaking the language. It takes them effort to get the pronunciation right, and they can spare that effort in the drills; but when they are actually speaking they have more important things to worry about.

10. Chomsky (1965:36–37) actually entertains the possibility that an evaluation measure is unnecessary: 'It is logically possible that the data might be sufficiently rich and the class of potential grammars sufficiently limited so that no more than a single permitted grammar will be compatible with the available data'. However, he finds it 'rather difficult to imagine how in detail this logical possibility might be realized'.

11. Here I gloss over the extremely important question of how rules are to be individuated. Without an answer to that question, one cannot tell whether one grammar has 'extra rules' relative to another.

12. [Transformational grammar has generally lumped together under the name of 'rules' two types of things that Stampe keeps separate. 'Rules' such as are alluded to in this paragraph, which are part of the child's innate language acquisition capacity and may be suppressed in the course of language acquisition, Stampe calls 'processes'; he reserves the term 'rules' for things that have to be learned and which need not be 'natural'.]

13. [My reference here to 'distance' between grammars is misleading, since 'distance' is normally a symmetric relationship (I'm as distant from you as you are from me), whereas the relationship between grammars that is under discussion here surely is asymmetric. Note, for example, that under the conception of language acquisition suggested by Haber 1975, in which rules (at least, rules in Stampe's sense) can be added to a child's grammar but normally not removed or revised, paths of development are one-directional. I am grateful to T. R. Hofmann for reminding me of this point.]

14. In alluding here to descriptivist linguists, I have in mind the fact that a remarkable number of descriptivists constructed pedagogical materials and practical orthographies on the basis of their analyses, and even claimed to be able to predict what characteristics of language A would be most difficult for speakers of language B to learn, despite the fact that their theory of language made no psychological claims and thus provided no basis for drawing any conclusions as to how a language is most effectively taught, what the difficulties

in learning it are, and what system of writing it is most useful. Bloch (1950:99) was a notable exception when he argued that the optimal practical orthography need not be a phonemic orthography. Strangely, transformational linguists, who do make psychological claims for their analyses, much more rarely draw conclusions about language teaching or the construction of orthographies.

15. [At the time I wrote this paper, I was unware of the fascinating study of morpheme relatedness by Derwing (1976), which confirms my conjectures that there is much individual variation in perceptions of morphemic relatedness and that phonological and semantic similarities between words contribute to the probability of their being felt to share a morpheme, whether or not the relation between the words can be taken to exemplify any otherwise attested rules.]

# Bibliography

Abbreviations:

*CLS* = *Chicago Linguistic Society* (papers from the regional meetings)
*FL* = *Foundations of Language*
*IJAL* = *International Journal of American Linguistics*
*LI* = *Linguistic Inquiry*

Abbott, Barbara. 1974. Some problems in giving an adequate model-theoretic account of CAUSE. Paper presented at summer meeting of Linguistic Society of America.

Abraham, R. C. 1940. The principles of Tiv. London: Crown Agents for the Colonies.

Akatsuka, Noriko. 1972. Emotive verbs in English and Japanese. *Studies in the Linguistic Sciences* 2 (fall):1–16.

Akmajian, Adrian; Steele, Susan; and Wasow, Tom. 1977. The category AUX in universal grammar. Paper presented at summer meeting of Linguistic Society of America.

Anderson, Lloyd. 1967. A left-to-right syllabic cycle. *Chicago Journal of Linguistics* 1:1–16.

Anderson, Stephen R. 1974. *The organization of phonology*. New York: Academic Press.

————. 1976. Concerning the notion 'base component of a transformational grammar'. In McCawley 1976*b*:113–28.

Antley, Kenneth. 1974. McCawley's theory of selectional restrictions. *FL* 11:257–72.

Arnott, D. W. 1964. Downstep in the Tiv tonal system. *African Language Studies* 5:34–51.

Aronoff, Mark. 1976. *Word formation in generative grammar*. Linguistic Inquiry Monograph, no. 1. Cambridge, Mass.: MIT Press.

Austin, J. L. 1962. *How to do things with words*. London: Oxford University Press.

Awobuluyi, Oladele. 1973. Terraced-level tone systems. Paper read at Fourth Annual Conference on African Linguistics, Queens College, New York.

Bach, Emmon. 1968. Two proposals concerning the simplicity metric in phonology. *Glossa* 2:128–49.

———.1976. "The position of embedding transformations in a grammar" revisited. In A. Zampoli, ed., *Papers from the International Summer School in Computational Linguistics* (Pisa).

Bach, Emmon, and Harms, Robert T. 1968. *Universals in linguistic theory.* New York: Holt, Rinehart, and Winston.

Bennett, Michael. 1976. A variation and extension of a Montague fragment of English. In Partee 1976:119–63.

Binnick, Robert I. 1968. On the nature of the 'lexical item'. *CLS* 4:1–13.

Bloch, Bernard. 1950. Studies in colloquial Japanese IV: phonemics. *Language* 26:86–125. Reprinted in Joos 1958:329–48.

Bloch, Bernard, and Trager, George. 1942. *Outline of linguistic analysis.* Baltimore: Linguistic Society of America.

Bloomfield, Leonard. 1917. *Tagalog texts.* Urbana: University of Illinois Press.

———. 1926. A set of postulates for the science of language. *Language* 2:153–64. Reprinted in Joos 1958:26–31.

———. 1933. *Language.* New York: Henry Holt.

———. 1939. Menominee morphophonemics. *Travaux du Cercle Linguistique de Prague* 8:105–15.

Breggin, Peter. 1974. Interview. *Reason* 6, 4:4–13.

Bresnan, Joan W. 1973. The syntax of the comparative clause construction. *LI* 4:275–343.

Browne, Harry. 1973. *How I found freedom in an unfree world.* New York: Macmillan.

Bunt, Harry. 1976. The formal semantics of mass terms. In F. Karlsson, ed., *Papers from the Third Scandinavian Conference on Linguistics*, pp. 81–94, Turku: Academy of Finland.

Carlson, Gregory. 1977. Reference to kinds in English. Ph.D. dissertation, University of Massachusetts.

Carter, Hazel. 1962. *Notes on the tonal system of Northern Rhodesia Plateau Tonga.* Colonial Research Study 35. London: Her Majesty's Stationery Office.

———. 1971–72. Morphotonology of Zambian Tonga: some developments of Meeussen's system. *African Language Studies* 12:1–30 and 13:52–87.

Chomsky, Noam A. 1951. Morphophonemics of Modern Hebrew. M.A. thesis, University of Pennsylvania.

————. 1955. *The logical structure of linguistic theory.* Ditto; privately circulated. Abridged ed. New York: Plenum, 1975.

————. 1957. *Syntactic structures.* The Hague: Mouton.

————. 1964. Current issues in linguistic theory. In Fodor and Katz 1964: 50–118.

————. 1965. *Aspects of the theory of syntax.* Cambridge, Mass.: MIT Press.

————. 1966. Topics in the theory of generative grammar. In Sebeok 1966:1–60. Also The Hague: Mouton.

————. 1968. *Language and mind.* New York: Harcourt Brace Jovanovich.

————. 1970a. Remarks on nominalization. In Jacobs and Rosenbaum 1970:184–221. Reprinted in Chomsky 1972:11–61. Page references in the text are to the reprint.

————. 1970b. Deep structure, surface structure, and semantic interpretation. In Jakobson and Kawamoto 1970:52–91. Reprinted in Steinberg and Jakobovits 1971:183–216 and in Chomsky 1972:62–119. Page references in the text are to the reprint in Steinberg and Jakobovits.

————. 1972. *Studies on semantics in generative grammar.* The Hague: Mouton.

————. 1975. *Reflections on language.* New York: Pantheon.

————. 1977. *Essays on form and interpretation.* Amsterdam and New York: North Holland.

Chomsky, Noam A., and Halle, Morris. 1968. *The sound pattern of English.* New York: Harper.

Cohen, David. 1972. *Limiting the domain of linguistics.* Milwaukee: University of Wisconsin at Milwaukee.

Cole, Desmond. 1967. *Some features of Ganda linguistic structure.* Johannesburg: Witwatersrand University Press.

Cole, Peter, and Morgan, J. L. 1975. *Speech acts.* Syntax and Semantics 3. New York: Academic Press.

Collingwood, R. G. 1938. On the so-called idea of causation. *Proceedings of the Aristotelian Society* 38:85–112. Also in H. Morris, ed., *Freedom and responsibility.* Stanford: Stanford University Press, 1961.

Cone, Fairfax M. 1973. *The blue streak.* Chicago: Crain Communications.

Davidson, Donald. 1967a. The logical form of action sentences. In N. Rescher, ed., *The logic of decision and action,* pp. 81–95. Pittsburgh: University of Pittsburgh Press.

————. 1967b. Truth and meaning. *Synthese* 17:304–23.

Davidson, Donald, and Harman, Gilbert. 1972. *Semantics of natural language.* Dordrecht: Reidel.

Davis, Steven, and Mithun, Marianne. In press. *Proceedings of the 1977*

*Albany Conference on Montague grammar.* Austin: University of Texas Press.

Derwing Bruce L. 1976. Morpheme recognition and the learning of rules for derivational morphology. *Canadian Journal of Linguistics* 21: 38–66.

Dougherty, Ray S. 1970a. A grammar of coordinate conjoined structures I. *Language* 46:850–98.

———. 1970b. Review of Bach and Harms 1968. *FL* 6:506–61.

Dowty, David. In press. Dative constructions in Montague grammar. In Davis and Mithun.

Edmondson, T., and Bendor-Samuel, J. T. 1966. Tone patterns of Etung. *Journal of African Languages* 5:1–6.

Elliott, Dale. 1971. The grammar of emotive and exclamatory sentences in English. *Ohio State Working Papers in Linguistics* 8:1–110.

Emonds, Joseph. 1970. Root and structure-preserving transformations. Ph.D. dissertation, Massachusetts Institute of Technology.

———. 1976. *A transformational approach to English syntax.* New York: Academic Press.

Feyerabend, Paul. 1970. Against method: outline of an anarchistic theory of knowledge. *Minnesota Studies in the Philosophy of Science* 4:17–130.

———. 1975. *Against method.* London: New Left Books.

———. 1976. On the critique of scientific reason. In R. S. Cohen, P. K. Feyerabend, and M. W. Wartofsky, eds., *Essays in memory of Imre Lakatos.* Dordrecht: Reidel.

Fillmore, Charles J. 1971. Verbs of judging: An exercise in semantic description. In Fillmore and Langendoen 1971:272–89.

Fillmore, Charles J., and Langendoen, D. T. 1971. *Studies in linguistic semantics.* New York: Holt, Rinehart, and Winston.

Firth, J. R. 1948. Sounds and prosodies. *Transactions of the Philological Society*, pp. 127–52. Reprinted in J. R. Firth, *Papers in linguistics 1934–1951* (London: Oxford University Press, 1957).

Fodor, Jerry A. 1972. Troubles about actions. In Davidson and Harman 1972:48–69.

Fodor, Jerry A., and Katz, Jerrold J. 1964. *The structure of language.* Englewood Cliffs: Prentice-Hall.

Forman, Don. 1974. The speaker knows best principle. *CLS* 10:162–77.

Fraser, Bruce. 1974. An analysis of vernacular performative verbs. In R. Shuy and C.-J. Bailey, eds., *Towards tomorrow's linguistics*, pp. 139–58. Washington, D.C.: Georgetown University Press.

Geis, Michael. 1970. Time prepositions as underlying verbs. *CLS* 6:235–49.

Goldsmith, John. 1976. *Autosegmental phonology.* Bloomington: Indiana University Linguistics Club.

Goodman, Nelson. 1947. The problem of counterfactual conditionals. *Journal of Philosophy* 44:113-28.

Grice, H. P. 1957. Meaning. *Philosophical Review* 66:377-88.

———. 1975. Logic and conversation. In Cole and Morgan 1975:43-58.

Gudschinsky, Sarah; Popovich, Harold; and Popovich, Frances. 1970. Native reaction and phonetic similarity in Maxakalí phonology. *Language* 46:77-86.

Haber, Lyn. 1975. The muzzy theory. *CLS* 11:240-56.

Halle, Morris. 1957. In defense of the number two. *Studies presented to Joshua Whatmough*, pp. 65-72. The Hague: Mouton.

———. 1959. *The sound pattern of Russian*. The Hague: Mouton.

———. 1962. Phonology in generative grammar. *Word* 18:54-72.

———. 1964a. Phonology in generative grammar (revised version of Halle 1962). In Fodor and Katz 1964:334-52.

———. 1964b. On the bases of phonology. Fodor and Katz 1964:324-33.

———. 1973. Prolegomena to a theory of word formation. *LI* 4:3-16.

Hankamer, Jorge, and Sag, Ivan. 1976. Deep and surface anaphora. *LI* 7:391-428.

Harms, Robert T. 1966. Stress, voice, and length in Southern Paiute. *IJAL* 32:228-35.

———. 1968. *Introduction to generative phonology*. Englewood Cliffs: Prentice-Hall.

Harris, Zellig. 1946. From morpheme to utterance. *Language* 22:161-83. Reprinted in Joos 1958:142-53.

———. 1951a. *Structural linguistics*. Chicago: University of Chicago Press.

———. 1951b. Review of Sapir 1949. *Language* 27:288-333.

Hart, H. L. A., and Honoré, A. M. 1959. *Causation in the law*. Oxford: Clarendon.

Heny, Frank. 1973. Sentence and predicate modifiers in English. In John Kimball, ed., *Syntax and Semantics* 2:217-45.

Heringer, James. 1970. Research on quantifier-negative idiolects. *CLS* 6:287-96.

———. 1976. Idioms and lexicalization in English. In M. Shibatani, ed., *The grammar of causative contructions*, pp. 205-16. Syntax and Semantics 6, New York: Academic Press.

Hirayama, Teruo. 1960. *Zenkoku akusento jiten* [All-Japan accent dictionary]. Tokyo: Tokyodo.

Hockett, Charles F. 1954. Two models of grammatical description. *Word* 10:210-31. Reprinted in Joos 1958:386-99.

———. 1966. Language, mathematics, and linguistics. In Sebeok 1966:155-304.

Hooper, Joan. 1976. *An introduction to natural generative phonology*. New York: Academic Press.

Horn, Laurence R. 1972. *On the semantic properties of logical operators in English*. Bloomington: Indiana University Linguistics Club.

Hornby, A. S; Gatenby, E. V.; and Wakefield, H. 1963. *The advanced learner's dictionary of current English*. 2d ed. London: Oxford University Press.

Hospers, John. 1967. *Introduction to philosophical analysis*. 2d ed. Englewood Cliffs: Prentice-Hall.

Householder, Fred W. 1965. On some recent claims in phonological theory. *Journal of Linguistics* 1:13–24.

Howard, Irwin. 1972. *A directional theory of rule application in phonology*. Bloomington: Indiana University Linguistics Club.

Jackendoff, Ray S. 1969. An interpretive theory of negation. *FL* 5:218–243.

———. 1972. *Semantic interpretation in generative grammar*. Cambridge, Mass.: MIT Press.

———. 1974. A deep structure projection rule. *LI* 4:485–505.

———. 1975. Morphological and semantic regularities in the lexicon. *Language* 51:639–71.

Jacobs, Roderick, and Rosenbaum, P. S. 1970. *Readings in English transformational grammar*. Waltham: Ginn.

Jakobson, Roman. 1948. Russian conjugation. *Word* 4:155–67. Also in R. Jakobson, *Selected writings* 2:119–29. The Hague: Mouton, 1971.

———. 1949. On the identification of phonetic entities. *Travaux du Cercle Linguistique du Copenhague* 5:203–213. Also in R. Jakobson, *Selected writings* 1:418–25. The Hague: Mouton, 1962.

Jakobson, Roman; Fant, C. G. M.; and Halle, Morris. 1951. *Preliminaries to speech analysis* Cambridge, Mass.: MIT Press.

Jakobson, Roman, and Kawamoto, S. 1970. *Studies in general and oriental linguistics: Essays presented to Shiro Hattori*. Tokyo: TEC.

Jenkins, Lyle. 1972. *Modality in English*. Bloomington: Indiana University Linguistics Club.

Johnson, C. Douglas. 1972. *Formal aspects of phonological descriptions*. The Hague: Mouton.

Joos, Martin. 1958. *Readings in Linguistics*. Chicago: University of Chicago Press.

Kachru, Braj, et al. 1973. *Issues in linguistics: Papers in honor of Henry and Renee Kahane*. Urbana and Chicago: University of Illinois Press.

Kamp, Hans. 1974. Free choice permission. *Proceedings of the Aristotelian Society* 74:57–74.

Karttunen, Lauri. 1976. Discourse referents. In McCawley 1976b:363–85.

Katz, Jerrold J. 1964. Semi-sentences. In Fodor and Katz 1964:400–416.

———. 1970. Interpretative semantics versus generative semantics. *FL* 6:220–59.

Katz, Jerrold J., and Fodor, Jerry A. 1963. The structure of a semantic theory. *Language* 39:170–210. Also in Fodor and Katz 1964:479–518.

Kaufmann, Walter. 1973. *Without guilt and justice.* New York: Wyden.

Kawakami, Shin. 1965. Accentuation of particles in present-day Japanese. Paper presented at First World Congress of Phoneticians, Tokyo.

Keenan, Edward. 1972. Semantically based grammar. *LI* 3:413–61.

Kenny, Anthony. 1963. *Action, emotion, and will.* London: Routledge, Kegan Paul.

Kenstowicz, Michael. 1973. On the application of rules in pregenerative phonology. Paper read at Indiana University Conference on Rule Ordering.

Kenstowicz, Michael, and Kisseberth, Charles. 1972. The multiple application problem in phonology. In C. Kisseberth, ed., *Studies in generative phonology*, pp. 13–41. Edmonton: Linguistic Research, Inc.

———. 1977. *Topics in phonological theory.* New York: Academic Press.

Kiparsky, Paul. 1965. *Phonological change.* Bloomington: Indiana University Linguistics Club.

———. 1966. Über den deutschen Akzent. *Studia grammatica* 7:69–98.

———. 1977. Paninian phonology. Paper read at Indiana University Conference on Current Phonological Theories.

Klima, Edward S. 1964. Relatedness between grammatical systems. *Language* 40:1–20.

Koutsoudas, Andreas; Sanders, Gerald; and Noll, Craig. 1974. The application of phonological rules. *Language* 50:1–28.

Kuhn, Thomas. 1962. *The structure of scientific revolutions.* Chicago: University of Chicago Press.

———. 1970. Reflections on my critics. In Lakatos and Musgrave 1970: 231–78.

———. 1974. Second thoughts on paradigms. In Suppe 1974:459–82.

Kuroda, Sige-Yuki. 1967. *Yawelmani phonology.* Cambridge, Mass.: MIT Press.

———. 1970. Some remarks on English manner adverbials. In Jakobson and Kawamoto 1970:378–96.

Lakatos, Imre, and Musgrave, Alan. 1970. *Criticism and the growth of knowledge.* London and New York: Cambridge University Press.

Lakoff, George. 1965. On the nature of syntactic irregularity. Ph.D. dissertation, Indiana University. Abridged version published as Lakoff 1970.

———. 1968. On instrumental adverbs and the concept of deep structure. *FL* 4:4–29.

———. 1970. *Irregularity in syntax.* New York: Holt, Rinehart, and Winston.

————. 1972. Linguistics and natural logic. In Davidson and Harman 1972:545–665.

————. 1973. Notes on what it would take to understand how one adverb works. *The Monist* 57:328–43.

————. 1977. Linguistic gestalts. *CLS* 13:236–87.

Lakoff, Robin. 1972. The pragmatics of modality. *CLS* 8:229–46.

————. 1975. *Language and woman's place*. New York: Harper Colophon Books.

Lamb, Sydney M. 1966*a*. Prolegomena to a theory of phonology. *Language* 42:536–73.

————. 1966*b*. *Outline of stratificational grammar*. Washington, D.C.: Georgetown University Press.

Laudan, Larry. 1976. *Progress and its problems*. Berkeley and Los Angeles: University of California Press.

Lawler, John M. 1972. Generic to a fault. *CLS* 8:247–58.

————. 1973*a*. Tracking the generic toad. *CLS* 9:320–31.

————. 1973*b*. Studies in English generics. Ph.D. dissertation, University of Michigan.

Leben, William. 1973. Suprasegmental phonology. Ph.D. dissertation, Massachusetts Institute of Technology.

Leben, William, and Robinson, Orrin W. 1977. 'Upside down' phonology. *Language* 53:1–20.

Lees, Robert B. 1960. *The grammar of English nominalizations*. The Hague: Mouton.

LeGrand, Jean Ehrenkrantz. 1975. *Or* and *any*: The semantics and syntax of two logical operators. Ph.D. dissertation, University of Chicago.

Leopold, Luna B., and Langbein, W. B. 1966. River meanders. *Scientific American* 214 (June 1966):60–70.

Lewis, David. 1973*a*. *Counterfactuals*. Cambridge, Mass.: Harvard University Press.

————. 1973*b*. Causation. *Journal of Philosophy* 70:556–67.

Lightner, T. M. 1971. On Swadesh and Voegelin's 'A problem in phonological alternation'. *IJAL* 37:227–37.

McCawley, James D. 1964*a*. What is a tone language? Paper read at summer meeting of Linguistic Society of America.

————. 1964*b*. Quantitative and qualitative comparison in English. Paper read at winter meeting of Linguistic Society of America. Annotated version appears in McCawley 1973*d*:1–14.

————. 1965. Statement versus rule in linguistic description. Paper read at conference of New York Linguistic Circle. In this volume.

————. 1967. Le role d'un système de traits phonologiques dans une théorie du langage. *Langages* 8:112–23. English original appears in this volume.

————. 1968a. *The phonological component of a grammar of Japanese*. The Hague: Mouton.

————. 1968b. The role of semantics in a grammar. In Bach and Harms 1968:124–69.

————. 1968c. Review of Sebeok 1966. *Language* 44:556–93.

————. 1968d. Concerning the base component of a transformational grammar. *FL* 4:243–69.

————. 1970a. A note on Tiv conjugation. *Studies in African Linguistics* 1:123–30. In this volume.

————. 1970b. English as a VSO language. *Language* 46:286–99.

————. 1970c. Some tonal systems that come close to being pitch accent systems but don't quite make it. *CLS* 6:526–32. In this volume.

————. 1971a. Prelexical syntax. *Georgetown University Monograph Series on Languages and Linguistics* 23:19–33.

————. 1971b. Interpretative semantics meets Frankenstein. *FL* 7:285–96.

————. 1971c. Tense and time reference in English. In Fillmore and Langendoen 1971:96–113.

————. 1972a. A program for logic. In Davidson and Harman 1972:498–544.

————. 1972b. On interpreting the theme of this conference. In Cohen 1972. In this volume.

————. 1973a. Syntactic and logical arguments for semantic structures. In Osamu Fujimura, ed., *Three dimensions of linguistic research*, pp. 259–376. Tokyo: TEC.

————. 1973b. Global rules and Bangubangu tone. In M. Kenstowicz and C. Kisseberth, eds., *Issues in generative phonology*, pp. 160–68. The Hague: Mouton.

————. 1973c. William Dwight Whitney as a syntactician. In Kachru, et al. 1973:554–68.

————. 1973d. *Grammar and meaning*. Tokyo: Taishukan, and New York: Academic Press.

————. 1974a. Review of Chomsky and Halle 1968. *IJAL* 40:58–88.

————. 1974b. Review of Bruce Derwing, *Transformational grammar as a theory of language acquisition*. *Canadian Journal of Linguistics* 19:177–88.

————. 1975a. Verbs of bitching. In D. Hockney, et al., eds., *Contemporary research in philosophical logic and linguistic semantics*, pp. 313–32. Dordrecht: Reidel. In this volume.

————. 1975b. Review of Chomsky 1972. *Studies in English Linguistics* 3:209–311.

————. 1976a. Some ideas not to live by. *Die neueren Sprachen* 75:151–65. In this volume.

————. 1976b. *Notes from the linguistic underground.* Syntax and Semantics 7. New York: Academic Press.

————. 1976c. Notes on Jackendoff's theory of anaphora. *LI* 7:319–41.

————. 1977a. Accent in Japanese. In Larry Hyman, ed., *Studies in stress and accent,* pp. 261–302. Southern California Occasional Papers in Linguistics 4. Los Angeles: University of Southern California Linguistics Department.

————. 1977b. Acquisition models as models of acquisition. In R. Fasold and R. Shuy, eds., *Studies in language variation,* pp. 51–64. Washington, D.C.: Georgetown University Press.

————. 1977c. The nonexistence of syntactic categories. *Proceedings of the 1977 Michigan State Conference on Linguistic Metatheory.* East Lansing: Michigan State University Linguistics Department.

————. 1978a. Conversational implicature and the lexicon. In P. Cole, ed., *Pragmatics,* pp. 245–59. Syntax and Semantics 9. New York: Academic Press.

————. 1978b. Notes on Japanese clothing verbs. In J. Hinds and I. Howard, eds., *Problems in Japanese Syntax and Semantics,* pp. 68–78. Tokyo: Kaitakusha.

————. In press *a.* What is a tone language? In Victoria Fromkin and S. R. Anderson, eds., *Tone: A linguistic survey.* New York: Academic Press.

————. In press *b.* Helpful hints to the ordinary working Montague grammarian. In Davis and Mithun.

————. In press *c.* Presupposition and discourse structure. In C.-K. Oh, ed., *Presupposition.* Syntax and Semantics 11. New York: Academic Press.

McCawley, Noriko A. 1973. Boy, is syntax easy! *CLS* 9:369–77.

McNeill, David. 1966. Developmental psycholinguistics. Frank Smith and George A. Miller, eds., *The genesis of language,* pp. 15–84. Cambridge, Mass.: MIT Press.

Makkai, Adam. 1971. Degrees of nonsense, or, Transformation, stratification, and the contextual adjustability principle. *CLS* 7: 479–92.

————. 1975. Madison Avenue advertising: a scenario. *The First LACUS Forum,* pp. 197–208. Columbia, S.C.: Hornbeam.

Martin, Larry W.; Bradac, James J.; and Elliott, Norman D. 1977. On the empirical basis of linguistics: a multivariate analysis of sentence judgements. *CLS* 13:357–71.

Masterman, Margaret. 1970. The nature of a paradigm. In Lakatos and Musgrave 1970:59–89.

Matthews, G. H. 1963. Discontinuity and asymmetry in phrase-structure grammars. *Information and Control* 6:317–46.

Meeussen, A. E. 1954. *Linguistische schets van het Bangubangu.* Tervuren: Koninklijk Museum voor Midden-Afrika.

———. 1963. Morphotonology of the Tonga verb. *Journal of African Languages* 2:72–92.

Miller, Casey, and Swift, Kate. 1977. *Words and women.* New York: Anchor.

Miller, George, and Johnson-Laird, Philip. 1976. *Language and Perception.* Cambridge, Mass.: Harvard University, Belknap Press.

Montague, Richard. 1974. *Formal philosophy.* Ed. Richmond A. Thomason. New Haven: Yale University Press. All page references to articles by Montague are to the 1974 reprintings.

Morgan, J. L. 1972*a.* Verb agreement as a rule of English. *CLS* 8:278–86.

———. 1972*b.* Syntactic form and conversational import: some interactions. In Cohen 1972:37–53.

———. 1973. Sentence fragments and the notion 'sentence'. In Kachru, et al. 1973:719–51.

Mufwene, Salikoko. 1978. Inside the li-/ma- nominal class in Lingala. Paper presented at Conference on African Linguistics, Michigan State University.

Pampell, John R. 1975. More on double modals. *Texas Linguistic Forum* 2:110–21.

Parret, Herman. 1974. *Discussing linguistics.* The Hague: Mouton.

Parsons, Terence. 1970. An analysis of mass terms and amount terms. *FL* 6:362–88.

———. 1972. The logic of grammatical modifiers. Davidson and Harman 1972:127–41.

Partee, Barbara H. 1971. Linguistic metatheory. In W. Dingwall, ed., *A survey of linguistic science,* pp. 650–79. College Park: University of Maryland.

———. 1975. Montague grammar and transformational grammar. *LI* 6:203–99.

———. 1976. *Montague grammar.* New York: Academic Press.

Pelletier, F. J. 1978. *Mass terms.* Dordrecht: Reidel.

Percival, W. Keith. 1976. The applicability of Kuhn's paradigms to the history of linguistics. *Language* 53:285–94.

Perlmutter, David. 1971. *Deep and surface constraints in syntax.* New York: Holt, Rinehart, and Winston.

Peterson, Philip L. 1978. On the logic of 'few', 'many', and 'most'. *Notre Dame Journal of Formal Logic* 19.

Postal, Paul M. 1964. Boas and the development of phonology. *IJAL* 30:269–80.

———. 1968*a. Aspects of phonological theory.* New York: Harper and Row.

———. 1968*b*. Linguistic anarchy notes, series F, no. 1: Plus one, or How about arithmetic? Duplicated, IBM Thomas J. Watson Research Center, Yorktown Heights, N.Y. Also in McCawley 1976*b*:215–22.

———. 1974. *On raising.* Cambridge, Mass.: MIT Press.

Pratt, Mary. 1972. Tone in Kikuyu verb forms. *Studies in African Linguistics* 3:325–77.

Prior, A. N. 1971. *Objects of thought.* Oxford: Clarendon Press.

Pullum, G. K. 1976. The Duke of York gambit. *Journal of Linguistics* 12:83–102.

Pullum, G. K., and Wilson, Deirdre. 1977. Autonomous syntax and the analysis of auxiliaries. *Language* 53:741–88.

Putnam, Hilary, as told to Frederick Suppe. 1974. Scientific explanation. In Suppe 1974:424–36.

Quine, Willard van Orman. 1960. *Word and object.* Cambridge, Mass.: MIT Press.

Rardin, Robert. 1975. Studies in derivational morphology. Ph.D. dissertation, Massachusetts Institute of Technology.

Rescher, Nicholas. 1964. *Hypothetical reasoning.* Amsterdam: North Holland.

Richardson, Irvine. 1959. *The role of tone in the structure of Sukuma.* London: School of Oriental and African Studies.

Ross, John Robert. 1967. *Constraints on variables in syntax.* Bloomington: Indiana University Linguistics Club.

———. 1976. To have have and not to have have. In Edgar Polomé, et al., eds., *Linguistic and literary studies in honor of Archibald A. Hill* 1:263–70. Lisse: Peter de Ridder.

Sadock, Jerrold. 1974. Read at your own risk: syntactic and semantic horrors you can find in your medicine chest. *CLS* 10:599–607.

Sapir, Edward. 1921. *Language.* New York: Harcourt Brace.

———. 1922. Takelma. In Franz Boas, ed., *Handbook of American Indian languages* 2:1–296. Washington, D.C.: Smithsonian Institution.

———. 1925. Sound patterns in language. *Language* 1:37–51. Also in Joos 1958:18–25 and Sapir 1949:33–45.

———. 1930. *Southern Paiute, a Shoshonean language. Proceedings of the American Academy of Arts and Sciences* 65, nos. 1–3.

———. 1939. *Nootka texts.* With Morris Swadesh. Baltimore: Linguistic Society of America.

———. 1949. *Selected Writings.* Ed. D. G. Mandelbaum. Berkeley and Los Angeles: University of California Press.

Schachter, Paul, and Fromkin, Victoria A. 1968. *A phonology of Akan: Akwapem, Asante, and Fante.* UCLA Working Papers in Phonetics 9. Los Angeles: University of California Phonetics Laboratory.

Schirmunski, V. M. 1962. *Deutsche Mundartkunde.* Berlin: Akademie-Verlag.

Searle, John. 1969. *Speech acts.* London: Cambridge University Press.

————. 1975. A taxonomy of speech acts. Keith Gunderson, ed., *Language, mind, and knowledge*, pp. 344–69. Minnesota Studies in the Philosophy of Science 7. Minneapolis: University of Minnesota Press.

Sebeok, Thomas A. 1966. *Current trends in linguistics* 3. The Hague: Mouton.

Shapere, Dudley. 1964. The structure of scientific revolutions. *Philosophical Review* 73:383–94.

Sharvy, Richard. 1978. The indeterminacy of mass predications. In Pelletier 1978.

Shibatani, Masayoshi. 1973. A linguistic study of causative constructions. Ph.D. dissertation, University of California at Berkeley.

Siegel, Dorothy. 1974. Topics in English morphology. Ph.D. dissertation, Massachusetts Institute of Technology.

Smith, Carlota. 1961. A class of complex modifiers in English. *Language* 37:342–65.

Snow, Catherine E., and Ferguson, Charles A. 1977. *Talking to children.* London and New York: Cambridge University Press.

Spaandonck, Marcel van. 1967. *Morfotonologische analyse in Bantutalen.* Leiden: E. J. Brill.

Stampe, David L. 1969. The acquisition of phonetic representation. *CLS* 5:433–44.

Stampe, Dennis. 1968. Toward a grammar of meaning. *Philosophical Review* 77:137–73.

Steinberg, Danny, and Jakobovits, Leon. 1971. *Semantics: An interdisciplinary reader.* London: Cambridge University Press.

Stevick, Earl W. 1969. Tone in Bantu. *IJAL* 35:330–41.

Stewart, J. M. 1964. *The typology of the Twi tonal system.* Legon: Institute of African Studies.

Stockwell, Robert P. 1962. On the analysis of English intonation. In A. A. Hill, eds., *Second Texas Conference on Problems of Linguistic Analysis in English*, pp. 39–55. Austin: University of Texas.

Stockwell, Robert P.; Bowen, J. Donald; and Martin, John W. 1965. *The grammatical structures of English and Spanish.* Chicago: University of Chicago Press.

Suppe, Fredericke. 1974. *The structure of scientific theories.* Urbana and Chicago: University of Illinois Press.

Swadesh, Morris, and Voegelin, C. F. 1939. A problem in phonological alternation. *Language* 15:1–10. Reprinted in Joos 1958:88–92.

Thomason, Richmond A. 1975. *A semantics for the Thomason 1976 fragment*. Pittsburgh: University of Pittsburgh.

———. 1976. Some extensions of Montague grammar. In Partee 1976:77–117.

Tucker, A. N. 1967. Introduction to R. A. Snoxall, *Luganda-English Dictionary*. Oxford: Clarendon Press.

Turvey, Michael T. 1974. Constructive theory, perceptual systems, and tacit knowledge. In Weimer and Palermo 1974:165–80.

Vendler, Zeno. 1957. Verbs and times. *Philosophical Review* 66:143–60. Also in Vendler 1967a:97–121.

———. 1967a. *Linguistics in philosophy*. Ithaca: Cornell University Press.

———. 1967b. Each and every, any and all. Vendler 1967a:70–96.

———. 1972. *Res cogitans*. Ithaca: Cornell University Press.

Voegelin, C. F. 1935. Tübatulabal grammar. *University of California Publications in American Archeology and Ethnology* 34:55–190.

———. 1958. Tübatulabal working dictionary. *IJAL* 24:221–28.

Voegelin, C. F. and Voegelin, F. M. 1963. On the history of structuralizing in twentieth century America. *Anthropological Linguistics* 5:12–35.

Weimer, Walter, and Palermo, David. 1974. *Cognition and the symbolic processes*. New York: Wiley.

Weitzman, Raymond S. 1969. Word accent in Japanese. Ph.D. dissertation, University of Southern California.

Whitney, William Dwight. 1867. *Language and the study of language*. New York: Scribner.

———. 1875. *The life and growth of language*. New York: Scribner.

———. 1889. *Sanskrit grammar*. 2d ed. Cambridge, Mass.: Harvard University Press.

Williamson, Kay. 1965. *A grammar of the Kolukuma dialect of Ịjọ*. London and New York: Cambridge University Press.

———. 1968. Deep and surface structures in tone languages. *Journal of West African Languages* 5:77–86.

Wright, G. H. von. 1963. *Norm and action*. New York: Humanities Press.

Ynge, Victor. 1961. The depth hypothesis. In R. Jakobson, ed., *Structure of language and its mathematical aspects*, pp. 130–38. Twelfth Symposium on Applied Mathematics. Providence: American Mathematical Society.

Zwicky, Arnold M. 1970a. The free-ride principle and two rules of complete assimilation in English. *CLS* 6:579–88.

———. 1970b. Greek-letter variables and the Sanskrit *ruki* class. *LI* 1:549–55.

———. 1971. In a manner of speaking. *LI* 2:223–33.

# Index

LIBRARY
BALDWIN-WALLACE COLLEGE

7/9/79

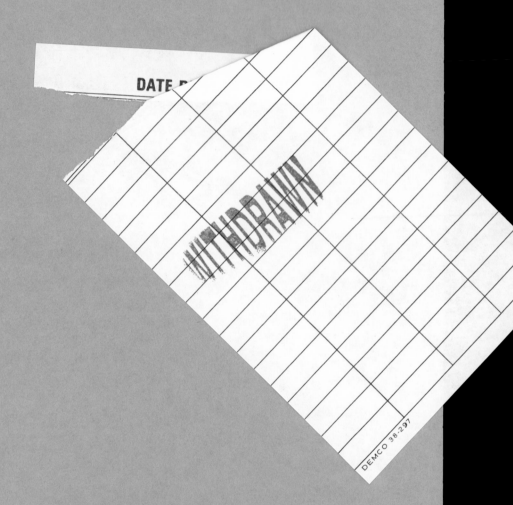

DATE D

WITHDRAWN

DEMCO 38-297